"Johnston is a pastor who rightly deserves the title 'pastor-scholar,' and his scholarly abilities and studies, as well as his pastoral sensibilities and sensitivities, are on full display in his commentary on the Psalms. As Johnston helps you exegete, illustrate, and apply the heart of the Old Testament in light of the person and work of Christ, I trust that your heart—like the men on the road to Emmaus—will burn within."

Douglas Sean O'Donnell, Senior Lecturer in Biblical Studies and
Practical Theology, Queensland Theological College; author,
The Beginning and the End of Wisdom

"While being sensitive to the original historical context of the Psalms as the prayer and songbook of the Jews, Johnston is keenly aware that there is a Christocentric end to which the Psalms point and a Son in whom they find fulfillment. Because of this, Johnston recognizes all the Psalms are messianic, and understood in this way means the Psalms are also the Christian's prayer, song, and life book. Reading this commentary results in thanksgiving and worship. Johnston's excellent commentary is a great addition to the Preaching the Word series. I commend it to you as both an aid to your preaching and as a companion to your devotional reading and praying of the Psalms."

Gregory C. Strand, Director of Biblical Theology and Credentialing,
Evangelical Free Church of America

"*Psalms* will be a treasured volume in this series. The original text is taken seriously and the gospel is made clear. In reading it, my own affections for Christ were delightfully energized. Johnston weds his love for God's poetry to his heart, which is so joyfully pledged to God's people."

David R. Helm, Pastor, Holy Trinity Church, Chicago; Chairman,
The Charles Simeon Trust

"More excellent fodder for sermons from this first-rate resource for preachers."

Josh Moody, Senior Pastor, College Church, Wheaton, Illinois; author,
Journey to Joy: The Psalms of Ascent

THE PSALMS
Volume 1

PREACHING THE WORD
Edited by R. Kent Hughes

(((PREACHING *the* WORD)))

THE PSALMS

REJOICE, *the* LORD IS KING

Volume 1 - Psalms 1 to 41

JAMES A. JOHNSTON

R. Kent Hughes
Series Editor

WHEATON, ILLINOIS

Psalms, Volume 1 - Psalms 1 to 41

Copyright © 2015 by James A. Johnston

Published by Crossway
        1300 Crescent Street
        Wheaton, Illinois 60187

Cover design: Jon McGrath, Simplicated Studio

Cover image: Adam Greene, illustrator

First printing 2015

Printed in the United States of America

Hardcover ISBN: 978-1-4335-3355-6
ePub ISBN: 978-1-4335-3358-7
PDF ISBN: 978-1-4335-3356-3
Mobipocket ISBN: 978-1-4335-3357-0

Library of Congress Cataloging-in-Publication Data

Johnston, James A., 1966–
   The Psalms : rejoice, the Lord is king / James A. Johnston ; R. Kent Hughes, series editor.
      volumes cm. — (Preaching the word)
   Includes bibliographical references and index.
   ISBN 978-1-4335-3355-6 (hc)
   1. Bible. Psalms—Commentaries. I. Title.
BS1430.53.J65   2015
223'.207—dc23   2014039270

Crossway is a publishing ministry of Good News Publishers.

VP		25	24	23	22	21	20	19	18	17	16	15
15	14	13	12	11	10	9	8	7	6	5	4	3	2	1

To my wife,
Lisa Johnston
Her delight is in the law of the Lord,
and on his law she meditates day and night.

Serve the LORD with fear,
and rejoice with trembling.
Kiss the Son,
lest he be angry, and you perish in the way,
for his wrath is quickly kindled.
Blessed are all who take refuge in him.

PSALM 2:11, 12

Contents

A Word to Those Who
Preach the Word

There are times when I am preaching that I have especially sensed the pleasure of God. I usually become aware of it through the unnatural silence. The ever-present coughing ceases, and the pews stop creaking, bringing an almost physical quiet to the sanctuary—through which my words sail like arrows. I experience a heightened eloquence, so that the cadence and volume of my voice intensify the truth I am preaching.

There is nothing quite like it—the Holy Spirit filling one's sails, the sense of his pleasure, and the awareness that something is happening among one's hearers. This experience is, of course, not unique, for thousands of preachers have similar experiences, even greater ones.

What has happened when this takes place? How do we account for this sense of his smile? The answer for me has come from the ancient rhetorical categories of *logos*, *ethos*, and *pathos*.

The first reason for his smile is the *logos*—in terms of preaching, God's Word. This means that as we stand before God's people to proclaim his Word, we have done our homework. We have exegeted the passage, mined the significance of its words in their context, and applied sound hermeneutical principles in interpreting the text so that we understand what its words meant to its hearers. And it means that we have labored long until we can express in a sentence what the theme of the text is—so that our outline springs from the text. Then our preparation will be such that as we preach, we will not be preaching our own thoughts about God's Word, but God's actual Word, his *logos*. This is fundamental to pleasing him in preaching.

The second element in knowing God's smile in preaching is *ethos*—what you are as a person. There is a danger endemic to preaching, which is having your hands and heart cauterized by holy things. Phillips Brooks illustrated it by the analogy of a train conductor who comes to believe that he has been to the places he announces because of his long and loud heralding of them. And that is why Brooks insisted that preaching must be "the bringing of truth through personality." Though we can never perfectly embody the truth we preach, we must be subject to it, long for it, and make it as much a part of our ethos as possible. As the Puritan William Ames said, "Next to the Scriptures, nothing makes a sermon more to pierce, than when it comes out of the inward affection of the heart without any affectation." When a preacher's *ethos* backs up his *logos*, there will be the pleasure of God.

Last, there is *pathos*—personal passion and conviction. David Hume, the Scottish philosopher and skeptic, was once challenged as he was seen going to hear George Whitefield preach: "I thought you do not believe in the gospel." Hume replied, "I don't, but he does." Just so! When a preacher believes what he preaches, there will be passion. And this belief and requisite passion will know the smile of God.

The pleasure of God is a matter of *logos* (the Word), *ethos* (what you are), and *pathos* (your passion). As you preach the Word may you experience his smile—the Holy Spirit in your sails!

R. Kent Hughes

Introduction

The Lord Reigns!

OPENING THE BOOK OF PSALMS

The Psalms are one of the most dearly loved books in the Bible. For generations, they have been one of our greatest treasures as God's people.

Most of the psalms were written for Israel's temple worship. We know
this because fifty-five are dedicated to the Director of Music, several more
were written for specific parts of the temple worship service, and twenty-four
are connected with temple musicians like the Sons of Korah.[1] The Psalms
reflect the prayer and praise of ancient Israel.

In the New Testament, Jesus probably sang Psalm 118 with his disciples
before they left the upper room for the Mount of Olives (Matthew 26:30).[2]
When Peter and John were arrested, the early church prayed with the words
of Psalm 2 (Acts 4:25ff.). Paul leaned heavily on the Psalms as he wrote the
book of Romans. Paul also commands us to "be filled with the Spirit, speaking
to one another in psalms and hymns and spiritual songs" (Ephesians 5:18b,
19a, NKJV). The Psalms were at the heart of spiritual life for the early church.

The Psalms were prominent in the Protestant Reformation in the 1500s.
Before Martin Luther nailed his 95 Theses to the church door in Wittenberg,
he had lectured on the Psalms for over two years.[3] His Christ-centered interpretation of the Psalms helped forge the doctrine of the Reformation. The
Psalms were also a key part of the development of Protestant worship. To
move away from the Latin Mass, the Reformers introduced congregational
singing based in large part on metrical psalms.[4] The Psalms were so important
to Protestant worship that the first book printed in North America was the
Bay Psalm Book in 1644. So we owe much of our worship and theology as
Protestants to the Psalms.

We treasure the Psalms in our own day too. Many of our favorite songs
and hymns are portions of a psalm or a paraphrase. We go to the Psalms when
we're laughing and when we're crying. Amazingly, they often say what we feel
but couldn't find the words to describe. We quote Psalm 104 at Thanksgiving.
After the September 11 attacks, the service held in the National Cathedral in
Washington, D.C. included portions from Psalm 46, Psalm 27, and Psalm 23.

So it is exciting to open the Psalms for ourselves. Charles Spurgeon called his commentary of the Psalms *The Treasury of David*—a good title because God's Word is "more to be desired . . . than gold, even much fine gold" (19:10). We are opening the door to a treasure chamber. If our hearts are open to God's Spirit, this focused time in the Psalms will change us. We will learn to pray as we pray with the psalmist. We will learn to praise as we worship God with David. The Psalms are as deep as the ocean; they are wide as human experience; they will carry us to spiritual heights.

We can set the table for our study of the Psalms by making three main observations about the Psalms in general. The Psalms are truth, the Psalms are poems, and the Psalms are a book.

The Psalms Are Truth

First, the Psalms are truth. They are Scripture that God inspired by his Holy Spirit to teach and instruct us. The Psalms are a rich source of doctrine. They speak to our minds.

The Psalms Are Torah

We see this emphasis on thinking in the opening verses of the Psalms. Psalm 1 introduces the whole book with these words.

> [B]ut his delight is in the law of the Lord,
>   and on his law he meditates day and night. (1:2)

The word *law* is the Hebrew word *torah*, which means instruction that comes from God.[5] The Psalms are divine revelation. We are to read and receive the Psalms as God's Word and think hard about what they say.[6] The call to meditate is a call to reflect and go deep.

This becomes even clearer when we notice that the Psalms are the whole Old Testament in miniature. In a real sense, this one book encapsulates Genesis to Malachi.

Think about how much of the Old Testament is in the Psalms. The Psalms deal with creation, the call of Abraham, the exodus, the Law of Moses, the monarchy, Israel's disobedience, the exile, the return, and the hope of a greater kingdom. The psalmists were reading their Bible, and often they reflected on what God had already said through Moses and the prophets as the Holy Spirit led them. On top of that, the Psalms make up the only book of the Old Testament that was written over the course of one thousand years of Israel's history.[7]

This means that to study the Psalms is to study the whole Old Testament.

Opening the Psalms is a call to think and reflect on Genesis through Malachi and beyond.

Most Quoted Book in the New Testament

Then add to this the fact that the Psalms are the Old Testament book most quoted in the New Testament. Jesus and the apostles consistently turned to the Psalms to preach the kingdom of God and establish key doctrines.

During the last week of Jesus' life, he used Psalms 8, 118, and 110 to silence the chief priests and scribes in the temple (Matthew 21:16, 42; 22:44). When the early church was wondering whether to replace Judas, they turned to Psalm 69 (Acts 1:20). When Peter preached at Pentecost, he used Psalms 16 and 110 to teach Christ's resurrection (Acts 2:25–36). Paul taught salvation by faith from Psalm 32 (Romans 4:6–8). Peter teaches believers to return good for evil based on Psalm 34 (1 Peter 3:9–12).

So the first observation I want to make as we start this study of the Psalms is that the Psalms are truth from God that is meant to teach and instruct us. The Psalms engage our minds with doctrine.

The Psalms Are Poems

The second observation is that the Psalms are poems. Not only do they speak to our minds, as poetry they speak to our hearts. Reading the Psalms engages both the right brain and the left brain, the intellect and the emotions, thinking and feeling.

We can see these two dimensions—the heart and the head—at the very beginning of the Psalms. Look again at Psalm 1:2.

> But his *delight* is in the law of the LORD,
>   and on his law he *meditates* day and night.

God blesses the man who both *delights* (heart) in his Law and *meditates* (head) on it. In fact, he mentions the heart first, suggesting that the reason a man thinks carefully about God's Word is because he has already come to love it. We treasure the Word before we ponder it and dwell on what it means.

As poetry, the Psalms are designed to engage our hearts so that our whole being will engage with God's Word.

Hebrew Poetry

Hebrew poetry is not based on rhyme, rhythm, and meter like most western poetry. Instead the main technique of Hebrew poetry is parallelism. So the key movements within a psalm are often from one line to another as the psalmist takes a thought and gives it a slight turn.

We should be very glad that, in God's providence, Hebrew poetry is not like ours. Western poetry does not translate well into other languages because it is usually based on rhyme, rhythm, and meter. If you know another language, try translating "Roses are Red, Violets are Blue." Chances are, it will fall flat.[8] But the genius of Hebrew poetry is that since it is based on parallelism, it "remains poetry in any language you translate it into."[9]

Poetry to Engage the Heart

As poetry, the Psalms engage our emotions in various ways. For one thing, they were meant to be sung. The name *psalm* comes from the Greek word *psalmos*, which is a translation of the Hebrew word *mizmor*. Both words mean a song accompanied by musical instruments, particularly a harp.[10]

The Psalms also engage our hearts with figures of speech. The writers are poets—artists with words. They paint pictures that linger like a good cup of coffee. The psalmist does not say, "The people are sad," but he says, "You have fed them with the bread of tears" (80:5). He doesn't say, "You made him happy," but he says, "God . . . has anointed you with the oil of gladness" (45:7). He doesn't just say, "Protect me," but he says, "[H]ide me in the shadow of your wings" (17:8). When we read the Psalms, we need to use our imaginations; we are supposed to picture and feel what we are reading.[11]

Poems that Express Emotions

Beyond the poetry, the men who wrote the Psalms also pour out an amazing array of emotions. Here is a short list.[12]

1. Loneliness: "I am *lonely* and afflicted" (25:16).
2. Love: "I *love* you, O LORD, my strength" (18:1).
3. Sorrow: "my life is spent with *sorrow*" (31:10).
4. Discouragement: "Why are you *cast down*, O my soul, and why are you *in turmoil* within me?" (42:5).
5. Shame: "*shame* has covered my face" (44:15).
6. Exultation: "In your salvation how greatly he *exults*" (21:1).
7. Fear: "Serve the LORD with *fear*" (2:11).
8. Peace: "in *peace* I will both lie down and sleep" (4:8).
9. Gratitude: "I will *thank* you in the great congregation" (35:18).
10. Confidence: "though war arise against me, yet I will be *confident*" (27:3).

The Psalms wake up our emotions to respond to God and to life like we should. No other book so powerfully shapes our minds and our hearts. Through the Psalms, we can adapt our thinking and feeling to be in line with the heart and mind of God.[13]

In case you're a man who thinks emotions are a sign of weakness, remember that David was a man's man—he could take down any three of us in hand-to-hand combat—yet his heart was soft toward God. He was a scholar, soldier, and poet at the same time. So the Psalms challenge us men especially to be more fully ourselves, to be true men like David.

The Psalms engage our hearts and minds, our thinking and feeling. They are truth, and they are poetry.

The Psalms Are a Book

Our third observation is that the Psalms are a book. More specifically, the Psalms are a book made up of five smaller books (Psalms 1—41; 42—72; 73—89; 90—106; 107—150). Each of these five smaller books is like a section of the larger book. Based on these five main sections, there is an order that runs through the book of Psalms as a whole.

When I was five years old, I was sitting with my mother in a chapel service at St. Paul Bible College[14] while my dad was preaching. Since I was fidgeting, my mom gave me her beaded necklace to look at, hoping that would keep me still. Well, wouldn't you know it, as I twisted the necklace in my hands, the string broke, and all the beads went clattering on the floor. To make it even worse, the chapel sloped forward and we were sitting in the back. So for twenty long seconds, these beads clattered down the tile floor toward the front—toward my dad.

Many people look at the Psalms like beads on a necklace—they are strung together, but they don't have much to do with each other. In fact, the Psalms have been carefully put together, in order, for a purpose.[15] This is a book.

A Book about Christ

The Psalms are a book about Christ. Jesus himself taught his disciples that the Psalms prophesied about him. He said in Luke 24:44, "Everything written about me in the Law of Moses and the Prophets and the Psalms must be fulfilled." Luke's grammar actually suggests that the apostles and early church counted the Psalms as part of the Prophets.[16] In fact, when Peter preached at Pentecost, he argued that David was indeed a prophet (Acts 2:30).

Psalms 1 and 2 are an introduction for the whole book of Psalms. Psalm 1 introduces us to the ideal man who loves God's Word and lives by it. Psalm 2 identifies this ideal man as the King God set on the throne.[17] The word "anointed" in Psalm 2 is the word *messiah* in Hebrew or *christ* in Greek. There are a number of issues involved here, but the New Testament is quick to recognize that Psalm 2 was pointing forward to Jesus (e.g., Acts 4:25, 26; 13:33; Hebrews 1:5; 5:5). As the Christ, he is God's King. "As for me, I have set my King on Zion, my holy hill" (2:6).

According to Psalm 2, the world hates this King; it schemes and fights against him. But God is on his side, and Christ will rule with power to judge the world.

In a real sense, the rest of the book of Psalms is about this King, his kingdom, and his people. What will happen to God's King? Will life be easy or will he have trouble? What will his enemies do? How will God protect him and give him victory? What will happen to his people? Will their lives be easy or hard? Will the world finally follow this King? The promise of a King in Psalm 2 is a key for understanding the whole book of Psalms.[18] Fundamentally this book is about Christ.

The background for this King is the covenant that God made with David in 2 Samuel 7.[19] God promised David that one of his descendants would rule forever.

> When your days are fulfilled and you lie down with your fathers, I will raise up your offspring after you, who shall come from your body, and I will establish his kingdom. He shall build a house for my name, and I will establish the throne of his kingdom forever. . . . And your house and your kingdom shall be made sure forever before me. Your throne shall be established forever. (2 Samuel 7:12, 13, 16)

This great Son of David is the King who is introduced in Psalm 2. David is not only his ancestor but also the model for who this King would be. David's experience as God's anointed king foreshadows what Christ experienced as God's greater Anointed King. These are not random poems as David reflects on his life. Augustine called Jesus *isti cantator psalmorum*, himself the singer of the Psalms, because when David speaks in the Psalms, he is speaking for Christ. In our day Old Testament scholar Derek Kidner said:

> It would scarcely seem too much to infer . . . that wherever David or the Davidic king appears in the Psalter . . . he foreshadows in some degree the Messiah.[20]

   With this in mind, the Psalms are about Christ in several ways. On the one hand, they make specific predictions that were fulfilled in Christ. On a deeper level, the Psalms point forward to Christ through the life, words, emotions, and experiences of King David as a whole.[21] In the Psalms King David is a model of the great King to come.

What Story Does It Tell?

With this in mind, then, we can sketch out the general shape of the Psalms as a whole book. To understand how the Psalms tell the story, think of a oratorio like Handel's *Messiah*. Maybe classical music isn't your thing, so think of a musical like *Oklahoma* or *Les Misèrables*. Each song can stand alone, but put them together in order and they tell a story. The Psalms are the same way— each can stand alone, but together they tell a story from beginning to end.

   This story begins with Israel during the time of David and Solomon, continues through the exile, and ends when God has returned the people to the land. Books 1 and 2 focus especially on David and his kingdom. Books 3 and 4 reflect the troubles and questions Israel faced during the exile in Babylon. Book 5 looks forward after the exile.

   Book 1 covers Psalms 1—41. All of these psalms were written by David except one (Psalm 33) or possibly two (though Psalm 10 may be part of Psalm 9, which was written by David). The focus is clearly on David's experience as king. Even though David was God's anointed, his life was hard and he faced deadly foes. If we had to summarize these first forty psalms, we could say that the theme of Book 1 is, "God rescues his king from his enemies."

   Psalm 41:11, 12 summarizes this first book well. David says,

> By this I know that you delight in me:
>   my enemy will not shout in triumph over me.
> But you have upheld me because of my integrity,
>   and set me in your presence forever.

   Book 2 includes Psalms 42—72. The first thing we notice is that David is not the author of the first nine psalms. Instead they are connected with a group of Levites called "the Sons of Korah" (Psalms 42—49)[22] and Asaph, one of David's choirmasters (Psalm 50). What's the point? The focus is no longer on David, the king, individually, but now these psalms describe the experience of God's people.

   Yet the people cannot be separated from the king; as the king goes, so goes the nation. Most of the psalms in Book 2 are still written by David. Yet since the book begins and ends by speaking for the people as a whole, David's psalms in Book 2 are framed by the people's experience.

The last psalm in this book, Psalm 72, reminds us that when the king is blessed, the whole world is blessed.

> May his name endure forever,
>   his fame continue as long as the sun!
> May people be blessed in him,
>   all nations call him blessed! (72:17)

To summarize Book 2, we could say that the theme is, "God rescues his people from their enemies through his king."

Psalms 2 and 72 seem like bookends that bind Books 1 and 2 together with their focus on the greatness of the king. Originally these first two books were probably the whole book of Psalms for Israel during the reign of David and the time of the monarchy. This is emphasized by 72:20, which marks the end of a collection of David's psalms.

Book 3 takes a sudden turn and reflects a different period in Israel's history. There is no longer a king on the throne; in fact, Jerusalem has been destroyed, and the temple has been burned.

> Direct your steps to the perpetual ruins;
>   the enemy has destroyed everything in the sanctuary! (74:3)

Since this psalm seems to describe the destruction of the temple, this book was probably compiled after Israel was taken in exile to Babylon. Many of the psalms in Book 3 are from an earlier time—psalms of David, Ethan, Asaph[23]— but they were arranged into this book to help Israel trust in God through the pain of the exile.[24] Book 3 asks some of the toughest questions in all the Psalms. How could God allow this? How long will this last? Is there any hope?

These questions come to a head in the last psalm of this book, Psalm 89. In a real sense this is the great hinge of the whole book of Psalms, the main crisis point. The first two-thirds of Psalm 89 celebrate God's covenant with David, his anointed king.

> You have said, "I have made a covenant with my chosen one;
>   I have sworn to David my servant:
> 'I will establish your offspring forever,
>   and build your throne for all generations.'" (89:3, 4)

And again,

My steadfast love I will keep for him forever,
    and my covenant will stand firm for him.
I will establish his offspring forever
    and his throne as the days of the heavens. (89:28, 29)

Then the psalmist dares to tell God he has gone back on his word!

But now you have cast off and rejected;
    you are full of wrath against your anointed.
You have renounced the covenant with your servant;
    you have defiled his crown in the dust. (89:38, 39)

How could this be? How could God promise David an eternal throne and let the kingdom be destroyed like this? How long will God let this go on? To summarize Book 3, the theme could be, "How could God abandon his king and his people?"

Book 4 was also compiled during the time of the exile. We conclude that this is the case because the book ends with a prayer for God to return the people from exile.

Save us, O LORD our God,
    and gather us from among the nations,
that we may give thanks to your holy name
    and glory in your praise. (106:47)

Evidently the people had not been brought home when this book was gathered together. Book 4 answers the questions of Psalm 89 by reaffirming that God is still King and Judge over all the earth. The people could see their captivity with new eyes. God is at work among the nations, and he is a refuge for his people wherever they may be scattered. A good theme might be, "God is still King over all the world."

Book 5 was compiled after the exile when God brought Israel back home. We say this because of the way it begins with Psalm 107:2, 3.

Let the redeemed of the LORD say so,
    whom he has redeemed from trouble
and gathered in from the lands,
    from the east and from the west,
    from the north and from the south.

What should Israel do now that they are back in the land? For one thing, they should love God's Word and keep his commandments. Since God had sent them into exile for disobedience, the logical thing now is to keep God's Word and not repeat their fathers' mistakes.[25] Psalm 119 is the center of gravity for this book with its celebration of God's Word. The Songs of Ascent (Psalms 120–134) also encouraged faithful pilgrims to keep the Passover.

The people should also look for another King, a King greater than David. They should have learned from the exile that there is more to God's plan than an earthly kingdom. In Psalm 110 David talks about a King who will rule from the throne of God in Heaven.

> The LORD says to my Lord:
>   "Sit at my right hand,
> until I make your enemies your footstool." (110:1)

So God's promise to David was not dead. Instead it was far more glorious and wonderful than they could have imagined. The Son of David would not be merely a human king—he would be great enough to sit on the throne of God in Heaven. How this could be would remain a mystery until the Incarnation when Jesus was born as the legitimate Son of David *and* the Son of God. From the perspective of the New Testament, we know that Jesus Christ is now seated at the right hand of God in power and glory where he will reign forever and ever.

Is he your King? If he is, you can say with the last verse of the Psalms, "Let everything that has breath praise the LORD! Praise the LORD!" (150:6).

1

Blessed Is the Man

PSALM 1

WHAT WILL MAKE YOU TRULY HAPPY? You have probably thought about this even if you haven't put it into words. Everyone wants to have a good life. What will make you truly blessed? Actually the Bible encourages us to look for true, lasting happiness.

The first words of the Psalms pull us in with the possibility of having this kind of life—a life that is blessed by God: "Blessed is the man . . ." (v. 1). This blessing means being supremely happy or fulfilled, a deep sense of well-being. His Word carries much joy, and some versions translate these words, "How happy is the man . . ." This is not superficial happiness that comes and goes but a deep sense of joy from God's grace in my life.[1]

Isn't that what we all want? Psalm 1 offers us true, lasting happiness by presenting a series of contrasts between the righteous and the wicked. It describes two kinds of people living two kinds of lives with two different outcomes. When we see the blessings of the godly next to the emptiness of the wicked, this stark contrast is supposed to make us choose life. The blessings God pours out are so beautiful and compelling that any sane man or woman would want them.

Psalm 1 is the introduction to the Psalms. The blessings God promises those who love his Word are supposed to whet our appetites to take in and to ponder every word of the Psalms.

We will walk through this psalm by asking three questions. Who is this blessed man? How is he blessed? And why is he blessed?

Who Is Blessed?

First, who is this blessed man? Psalm 1:1, 2 describe an ideal man, the kind of person God is looking for.

The Blessed Man Does Not Sin

This ideal man is known first by what he does not do.

> Blessed is the man
> who walks not in the counsel of the wicked,
> nor stands in the way of sinners,
> nor sits in the seat of scoffers. (1:1)

There is a downward spiral in these three negative descriptions. A man or woman settles into sin by stages—he walks, then he stops and stands, and finally he sits down. First he is influenced by the sinners, then he identifies with them, and finally he spreads sin to others through his laughter and sarcasm.

Sin will take you from bad to worse. First, you will be influenced; you start by listening to what the wicked say. You laugh at sin on talk shows and movies. You look up to an ungodly woman at work. You admire a celebrity who is far from God. You spend more and more time with a questionable friend. You listen to music that makes sin sound appealing. As you listen to sinners, you want to be like them. You meditate on sin, although you might not call it that.[2] You begin walking "in the counsel of the wicked" (v. 1).

Next, you identify with sinners. You stop and take your stand with them. The word "way" refers to a lifestyle, a path you follow through life. Their sinful lifestyle becomes your lifestyle; their attitude is your attitude; their habits become your habits.

Then there is one step further as you sit "in the seat of scoffers" (v. 1). Scoffers are funny—they'll make you laugh as you turn away from God. Mockers are missionaries of wickedness. They tell jokes as they call good evil and evil good. They want to make you feel stupid for trying to follow God. If you listen to them long enough, you will walk in their counsel, you will take your stand with them, and you will become like them.

This first verse presents us with a problem that we cannot ignore. If we are honest, you and I will admit that we do listen to the counsel of the wicked all too often. We have stood with sinners. We may have laughed and made fun of someone who is obeying God. To say it another way, you and I are sinners (1 John 1:8).

This is a problem because the grammar of verse 1 requires complete obedience. The blessed man has never sinned.[3] Willem VanGemeren, a noted Old Testament scholar, points this out.

> The perfect mood of the verbs in each case emphasizes that the godly are *never* involved with anything tainted with evil.[4]

So the blessings of Psalm 1 are for those who are and always have been separate from sin. Who can inherit this blessing? Who can hope to have the truly happy life this psalm lays out for us? Is the psalmist tempting us with something we can never have?

In fact, only one man in history has lived out the reality of Psalm 1. Augustine, the great North African theologian of the fourth century, says boldly about this verse, "This is to be understood of our Lord Jesus Christ."[5] From Adam onward, no other man has lived up to Psalm 1:1.

A man named Joseph Flacks was visiting Palestine in the early twentieth century. He had an opportunity to address a gathering of Jews and Arabs and decided to speak on the first psalm. He read it in Hebrew and discussed the verb tenses. Then he asked the question, "Who is this blessed man of whom the psalmist speaks? This man never walked in the counsel of the wicked or stood in the way of sinners or sat in the seat of mockers. He was an absolutely sinless man."

Nobody spoke. So Flacks said, "Was he our great father Abraham?" One old man said, "No, it cannot be Abraham. He denied his wife and told a lie about her."

"Well, how about the lawgiver Moses?" "No," someone said. "It cannot be Moses. He killed a man, and he lost his temper by the waters of Meribah."

Flacks suggested David. It was not David; he committed both murder and adultery.

There was a long silence. Then an elderly Jew arose and said, "My brothers, I have a little book here; it is called the New Testament. I have been reading it, and if I could believe this book, if I could be sure that it is true, I would say that the man of the first Psalm was Jesus of Nazareth."[6]

Amazingly, the very first verse of the Psalms points to Christ. Ancient Jews who read this psalm would recognize that David and the kings after him did not live up to the ideals of this opening psalm. Like this elderly Jewish man, Psalm 1:1 would prompt them to look for the kind of messiah who did please the Lord and who did not sin against him.[7] Now that Jesus has come, we can see that he is the only one whose sinless life and delight in God's Word has earned him God's blessing. He is the one truly and supremely happy man (cf. 45:7). Jesus is the blessed man of Psalm 1!

So where does this leave us? The good news, the gospel, is that all the blessings of Psalm 1 become ours through his obedience. We have been joined together with Jesus by trusting in his death and resurrection. If you are in Christ, your life is wrapped up in him, and his life is wrapped up in yours. On the cross he took our sin and gave us his righteousness. The Scriptures say,

For our sake he [God] made him [Jesus] to be sin who knew no sin, so that
in him we might become the righteousness of God. (2 Corinthians 5:21)

God gives us Jesus' righteousness—his obedience is counted as ours.
And since Jesus' righteous obedience is imputed to us, then all the blessings
of Psalm 1 are ours as well. Not only so, but if the Spirit of Christ is living in
us, Christ himself will help us turn away from sin, delight in his Word, and
meditate on his Word. To live out Psalm 1, we need to become like Christ
through the power of the Holy Spirit.

The Blessed Man Loves God's Word

The description of the blessed man continues in verse 2. God blesses the one
who constantly and intentionally focuses on his Word.

[B]ut his delight is in the law of the LORD,
    and on his law he meditates day and night. (1:2)

This was supremely true of Christ, of course. As a child, he amazed the
teachers in the temple with the depth of his knowledge and understanding.
When he was tempted by Satan in the wilderness, Jesus answered each time
with the Scriptures. Jesus began and ended his earthly ministry teaching the
Scriptures (Luke 4:14–21; 24:44–47).

This is also true of everyone who belongs to Christ. Those who inherit the
blessings of Psalm 1 are known by their heart and their head. First, their hearts
delight "in the law of the LORD" (v. 2). One important sign that someone has
genuinely come to faith is that he or she has a new hunger for God's Word.
He or she loves to read it.

The word "law" is the Hebrew word *torah*, which means instruction. This
often means the Law of Moses, but in this context it refers to the Scriptures as
a whole and especially the Psalms. The blessed man finds unspeakable joy in
God's Word because he loves God and he wants to learn how to please God.
You will only delight in God's Law if you already delight in God himself.

Some people do not delight "in the law of the LORD" (v. 2) because they
are not humble enough to be taught. "The law of the LORD" (v. 2) is his instruction, and they don't want anyone to tell them what to do. If you are full
of yourself, the captain of your soul, it will be impossible for you to love
God's Word.

Some people do not delight "in the law of the LORD" (v. 2) because they
assume they already know God. When I was in high school, our football coach

gave us a chalk talk before games on Saturday morning. He would always end by giving us a moment of silence to pray to God "however we understood him to be." No judgments—pray to the God you choose for yourself.

If you imagine that you can know God just by looking inside yourself, you are like a man looking down a well. The reflection you see is your own face. You assume that God is like you (Psalm 50:21). But God's ways are high above our ways; he dwells in unapproachable light. We can only know him if he reveals himself to us (Isaiah 55:8, 9; 1 Timothy 6:16). This is why we need the Bible. Some people don't love God's Word because they think they already know him.

God's blessing is for those whose hearts love his Word. If your heart is engaged, your head will be engaged too: "and on his law he meditates day and night" (v. 2). The word "meditate" means to murmur or to mutter. This has the sense of talking to yourself, speaking under your breath as you ponder God's Word. This is also an imperfect verb, which suggests that this is an ongoing action; we ponder God's Word "day and night" (v. 2) like a program running constantly in the background on a computer. The Word of God releases its flavor as we chew on it over time.

How can we meditate on God's Word? The foundation is to spend time reading God's Word. You cannot be deeply influenced by something you don't know. As we read, we can reflect on God's Word in a number of ways. When I pray at the end of my devotions, I try to pray two or three things that stood out to me. This helps reinforce some things I can think about all day. We can write down a verse or two on a Post-it and keep it in our pocket. Music is a powerful way to meditate on God's Word for both children and adults. My family has a set of CDs called *Good Seed* that are Scripture put to music, and we know all the words. Some people set an alarm on their watch to remind them to think about God's Word throughout the day.

And, of course, there is no substitute for memorizing God's Word. When I wake up at night worrying, afraid, or feeling sorry for myself, God sends me light in the darkness through the Word that I have committed to memory.

The goal of meditating on God's Word is to look at it long enough so that we see its beauty and our hearts catch fire. Pondering the Psalms will wake up our hearts to find joy in Christ. Our goal is not to master the Psalms but to be mastered by them.

Who is this blessed man of Psalm 1? The true blessed man is our Lord Jesus Christ. Every man or woman who belongs to Christ also receives these blessings through him. And if we belong to him, we make it our goal to live out the pattern God sets for us in this psalm. Blessed is the man who turns away from sin to find joy in God's Word.

How Is the Godly Man Blessed?

This leads us to our second main question. What does this blessing look like? How was Jesus blessed through his obedience, and how are we blessed in him? What does God's favor look like?

The psalmist paints a picture of the green and growing blessings of the righteous. These blessings are even more compelling because they stand in contrast with the empty wasteland of the ungodly.

The Blessing of Life

The blessings of the righteous remind us of the beauty of the garden of Eden.

> He is like a tree
>   planted by streams of water
> that yields its fruit in its season,
>   and its leaf does not wither.
> In all that he does, he prospers. (1:3)

The image of a flourishing tree is a rich image to describe a believer's life. There are five specific blessings in this picture.

First, this tree doesn't merely grow; it is "planted" (v. 3). Trees grow randomly in a forest; it takes a landscaper or gardener for a tree to be planted. A landscaper plans where to plant her trees for height, for color, for shade, and for a host of other reasons. In the same way, God chooses where to place us for our good to bring order and beauty in this world. There is a purpose and plan to the life of a believer. Nothing in your life is haphazard. The Scriptures say,

> all the days ordained for me were written in your book
> before one of them came to be. (Psalm 139:16 NIV)

This sense of God's planning grows in the second blessing. This happy man or woman is planted "by streams of water" (1:3). The word "streams" is literally "canals." This tree is intentionally planted by not one but several irrigational canals that flow with life-giving water.[8]

The third blessing of this tree is that it "yields its fruit in its season" (v. 3). As you delight and meditate on God's Word, you will produce fruit in every season of life. The psalmist doesn't name these fruits because they are innumerable. The godly man or woman produces thanksgiving in seasons of plenty, faith in seasons of doubt, patience in suffering, peace in turmoil, mercy when wronged, gentleness when falsely accused, strength in temptation, humility in leadership, and prayer in all seasons.

The fourth blessing of this tree is, "its leaf does not wither" (v. 3). In the middle of summer, the grass might be brown as the sun beats down and turns the land into a skillet. But this man has roots that go below the surface to drink from the waters his gardener supplies. When an unbelieving world sees a man put out leaves while he is torched by the hot winds of life, there can only be one explanation.

I think of a dear friend, Don McKinzie, whose "leaf did not wither." As his cancer advanced, Don continued to work security at the door of the church. When I left in the late afternoon or came back in the evening, Don was always upbeat, even after a hard day of chemo. Deep beneath the surface, his roots drank from streams of living water.

The fifth blessing comes at the end of verse 3, "In all that he does, he prospers" (v. 3). Prosperity preachers read this verse with dollar signs in their eyes. But the Hebrew verb translated "prospers" means "to succeed, to accomplish the work you set out to do."[9] Jesus, the truly blessed man, accomplished his work through the cross; he succeeded through suffering and death. Isaiah says this about him:

> Yet it was the will of the LORD to crush him;
>   he has put him to grief;
> when his soul makes an offering for guilt,
>   he shall see his offspring; he shall prolong his days;
> the will of the LORD shall prosper in his hand.
> Out of the anguish of his soul he shall see and be satisfied.
>   (Isaiah 53:10, 11)

In God's economy, the work he gives us often prospers through our own suffering and humiliation. The blessing, though, is that this pain and confusion is not pointless. The work God gives us to do in the place he plants us will prosper as we faithfully turn from sin, delight in God's Word, and meditate on the Word.

The Wasteland of the Wicked

The psalmist contrasts the blessings of a godly man with the wasteland of the wicked. The life of the ungodly is futile.

> The wicked are not so,
>   but are like chaff that the wind drives away. (1:4)

The picture here is of the threshing floor during harvesttime. First the heads of wheat were crushed to separate the kernel from the husk. Then it was tossed in the air so that the wind would carry away the lighter husks, the chaff, while the heavy kernels fell back down to the ground. To picture chaff today, think of a combine harvesting a Kansas wheat field. Dust and bits of straw blow in a cloud across the open prairie behind it.

Nothing could be farther from the picture of the blessed man. Instead of a solid tree, the wicked is a hollow shell. He doesn't produce fruit; his life is a husk. He has no roots to hold him steady and reach the water. He is blown by the wind. The wicked are rootless, weightless, useless, worthless. In fact, chaff is in the way; you have to remove it to find the useful grain.

An empty husk is not always obvious on the surface. Many who are chaff mask it well, even some who go to church. But eventually the winnowing and the winds will reveal the truth. Sometimes a crisis hits them or one they love, and they do not survive spiritually; the wind blows them away. And ultimately a final judgment is coming.

> Therefore the wicked will not stand in the judgment,
>> nor sinners in the congregation of the righteous. (1:5)

The end of the wicked may not be visible in this life. But since they are chaff, they will not survive the day of judgment. They will collapse; they "will not stand" (v. 5). They will also be driven away because they don't belong with God's people.

So there are two drastically different pictures before us. On the one hand, the blessings God promises those who love him are like the garden of Eden. On the other hand, the emptiness and judgment that come to the wicked are terrifying. Which life is yours? Which life do you want to be yours?

Why Is the Godly Man or Woman Blessed?

This brings us to the final question. Why is the godly man or woman blessed?

> [F]or the LORD knows the way of the righteous,
>> but the way of the wicked will perish. (1:6)

The reason the godly flourish is because God is watching over them. When all is said and done, the real question in life is not whether I know God but whether he knows me. During the 1996 Presidential elections Bob Dole, the Republican candidate, came to march in our town's Fourth of July Parade. Thousands of people lined the parade route, yelling and cheering as he went by. It was exciting to have a national candidate in our little town outside Chicago. All of us knew who Bob Dole was, but if I wanted to see him, the Secret Service would not have let me near him unless he knew me. When it comes to God's blessing today and in eternity, the question is not, "Do I know God?" but "Does God know me?" Does he know your way?

No one watches over the wicked to protect and bless them. To describe the totality of their destruction, it's not just the wicked themselves who perish, but "the way of the wicked will perish" (v. 6). The godless path they blazed through life will be destroyed when God purges sin from his world. Every trace of the wicked, even their footsteps, will be wiped away.

When our family still lived in the Twin Cities, the bridge over I35W collapsed during the afternoon rush hour on August 1, 2007. The eight-lane bridge was the fifth busiest bridge in Minnesota, carrying over 140,000 commuters daily. When the bridge fell, one hundred vehicles and eighteen construction workers plunged down 112 feet to the Mississippi River below. One minute the bridge was there, the next it was gone. When the way of the wicked disappears, the wicked will disappear with it. Even their place is gone. There will be nowhere for them.

Closing Thoughts

Jesus Christ is the true righteous man of Psalm 1. God blessed him and prospered him as our sinless Savior. If you belong to him, the blessings of Psalm 1 are yours through him. If you belong to him, Psalm 1 will be the pattern of your life.

This is the way to true happiness. This is the path of God's blessing. I pray it is your path.

2

Let Earth Receive Her King

PSALM 2

KIM UN GUK was the second North Korean weightlifter to win a gold medal at the London Olympics. After his world record lift, he told reporters, "I won first place because the shining supreme commander Kim Jong Eun gave me power and courage."[1] We laugh because this sounds funny to us. But this is a reminder that the nation of North Korea remains officially atheistic and set against Christ.

As Christians, what should we think when we see this kind of opposition to God? North Korea is one of thousands of obvious examples of a world in rebellion against God.

Christians in Egypt are nervous about the future as the Muslim Brotherhood strengthens its grip on power in that nation. Here at home the Parents Research Council released a recent report that full nudity on prime-time television rose 407 percent from 2011 to 2012.[2] Violence is so common it hardly raises an eyebrow. After a recent shooting at the Empire State Building, I overheard one man ask, "Was anyone killed in this one?" There was hardly a flicker of emotion in his voice.

Usually, though, our rebellion is less dramatic. Many people we know simply ignore God and do life their own way. They go to school, raise their kids, and pay their taxes without the slightest thought of following Jesus Christ. This is suburban rebellion.

It's not immediately obvious that the cause of Christ is winning in our world or in our neighborhoods. We live in a world that openly opposes God in big and small ways. What should we think about this? Will God do anything about it?

The message of Psalm 2 is that God has powerfully and decisively set his Son on the throne to end this world's rebellion. This uprising began when Adam and Eve, our parents, first sinned in the garden of Eden. God will not let this go on forever. He has raised up a King with authority over every person and every nation.

Psalm 2 continues the contrast between the righteous and the wicked that began in Psalm 1. These first two chapters stand as an introduction to the book. Psalm 1 begins with, "Blessed is the man" and Psalm 2 ends with another blessing, "Blessed are all." These bookends suggest that the first two Psalms are meant to be read together as an introduction to the Psalms.

In Psalm 2, "the way of sinners" (Psalm 1:1) becomes more specific and more serious. It is a violent insurrection against the God of Heaven and the King he set in authority to rule the world. On the other hand, the righteous man of Psalm 1 becomes more specific and clear too. He is the Son of God who inherits a throne—God gives him complete authority over all nations. The world hates God's anointed King, but the righteous embrace him and are blessed. So the Psalms open with two ways to live: we can refuse Christ or take refuge in him.

The purpose of this psalm is to convince us that it is foolish and futile to fight against Christ. For Christians, this is a message of hope and encouragement. The world is lined up against God, and yet Jesus will conquer all nations and peoples.

If you don't know Jesus, God is appealing to you through this Psalm. Be wise. Be reasonable. You can't fight God. You need to bend your knee to Jesus and honor him with joy today. True blessing doesn't come from being free to live your own life; true happiness comes from following Jesus Christ.

Harry Ironside speaks of four voices in this psalm in its four sections: the voice of the world, the voice of the Father, the voice of the Son, and the voice of the Holy Spirit.[3] Let's listen to each of these voices in turn.

The World Shouts

We begin with the world's rebellion. The psalmist is amazed that anyone would be foolish enough to fight God.

> Why do the nations rage
>   and the peoples plot in vain?
> The kings of the earth set themselves,
>   and the rulers take counsel together,
>   against the LORD and against his Anointed, saying,
> "Let us burst their bonds apart
>   and cast away their cords from us." (2:1–3)

If we could see the psalmist as he writes this, he would be shaking his head in disbelief. Don't they know they can't win? Why are they raging? Why are they scheming? The word translated "plot" (v. 1). is the same word translated "meditates" in Psalm 1:2. It means to murmur or to talk under your breath. The righteous murmur about God's Word; the wicked murmur about rebellion.

Worldwide Rebellion

This uprising is not limited to a specific country or continent. All the nations and peoples of the world are in this together. This uprising is also not limited to any social class. Both the people and their leaders—the upper class and the lower class—have set themselves against God.

This rebellion is worldwide because it is rooted in the sin nature we all inherited from Adam. If you trek five days into the jungle, the people you meet are set against God. If you ride the crowded subways of New York City, the people pushing by you are set against God.

Rebellion against God and His Christ

Who are they fighting against? The word "Anointed" (v. 2) is the name *messiah* in Hebrew and *christ* in Greek. In ancient Israel, kings, prophets, and other leaders were anointed with oil to show that they were set apart for God's work. Because of this, some Old Testament scholars think Psalm 2 was written for the coronation of David or another king after him in Jerusalem.

Is that where this psalm comes from? I don't think it's likely that this psalm was used to crown any of the kings in Jerusalem. For one thing, this psalm is not linked to a coronation anywhere in the Old Testament. Some think this *should* have been used at a coronation, but there is no evidence that it actually *was*.[4] In fact, the evidence points in the other direction. Very few of the kings in Jerusalem had neighboring countries under their control who could rebel the way verses 1–3 describe.[5] Except for the reigns of David and Solomon, Israel was mostly a minor power in the Ancient Near East. For much of their history, it would have been laughable for a king in Jerusalem to think he was a major player on the world stage.[6] So with the worldwide scope of Psalm 2, these words fit the kings in Jerusalem like NFL shoulder pads on a little boy. The words of this psalm are simply too big for them.

In fact, this psalm points to someone greater than David or any king of Israel or Judah. F. F. Bruce concludes,

It is inconceivable that such notions were entertained in any directly personal way concerning the line of monarchs who followed in Judah. We have here, therefore, either the most blatant flattery the world has ever heard, or else the expression of a great ideal.[7]

Psalm 2 could apply to only one king in all human history, the Lord Jesus Christ. This is not an armed insurrection in the Ancient Near East against David or the kings after him in Jerusalem. Psalm 2 describes the rebellion of the human heart against God. This psalm is a prophecy that points forward to Jesus.

In fact, this is one of the psalms most often quoted in reference to Jesus Christ in the New Testament. When God the Father spoke from Heaven at Jesus' baptism, he used the words of Psalm 2:7, "This is my beloved Son" (Matthew 3:17). The author of Hebrews quotes Psalm 2 to show that Jesus is greater than the angels and that he is a greater high priest than the Old Testament priests (Hebrews 1:5; 5:5). Paul preached Christ's resurrection from Psalm 2 (Acts 13:33). The book of Revelation shows several ways that Psalm 2 is fulfilled in Jesus (Revelation 1:5; 2:27; 12:5).

Since Jesus is God's Son, those who rebel against him are rebelling against God himself. This rebellion is against "the LORD *and* against his Anointed" (v. 2). The kings want to break "*their* bonds" and "*their* cords" (v. 3), meaning the chains of obedience to God and his Christ. You can't be for God and against Christ—they cannot be separated. If you are against Christ, you are against God. If you ignore Christ, you ignore God. This is why the Scriptures say, "No one who denies the Son has the Father. Whoever confesses the Son has the Father also" (1 John 2:23).

The world has not set itself against the idea of God in general. In fact, people around the world are usually religious. By nature, though, we are against the God who has revealed himself in Jesus Christ. Human beings across the globe are offended by the God of the Bible, and we rage against him.

Fulfilled in Jesus Christ

Kings and leaders did rise up against Jesus. Herod fought against Christ when Jesus was just a baby. The leaders of Israel gathered together to plan how to kill Jesus (Matthew 12:14; 26:3, 4). The early church saw that Psalm 2 was fulfilled in Jesus' life. When they were persecuted, they applied the words of Psalm 2 to Jesus in their prayer.

And when they heard it, they lifted their voices together to God and said, "Sovereign Lord, who made the heaven and the earth and the sea and everything in them, who through the mouth of our father David, your servant, said by the Holy Spirit,

> 'Why did the Gentiles rage,
>   and the peoples plot in vain?
> The kings of the earth set themselves,
>   and the rulers were gathered together,
>   against the Lord and against his Anointed'—

for truly in this city there were gathered together against your holy servant Jesus, whom you anointed, both Herod and Pontius Pilate, along with the Gentiles and the peoples of Israel, to do whatever your hand and your plan had predestined to take place." (Acts 4:24–28)

Rebellion against Jesus did not end with his death and resurrection. Saul of Tarsus was traveling to Damascus to put Christians in chains when Jesus appeared to him and said, "Saul, Saul, why are you persecuting me?" (Acts 9:4). Whenever people persecute Christians, they are raging and fighting against Christ.

Near the end of his reign, Emperor Diocletian (AD 284–305) set up two massive pillars in Spain declaring victory over Jesus Christ. The inscription on the pillars read:

> Diocletian Jovian Maximian Herculeus Caesares Augusti, for having adopted Galerius in the east, for having everywhere abolished the superstition of Christ, for having extended the worship of the gods.[8]

This rebellion against Christ continues in the twenty-first century, of course. North Korean weightlifter Kim Un Guk is just one example. We can each think of many more.

God Responds

Where is God in all this? What is God going to do about this mutiny?

God Laughs

God is not in Heaven wringing his hands. He doesn't call in his generals. He doesn't hurry into a fortified bunker.

> He who sits in the heavens laughs;
>   the Lord holds them in derision. (2:4)

This is the only place in the Bible where it says that God laughs. When a creature shakes his fist at the Creator, it's so ridiculous that laughter is the only response.

God laughs because this uprising doesn't threaten him in the least. The nations rage, but God doesn't have to rage. He doesn't have to set himself like the kings of the earth do. He doesn't take counsel with anyone. He doesn't need to plot. In fact, God doesn't bother to stand up; he "sits in the heavens." Isaiah says,

> Behold, the nations are like a drop from a bucket,
>   and are accounted as the dust on the scales;
>   behold, he takes up the coastlands like fine dust. (Isaiah 40:15)

God's laughter humiliates his enemies. He "holds them in derision." God is not laughing because the world's rebellion is some kind of silly joke. God takes sin seriously. In our disobedience we spit on his glory. We drag his name through the mud, we ruin his world, we harm men and women who bear his image, and we war against his Son. Part of God's triumph is holding his enemies up to public disgrace. He did this supremely through Jesus' death. The Scriptures say that God "disarmed the rulers and authorities and put them to open shame, by triumphing over them" on the cross (Colossians 2:15). God's mocking laughter is part of his judgment on sinners.

God Speaks

With all the nations gathered for war, God merely opens his mouth.

> Then he will speak to them in his wrath,
>   and terrify them in his fury, saying,
>   "As for me, I have set my King
>   on Zion, my holy hill." (2:5, 6)

God's Word stands firm in spite of the nations' hatred, their gathered strength, the wisdom of their council chambers, their plotting, and their rage. In the beginning "God said, 'Let there be light,' and there was light" (Genesis 1:3). God has established his King with his word, the same powerful word that spoke creation into being.

All the power in the world will not stop God's word. Pharaoh tried to destroy the Israelites, but he ended up caring for Moses and educating him in his own palace. Haman plotted to destroy the Jews, but he was hung on the gallows he built for another. The leaders of Israel put Jesus to death and thought they had destroyed him. Instead God used the cross to triumph over sin and save his people. Paul and Silas were beaten and thrown in jail; through their suffering, the jailer was saved. The Emperor Diocletian set up pillars proclaiming victory over Christ, but seven years later Constantine came to the throne, and Christianity became the official religion of the Roman Empire.

God's Word still stands today. Jesus is still God's King by the strength of an unbreakable Word. In spite of opposition, the kingdom of Christ has grown to the point where 70 percent of the Christians in the world do not come from the West (North America and Europe). At least 50 percent of Christian missionaries today come from the non-western world. In the Middle East more people have come to Christ in the last twenty-five years than came to Christ in the previous fourteen hundred years, since the birth of Islam. There are at least three million Christians in the Arab world, and roughly two million of them have come to Christ from a Muslim background.[9]

God has spoken. His Word will stand. He has set Jesus Christ as King over all creation.

Christ Proclaims

In the third section of this psalm, the Messiah speaks for himself. God's King is not the strong, silent type. God's King is a preacher.

When an Army officer arrives to take a new command, he brings his orders with him to show that he has the right to be in charge. If a man takes over without orders, he is breaking the chain of command and is acting on his own. Christ repeats God's decree to prove that he has the legitimate right to rule the world. In verses 7–9 the King announces his identity, his destiny, and his authority.

Christ's Identity

First, Christ announces his identity.

> I will tell of the decree:
> The Lord said to me, "You are my Son;
>   today I have begotten you." (2:7)

When Christ declares that he is God's Son, he identifies himself in two ways. As God's Son, he is connected horizontally to his people and vertically to God.

As the Son of God, Christ identifies himself vertically in relationship to God. As a son, he is close to God; he knows God as a son knows his father (Matthew 11:27). He is subordinate to God; he obeys as a son obeys his father

(Philippians 2:5–8). He represents God as a son represents his father (Hebrews 1:3). He shares God's life as a son has life from his father. And because he is God's Son, he is the legitimate heir to the throne.

When our son was born, my wife and I took time to settle on his name. Since he was our last child, we knew that he would be the only boy in our family. After talking about names for several weeks, we finally decided to give him my name, but in reverse order. I am James Andrew Johnston; he is Andrew James Johnston. And as it turns out, he looks an awful lot like me. There is a bond between father and son that is deep and special. As God's Son, Christ shares the very life and being of God himself.

As God's Son, Christ is also connected horizontally to God's people. How so? Much earlier in the Old Testament, God had called Israel his son. When God sent Moses to Pharaoh, he instructed him,

> Then you shall say to Pharaoh, "Thus says the LORD, Israel is my firstborn son, and I say to you, 'Let my son go that he may serve me.' If you refuse to let him go, behold, I will kill your firstborn son." (Exodus 4:22, 23)

God called the whole nation of Israel his son several times in the Law and the Prophets as well (Deuteronomy 1:31; Jeremiah 31:9; Hosea 11:1). Being God's son was at the heart of what it meant for Israel to be God's covenant people.[10]

The King is God's Son because he represents all the people. So when God promised David that one of his descendants would sit on his throne forever, God said, "I will be to him a father, and he shall be to me a son" (2 Samuel 7:14). God's covenant with his people would be focused on their representative, the King.

When Christ announces that he is God's Son, he claims to represent all God's people as their King. It is a horizontal statement. This reality is at the heart of our salvation. He embodies us in himself so completely that his obedience can be counted as our obedience, his death can be counted as our death, his resurrection is our resurrection, his unending life is our life. We are saved because Jesus is the Son of God, our representative.

So when Christ proclaims God's decree, "You are my Son; today I have begotten you," he is proclaiming his relationship with God and with God's people.

Christ's Destiny

Then Christ proclaims his destiny.

> Ask of me, and I will make the nations your heritage,
>   and the ends of the earth your possession. (2:8)

God has promised to give him the farthest corners of the world as his inheritance. His destiny is to rule the planet.

Christ's Authority

And finally Christ proclaims his authority.

> You shall break them with a rod of iron
>   and dash them in pieces like a potter's vessel. (2:9)

God commissioned the Messiah to use whatever force is necessary to subdue the world and take his inheritance. The word "shall" implies that many will resist and be shattered by Christ. A king may need to send troops to put down an uprising in a rebellious province. First he sends messengers under a flag of truce. If they are rejected, then he will have to use force. He is acting for the good of the nation even though he hopes he will not have to take such a drastic step. In the same way, Christ calls people everywhere to repent before he must use force. God has charged him to end this world's rebellion. He has the power and authority to complete the work that God gave him to do.

When did Christ announce these things? Christ declared his identity, his destiny, and his authority during his earthly life, of course. After the Resurrection, Christians preached Jesus in all the world (Colossians 1:6, 23). The apostles announced the news that Jesus is "both Lord and Christ" (Acts 2:36). After them, evangelists, pastors, and teachers have carried on the preaching of Jesus Christ.

When Christ's ambassadors speak, it is Christ himself speaking through them to the world. For example, the church in Ephesus was established by Paul and others. Yet Paul says that it was actually Christ who was speaking through these missionaries.

> And he [that is, Christ] came and preached peace to you who were far off
> and peace to those who were near. (Ephesians 2:17)

Christ speaks today through the messengers he sends with his Word. Calvin says, "As often, therefore, as we hear the gospel preached by men, we ought to consider that it is not so much they who speak, as Christ who speaks by them."[11]

This means that the missionaries, evangelists, and preachers Christ raises up and sends out are fulfilling the Son's proclamation from Psalm 2. Christ extends his rule throughout the world by extending his Word throughout the world.

The Spirit Invites

The psalmist closes with this invitation:

> Now therefore, O kings, be wise;
> be warned, O rulers of the earth. (2:10)

This appeal is God's mercy and patience as he holds out his hands to a rebellious world. The work of the Holy Spirit is to lift up Christ and draw us to him, which is what these final verses are doing. After the thunder of the iron rod and crashing pottery in verse 9, Ironside calls this "a very gentle, a very loving, a very tender voice."[12]

This tender voice calls for us to be sensible, to be wise. He invites you to examine yourself and to consider God's decree. The words "Now therefore" (v. 10) mean that this is not a knee-jerk, emotional response. We need to make a logical conclusion from what we have just read.[13] We need to come to our senses. God's Spirit is patiently reasoning with us.

> Serve the LORD with fear,
> and rejoice with trembling.
> Kiss the Son,
> lest he be angry,
> and you perish in the way,
> for his wrath is quickly kindled. (2:11, 12a)

This is a mature, complex response. To respond rightly to God, we need to see his beauty and goodness so clearly that we respond with joy because we love him. And yet we also need to see his terrifying power so clearly that we tremble.

There is a blessing for those who love and honor Christ.

> Blessed are all who take refuge in him. (2:12b)

Our only hope is to embrace Jesus Christ. God has set him on the throne to deal decisively with this world's rebellion. There is no refuge from him. Our only refuge is in him.

3

God Save the King

PSALM 3

THERE ARE FEW CRIMES more horrifying than when a son attacks his own father. On April 16, 2012, nineteen-year-old Tucker Cipriano broke into his parents' home in Dearborn, Michigan at 3:00 a.m. Tucker broke in with his friend Mitchell Young, looking for drug money. They had even planned what they would do, practicing the break-in when no one was there. The plan was to kill the Cipriano family, steal the contents of the family safe, and flee to Mexico.

The police found Tucker's father, Robert Cipriano, beaten to death. His mother, Rose, and brother, Salvatore, had been savagely attacked but survived. Tucker was arrested a short time later.

What a horrifying crime! The name for killing one's own father is patricide. It is an especially gruesome, wicked sin when a son turns his hand against the man who gave him life.

This sort of horror is the background behind Psalm 3. The superscription gives us the historical setting for these words.

A PSALM OF DAVID, WHEN HE FLED FROM ABSALOM, *HIS SON.*

This is the first Psalm that comes with a superscription. The word "psalm" in this case is the Hebrew word *mizmor*, which means a song that is accompanied by stringed instruments. Of the seventy-three psalms we have that were written by David,[1] thirteen include historical details; here we have a reference to Absalom's rebellion.

These superscriptions are part of the psalms; in fact, they are numbered as verse 1 in the Hebrew Bible. In the New Testament, Jesus treated the superscription of Psalm 110 as if it was authoritative Scripture (Matthew 22:43, 44). The Holy Spirit inspired these superscriptions to give important background details to understand a particular psalm. Not all the psalms have a superscription, but when they do we need to notice them.

David's flight from Absalom was a particularly horrifying moment in his life. The insurrection was unexpected. It came at a time when David was strong and well-established as king. Israel was something of a superpower in the region, but this attack did not come from an outside enemy—his own family turned on him. It was all too common in the ancient world for a son to murder his father to take the throne. Even mighty Sennacherib, the King of Assyria who laid siege to Jerusalem, was killed by two of his own sons (2 Chronicles 32:21).

The story of Absalom's rebellion is found in 2 Samuel 15—19. Absalom already had blood on his hands; years before, he had murdered his brother Amnon. Now Absalom began plotting to take the throne. While David was busy governing the nation, Absalom charmed the people and won their hearts. The rebellion began in Hebron, about twenty-five miles from Jerusalem, and the people of Israel rallied to him there.

David barely escaped with his life. He fled his palace with the men still loyal to him, walking up the Mount of Olives, weeping, barefoot, and with his head covered. Along the way one of Saul's relatives, a man named Shimei, cursed David up and down.

> And Shimei said as he cursed, "Get out, get out, you man of blood, you worthless man! The LORD has avenged on you all the blood of the house of Saul, in whose place you have reigned, and the LORD has given the kingdom into the hand of your son Absalom. See, your evil is on you, for you are a man of blood." (2 Samuel 16:7, 8)

David's enemies came out of the woodwork. Anyone who had a grudge against him rallied to Absalom. Most of the people were swept up by the current and joined the uprising. David and his followers marched all night, and by daybreak they had crossed the Jordan.

This is the background for Psalm 3. David's flight from Absalom was not a vague sense of disappointment that life hadn't turned out the way he wanted. It meant pumping adrenaline—a fight or flight response. This flight was the bone weariness of a forced march, the stabbing pain of betrayal. *Who can I trust? Where can I go? Is there a spy in my camp? Will one of these men turn me over to Absalom?*

And to make it worse, David still dearly loved his son Absalom (2 Samuel

18:5, 33). I know parents who have not pressed charges against their son even though he stole money from them to buy drugs. A father may not have talked to his son in years, yet even though they are estranged, he will drive to another state to help his son when he is in trouble. David was a father. When his soldiers went out to fight against Absalom and his army, he begged his generals to go easy on the young man and spare his life. His heart was torn as a father.

Thousands of men died in this civil war. Something died inside David too. His own son wanted him dead. Absalom broke his heart. The faith of Psalm 3 was forged in a hot furnace. God literally delivered David from death and betrayal.

It is no accident that Psalm 3 comes immediately after Psalm 2, the great song of God's King. The second Psalm predicts that rulers and nations will rise against God's Anointed. Psalm 3 begins to chronicle what God's anointed actually experiences in this world. This is what life is like for God's king—he is betrayed by those closest to him.

As David reflected on the way God rescued him, we see his complaint, his confidence, his calm, and his cry. David is not just speaking for himself though. This psalm points us forward to Christ.

David's Complaint

David voices his complaint in verses 1, 2.

> O LORD, how many are my foes!
>   Many are rising against me;
> many are saying of my soul,
>   there is no salvation for him in God. *Selah*

David's complaint hinges on the word "many." He has "many . . . foes," "many" rose against him (v. 1), and "many" claimed that God had rejected him (v. 2). David is completely outnumbered and overwhelmed.

David is surrounded by "many . . . foes" (v. 1). Literally, David describes his enemies as "oppressors." The word has the sense of people pressing down on David, closing in on him like a hunted man. He is backed into a corner. His enemies are squeezing like the coils of a boa constrictor.[2] He is hemmed in—there is no escape.

To make it worse, David's enemies were not foreigners. He had fought battles against the Philistines, Ammonites, and Edomites, but these were fellow Jews. The tribe of Benjamin jumped at the chance because King Saul had been from their tribe. They resented David, the son of Jesse, from the tribe of

Judah, and this was payback. The uprising grew and multiplied as his friends betrayed him, including many in his own army.

The worst stroke of all, though, was the accusation that God had abandoned him. As they closed in for the kill, maybe they thought that God had tossed David aside because of his sin with Bathsheba. God wouldn't help him now. When you and I have sinned, it is easy to think that God wants nothing more to do with us. This is the very definition of hopelessness. So they taunted David that God had abandoned his anointed one.

David's complaint ends with the word *Selah*. This probably means a pause in the singing while the music continued. As the people sang this psalm in the temple, this was a moment to reflect on David's hopeless situation: many foes, many rising, many accusing. How would he respond? How would you respond?

David's Confidence

David was confident in the face of this overwhelming flood.

> But you, O Lord, are a shield about me,
>   my glory, and the lifter of my head. (3:3) ·

David is confident in God's protection. As a "shield," God absorbs the blows that are aimed at him. God is blocking the blows that come from the front and from behind; God is "a shield about me" (v. 3). The Lord was watching his back.

David is also confident of his relationship with God. "You, O Lord, are . . . my glory" (v. 3). David's honor and dignity came from being the one God had anointed as king.

David knew God would vindicate him—he would lift his head. In the ancient world, kings would humiliate their enemies by putting their foot on the neck of a conquered king. This sounds bad enough to us, but in a culture based on shame and honor, this was the ultimate humiliation—to be helpless and vulnerable, shamefully beneath the sole of your enemy's foot. David was confident that God is "the lifter of my head" (v. 3). He would not be humiliated under Absalom's foot; God would publicly honor him.

How could David be so sure this would happen? Was this a gut feeling David had? No. David trusted in God's promises. God made a covenant with David in 2 Samuel 7 that he would establish his kingdom and place one of his descendants on his throne forever. Psalm 2 echoes this Davidic covenant as God pledged to defend his anointed king.

> Then he will speak to them in his wrath,
>   and terrify them in his fury, saying,
> "As for me, I have set my King
>   on Zion, *my holy hill.*" (Psalm 2:5, 6)

David's confidence echoes this promise.

> I cried aloud to the LORD,
>   and he answered me from *his holy hill. Selah* (3:4)

Literally David says, "My voice cried out to the LORD"—an audible shout. If someone tries to mug you on the street, you'll yell for help. That's the idea here. David yelled for help, and God answered. His enemies tried to convince him that God would not save him. David knew better. God always keeps his word.

David's confidence is something to think about. The *selah* at the end of verse 4 is a time for reflection on God's promises.

> And my God will supply every need of yours according to his riches in glory in Christ Jesus. (Philippians 4:19)

> Let not your hearts be troubled. Believe in God; believe also in me. In my Father's house are many rooms. If it were not so, would I have told you that I go to prepare a place for you? And if I go and prepare a place for you, I will come again and will take you to myself, that where I am you may be also. (John 14:1–3)

The same God who heard David will hear you today. Do you trust him like David did?

David's Calm

David's confidence was the source of David's calm.

> I lay down and slept;
>   I woke again, for the LORD sustained me.
> I will not be afraid of many thousands of people
>   who have set themselves against me all around. (3:5, 6)

Anxiety will keep you awake at night—I know this from personal experience. Sometimes I can chalk up my insomnia to a physiological reason—jet lag or too much coffee. But more often than not, there is a spiritual root to my sleeplessness. When I lie tossing and turning on my bed, I've learned to take inventory of my soul, asking, "What do I need to turn over to the Lord?"

> Hear my anxious prayer
> The beating of my heart
> The pulse and the measure of my unbelief
> Speak your words to me
> Before I come apart
> Help me believe in what I cannot see.[3]

It's not a quick fix. I may not be able to put my finger on the root of my unbelief for several days. But this is the first step to strengthen my faith and get to the point where I can sleep soundly.

David's sleep is beautiful evidence that he was resting in God's promises. His mind was at rest. He allowed his body to rest because he knew that the God who sustains him never sleeps.

David's sleep doesn't mean we should fold our hands and not do anything for ourselves—let go and let God. God expects us to think and be wise. In fact, when David fled from Absalom, he crossed the Jordan River during the night to safety. "By daybreak not one was left who had not crossed the Jordan" (2 Samuel 17:22b). David *didn't* sleep the first night he fled from Absalom. But at some point later during the rebellion, he laid down and slept.

We need to be wise, make decisions, and take precautions when we can. But when we have done what we can, we can lie down and sleep if we trust God.

David's Cry

David's calm led to David's cry.

> Arise, O Lord!
>   Save me, O my God!
> For you strike all my enemies on the cheek;
>   you break the teeth of the wicked. (v. 7)

David echoed the war cry of Israel. When Israel broke camp in the wilderness, the ark of the covenant led the way, and Moses would pray, "Arise, O Lord, and let your enemies be scattered, and let those who hate you flee before you" (Numbers 10:35).

God's presence was not limited to the ark of the covenant. God's presence was also with his anointed king. So David called out his battle cry to the Lord: "Arise, O Lord!" (v. 7). God would shame and humiliate his enemies by slapping them on the cheek. He would disarm them. A mighty lion is powerless if his teeth are broken. God would break their fangs.

Even in this, David's heart still beat for the good of his people. He could have been utterly vindictive—"you rejected me and followed Absalom!" Instead he teaches them to trust God.

> Salvation belongs to the LORD;
>   your blessing be on your people! *Selah* (v. 8)

God would bless his people through the king they rejected. By delivering David from their foolish rebellion, God did them good.

David's Greater Son, Christ

What does David's rescue from Absalom mean for us today?

On the one hand, we can imitate David's faith and trust God's promises like he did. We have thought about several ways we can do this in this psalm. On another level, though, there is something more to Psalm 3. David's deliverance from Absalom was a physical rescue from real, deadly danger. He called out to God to save his life, and God literally saved his life.

The problem is that many times God does not save the lives of his people when we call out to him. God doesn't always deliver us like he delivered David. Sometimes we lie down to sleep and we don't wake up. So what does this psalm mean for us?[4]

We often think of the way God rescued Peter from prison. He sent an angel to open the doors and lead him to safety (Acts 12:6–19). But just days before, one of the other apostles was not rescued.

> About that time Herod the king laid violent hands on some who belonged to the church. He killed James the brother of John with the sword, and when he saw that it pleased the Jews, he proceeded to arrest Peter also. (Acts 12:1–3)

Peter was rescued, but James was not. This is a story that is repeated throughout the centuries for God's people. Two young men from the same church go off to war; one returns while the other is killed. Both men loved the Lord; both families prayed fervently; one was delivered like David, but the other was not.

We can expand this to other dangers and trials too. A loved one is in an accident and does not recover even though we pray fervently for him. A woman calls out to the Lord for her marriage, but her husband still leaves her. A man is painted into a corner by office politics; he calls out to God but still loses his job. I know one young woman who was the only believer in her family. As a teenager she was violently attacked by a group of men. When she went home, her father asked her, "So where is your God now?" Often our enemies seem to win.

We are not always delivered from trouble and danger like David was when Absalom betrayed him. God doesn't always rescue us from physical danger when we call to him. So how can we be strengthened by this psalm? What does David's rescue mean for us today?

If we are going to be fed by Psalm 3, we need to remember that David was a model of the greater King who was to come. As God's anointed king, David points forward to Christ. When Peter preached at Pentecost, he said David was a prophet (Acts 2:29, 30). Tertullian, the great North African theologian from the second century, said about David, "He sings to us of Christ, and through his voice Christ indeed also sang concerning Himself."[5]

Psalm 3 is a prophecy pointing forward to Christ. David's experience as God's anointed is a model for Jesus' experience as God's Anointed. Charles Spurgeon gives this reminder:

> Remember that David in this was a type of the Lord Jesus Christ. He, too, fled; he, too, passed over the brook Kedron when his own people were in rebellion against him, and with a feeble band of followers he went to the garden of Gethsemane.[6]

David's rejection by his own family points forward to Jesus' rejection. As John opens his Gospel, he says Jesus "came to his own, and his own people did not receive him" (John 1:11).

Jesus was also rejected as king. His family thought he was insane; his hometown would not believe in him. As Jesus hung on the cross, the chief priests complained to Pilate, "Do not write, 'the King of the Jews'" (John 19:21). Israel rejected Jesus.

David's enemies taunted him saying, "there is no salvation for him in God." When Christ hung on the cross, his enemies taunted him: "He trusts in God; let God deliver him now, if he desires him. For he said, 'I am the Son of God'" (Matthew 27:43).

David's lying down, sleeping, and waking again points forward to Jesus' death, burial, and resurrection. Sleep is a common way to describe death in the Old Testament. When King David died, for instance, the Scriptures say, "Then David slept with his fathers and was buried in the city of David" (1 Kings 2:10). This beautiful expression means that death is no more permanent than sleep to God. He wakes his people from death like we wake our children in the morning.

When Augustine comments on Psalm 3, he says,

> The words, 'I slept, and took rest; and rose, for the Lord will take me up,' lead us to believe that this Psalm is to be understood as in the Person of Christ.[7]

God saved David, his anointed, *from* physical death. God saved Jesus, his great anointed, *through* physical death.

Finally, David's love for the people who turned against him anticipates Christ's love for those who rejected him. David said, "[Y]our blessing be on your people!" (v. 8). Jesus said, "Father, forgive them" as he was being crucified (Luke 23:34).[8] The only hope for rebellious people like you and me is through this very King we have betrayed.

This psalm is pointing forward to a greater king and a greater salvation. This makes all the difference for us as Christians. Psalm 3 strengthens us through the gospel. We look to Christ, the author and perfecter of our faith, and in this psalm we see the pattern of his life. His suffering led to glory because God sustained him.

God may not save you *from* shame and death like he saved David, but he will save you *through* shame and death like he saved Christ.

> For if we have been united with him in a death like his, we shall certainly be united with him in a resurrection like his. (Romans 6:5)

You may be hard-pressed. Your family or close friends may turn against you. You might lose your job. You might lose your life. Your own children may turn against you, steal from you, hurt you. The promise of the gospel is that you will lie down, sleep, and wake up again, for the Lord will sustain you.

> [H]e who raised the Lord Jesus will raise us also with Jesus and bring us . . . into his presence. . . .
> So we do not lose heart. Though our outer nature is wasting away, our inner nature is being renewed day by day. For this light momentary affliction is preparing for us an eternal weight of glory beyond all comparison, as we look not to the things that are seen but to the things that are unseen. For the things that are seen are transient, but the things that are unseen are eternal. (2 Corinthians 4:14, 16–18)

If you believe this, you will be able to sleep in peace. You will be able to face death with confidence, knowing that God will sustain you.

4

Trusting God in a Bad Economy

PSALM 4

THE ECONOMY IS A POWERFUL ISSUE in many elections. In 1980 Ronald Reagan famously asked, "Are you better off than you were four years ago?" Bill Clinton and Barack Obama also promised to fix a weak economy. A bad economy puts enormous pressure on our leaders.

Many think that a bad economy is the background for Psalm 4.[1] More specifically, David seems to be crying out to God when the crops have failed. A bad harvest spelled disaster in an ancient agrarian society. As the king, David was feeling the heat. Even his own officials turned against him as the famine wore on.

The superscription doesn't give us any historical details, but several clues do suggest that a famine is the background for the psalm. Verses 6, 7 give us the sense of the nation's mood.

> There are many who say, "Who will show us some good?". . .
> You have put more joy in my heart
>   than they have when their grain and wine abound.

This probably reflects David's historical situation as he was writing. David seems to mention "grain" and "wine" (v. 7) because this is what people were longing for. Reading between the lines, we see a famine, a nation suffering an economic and humanitarian crisis. When the poll numbers show that people are unhappy with the economy in an election year, a sitting president is in trouble.

The leaders of the people turned against David in this famine. The word "men" in verse 2 is literally "sons of men." These are the wealthy, the landowners, the prominent, the powerful.[2] Today these are the major donors, business leaders, union bosses, and senior political party leaders. Politicians will listen to CEOs of large corporations because they have money and they have clout. David's enemies were the movers and shakers of Israel in his day. Any king needs them on his side if he is going to govern well.

Not only did the leaders turn against David, they turned away from God. We understand how this happens when the bottom falls out today. There are few things that will test your faith like a layoff, unemployment, bankruptcy, crippling debt, financial ruin, or being homeless. If you are a husband and father, you ask yourself how you will feed your family. *Has God forgotten me? Does God see? I have been following Jesus and look where it has gotten me.*

The people in David's day were tempted just like we are. Since God did not seem to be providing for them, they ran into the arms of foreign idols who promised blessings, prosperity, and plenty of food. "Our neighbors worship fertility gods, and their fields are full of grain," they said, "We would be better off if we worshiped their gods too."[3]

In Psalm 4 David appeals to these unfaithful leaders to stay faithful to God during this famine. As a faithful prophet and king, David calls the people back to God. This is a call to trust God in a bad economy.

Since this psalm was given "to the choirmaster," this is not a private prayer or an appeal that David made behind closed doors. Generations of Israelites sang this song in the temple to strengthen their faith. And through this psalm they also learned what to expect from the Messiah. Christ would be like the great King David. He would be faithful to God even when the leaders of Israel had turned away.

The word *selah* appears twice in this Psalm, suggesting natural breaks we will follow. David makes his appeal with a call, counsel, and correction.

David's Call

David's opening call comes in two parts: he calls out to God, and he calls out to men. Our lives are both vertical and horizontal; we live in the presence of God and of fellow human beings. David appeals to both in his opening call.

A Plea to God

David first pleads with God to answer his prayer.

> Answer me when I call, O God of my righteousness!
> You have given me relief when I was in distress.
> Be gracious to me and hear my prayer! (4:1)

It's significant that David pleads with God before he pleads with the leaders of Israel to repent. There is divine wisdom in this order—we need to speak with God before we speak with men.

This was especially important because David was going through the same crisis they were. Before he could ask them to trust God, he himself had to fix his hope on God. David prepared his own soul with this prayer of faith. Charles Spurgeon said, "Surely we should all speak the more boldly to men if we had constant converse with God. He who dares to face his Maker will not tremble before the sons of men."[4] Prayer should be our first response.

David strengthened his faith by remembering God's character. A better way to translate the phrase, "O God of my righteousness" (v. 1) would be "O my righteous God."[5] David remembers that God is a righteous God who keeps his commitments to his people. The gods of the nations were fickle. Their idols had feuds and were forgetful. They might lie or play tricks on their people. If you have sat through Wagner's *Ring of the Nibelung*, you have seen how the gods of Norse mythology are fickle and scheming. The movie *Thor* shows such plotting and scheming. The gods of the Canaanites behaved in much the same way.

But the God of Israel is a righteous God. Here the sense of God's righteousness is that he does what is right in all his relationships.[6] He is committed to his people as a father is committed to his children—he will do right by them. What father will not pick up the phone when his son or daughter is in trouble? Since God is righteous, David was convinced God would answer when he called. Your God is a righteous God. He will do right by you too. If you are his child, he will hear your prayer.

David also strengthened his faith by remembering what God had done for him in the past: "You have given me relief when I was in distress" (v. 1). He could look back on those years when Saul had hunted him and closed in for the kill. Again and again his life hung in the balance; yet God had rescued him out of all his troubles.

One of the great ways to strengthen your faith when the bottom falls out is to look back on your own stones of remembrance. When I was in seminary, I never knew how God was going to provide tuition for each quarter of school. One year God allowed me to line up three painting jobs during spring break. I worked fourteen-hour days and paid cash for the next quarter. Another year I received an award that came with a scholarship.

When Lisa and I look back together, one of our great stones of remembrance was the way God provided a place for our family to live when I was finishing up my doctoral dissertation. We returned from a year overseas and got off the plane with four children, no home, no job, and no income. We were literally homeless and unemployed. Some dear friends stepped in and offered to let us live in their summer home on beautiful Lake Alexander near Brainerd, Minnesota. They would not even let us pay for utilities for the nine months we stayed there. We will never forget their kindness. We had no idea how God was going to provide, and this turned into one of the sweetest years for our family.

Has the bottom fallen out for you? Remember God's character—he is a righteous God. Remember what he has done—look back over your stones of remembrance. Teach your heart to trust in God, and cry out to him in faith. He has come through six times; you can count on him to come through a seventh time.

Rebuke to Men

After David spoke to God, he was ready to speak to men. God's king not only prays, he also preaches. David calls the leaders to account by twice asking, "How long?"

First, he calls them to account for despising him as king: "O men, how long shall my honor be turned into shame?" (4:2a).

They should have honored God's chosen king just like we should honor the leaders God gives us today. All Israel knew that the prophet Samuel had chosen David from among his brothers and poured oil over his head to anoint him as king (1 Samuel 16). David did not choose this honor for himself; God chose it for him. But instead of respecting him, they turned his "honor . . . into shame" (Psalm 4:2).

In this way David points forward to Jesus Christ. When Jesus came as the rightful King of Israel, the chief priests and elders did not welcome him and honor him. Instead they mocked him and said, "He is the King of Israel; let him come down now from the cross, and we will believe in him" (Matthew 27:42). When Jews for Jesus had one of their summer campaigns in New York City several years ago, a local radio station interviewed a rabbi to get his reaction. The rabbi was dismissive, of course, and pointed out that most Jews had rejected Jesus in his lifetime. "We weren't impressed with him then," he said, "and we're not impressed with him today."

This rabbi didn't go back far enough. Not only were the Jewish people not impressed with Jesus, they weren't impressed with David either. Nor, for that matter, were they impressed with Joseph, Moses, Isaiah, or the other prophets during their lifetimes (Acts 7:52). By and large, Israel rejected the leaders God sent her. Here they despised David and turned his "honor . . . into shame" (v. 2). In the same way most Jews despise Jesus Christ even today.

Second, the leaders turned to other gods: "How long will you love vain words and seek after lies? *Selah*" (4:2b).

These men may have been lying about David, but the main issue here is probably idolatry. The prophet Amos uses the word "lies" as another name for the idols Israel worshiped (Amos 2:4). "[S]eek after lies" (v. 2) probably means praying to these gods, seeking help from them. "[V]ain words" (v. 2) is a good description of worthless worship to false gods who cannot save.[7] The leaders not only rejected David as God's king, they rejected God himself. They loved false gods and prayed to idols. David calls them to account.

David's Counsel

David followed up his call with counsel to the leaders who had buckled under the pressure of this famine and wandered from God.

Be Sure God Knows

First, David counsels his enemies to recognize that God knows those who belong to him and those who don't.

> But know that the LORD has set apart the godly for himself;
>   the LORD hears when I call to him. (4:3)

The word "godly" here has the sense of being faithful to God and committed to his covenant.[8] A godly man remains loyal to God, and God hears his prayer. Here again David points forward to Jesus, the true godly man. He is the only man who never sinned but was always faithful to God. He called out to God, and God heard him. Through his suffering and obedience, Jesus became our Savior (Hebrews 5:7–9). On the flip side, the leaders of Israel were spiritual traitors, and God would not hear their prayers. God knows those who are faithful to him and those who are not.

Interestingly, the only other place the Old Testament uses this verb "set apart" is to describe the way God makes a distinction between Israel and Egypt in the exodus.[9] He set apart the Israelites and their land so that none of the plagues affected them while the Egyptians felt the weight of his anger.[10] By using this word from the exodus, David warns these prominent men that God had set him apart from them like he set apart the Israelites from the Egyptians. The leaders were behaving like Pharaoh and his officials. If they would not repent, God might deal with them like he dealt with the Egyptians.

Repent

It is sobering to realize that God knows those who are loyal and those who are traitors to his name. This is why David's second piece of advice is to repent.

> Be angry, and do not sin;
>   ponder in your own hearts on your beds, and be silent. *Selah* (4:4)

David prescribes four dimensions of repentance. Literally the words "Be angry" (v. 4) should be translated "tremble." If you realize the danger of wandering away from God, you should shake with fear. It is a terrifying thing to face God's judgment. Then David says, "[D]o not sin" (v. 4). If you fear God in this way, you will stop repeating your sinful actions. The phrase "ponder in your own hearts" (v. 4) is literally "speak in your heart." In the privacy of your bedroom where you can be honest before God, repentance means reflecting on what God expects from you. And as a final dimension of repentance, David says, "[B]e silent" (v. 4). Be still before God.

The word *Selah* tells us to pause and think about what David just said. Is your heart at rest? Does God recognize you as one of his people? Can you be sure that God will hear you when you pray? Are you an Israelite or an Egyptian to him?

God knows his children. When I was in seminary, our church had a dinner every Wednesday night so families could eat together before the Bible studies and children's programs. I was helping clean the fellowship hall one Wednesday night when a girl came running up behind me as I was wiping a table. "Dad, Dad," she said, "can I go out with Christy's family after church? Mom said it's OK!"

I was still single, so I knew something was wrong. I also knew that I look a lot like another man in our church, and people sometimes confused the two of us. I turned around, and sure enough, it was one of his daughters. So I said, "I'm not your father, but it's okay with me." She was mortified, of course— she turned bright red and ran away.

Are you one of God's children? Will he recognize you when you come running to him? Is he watching over you? The good news is that you yourself can become a child of God through Jesus Christ his Son. The Apostle John says this at the beginning of his gospel:

> He came to his own, and his own people did not receive him. But to all who did receive him, who believed in his name, he gave the right to become children of God. (John 1:11, 12)

You can become one of God's dearly loved children by turning to Jesus today. He died on the cross to carry your sin and guilt. He rose again from the dead to give you new life. If you turn to follow Jesus, you can know that God has set you apart for himself. He does not adopt you because you deserve it by being godly. He adopts you because Jesus is the godly one who died and rose again to be our Savior.

David's Correction

David ends his appeal with correction. If the elders and wealthy men of Israel heard him and repented, they would be crying out, "What should we do?" David gives three directions.

Offer True Worship

First, they needed to offer true worship: "Offer right sacrifices, and put your trust in the LORD" (4:5).

The right sacrifices are the ones God asks for in the Law of Moses. Instead of offering gifts to other gods in the fields and high places, David commands the men to offer sacrifices on God's altar.

But rituals are not enough. For these sacrifices to be accepted, they must be offered in faith by people who genuinely trust God and look to him to provide. It's not enough to go through the motions of religion. "The sacrifices are only 'righteous' when they are acts of devotion flowing out of a right relationship with God."[11] It is easy to be a moral person with a religious veneer of Christianity. If you start going to church, it doesn't take long to learn how to behave like a "Christian." You learn the right words to say and how to behave, and you volunteer to serve. But with all that, your heart can still be far from God. God is not looking for people who are good at doing religious things. God is looking for men and women who love him and obey him sincerely from the heart.

Desire True Good

Secondly, David urges them to hunger and thirst for the right things. God is infinitely more good, more satisfying, and more full of joy than barns full of wheat.

> There are many who say, "Who will show us some good?
> Lift up the light of your face upon us, O LORD!" (4:6)

As the famine took its toll, people wondered where help would come from. The "who" in this question refers to the many idols around them. In essence David suggests the question many people were asking: "Which god should we follow who can help us?" Tragically the people were ready to sell their souls.

David's answer reminds the people that God himself is the greatest blessing: "Lift up the light of your face upon us, O LORD!" This echoes the priestly blessing Aaron and his sons used as a benediction over Israel.

> The LORD bless you and keep you;
> the LORD make his face to shine upon you and be gracious to you;
> the LORD lift up his countenance upon you and give you peace.
>   (Numbers 6:24–26)

To see God's face is to be in God's presence, which is the greatest good for which any human being can long. The tragedy is that we settle for so much less. No food, no amount of money, no clothes, no car, no house, no retirement package, no vacation, no travel destination can possibly compare with the overwhelming glory of seeing God's face. But many people live just to get more stuff. They walk through life with their eyes focused down on the ground like a cow grazing in a field. Lift up your eyes! See what is truly good and satisfying. C. S. Lewis put it this way:

> Indeed, if we consider the unblushing promises of reward and the staggering nature of the rewards promised in the Gospels, it would seem that Our Lord finds our desires not too strong, but too weak. We are half-hearted creatures, fooling about with drink and sex and ambition when infinite joy is offered us, like an ignorant child who wants to go on making mud pies in a slum because he cannot imagine what is meant by the offer of a holiday at the sea. We are far too easily pleased.[12]

God himself is the best and most satisfying good thing we can imagine. He has placed echoes and shadows of his glory in our lives to make us long for something more. The majestic roar of a waterfall shakes our bodies. The mystery of space tugs at us through a telescope. We feel the burning heat of love. We watch the sun rise over the fields. These wondrous things are appetizers that are meant to make us hungry for the God who created them. You were made to love him and worship him. Nothing less will please you.

What's more, when you have him, you can enjoy the world he has created. With him, the world is full of joy and wonder. Without him, the world is dry and stale like an old tortilla. The light of God's face brings joy to life.

When I was a boy, my father used to come back from trips and tell us about the things he had done. Sometimes he would tell us about a great meal he'd had in a restaurant—medium rare steak, sautéed asparagus, a wonderful dessert—and he would end by saying, "But I didn't really enjoy it because I wasn't with you." Now that I am a husband and father, I know what he meant. I enjoy peanut butter and jelly with my wife and children more than a steak sitting by myself. It's the relationship that makes the meal.

And it's the relationship with God that makes this world a meal to enjoy. The light of God's face transforms this world into a feast. Movie stars will tell you that a Hollywood mansion is empty and cold without love. A friend of mine was given almost a quarter of a million dollars when his family sold their business. "Aren't you happy?" they asked him. As he thought about it, he realized that no, this didn't make him happy. He never felt loved and accepted by them. This gift was certainly generous, but it didn't give him joy. He wanted them, not their money.

God gives us the greatest thing. He doesn't just give us stuff—he gives us himself. And he is more than enough. David testifies to the joy he has from knowing and loving God without the gifts God gives. Before the famine broke, he said,

> You have put more joy in my heart
>> than they have when their grain and wine abound. (4:7)

Where did that joy come from? The light of God's presence. God himself is true joy.

Rest in True Security
The result of God's joyful presence is lasting peace.

> In peace I will both lie down and sleep;
>> for you alone, O LORD, make me dwell in safety. (4:8)

David still felt the political pressure. The land was still suffering from an economic and humanitarian disaster. Yet David was able to rest. "I will not stay up in fear; I will lie down. I will not lie awake worrying; I will lie down and sleep."

If you know Jesus Christ, this rest is yours too, even in a bad economy. David's song finds its fulfillment in him. Jesus left us with his peace.

> Peace I leave with you; my peace I give to you. Not as the world gives do I give to you. Let not your hearts be troubled, neither let them be afraid. (John 14:27)

Christian, you can lie down and sleep. Your Savior loves you and cares for you.

5

The God Who Hears Prayer

PSALM 5

IN PSALM 5 David prays for God to rescue him from his enemies. We're not sure what was happening in David's life at this point. The superscription doesn't give us any historical information.

Whatever the situation was, David's confidence stands out. He is certain that God will rescue him.

> Give ear to my words, O LORD;
>   consider my groaning.
> Give attention to the sound of my cry,
>   my King and my God,
>   for to you do I pray.
> O LORD, in the morning you hear my voice;
>   in the morning I prepare a sacrifice for you and watch. (5:1–3)

David is completely confident in his relationship with God. David knows God well enough to cry out to him with his whole being—his words, his groans, his cry for help. David does not just pray to God with spoken words. He also asks God to pay attention to the unspoken groaning of his heart. And he is sure that God will not be offended even if he shouts with a loud cry for help.

People who don't know God well think they have to pray with special words. Their prayers sound like a formula with set words and phrases. But if you know God, you can come to him without putting on your makeup. You pour out your unvarnished thoughts to him. If you had a good father, you talk to God the way you would talk to your dad—you are respectful but completely comfortable that he loves you and understands.

David was also confident that God heard his prayer and would answer. "[I]n the morning" (v. 3), at the beginning of the day, David offered his sacrifice and waited to see what God would do for him. The word "watch" (v. 3) has the sense of looking with expectation. It is the same root in Hebrew as the word *watchman* or *watchtower*. When the grandparents come for a visit, our children wait for them all day. When Grandma and Grandpa are getting close, sometimes the kids will climb the trees in our front yard to watch for them. That is the sense here—he is looking with eager expectation. David was confident that his prayer had risen to the throne room of Heaven, and he watched eagerly to see what God would do.

Where does this confidence come from? How can David pour out his heart so freely to God? How can he be so sure God will answer him and rescue him? The message of Psalm 5 is that David's hope is grounded in the character of God. He is confident because he knows who God is.[1]

God's character may seem like a strange place for David to find his confidence as he prays. But there is nothing more solid than the unchanging, unwavering, unshifting, unshakable character of God. If you are a follower of Jesus Christ, God will answer your prayer because he cannot deny himself. Because of who God is, we are absolutely certain that God will hear and save everyone who takes refuge in him.

David interacts with four aspects of God's character in this prayer: God is holy, God is loving, God is just, God is kind. These aspects of God's character are joined together in two pairs: God is holy, and he is loving; God is just, and he is kind.

God Is Holy

First, David focuses on God's holiness in verses 4–6. God absolutely rejects evil and everyone who does evil.

God is holy because he infinitely loves everything that is good and beautiful and true. And because God infinitely loves everything good, he infinitely hates everything that goes against it. If you love your daughter, you will be furious at someone who abuses her. If you are not angry and you allow her to go on being hurt, she will look at you and say, "You don't love me." God hates sin precisely because he is a loving God. His love and his wrath are two sides of one coin. The purity of God's unbounded delight in goodness and his perfect hatred for evil is what makes God holy, set apart from every other thing in the universe. God's love and his wrath are not at odds with each other—they are the two complementary sides of his holiness. The prophet

Habakkuk says, "You . . . are of purer eyes than to see evil and cannot look at wrong" (Habakkuk 1:13).

As the first foundation for his confident prayer, David presents God's holy anger at sin like six steps in a staircase.

God Does Not Delight in Sin

First, God does not think sin is fun or funny: "For you are not a God who delights in wickedness" (5:4). God doesn't find sin attractive or entertaining in any way. God is repulsed by evil and wickedness wherever and whenever he sees it. This is a warning to us because sin is central to many TV shows and movies. We might chuckle when a couple hooks up on a sitcom. We might laugh at the gossip and jealousies of reality TV. Sin will desensitize you if it entertains you. But God does not delight in wickedness—ever.

This is why God never tempts anyone to sin. James says:

> Let no one say when he is tempted, "I am being tempted by God," for God cannot be tempted with evil, and he himself tempts no one. But each person is tempted when he is lured and enticed by his own desire. (James 1:13, 14)

God never tries to get someone to do wrong, because he himself is repulsed by it. Sin grows from the evil in our own hearts.

Evil Cannot Exist in God's Presence

The second step on this staircase of holiness is that evil cannot exist in God's presence. "[E]vil may not dwell with you" (v. 4). The word "dwell" means "to sojourn or to visit." The picture is of a nomad passing through and living in a tent. "God is so incompatible with sin that even the most temporary coexistence is utterly impossible."[2] Evil cannot even visit his presence. His holiness is active—it purifies everything that comes in contact with him. The writer of Hebrews says, "Our God is a consuming fire" (Hebrews 12:29). Evil cannot dwell in God's presence because his holiness actively consumes sin like coals consume ketchup.

This is why it is impossible for a genuine believer to continue in an ongoing lifestyle of sin. John says, "No one born of God makes a practice of sinning" (1 John 3:9). The Spirit of God lives inside you, and he cannot tolerate sin. If the Holy Spirit is at work in you, you will work to cleanse your lives from evil. The Scriptures also say,

> beloved, let us cleanse ourselves from every defilement of body and spirit, bringing holiness to completion in the fear of God. (2 Corinthians 7:1)

We learn the fear of God when we realize that he is a consuming fire. Personal holiness begins in this life by the Holy Spirit's power at work in us. Sanctification is a progressive process; we become more and more obedient to Jesus Christ. It will be completed when we are raised to new life in God's presence. God will make us holy because we cannot enter God's presence with even the slightest bit of evil.

God's intolerance for evil was David's great hope as he prayed, just as it is for us today. Your enemies for the sake of Christ will not have the last word because evil cannot exist in God's presence.

God Will Not Tolerate the Arrogant

This leads us naturally to the third step of God's holiness. "The boastful shall not stand before your eyes" (v. 5). When David's enemies had their way, they swaggered. When you are shamed and hurt for the sake of Christ today, people will swagger too. They boast because they think they've won. David was confident because he knew his enemies would not stand on the day when God judges the secrets of men's hearts.

God Hates Those Who Do Evil

The fourth step is God's hatred for those who do wicked things. "[Y]ou hate all evildoers" (v. 5). This sounds strange to our ears because we are used to the phrase, "God hates the sin but loves the sinner." What should we make of this verse?

These words mean what they say. God thoroughly hates everyone who does evil. God cannot coexist with evil, and he cannot tolerate those who do evil. This might seem to clash with what the Bible says elsewhere, "God so loved the world" (John 3:16). Let's dig into this a little deeper and explain this hard word.

Who are these "evildoers"? Since the Hebrew verb behind "evildoers" is a participle, the grammar tells us that an evildoer is someone who sins as a way of life.[3] If you are a Christian, this should not describe you because the Holy Spirit will not let sin be your normal lifestyle. As a result, you are working to cleanse yourself from sin. But this does describe everyone who is apart from Christ.

> [W]e all once lived in the passions of our flesh, carrying out the desires of the body and the mind, and were by nature children of wrath, like the rest of mankind. (Ephesians 2:3)

We will never grasp the greatness of God's love and mercy unless we first understand his hatred and wrath for sin and sinners. God's anger against unrepentant sinners is never fashionable, but it is the bedrock and foundation of the gospel. If you think it was no big deal for God to save you because you were already a pretty good person, then the gospel will be ho-hum. The good news is not good unless you understand that God is furious against each and every sinner.

God's burning anger against sinners is also a key reason we fight against sin in our own lives. If we understand that God hates evildoers, we will do everything in our power not to be evildoers (Hebrews 10:26–31). We will never be serious about sanctification until we understand the depth of his fury and hatred for everyone who makes a practice of doing wrong.

When you understand that God "hate[s] all evildoers" (v. 5), the gospel explodes with God's glory and goodness and grace and transforming power. Listen to the Scriptures.

> God shows his love for us in that *while we were still sinners*, Christ died for us. Since, therefore, we have now been justified by his blood, much more shall we be saved by him *from the wrath of God*. For if *while we were enemies* we were reconciled to God by the death of his Son, much more, now that we are reconciled, shall we be saved by his life. (Romans 5:8–10)

The good news is that God saves sinners. We were "evildoers," but God reached out to us in love to save us from his wrath against sin.

God Destroys Liars

Fifthly, David says, "You destroy those who speak lies" (v. 6). This also sounds strange to our ears because we don't think lying is a big deal. After all, it's just words. But God takes truth and honesty very seriously. Why?

God is a speaking God. Language is his gift to us from the first days of creation. He is not silent but communicates to us in words. Since you and I are created in the image of God, the way we use words reflects on him and his words. And on top of that, our words can spread sin in his world like a virus. Sin entered the world through Satan's words (Genesis 3:1–5). James says, "[T]he tongue . . . is a restless evil" (James 3:8).

It is significant that when Isaiah saw God in his glory sitting on his throne above the temple, he summarized his sinfulness by saying, "I am a man of unclean lips" (Isaiah 6:5). When we see God in his overwhelming majesty, even a good man like Isaiah is immediately aware of his lies and deceit. Some of the very last words of Scripture warn us that those who practice falsehood will not be allowed into Heaven (Revelation 22:15).

Make no mistake: God's holiness means that he deals drastically with liars. This was a comfort to David as he cried out to God—his enemies lied about him, but they would not succeed. It is a warning to us to guard our tongues.

God Abhors Murderers and Deceivers

The sixth step of God's holiness in these verses is found at the end of verse 6. "[T]he LORD abhors the bloodthirsty and deceitful man." Both liars and murderers are desperately wicked. We don't see it that way, of course. We can understand why God abhors murderers. Liars don't seem as bad to us. But the same evil is at work in both "the bloodthirsty" and the "deceitful." A liar is a potential murderer in certain situations. God abhors both.

It is sobering to step back and look at these six steps of God's holiness. We cannot read these words without realizing that we fall short.

God Is Loving

God's wrath against sin is not the last word. If it were, then David himself would be without hope. David lied several times during his life. He lied twice to Achish, the king of Gath, and deceived him on two separate occasions (1 Samuel 21:12–15; 27:8–12). He also lied to Ahimelech, the priest. As he was fleeing Saul, he told Ahimelech that he was on a secret mission. As a result of his deception, Saul slaughtered eighty-five priests in Ahimelech's family (1 Samuel 21:2; 22:18). And finally when David sinned with Bathsheba, he committed both murder and deception (2 Samuel 11). David was guilty by his own words.

And yet David sets himself apart from sinners who will be destroyed with the words, "But I" (Psalm 5:7). David's hope is not only in God's holiness—he also rests his hope in a second aspect of God's character: God is loving. David sings about his experience of God's love in verses 7, 8.

> But I, through the abundance of your steadfast love,
>   will enter your house.
> I will bow down toward your holy temple
>   in the fear of you.
> Lead me, O LORD, in your righteousness
>   because of my enemies;
>   make your way straight before me.

The words "steadfast love" (v. 7) are translated as "mercy" or "loving-kindness" in some translations. It is the Hebrew word *chesed*, God's covenant loyalty or committed love for his people. David knows he does not deserve to come before God. He doesn't say, "I will enter your house because I have been such a good man." As a sinner, David was confident he could enter God's presence because of God's unfailing, faithful, covenant love.

The world rejects God's love like it rejects God's holiness. We reject God's love in one of two ways. On the one hand some people say, "I'm not even going to try to please God. I'm going to live the way I want." This is the path of irreligion, and many live like this today. If you're a Christian, it is easy to spot the irreligious. They are usually not in church on Sunday. They don't do Christian things. They live however they want.

But there is another way we can reject God's love, and that is by being good, moral people. We think, "If I do the right things and clean up my life, God will be pleased with me and bless me." This is the path of religion. People on this path obey carefully so that they don't need to depend on his love. They only come to Jesus to fill in the gaps between the good things they do to earn God's approval. In Flannery O'Connor's novel *Wise Blood*, her main character, Hazel Motes, says at one point, "The way to avoid Jesus was to avoid sin."[4] You can work hard to be a good, moral person to avoid having to rely on God's love. Americans like to be self-reliant—it's humbling to accept that not a single good thing I do can make me right in God's eyes. I have to depend completely on his love. Religious people are very upright and moral, but their hearts are far from God. Both religion and irreligion reject God's love but in different ways.

To embrace the love of God like David did, we need to humble ourselves and call out to God for mercy. Sin will keep you out of God's presence, but obedience will not get you in.[5] The only way for a sinner to come before God is through his lovingkindness, his undeserved covenant love, his *chesed*.

God offers us his mercy and covenant love through Jesus Christ. That is why the Scriptures say,

> But when the *goodness* and *loving kindness* of God our Savior appeared, he saved us, *not because of works done by us in righteousness*, but according to his own *mercy*, by the washing of regeneration and renewal of the Holy Spirit, whom he poured out on us richly through Jesus Christ our Savior. (Titus 3:4–6)

God's unwavering love for you in Jesus Christ should give you immense confidence as you pray. He will not abandon you. He will rescue you from all your enemies. You can count on him to hear and to answer when you call, even if your prayer is the wordless groaning of your heart.

God Is Just

David also based his confidence on a third aspect of God's character: God is just.

David appeals to God the way a prosecutor appeals to a judge. When I was called for jury duty, I had the opportunity to watch a district attorney do his work. He began laying the ground for his case even as they were selecting the jury. David prays to God like a DA in verses 9, 10.

The Evidence

First, David lays out the evidence.

> For there is no truth in their mouth;
>   their inmost self is destruction;
> their throat is an open grave;
>   they flatter with their tongue. (5:9)

David focuses his attention on his enemies' words again. Nothing they say is true. This may be a window on David's historical situation as to when he cried out to God. His enemies may have been lying about him and spreading rumors to overthrow him as king.

David traces the source of their lying to their hearts. Jesus said, "Out of the abundance of the heart the mouth speaks" (Matthew 12:34). David's enemies were lying because "their inmost self is destruction" (v. 9). Their words are destructive because their hearts are "destruction." David follows this up with a graphic word picture: "their throat is an open grave" (v. 9). The words that come from their mouths are like the stench rising from a rotting corpse. When they speak, it is like opening a casket.

The words "mouth," "inmost self," "throat," and "tongue" are all singular even though David's enemies are many. Their many words come from one heart and one mouth as if he is facing a single person.[6] Their many voices are the one voice of sin. This may be why Paul applies this verse to all humanity in Romans 3:13 to show that Jews and Gentiles alike are under the power of sin. All of us are profoundly deceitful apart from Christ.

The Prosecutor's Final Argument

As a prosecutor, David presents his closing argument to God as a just judge and asks for a guilty verdict.

Make them bear their guilt, O God;
>   let them fall by their own counsels;
because of the abundance of their transgressions cast them out,
>   for they have rebelled against you. (5:10)

This is the first prayer in the Psalms asking God to judge the wicked. These prayers for God's judgment are called imprecatory prayers. They may sound harsh to our ears today. Since we emphasize God's mercy, it sounds cruel when David asks God to "cast out" his enemies (v. 10). What should we make of this?

David's anger at his enemies is not personal. He asks God to judge them not because they have harmed him but because "they have rebelled against you" (v. 10). As God's anointed king, his enemies were not just attacking him; they were attacking God himself (cf. Psalm 2:1–3). David asks God to condemn sinful behavior and to banish those who plot and plan against God.

These words asking for judgment are appropriate for David but not for us. As God's anointed king, he was a model pointing forward to Christ, and he held a unique place in salvation history. We should not flatter ourselves by thinking we can curse our enemies like David did. Our hearts are deceitful, and we can find ourselves thinking that the people we don't get along with are God's enemies too. What was right for David can be very wrong for us.[7] Who knows but that one of God's greatest enemies can be transformed by the gospel, like Paul was transformed into a powerful servant of God?

God Is Kind

This transformation is possible because of the fourth aspect of God's character that David prays about in this psalm: God is kind.

But let all who take refuge in you rejoice;
>   let them ever sing for joy,
and spread your protection over them,
>   that those who love your name may exult in you.
For you bless the righteous, O LORD;
>   you cover him with favor as with a shield. (5:11)

God's justice is met by God's generous kindness to sinners. David broadens his prayer to include many people. He encourages anyone and everyone who has taken "refuge" in God (see 2:12). Taking refuge in God is not temporary like a quick shelter in a rainstorm. It means committing your life and destiny to God, relying on his power and protection. This is the essence of trusting God with saving faith. Everyone who runs to him will find joy, protection, and favor.

When Martin Luther was making his way to Augsburg to appear before Cardinal Cajetan and answer for his writings, one of the Cardinal's servants taunted him, "Where will you find shelter if your patron, the Elector of Saxony, should desert you?" "Under the shelter of heaven," Luther answered.[8]

This was David's answer when his enemies pressed in against him. May it be your answer too. If you are God's child, you can pray with confidence to this God. You can trust his unchanging, unwavering, unshifting, unshakable character. He hears your prayers.

6

How Long, O Lord?

PSALM 6

ONE OF THE MOST IMPRESSIVE EXPERIMENTS I've seen is testing the tensile strength of a stainless steel rod. This is not a test to bend the rod. Instead engineers place the steel in a testing machine that pulls the rod from either end like a candymaker pulling taffy.

The yield strength measures the point at which the solid steel first begins to stretch. Then they can test the steel to failure. At first it looks like the rod is indestructible. But as the machine continues pulling the steel, something amazing happens. The thick rod dimples in the middle like an hourglass, and the steel stretches until it snaps.

God tests his people like an engineer tests his materials. He does not test us to failure, but he will take us almost to the breaking point. In one of the most grueling tests any man ever endured, God tested Abraham by asking him to sacrifice his son.

> After these things God tested Abraham and said to him, "Abraham!" And he said, "Here I am." He said, "Take your son, your only son Isaac, whom you love, and go to the land of Moriah, and offer him there as a burnt offering on one of the mountains of which I shall tell you." (Genesis 22:1, 2)

What agony! God did not allow him to go through with the sacrifice, of course. God stopped him and said:

> Do not lay your hand on the boy or do anything to him, for now I know that you fear God, seeing you have not withheld your son, your only son, from me. (Genesis 22:12)

God stretches all his children to train us for our good. James says:

> Count it all joy, my brothers, when you meet trials of various kinds, for you
> know that the testing of your faith produces steadfastness. And let stead-
> fastness have its full effect, that you may be perfect and complete, lacking
> in nothing. (James 1:2–4)

Youcef Nadarkhani is an Iranian pastor who was freed on September 8,
2012 after being sentenced to death for his faith. In an open letter to his sup-
porters, he wrote,

> Indeed I have been put to the test, the test of faith which is, according to the
> Scriptures "more precious than perishable gold." The Lord has wonderfully
> provided through the trial, allowing me to face the challenges that were
> in front of me. As the Scriptures says, "He will not allow us to be tested
> beyond our strength. . . ."[1]

In Psalm 6 God has stretched David to the breaking point. We don't
know the historical situation. David was tested to the limit several times. He
mentions his "foes" (v. 7) and "workers of evil" (v. 8); so his enemies were attacking him in some way.[2] Whatever the specific situation, David was almost
overcome by anguish.

But testing ends with victory. "Weeping may tarry for the night, but joy
comes with the morning" (Psalm 30:5). God's discipline is agony when we're
going through it. Afterward it "yields the peaceful fruit of righteousness"
(Hebrews 12:11). In Psalm 6 David's plea leads to David's victory. This is the
pattern for everyone who endures God's testing.

David's Plea

Psalm 6 begins with David's plea. It is the anguished prayer of a man who is
on the edge as he pours out his heart to God.

Not in Anger

His first concern is to ask God not to deal harshly with him.

> O Lord, rebuke me not in your anger,
>   nor discipline me in your wrath. (6:1)

God's "discipline" (v. 1). feels so harsh to David that God seems to be
angry with him. The word order in Hebrew puts the emphasis on God's wrath.
To get the sense, we could translate this verse, "O Lord, do not in your anger
rebuke me, nor in your wrath discipline me." David is not asking God to stop
correcting or training him. A wise man or woman welcomes God's instruc-

tion; only a fool refuses correction and discipline. Yet he doesn't want God to treat him like the wicked who are under his judgment (Psalm 5:4–6). He asks God not to discipline him in the heat of his anger.

The prophet Jeremiah prayed the same thing when God's hand was heavy on him. "Correct me, O LORD, but in justice; not in your anger, lest you bring me to nothing" (Jeremiah 10:24). As David wilted under the grueling discipline of God's spiritual training, it was so painful that he worried that God had turned against him.

Any parent knows the difference between discipline done in anger and discipline—even painful discipline—that is self-controlled and loving. Mom and dad, your children know the difference too. Sometimes you need to walk away to get your own heart right before you deal with your child's behavior. I have had to go back to my children and ask for their forgiveness because I disciplined in anger. What they did was wrong, but my response was wrong too. The spirit behind the punishment makes all the difference. David asked God not to discipline him in anger.

What brought on this rebuke and discipline? Some think that David implies that he has sinned. This psalm is one of the seven Penitential Psalms or Psalms of Confession of the early church (Psalms 6, 32, 38, 51, 102, 130, 143). Traditionally these Psalms were read on Ash Wednesday to begin a season of repentance during Lent. But God's "rebuke" (v. 1) does not necessarily mean that David had sinned; the word "rebuke" may refer to judgment, or it may mean teaching a hard life lesson.[3]

If we read Psalm 6 carefully, David does not confess any sin and he does not repent from sin. David feels like Job, a man who is suffering even though he is righteous.[4] In fact, God sometimes puts his children through the wringer not because they have sinned but because he loves them and wants them to grow. Wise King Solomon gave this advice to his son:

> My son, do not despise the LORD's discipline
>   or be weary of his reproof,
> for the LORD reproves him whom he loves,
>   as a father the son in whom he delights. (Proverbs 3:11, 12)

These are the exact same root words that David uses in Psalm 6, "rebuke" and "discipline." They are often found together in the Bible's wisdom literature. God may send difficulty in your life because of sin—we shouldn't minimize that. But if you are a believer with a clear conscience, God may discipline you because he is delighted with you and pleased at what he sees in you.

The temptation is to assume that God is angry with you when things go wrong. God's hand can be so heavy that it feels like he has it in for you. David doesn't turn away from God's discipline; he wants to learn the lessons God has for him. But he pleads with God not to judge him like the wicked and deal with him in anger.

Grace

Instead David pleads for grace.

> Be gracious to me, O LORD, for I am languishing;
>   heal me, O LORD, for my bones are troubled.
> My soul also is greatly troubled.
>   But you, O LORD—how long? (6:2, 3)

Although God is the one who has brought such anguish into his life, David does not try to run from God or shake his fist at him. Instead he appeals for kindness from the very God who seems angry with him. He appeals for healing to the God who has wounded him. Three times in these two verses David uses God's personal covenant name, Yahweh ("LORD"). He knows God, and his heart turns to God with faith that could not grow in any other soil. There are many types of faith that we simply cannot have except in times of trouble. You can't trust God with your life unless your life is on the line. You can't really trust God to provide unless you have nothing and cannot provide for yourself. You can't fully hope in God unless you have no other hope.

A young woman went to her mother and told her about how hard things were for her. She wanted to give up. She was tired of fighting and struggling. It seemed like God had it in for her.

Her mother took her to the kitchen and brought three pots to boiling on the stove. In the first pot she placed carrots, in the second she placed eggs, and in the last she placed coffee. She let them simmer, and in twenty minutes she turned off the burners. She scooped out the carrots and placed them in a bowl. She pulled out the eggs and placed them in another bowl. Then she poured the coffee into two cups.

Turning to her daughter, she asked, "Tell me what you see." "Carrots, eggs, and coffee," she replied.

"Feel the carrots," her mother said. They were soft and limp, of course. Then her mother asked her to peel one of the eggs. The daughter tapped the egg on the counter and pulled off the shell, revealing a hard-boiled egg. Finally her mother smiled and handed her a cup of coffee. Then the girl asked, "What does this mean, Mom?"

Each of these objects had faced the same adversity: boiling water. Each reacted differently. The carrot went in strong and hard. After twenty minutes in boiling water, it was limp. The egg had been fragile and delicate, but now it was hard. The coffee was different. The coffee had released its fragrance and flavor in the water.

"Which are you?" this wise mother asked her daughter. "When God brings trouble into your life, will you go limp like a carrot, will you harden like an egg, or will you release the fragrance of faith?"

David released the fragrance of faith. He pled for grace from the very God who had placed him in such turmoil.

David's faith becomes even more beautiful when we notice how deeply his trouble affected him. The word "languishing" (v. 2) has the sense of a plant wilting and withering; its life is wasting away. The word "troubled" is more literally "terrified"; his soul was panicked and trembling. It is the same word in Psalm 2:5 when God speaks and terrifies his enemies. Here, though, it is God's anointed king who is terrified by God's hand—God seems to be treating David like an enemy. David is terrified physically, and his very soul, the breath of life within him, is even more terrified. He is almost scared senseless.[5]

Has your heart ever been gripped by real terror because of the trouble God brought into your life? Martin Luther said, "No one who has not been profoundly terrified and forsaken prays profoundly."[6] David felt it, and so did our Lord Jesus Christ. When Jesus turned his face to walk to the cross, he was gripped by the horror of what God had set before him, and he echoed the words of Psalm 6.

> Now is my soul troubled. And what shall I say? "Father, save me from this hour"? But for this purpose I have come to this hour. (John 12:27)

David's inner torment points forward to Christ's inner torment as our Savior. Jesus did not go through life like a statue of Buddha with a peaceful, distant half-smile, unmoved and untouched by the world. He was fully human; he endured anguish and agony as he obeyed the Father. This is a major comfort for every believer. Our Savior knows. Our Savior can care for us and pray intelligently for us because he has felt what we feel when we suffer in God's will.

Rescue
David continues his plea by calling on God to rescue him.

Turn, O LORD, deliver my life;
    save me for the sake of your steadfast love. (6:4)

Several translations say, "Return, O LORD." This gives more of the sense
of change for which David is asking. The prophets often used this word "turn"
(v. 4) as a call to repentance, a call to turn away from sin to follow God again.
David is obviously not asking God to turn from sin because God has never
sinned. But he is asking God for a drastic change. It felt like God was set
against him or had abandoned him. He wanted God dramatically to change
course and return to him, end this trial, and heal him.

The reason David could be so bold is because he knew God. "Steadfast
love" (v. 4) is part of God's character. We human beings would have no reason
to expect anything good from almighty God except for the fact that he himself is good and he is unwaveringly faithful to his people. If he is your God,
you can count on him to be faithful and loyal to you. Your friends may turn
against you, your own family may leave you, but God will always be faithful
and loyal to you because his very character is to love his people with rock-
solid, steadfast love. David appeals for rescue on the basis of God's covenant
loyalty, his steadfast love.

He also pleads with God to rescue him for God's own glory.

For in death there is no remembrance of you;
    in Sheol who will give you praise? (6:5)

The word "remembrance" means more than having data in your memory
like gigabytes on a flash drive. It has the sense of recounting and repeating
the things God has done. When David is dead and gone from the land of the
living, how will he be able to tell others the great and mighty things God has
done?

This last appeal may be the most powerful of all because God is passionate for his own fame and glory. As a holy God, he perfectly and infinitely
loves everything good, beautiful, and true, and he perfectly hates everything
false and wicked (Psalm 5:4–6). God himself is the most infinitely good, true,
and beautiful thing in the universe. There is nothing more glorious, great, and
grand than him. So it follows that God must love himself above all else if he
is true to his character as a holy God. If God loved anything else more than he
loved himself, even for a moment, he would commit idolatry and be guilty of
sin—unthinkable! Since God rightly loves himself more than anything else,
he is passionate for his glory.

What's more, as men and women we should perfectly love everything good, beautiful, and true too. If you think about it, we find our greatest joy in appreciating good and beautiful things: the smile on a six-year-old's face, the turning leaves, a perfect dovetail joint. When we see goodness, beauty, and truth, it fills our hearts. God is the most good, beautiful, and true being in the universe! When we see him in his glory, the sight of him fills our hearts with joy.

So God's passion for his own glory is not at odds with my pleasure and my good. In fact, I am most joyful and satisfied when I see God most clearly in his glory. The best thing God could do for me is to be passionate for his own glory. When I have him, I have everything. When I see his beauty, I am filled with joy.

So David's final appeal to God is his trump card. "For in death there is no remembrance of you; in Sheol who will give you praise?" *Turn and rescue me, Lord, for the sake of your great glory. If I am gone from this earth, who will recount your praise?*

This is a powerful perspective for us to hold on to when God stretches us. *Lord, what I want most in this situation is for you to bring glory to yourself. I want the pain to end, of course. Please rescue me, because I am about to break. But save me so that I can tell others about your great glory and power. At the end of the day, this is about you, Lord. Whatever brings you praise will ultimately bring me pleasure. Whatever brings you glory is for my good.*

Exhaustion

David ends his plea by reminding God that he is exhausted and depressed.

> I am weary with my moaning;
>   every night I flood my bed with tears;
>   I drench my couch with my weeping.
> My eye wastes away because of grief;
>   it grows weak because of all my foes. (6:6, 7)

If you are going through something like this as a Christian, it is good to know that you are not alone. God's servants are not immune from dark nights and deep valleys. Under the immense pressure of the Reformation, with Pope and princes pressuring him, Martin Luther was known for bouts of depression, his famous *anfechtungen*. Many other Christians have gone through the same thing.

On an unforgettable Sunday morning in 1866, the great C. H. Spurgeon stunned his five thousand listeners when from the pulpit of London's

Metropolitan Tabernacle he announced, "I am the subject of depressions of spirit so fearful that I hope none of you ever gets to such extremes of wretchedness as I go to." For some of his audience it was incomprehensible that the world's greatest preacher could know the valley of despair. Yet twenty-one years later in 1887 he said from the same pulpit, "Personally I have often passed through this dark valley."[7]

It is exhausting to be stretched and tested by God, even though we know it is for our good. Many believers could echo Spurgeon and Luther. David himself ends his prayer with a moan.

David's Victory

The darkness of David's night makes the sunrise all the more beautiful. After David's plea in 6:1–7, the last three verses record David's victory.

The King Banishes the Wicked

We can feel the change in David's heart with the new energy in his command. The king is out of bed, taking charge with confidence.

> Depart from me, all you workers of evil,
>> for the LORD has heard the sound of my weeping. (6:8)

David asserts his power as king to purge his kingdom and banish the wicked.[8] Psalm 5:5 teaches that God hates all evildoers and drives away the arrogant. Evildoers are those whose lifestyle is marked by unrepentant sin. David's response in Psalm 6:8 tell us *how* God drives the wicked away— God's king puts God's will into effect. David is the agent of God's will by banishing the wicked from his presence.

It is significant, then, that Jesus quotes these exact words from David at the end of the Sermon on the Mount.[9] As the Great King, Jesus will banish all the wicked in the last day.

> Not everyone who says to me, "Lord, Lord," will enter the kingdom of heaven, but the one who does the will of my Father who is in heaven. On that day many will say to me, "Lord, Lord, did we not prophesy in your name, and cast out demons in your name, and do many mighty works in your name?" And then will I declare to them, "I never knew you; *depart from me, you workers of lawlessness.*" (Matthew 7:21–23; see also Luke 13:27)

Jesus' shame and anguish on the cross were not the end of the story. After the agony of his soul, the risen Christ will judge the world and purge everyone who practices sin from his kingdom. David's banishment of the wicked points forward to the work of his greater son, the King Jesus Christ.

The King's Faith

David's confidence and victory were full of faith.

> The LORD has heard my plea;
>   the LORD accepts my prayer.
> All my enemies shall be ashamed and greatly troubled;
>   they shall turn back and be put to shame in a moment. (6:9, 10)

Nothing seems to have changed for David except for the fact that God has heard him. But David stood up once he knew God had heard and accepted him even though his enemies had not yet been turned back. By faith David trusted the promise implied in God's acceptance of his prayer. And with this confidence he boldly took action as God's agent to cleanse his kingdom from all the wicked.

Closing Thoughts

Is God testing you? Is he stretching you? You might feel like a stainless steel rod being pulled from both ends. God knows what he is about. He will not test you beyond what you are able to bear. David's plea led to victory.

Take comfort from the example of our Lord Jesus Christ.

> [L]et us run with endurance the race that is set before us, looking to Jesus, the founder and perfecter of our faith, who for the joy that was set before him endured the cross, despising the shame, and is seated at the right hand of the throne of God. (Hebrews 12:1, 2)

7

A Prayer for Justice

PSALM 7

FEW THINGS ARE MORE PAINFUL and frustrating than being accused of something you did not do. A coworker doesn't follow through with the customer, and your manager pins the low sales figures on you. I know men and women who have been deeply hurt when a brother or sister accused them of cheating as they sorted out their parents' estate. A friend might accuse you of sharing a secret when you haven't told anyone. You might have been accused of stealing something that went missing.

Sometimes injustice can be deadly serious. A recent PBS documentary presented the case of Paco Larrañaga. The nineteen-year-old was arrested for a double murder he cannot possibly have committed. On July 16, 1997 two girls disappeared from a mall in the Philippines. At the time, Paco was at school in Manila, 350 miles away on another island. Thirty-five classmates and teachers testified that Paco was with them in Manila that night and early the next morning. They had pictures and school records to back them up, along with the security log of Paco's apartment building. Yet Paco was arrested. After a rigged trial before a judge who repeatedly fell asleep, Paco was convicted of murder. It so happens that the father of the girls who disappeared worked for a drug lord who was known to be paying off the police and several judges. Needless to say, no one ever followed up on this line of investigation.

Psalm 7 is about this sort of injustice. David was in deadly danger because a man named Cush had falsely accused him. We don't have the specific details of David's problem, but there is enough in the superscription for us to connect the dots.

Cush was from the tribe of Benjamin, the tribe of King Saul, David's predecessor. Saul was immensely jealous of David and tried to kill him several times. As his hatred grew, Saul called on his tribe's allegiance in his feud with David.

> Saul said to his servants who stood about him, "Hear now, people of Benjamin; will the son of Jesse give every one of you fields and vineyards, will he make you all commanders of thousands and commanders of hundreds, that all of you have conspired against me?" (1 Samuel 22:7, 8)

The tribe of Benjamin was Saul's power base and remained loyal to his family. When Saul was killed by the Philistines, Israel was divided by a civil war between those who followed David and those who were loyal to Saul (2 Samuel 3:1). Naturally Benjamin was the spearhead of the opposition (see 2 Samuel 2:15, 25, 31). It took about eight years for David to be established as king over all Israel.

The people of Benjamin held their grudge against David for a long time. When David's son, Absalom, rebelled against him, a man from Benjamin, named Shimei, cursed David as he fled Jerusalem.

> And Shimei said as he cursed, "Get out, get out, you man of blood, you worthless man! The LORD has avenged on you all the blood of the house of Saul, in whose place you have reigned, and the LORD has given the kingdom into the hand of your son Absalom." (2 Samuel 16:7, 8)

After the rebellion was put down, a different man from Benjamin named Sheba led another revolt against David (2 Samuel 20:1). It is easy to understand how another false accusation flared up from the smoldering hostility of this tribe.

We're not sure at what point this accusation came in David's life. My best guess is that it was during the years when David was running from Saul. As he ran away, David said to Jonathan, "What have I done? What is my guilt? And what is my sin before your father, that he seeks my life?" (1 Samuel 20:1). This sounds very similar to the psalm we are reading. It would have been easy to accuse David of almost anything during those days. Saul wanted to believe the worst about him.

What can we do when we are faced with false accusations? You can't "give as good as you got" because that drags you down to their level. Sometimes you can clear your name and protect yourself. But if you deny it far and wide, sometimes you fan the flame—people might assume that where there's smoke, there's a fire.[1] Sometimes there is nothing you can do—there is no way to show you are innocent.

Ultimately you need to bring your problem to God. This is what David did and, as we will see, this is what our Lord Jesus Christ did too. Your God is a righteous Judge. There is nothing hidden that will not be made known. "Commit your way to the LORD; trust in him and he will do this: He will make your righteous reward shine like the dawn, your vindication like the noonday sun" (Psalm 37:5, 6 NIV).

We see four steps as David brings his false accusation to God in Psalm 7. David cries for deliverance, claims his innocence, calls for judgment, and closes with worship.

A Cry for Deliverance

First, we need to turn to God. David calls out to God for rescue.

> O LORD my God, in you do I take refuge;
>   save me from all my pursuers and deliver me,
> lest like a lion they tear my soul apart,
>   rending it in pieces, with none to deliver. (7:1, 2)

David is not calling out to a stranger. He calls out to God because he knows him and has a relationship with him. As mentioned previously, the name "LORD" in capital letters is a translation of God's name, Yahweh. David cries out to Yahweh as "my God" (v. 1), based on a personal relationship.

David runs to God the way we run to a safe room during a tornado. Taking refuge in God means trusting that he can and will protect you. He is strong enough to shield you and is faithful to guard you. God does not merely protect—he himself is protection. We take refuge *in* him.

This kind of faith is intensely practical. David's enemies are like a lion ready to tear him apart. When I was a boy, I used to watch Mutual of Omaha's *Wild Kingdom* on Saturday night. The host would take us on safari where a pride of lions was chasing down their prey on the African savannah. One of the lions takes down a wildebeest and begins tearing into it, ripping out great chunks of flesh, blood staining the fur around his mouth. This grisly sight is a picture of the violence David's enemies have planned for him. Does the God you know protect you from real-life violence and trouble? David took refuge in a God who stands guard around his people to protect them from real danger.

This kind of practical faith is also the pathway to blessing, a promise we have already seen in the Psalms. Psalm 2 ends with the promise, "Blessed are all who take refuge in him" (Psalm 2:12). Psalm 5:11 says again, "But let all who take refuge in you rejoice; let them ever sing for joy, and spread your protection over them, that those who love your name may exult in you." When you place yourself in God's protective care, you will find blessing and joy in the shelter of his wings.

Taking refuge in God does not mean doing nothing. David's enemies pursued him, which implies that he was running away. He did what he could to escape, but ultimately he trusted God to shield him. When Nehemiah rebuilt the wall of Jerusalem, he prayed and set a guard (Nehemiah 4:9). You should do what you can to protect yourself and clear your name, if possible. But ultimately your hope needs to be in God.

If your ultimate hope is not in God, anxiety will churn you up inside when you cannot reverse injustice. The false accusation will eat you up when can't do anything about it.

You will also be tempted to overreact. In Herman Melville's novel *Billy Budd*, Billy is a young, handsome seaman, well-liked with a good future ahead of him. Claggart, the Master-at-Arms, has it in for him. Eventually he goes to Captain Vere to accuse Billy of leading a mutiny, a crime punishable by death. Billy Budd is called to the captain's quarters to answer this charge. Claggart walks up to Billy and repeats the lie inches from his face.

> The next instant, quick as the flame from a discharged cannon at night, his right arm shot out, and Claggart dropped to the deck. Whether intentionally or but owing to the young athlete's superior height, the blow had taken effect full upon the fore-head . . . so that the body fell over lengthwise, like a heavy plank. . . .
>
> "Fated boy," breathed Captain Vere in a tone so low as to be almost a whisper, "what have you done!"
>
> . . . The twain raised the felled one . . . up into a sitting position. The spare form flexibly acquiesced, but inertly. It was like handling a dead snake.[2]

Billy Budd killed the Master-at-Arms, setting up the moral dilemma of Melville's novel. This tragic punch is a classic example of overreacting in the heat of the moment when we are falsely accused. If God is not your refuge, you will be set up to lash out when someone lies about you. You might gossip about your accuser and say hateful things in return—which is sin. You might become violent. You might destroy something they love in order to get back at them. You will take matters into your own hands and sin.

If God is your refuge, you will do what you can to defend yourself and clear your name. But since you believe that God is in control and is working for your good, you will have the confidence to be self-controlled and godly even when people lie about you.

A Claim of Innocence

Next David claims his innocence. Cush's words truly were a false accusation, and David's conscience was clear.

Sometimes you can fool people into thinking you're the victim. You can gather friends to your side even though your hands are dirty. Their sympathy makes you feel good, and it's nice to hear how they are outraged at what supposedly happened to you. You can be like a football player who gives a cheap shot and then acts all innocent when the other guy retaliates and draws the flag.

We can fool others, but there is no fooling God. He knows our hearts. So it is significant that David claims to be innocent before God himself.

> O Lord my God, if I have done this,
>   if there is wrong in my hands,
> if I have repaid my friend with evil
>   or plundered my enemy without cause,
> let the enemy pursue my soul and overtake it,
>   and let him trample my life to the ground
>   and lay my glory in the dust. *Selah* (7:3–5)

The word "if" is repeated three times, signaling a progression in verses 3, 4 that helps us tease out the essence of the accusation leveled against him. When David says, "[I]f I have done *this*" (v. 3), he is referring to the specific sin or crime of which he has been accused. He is not claiming complete innocence. When a defendant pleads "Not guilty" in court, he is not saying that he is completely and utterly without guilt; he is claiming to be innocent of this particular crime.

The content of the charge becomes more specific: "if there is wrong in my hands, if I have repaid my friend with evil or plundered my enemy without cause" (v. 4). Cush was accusing David of treachery to his friends and his foes. Actually David was known for his integrity. He could have taken Saul's life several times, but he held his hand.

David is so sure of his innocence that he calls down curses on himself. The word "trample" (v. 5) is particularly graphic. A potter tramples the clay, mashing it with his feet so he can work with it. When grapes have been harvested, vintners trample the grapes to crush them and release the juice that flows like blood. This word was even used of the horses trampling wicked Queen Jezebel into the dust (2 Kings 9:33). David's curse ends by calling for his "glory" to be laid "in the dust" (Psalms 7:5). I take David's "glory" to mean his position as God's anointed king with the fame and accomplishments that came with his role. He puts his crown on the line. The weight of these curses that David willingly calls down on himself shows that he is not guilty.

When you feel like you have been falsely accused, make sure your conscience is as clear as David's was. God knows our hearts. He sees everything we do; he hears everything we say; he knows what we intend. Ask God for the clarity to see your own role in the situation. Sometimes what feels like a false accusation is actually true. Ask a close friend for his opinion; he may see something in you that you cannot see yourself. There have been several times when my wife, Lisa, has helped me see my part in a conflict with someone else. You need to be honest and humble enough to face the truth, even when it hurts.

Sometimes you are genuinely innocent. If you are, then know that you are in good company. David didn't do what they said about him either, and neither did our Lord Jesus Christ.

A Call for Judgment

Because of his innocence, David calls for God to sit in judgment and bring him justice.

> Arise, O Lord, in your anger;
>   lift yourself up against the fury of my enemies;
>   awake for me; you have appointed a judgment. (7:6)

When someone lies about you, it can seem like God is asleep. But the Scriptures are clear that God can never wake up because he never sleeps. "Behold, he who keeps Israel will neither slumber nor sleep" (Psalm 121:4). When David asks God to wake up, he is using a figure of speech. It is a dramatic way of asking God to take action.

David knows that God is the Judge of all the world (Genesis 18:25). His great hope is that God will give him justice in his heavenly courtroom. You may go to your grave wrongfully accused; the history books may be wrong about you and slander your name to the coming generations. But there is a final justice in this world, and it comes from God himself, the great Judge. God is bigger than lies. Truth will triumph.

The Judgment Day

David looks forward to the judgment day with the hope of a man who waits for his day in court.

> Let the assembly of the peoples be gathered about you;
>   over it return on high. (7:7)

David arranges the judgment scene. All the nations are gathered in a great circle around God for him to sit in judgment. God will be utterly and completely just. "For according to the work of a man he will repay him, and according to his ways he will make it befall him" (Job 34:11). Then God will return to the heights of Heaven in victory.[3]

David can trust God to see through this one false accusation and give him justice.

> The LORD judges the peoples;
>   judge me, O LORD, according to my righteousness
>   and according to the integrity that is in me.
> Oh, let the evil of the wicked come to an end,
>   and may you establish the righteous—
> you who test the minds and hearts,
>   O righteous God! (7:8, 9)

It might surprise you that David can be this bold as he looks forward to the coming judgment. He is not afraid in the least. But David is a sinner just like the rest of us. Since God "tests the minds and hearts" (v. 9), how could David face God's great, final judgment with such confidence? One suggestion is that David is just thinking of this particular false accusation. This does not seem likely to me, though, because he seems to refer here to God's general judgment over all the nations. David may have been innocent of this one crime, but he was guilty in other ways that would come out at the last day.

The solution is that David was a prophet. His appeal to God's judgment points forward to the Messiah, the Lord Jesus Christ. Jesus was the ultimate falsely accused man, and David spoke for him. No one has faced worse injustice than Jesus Christ—no one has ever been so good as Jesus and so hatefully treated.

Jesus came to this earth doing nothing but good. The lame walked, the deaf heard, the mute spoke, the blind received their sight. Never did a man do the wonderful things he did. Yet the Pharisees accused him of being in league with Satan and performing his miracles by the power of Beelzebul (Matthew 9:34; 10:25; 12:24). He was accused by false witnesses at his trial (Matthew 26:59, 60). He was hated and put to death, the most unfair and unjust act in the history of the world.

Jesus handled this injustice by trusting God to judge like David did. The Apostle Peter describes Jesus' response to false accusations.

> He committed no sin, neither was deceit found in his mouth. When he was reviled, he did not revile in return; when he suffered, he did not

threaten, but continued entrusting himself to him who judges justly. (1 Peter 2:22, 23)

Jesus, the Son of David, was totally sinless, and he waited for God's judgment with eager hope and anticipation. David was not guilty of the specific crime of which Cush accused him. But Jesus was not guilty of anything ever. Of all men who ever lived, Christ could ask God to judge him according to his righteousness and integrity.

Jesus was not only righteous and sinless for his own good. He obeyed God and endured false accusations to become our Savior. Peter goes on to say,

He himself bore our sins in his body on the tree, that we might die to sin and live to righteousness. By his wounds you have been healed. (1 Peter 2:24)

If you belong to Jesus, you can face God's judgment with confidence. Christ's perfect obedience has been credited to you, deposited into your account. His righteousness is your righteousness. If you are a follower of Christ, you need not fear the great and final judgment that is coming on the world. Your sins have been taken from you as far as the east is from the west. That judgment day will be a day of joy and vindication for you (Revelation 19:1–3).

Judgment Today

God does not hold all his judgment for that final day though. He brings justice and punishment today too, rewarding those who do good and punishing the wicked. The final judgment is the finale of judgment that God is constantly handing down throughout history.[4]

My shield is with God,
    who saves the upright in heart.
God is a righteous judge,
    and a God who feels indignation every day.

If a man does not repent,God will whet his sword;
    he has bent and readied his bow;
he has prepared for him his deadly weapons,
    making his arrows fiery shafts.
Behold, the wicked man conceives evil
    and is pregnant with mischief
    and gives birth to lies.
He makes a pit, digging it out,
    and falls into the hole that he has made.
His mischief returns upon his own head,
    and on his own skull his violence descends. (7:10–16)

The principle is that you will reap what you sow in this life. Those who do evil will suffer evil themselves. God's judgment is not being held for the last day; it is a present, daily threat for those who do not obey him.

When an archer "has bent . . . his bow" (v. 12), all he has to do is relax his fingers to let the arrow fly. He cannot hold it long before his arm begins to shake and his fingers grow numb. What a striking picture of God's judgment! Don't think it is a long way off! Every day God brings violence back on the violent. He brings cheating back on cheaters. Liars believe lies. His judgment is at work in this world through his divine providence. If you do not know God, this means you need to repent today and turn to Christ.

God's judgment today is also a comfort for believers! It means God is a shield for those who know him like David did. He also saves today. He rescues today.

No wonder David closes with worship.

> I will give to the LORD the thanks due to his righteousness,
>   and I will sing praise to the name of the LORD, the Most High. (7:17)

Nothing had changed on the outside. Cush was still lying about him. But David had changed inside. His heart was set on God.

God's righteousness is our hope. Can you imagine a world where there is no final justice? Where liars have the last word? Where the powerful crush the weak with no consequences ever? Where government inspectors get away scot-free with bribes? Where murders go unsolved forever? Where Paco Larrañaga is never cleared? Where someone steals and is never caught?

Praise God for his righteousness. When you are falsely accused, cry out to him and trust him to judge.

8

How Majestic Is Your Name!

PSALM 8

THE EISENHOWER TUNNEL carries Interstate 70 under the Continental Divide fifty miles west of Denver. Before it was completed in 1979, the way west lay over Loveland Pass, which is much longer and can be closed by winter storms. Driving out of this long tunnel on a sunny day is a glorious experience. After a mile and a half underground, you emerge again into the glory of the Rockies at 11,000 feet. It feels like the roof of the world.

Psalm 8 gives us the same sort of transition. The five previous psalms feel like a tunnel as David prays to be rescued from his enemies. Here we come out into the sunshine again to celebrate the majesty of God. The view is breathtaking! David begins and ends with the same words: "O LORD, our Lord, how majestic is your name in all the earth!" (8:1, 9).

These identical bookends are a literary device called *inclusio*. They are set at the beginning and end like a picture frame to signal that the whole psalm is about the majesty of God. We will begin by looking more closely at this theme verse, then will look at the ways God makes his name majestic.

The Majesty of God's Name

Our English translations sound redundant by repeating the word *Lord* in the opening line, "O LORD, our Lord." When I learned this psalm as a boy, I assumed that this was a sort of pledge of allegiance, that David was making the point that God is "*our* Lord." In fact, this is the first time in the psalms that David uses the plural and invites God's people to join him. God is *our* ruler and king.

The two words for *Lord* are not the same in Hebrew, however. Most English Bibles translate God's name Yahweh with the word *Lord* in capitals out of respect for God's personal name. The second *Lord* is a different word in Hebrew, *adonai*, which means lord in the sense of a ruler, master, or king. If we sharpen our translation, David is speaking to God saying, "O Yahweh, our King, how majestic is your name in all the earth!"

God's name Yahweh is majestic throughout the earth. The name Yahweh probably means, "I am who I am" or "I will be who I will be."[1] The significance of this name is that God exists in and of himself. Yahweh created the heavens and the earth (Genesis 2:4). By his own will and power, he existed before the universe came into being. He is the uncreated Creator, the self-existing one, and he is absolutely complete in himself. Yahweh is also God's personal name, the name he revealed to Israel as he brought them out of Egypt (Exodus 3:14, 15; 6:2, 3). This Yahweh is our king and ruler, the living God who created the world and redeems his people.

This name also means that Yahweh will be true to himself. He cannot be manipulated or forced into anything—he will be who he will be. God defines himself; he does not change to fit what we expect or demand him to be. God will be true to himself at all times and in all places. God is today who he was yesterday and who he will be tomorrow. He revealed himself to Israel as Creator and Savior. He will not suddenly change. We can depend on him because he is a consistent, faithful, trustworthy God.

Yahweh has made his glory visible on the earth below and in the sky above.

> O Yahweh, our King,
>   how majestic is your name in all the earth!
> You have set your glory above the heavens. (8:1)

By mentioning both earth and Heaven, David includes everything in between. This is a literary technique called *merism*. All of creation is permeated with the majestic name of Yahweh. The word "majestic" points to God's visible power and might. The word "glory" in this verse is often translated "splendor," the visible display of God's greatness. David focuses our attention on the outward display of God's power and glory. His majesty is so impressive that his power is almost intimidating.[2] Gerard Manley Hopkins put it well.

> The world is charged with the grandeur of God.
> It will flame out, like shining from shook foil. . . .[3]

How does Yahweh display his glory in our world? How does he make his name majestic?

The answer is surprising and counterintuitive. The message of Psalm 8 is that Yahweh reveals his majesty in this world by using weak people to do his great work. God reveals his majesty by defeating his enemies through the weakness of children (v. 2). He also reveals his majesty by ruling the world through weak, mortal human beings (vv. 3–8).[4] God does his greatest work through human weakness.

When God uses weak people to do great and mighty things, his glory shines because it is obviously his power and not ours. The Apostle Paul says the same thing.

> But God chose what is foolish in the world to shame the wise; God chose what is weak in the world to shame the strong; God chose what is low and despised in the world, even things that are not, to bring to nothing things that are, so that no human being might boast in the presence of God. (1 Corinthians 1:27–29)

Weak children and mortal men could not possibly be responsible for the power that works through them. The glory goes to Yahweh whose majestic name permeates Heaven and earth.

This is an important perspective at this point in the Psalms because it helps us understand why God's anointed king suffers like he does. God allows his king to be weak and oppressed so that his own glory and power will shine more brightly. When David then triumphed over his enemies, it was obvious that the power came from God. Christ conquered through the shame and weakness of the cross. God often allows us to be weak and oppressed too, so that it is obvious that the power comes from God and not from us. Again Paul says,

> But we have this treasure in jars of clay, to show that the surpassing power belongs to God and not to us. We are afflicted in every way, but not crushed; perplexed, but not driven to despair; persecuted, but not forsaken; struck down, but not destroyed; always carrying in the body the death of Jesus, so that the life of Jesus may also be manifested in our bodies. (2 Corinthians 4:7–10)

God makes his name majestic by using weak people like you and me to do his great work.

God Triumphs over His Enemies through Weak Children

Notice how God triumphs over his enemies through weak children.

> Out of the mouth of babies and infants,
> you have established strength because of your foes,
>   to still the enemy and the avenger. (8:2)

Out of the Mouths of Children

What does this mean? A better translation for "babies" is "children" (see NIV). Jeremiah uses the same Hebrew word (*'ôlēl*) to describe children playing in the street, so these are not necessarily babes in arms like the English word suggests (cf. Jeremiah 6:11; 9:21). The word "infants" might be a bit misleading too. Literally it refers to nursing children. But most women in the ancient world (including Jewish mothers) generally nursed their children until age two or three.[5] So the phrase "babies and infants" (v. 2) is broad enough to include grade school children and toddlers just learning to speak.

God creates power and might for himself from the lisping, learning, stammering tongues of young children. Rather than establish strength through the lips of the wise and the aged, Yahweh reveals his majesty most clearly through little boys and girls. He brings himself glory through the youngest, weakest, most vulnerable human beings. When little children lisp the gospel, God unleashes power beyond comprehension.

Karl Barth was one of the greatest theologians of the twentieth century. Many evangelicals do not agree with him at various points, yet he towered over the landscape for at least half a century. After the Nazis expelled him from Germany, Barth was a leading figure in the Christian opposition to Hitler from his post at the University of Basel, Switzerland. He was primarily responsible for writing the famous Barmen Declaration, which affirmed that Christ is the head of the Church. His commentary on Romans was a landmark in New Testament studies. His thirteen-volume *Church Dogmatics* is one of the longest systematic theologies ever written.

In the early 1960s Barth made his only trip to the United States. At one of his stops he took part in a panel discussion at the University of Chicago's Rockefeller Chapel, an enormous Gothic cathedral. During the question and answer time, a young student stood up and asked the great man, "Professor Barth, could you summarize your entire life's work in a few words?" The audience gasped, but Barth only paused for a second. "Yes. In the words of a song my mother taught me when I was a child: 'Jesus loves me, this I know, for the Bible tells me so.'"[6]

When toddlers lisp the gospel, they utter powerful, profound truth. Theologians may tease out and develop the nuances of God's Word more fully, but a faithful scholar cannot leave behind the simple, glorious truths that come from the lips of young children. God gets all the glory because toddlers are so weak, so vulnerable that the power of the truth cannot be from them.

The universe is stunned at the magnificent majesty of God when toddlers pray before bedtime and sing in Sunday school. God creates victorious power from the lips of children who confess him.[7] God makes himself great through the weakness of the weak. This should be a huge encouragement for young mothers who spend their days wiping noses, cleaning up spills, folding little hands before meals, and singing songs while changing diapers. Step back and see the big picture: God is making his name majestic in this world through you. God is establishing his strength in this world through your children as they learn to praise him.

God Defeats His Enemies

The strength God establishes through children is no small thing. God uses the lisping words of toddlers to defeat mighty enemies. The world is set against God. The nations rage, and kings gather together against Yahweh and his anointed king (Psalm 2:1–3). God silences these mighty foes with the chubby lips of children. For all his strength and fury, Satan himself cannot stand against the simple truth, "Jesus loves me, this I know."

God won victory through the lips of children during Jesus' earthly life. Jesus applied Psalm 8 in the temple as he answered the Jewish leaders.

> And the blind and the lame came to him in the temple, and he healed them. But when the chief priests and the scribes saw the wonderful things that he did, and the children crying out in the temple, "Hosanna to the Son of David!" they were indignant, and they said to him, "Do you hear what these are saying?" And Jesus said to them, "Yes; have you never read,
>
> 'Out of the mouth of infants and nursing babies
> you have prepared praise'?" (Matthew 21:14–16)

The children recognized Jesus as the Messiah who brought God's salvation. The chief priests and scribes were horrified that Jesus would allow the children to say this.

When Jesus accepted the praise of these children, Psalm 8 was fulfilled in two ways. First, the chief priests and scribes were defeated. God's enemies were silenced—the children's praises won the day. Their "Hosanna" still wins the day as people read their words and recognize that Jesus truly is the Messiah, the Savior of the world. God established strength through their lips.

Psalm 8 was also fulfilled because Jesus accepted the praise of God for himself. When you compare Psalm 8 in our Bibles with Psalm 8 as Jesus quoted it, you will notice they are slightly different. The Hebrew Old Testament says, "you have established strength" (v. 2), but Jesus quotes the Greek translation of the Old Testament that says, "you have prepared praise" (v. 16). The Greek version is a paraphrase that tells us how God establishes strength from children—by preparing praise from them. Jesus affirms this interpretation and applies it to himself. This was a stunning claim—when the children praised him, they were praising God! God used the weakness of those children to bear witness to the world that Jesus is the Son of David, the Messiah, and God himself.

God Rules the Whole World through Weak Mortals

The second way God makes his name majestic in Psalm 8 is by ruling through the weakness of human beings. We are mortal and frail, yet God has placed us over all creation. Here again God makes his glory clear to the watching universe by using weak people to do great work.

Human Frailty

David shows us our frailty and finitude as human beings. To show us how small we are, David lifts our eyes to the night sky.

> When I look at your heavens, the work of your fingers,
>   the moon and the stars, which you have set in place . . . (8:3)

Have you ever walked out onto a dock at night? The lake is calm, small waves whisper on the shore, and a loon cries off in the distance. Then you look up and see the vast sky spread above you like diamonds on black velvet. The Milky Way glows like a wide ribbon across the heavens. Our galaxy looks like a cloud, but this glow is actually the light of 200–400 billion stars turning like a giant pinwheel some 100 light years across. In the 1920s Edwin Hubble showed that our galaxy is one of many galaxies in the universe. The best estimate is that there are roughly 170 billion galaxies gathered in clusters and strung like filaments across space. Now the Hubble Space Telescope gives us a front-row seat to see the wonders of the Tarantula Nebula, the Magellanic Clouds, or the collision of a comet with Jupiter. All this is the work of God's fingers! The vast distances and the nuclear explosions of the stars are not rough, sweaty work like heavy construction or road building for God. Creating the galaxies is detailed, delicate work for him, like a woman weaving lace.

No wonder David asks, "what is man that you are mindful of him, and the son of man that you care for him?" (8:4). William Beebe, the naturalist, used to tell a story about Teddy Roosevelt. At Sagamore Hill, after talking for the evening, the two would go out on the lawn and search the skies for a certain spot of star-like light near the lower left-hand corner of the Great Square of Pegasus. Then Roosevelt would recite: "That is the Spiral Galaxy in Andromeda. It is as large as our Milky Way. It is one of a hundred million galaxies. It consists of one hundred billion suns, each larger than our sun." Then Roosevelt would grin and say, "Now I think we are small enough! Let's go to bed."[8]

It is healthy to gaze at the vast beauty of the night sky and feel small. The greatest mystery, though, is not that I am so small but that God's love is so big. He is mindful of men and women who are mere microscopic specks in the universe. He cares for us. There are several words for *man* that David could have used at the beginning of verse 4. He chose the word *'enôsh*, a word that emphasizes our frailty and mortality. To emphasize our mortality, he pairs that with the name "son of man," which probably emphasizes the fact that our lives are not our own.[9] We owe our life to our parents. Yahweh is self-existent; we are not.

God showed the depth of his love for us small, weak creatures through Jesus Christ. Jesus took the name "Son of Man" for himself, emphasizing his humanity.[10] As the Son of Man, Jesus was vulnerable; he took on mortal flesh to be our Savior. The great mystery is God's great love for tiny people. He is mindful of insignificant creatures; he cares for us.

Human Dignity

David then pairs our frailty with the dignity God has given us as human beings.

First, we have the dignity of our position. "Yet you have made him a little lower than the heavenly beings" (v. 5). The word translated "heavenly beings" is literally "God" or "gods"; it can refer to angels, and that is how many English versions take it. God has given us the highest honor of any earthly being. On the one hand, we are earthly, fashioned from the dust of the earth. We are not mere animals, though, because God breathed his life into us (Genesis 2:7). God gave us a unique and exalted position in his created world.

Second, we have the dignity of our crown. God "crowned him with glory and honor." Since glory and honor ultimately belong to God, I take this to mean that we were created in God's image. The picture of a beautiful woman reflects her beauty. In the same way God made us in his likeness to reflect his glory.

Third, we have the dignity of our authority.

You have given him dominion over the works of your hands;
    you have put all things under his feet,
all sheep and oxen,
    and also the beasts of the field,
the birds of the heavens, and the fish of the sea,
    whatever passes along the paths of the seas. (8:6–8)

God appointed us to rule over all creation as his representatives. Nothing on earth is left outside our control, whether in the sky, on the earth, or in the sea. The depths of the sea are the most mysterious part of our planet to us, the last unexplored frontier. But David does not leave out the hidden sea creatures—"whatever passes along the paths of the seas" (v. 8). God has made us ruler over absolutely everything on earth.

The problem, though, is that this is not the way things are. Adam and Eve had this kind of authority, but it is long gone. We are not rulers over all the earth. We can subdue some creatures and train them to obey us, but since the time of Noah our rule over the animals is at best superficial (Genesis 9:2). If you don't believe me, watch bull riding at the rodeo. Those massive animals are definitely not submitting to the man on their back.

The writer of Hebrews saw this problem, too, and recognized that it points us forward to Christ.

For it was not to angels that God subjected the world to come, of which we are speaking. It has been testified somewhere,

"What is man, that you are mindful of him,
    or the son of man, that you care for him?
You made him for a little while lower than the angels;
    you have crowned him with glory and honor,
    putting everything in subjection under his feet."

Now in putting everything in subjection to him, he left nothing outside his control. At present, we do not yet see everything in subjection to him. But we see him who for a little while was made lower than the angels, namely Jesus, crowned with glory and honor because of the suffering of death, so that by the grace of God he might taste death for everyone. (Hebrews 2:5–9)

It's obvious that creation is not under our control as human beings the way God originally intended. But creation is under the control of one man. Christ has risen from the dead, and everything *is* under his feet. Everything on earth—beasts of the field, birds of the air, fish of the sea—submits to his authority. Everyone who is in Christ will reign with him as well (2 Timothy

2:12). Psalm 8 is looking forward to the day when God's people will be renewed and take their rightful rule over the world.

How did Jesus take up his authority over all creation? Through the weakness of the cross. Christ crucified looked foolish, helpless, and weak. Yet through the cross God displayed his majesty most fully and brightly in this world.

God makes his name majestic through human weakness. He creates strength through the lisping words of babies. He rules creation through puny people. He saves the world through a crucified Messiah.

Do you feel weak? Has God given you a task that seems impossible? Then you are in a good place. God reveals his strength in our weakness.

[W]e have this treasure in jars of clay, to show that the surpassing power belongs to God and not to us. (2 Corinthians 4:7)

9

Praise Him for His Justice

PSALM 9

ONE OF THE MOST FAMOUS STORIES in the Old Testament is Solomon's judgment between two women who both claimed the same baby. It seemed like an impossible case to decide. Here is the way it was presented to Solomon.

> The one woman said, "Oh, my lord, this woman and I live in the same house, and I gave birth to a child while she was in the house. Then on the third day after I gave birth, this woman also gave birth. And we were alone. There was no one else with us in the house; only we two were in the house. And this woman's son died in the night, because she lay on him. And she arose at midnight and took my son from beside me, while your servant slept, and laid him at her breast, and laid her dead son at my breast. When I rose in the morning to nurse my child, behold, he was dead. But when I looked at him closely in the morning, behold, he was not the child that I had borne." But the other woman said, "No, the living child is mine, and the dead child is yours." The first said, "No, the dead child is yours, and the living child is mine." Thus they spoke before the king. (1 Kings 3:17–22)

How could any judge solve this dilemma? Today we would use DNA testing, but that was not an option.

What did Solomon do? Most of us know the rest of the story.

> And the king said, "Divide the living child in two, and give half to the one and half to the other." Then the woman whose son was alive said to the king, because her heart yearned for her son, "Oh, my lord, give her the living child, and by no means put him to death." But the other said, "He shall be neither mine nor yours; divide him." Then the king answered and said, "Give the living child to the first woman, and by no means put him to death; she is his mother." And all Israel heard of the judgment that the king had rendered, and they stood in awe of the king, because

they perceived that the wisdom of God was in him to do justice. (1 Kings 3:25–28)

Solomon's answer is so legendary that versions of this story have traveled the world. The thirteenth-century Chinese writer Li Quianfu wrote a classical play called *The Circle of Chalk* with a similar plot. The wise judge, Bao Zheng, puts the two mothers in a circle of chalk and orders each mother to pull the baby out of the circle. The true mother lets go, of course, because she doesn't want to harm her son. In 1944 Berthold Brecht gave this story a twist in his famous play *The Caucasian Chalk Circle*.[1]

Why does this story capture our imaginations? We long for justice. We long for a judge who will be fair and honest—a judge who will see through lies and deceit to make things right. This longing is buried deep in every human heart. Ultimately this longing leads us to God because he is the just ruler and judge of the universe. This reality is at the heart of Psalm 9.

> But the LORD sits enthroned forever;
>   he has established his throne for justice,
> and he judges the world with righteousness;
>   he judges the peoples with uprightness. (9:7, 8)

Every human judge is a reflection of him, and our longing for fairness and justice is an echo of our deeper longing for God. This is why Psalm 9 speaks so powerfully to our hearts today. God brings himself glory by ruling and judging the world with justice.

This is the first direct psalm of praise in the book of Psalms. David begins by praising God himself, and he commands all of us to praise God as well (v. 11). Significantly, this first psalm of praise lifts God's name because he is a wise, fair, and just judge. When we see God's glory as the Judge of all the world, our hearts should sing to him.

In some translations, Psalms 9 and 10 are one psalm of thirty-nine verses. This shifts the chapter numbering for many of the Psalms that follow in those Bibles: Psalm 11 is now Psalm 10, Psalm 23 is Psalm 22, and so on.[2] This is because early Greek and Latin translations (Septuagint and Vulgate) combine Psalms 9 and 10 as one psalm. Some Orthodox and Roman Catholic Bibles follow that order or print the alternate chapter numbers in brackets. Most modern English translations follow the Hebrew order and keep Psalms 9 and 10 as individual psalms, however.[3]

Psalm 9 is an acrostic psalm built on the first eleven letters of the Hebrew alphabet. Verse 1 begins with *aleph*, and verse 18 begins with the letter *kaph*.[4]

These alphabetical lines build on one another as David pours out his praise to the God who judges justly. We can divide this psalm into David's Praise (vv. 1–12) and David's Prayer (vv. 13–20).

David's Praise

David sets the tone for this song in the first two verses.

> I will give thanks to the LORD with my whole heart;
>> I will recount all of your wonderful deeds.
> I will be glad and exult in you;
>> I will sing praise to your name, O Most High. (9:1, 2)

The Heart of Praise

David worships with five synonymous verbs: "give thanks," "recount," "be glad," "exult," "sing praise" (v. 1, 2). His whole being is involved in praising God. His mind is engaged: he knows what God has done. His praise is sincere. He is not just saying what he knows he is supposed to say, but he really means it—he thanks "the LORD" (Yahweh) with his "whole heart" (v. 1).

Worship is not wishful thinking. David's praise is grounded in reality: "I will recount all of your wonderful deeds." God's mighty acts in creation and history are beyond human comprehension—they are truly awe-inspiring and jaw-dropping.[5] David's praise is also public. As he recounts God's wonders, he tells others about God. He is the majestic and mighty creator of the constellations. He is the Savior who led his people out of Egypt and settled them in a land of their own. Praise has an intellectual component; it is a rational retelling of historical reality. Praise is also emotional. If our praise is only cerebral, we are missing the heart response we should have when we see God. Praise is the joyful, happy gladness of exulting in God himself. David breaks out in a song of joy to God Most High.

Why Praise?

This raises a question. Why does God ask us to praise him? Why is Psalm 9 a psalm of praise? Why are the Psalms full of praise? We need to answer this as we consider this first psalm of praise.

Some people have a problem with God asking us to praise him for his justice or for anything else. What kind of God needs his people to praise him? We look down on people who are so insecure that they need to be built up and told how smart they are. We admire people who are confident and composed, who don't fish for compliments. We don't like businessmen who have to tell us how well they time the markets. We don't like athletes who brag about their gold medals. We don't like an actress who is self-absorbed. Is God like that? We despise the crowds of people that fawn over dictators or billionaires and feed their egos. Is that what we are doing when we praise God?

One thing we need to be sure of is that God is not weak, he is not insecure, he doesn't need to be built up to feel good about himself. When Paul was preaching in Athens, he said,

> The God who made the world and everything in it, being Lord of heaven and earth, does not live in temples made by man, nor is he served by human hands, as though he needed anything, since he himself gives to all mankind life and breath and everything. (Acts 17:24, 25)

There is nothing we have that God could possibly need. C. S. Lewis put it this way.

> The miserable idea that God should in any sense need, or crave for, our worship like a vain woman wanting compliments, or a vain author presenting his new books to people who never met or heard him, is implicitly answered by the words, "If I be hungry I will not tell thee" (Ps. 50:12). Even if such an absurd Deity could be conceived, He would hardly come to us, the lowest of rational creatures, to gratify His appetite. I don't want my dog to bark approval of my books.[6]

God has no needs. If God did have any needs, puny people like us couldn't fill them. So why does God command us to praise him?

Think about the reason you praise something. We praise the things that bring us joy. We look at a baby's tiny fingers and we gush, "Look how perfectly formed they are!" You walk by a lilac bush and say to your wife, "Doesn't that smell wonderful?" Your team scores a touchdown and you shout, "Did you see that pass?" You point out the red maple on the corner as it changes color. We instinctively praise the things we enjoy.

God himself is the most beautiful, most exciting, most captivating thing in the universe. If we see him, our hearts will leap to praise him. So the command to praise God is a command to open our eyes to see God for who he is so that we respond with joy and pleasure as we admire him. The only reason someone would not praise God is because they are blind to who he is. The Psalms are constantly lifting our eyes to see God for who he is, filling out our picture of him, exalting another aspect of his character, displaying another of his mighty works. When we see him, he is so thrilling and glorious that we naturally praise him.

The command to praise God is also a command to be truly happy and joyful. Praise is the natural conclusion for the things we enjoy. If you can't smack your friend on the leg and say, "Wasn't that a great play?" you don't enjoy the game as much. This is why people go to a sports bar to watch a game when they have a perfectly good TV at home. Joy is incomplete until we express it in praise. Again C. S. Lewis puts it well.

> The world rings with praise—lovers praising their mistresses, readers their favorite poet, walkers praising the countryside, players praising their favorite game—praise of weather, wines, dishes, actors, horses, colleges, countries, historical personages, children, flowers, mountains, rare stamps, rare beetles, even sometimes politicians and scholars. My whole, more general difficulty, about the praise of God depended on my absurdly denying to us, as regards the supremely Valuable, what we delight to do, what indeed we can't help doing, about everything else we value.
>
> . . . I think we delight to praise what we enjoy because the praise not merely expresses but completes the enjoyment; it is its appointed consummation. It is not out of compliment that lovers keep on telling one another how beautiful they are, the delight is incomplete till it is expressed.[7]

The bottom line is that our joy in God is incomplete until we can express it in praise. We see this clearly in the opening verses of Psalm 9. David recounts God's wonderful deeds and exults in God in the same breath. He tells others what God has done and rejoices in God all at the same time.

So why does God ask us to praise him? He is worthy of praise, of course, but he does not need our praise in the slightest; he is infinitely perfect and complete in himself. God lifts up his glory before us and commands us to praise him because the kindest thing God could do for us is to demand that we make much of him. He compels us to lift our eyes and see that he is the most beautiful and exciting being in the universe. He compels us to be glad, happy, and joyful by admiring the greatness of his glory. He compels us to see his light and find true life.

If God were angry with us, he would hide himself so we could not see him. Instead God reveals himself to us because he loves us. He offers us full-hearted joy in praising him.

The Content of David's Praise

This brings us to the content of David's praise in Psalm 9. David recounts God's wonderful deeds in the verses that follow. God judges the world with justice, delivering his people and condemning the wicked.

First, David praises God for delivering him personally.

When my enemies turn back,
    they stumble and perish before your presence.
For you have maintained my just cause;
    you have sat on the throne, giving righteous judgment. (9:3, 4)

The word "when" (v. 3) tells us that David's enemies have not turned back yet. The grammar indicates that David is looking forward to God's deliverance.[8] The context also suggests that we should take the Hebrew verbs in verses 4–7 as referring to the future.[9] In other words, here David does not praise God for things he has already received. David is praising God in faith.

This is hugely important for us because we often have to look past our circumstances to praise God in faith ourselves. God may not deliver you now, but if you know that he is on the throne, you can praise him in faith. If you know God, you know that he will judge justly and rescue you from every trial and trouble in this life.

Second, David praises God for his justice in rescuing his people. As the king of Israel, David felt responsibility for the well-being of the whole nation. He praises God for the victory he would give over the people's enemies. David continues to talk about the future as if it had already happened.

You have rebuked the nations; you have made the wicked perish;
    you have blotted out their name forever and ever.
The enemy came to an end in everlasting ruins;
    their cities you rooted out;
    the very memory of them has perished. (9:5, 6)

Does David hate foreigners? Does he want God to rebuke the nations simply because they are a different nationality? Two key observations tell us that this is not the case. First, the word "nations" is parallel with the words "wicked" and "enemy" in these verses. The second observation is that we have already met these nations in the Psalms. Psalm 2 tells us that kings and nations rage against God and his anointed king (Psalm 2:1–3). These are not just any foreigners; they are the evil enemies of God and his king.

In fact, Israel was friendly with the nations that lived with them in peace. Hiram, king of Tyre, loved David, and men from Tyre helped build the temple and its furnishings (1 Kings 5; 2 Chronicles 2:11–16; 4:11–18). David was not hateful and xenophobic. But, he was confident that God's enemies would be so completely destroyed that they would be utterly forgotten.[10]

God, on the other hand, will reign and rule forever.

But the LORD sits enthroned forever;
    he has established his throne for justice,

and he judges the world with righteousness;
  he judges the peoples with uprightness. (9:7, 8)

As king, God will judge the world through David's greater son, the Lord
Jesus Christ. When Paul was preaching in Athens to the philosophers on Mars
Hill, he applied this verse to Christ.

> The times of ignorance God overlooked, but now he commands all people
> everywhere to repent, because he has fixed a day on which *he will judge*
> *the world in righteousness* by a man whom he has appointed; and of this he
> has given assurance to all by raising him from the dead. (Acts 17:30, 31)

David's hope is fulfilled in Christ! God displays his glory in the world by
judging the world with justice through Jesus. When we read about the majesty
of God's judgment in Psalm 9, we are ultimately reading about the reign and
rule of Jesus Christ.[11]

Third, David praises God for judging all humanity with justice.

The LORD is a stronghold for the oppressed,
  a stronghold in times of trouble.
And those who know your name put their trust in you,
  for you, O LORD, have not forsaken those who seek you. (9:9, 10)

God is the hope of all peoples, the champion of the weak.[12] He cares for
everyone who is beaten down and oppressed. He is a refuge for migrant workers paid below minimum wage, trapped in a vicious cycle of poverty. He cares
for girls caught in human trafficking. He doesn't forget the atrocities of civil
war in Syria. He is a good and just ruler who cares for everyone trampled and
abused in this world. Psalm 146 says that God is the one

who executes justice for the oppressed,
  who gives food to the hungry.

The LORD sets the prisoners free;
  the LORD opens the eyes of the blind.
The LORD lifts up those who are bowed down;
  the LORD loves the righteous.
The LORD watches over the sojourners;
  he upholds the widow and the fatherless,
    but the way of the wicked he brings to ruin. (Psalm 146:7–9)

God is the hope of all the oppressed. He cares for the weak and vulnerable. If he cares for all peoples, how much more will he care for his own
people who know him and call on him by name.

God's purpose is to bless the whole world. David calls all people to praise him.

> Sing praises to the LORD, who sits enthroned in Zion!
>   Tell among the peoples his deeds!
> For he who avenges blood is mindful of them;
>   he does not forget the cry of the afflicted. (9:11, 12)

David calls everyone who hears and reads this psalm to praise God along with him. God's salvation will be proclaimed from Zion, the city of God, to the whole world. This theme will be repeated throughout the book of Psalms: God's goodness flows from Israel to all peoples. In a real sense this is one of David's Great Commission texts!

This worldwide emphasis is reflected in the phrase "he who avenges blood" (v. 12). This name for God echoes the covenant God made with Noah and all his descendants, a covenant with all humanity. God said to Noah, "I will require a reckoning for the life of man . . . for God made man in his own image" (Genesis 9:5, 6). Every human life is precious to God because every human being is a picture of God. God remembers every man and woman, every boy and girl because he or she bears his image. And he demands an accounting for the way they are treated.

This means that the ends of the earth should praise him! He does not forget the youngest child or miss the tears of the weak. If the world lifts up its eyes to see the beauty and majesty of this God, the peoples of the world will praise him. God brings himself glory by ruling the world with justice. He saves the weak and powerless. He will judge the world in righteousness by the man he appointed, the Lord Jesus Christ.

David's Prayer

The second main section of this psalm is David's prayer. David is still on the same topic, however, because his prayer centers back on the glory of God in judging the world with justice.

Deliver Me

David first petitions God to deliver him personally.

> Be gracious to me, O LORD!
>   See my affliction from those who hate me,
>   O you who lift me up from the gates of death,
> that I may recount all your praises,

that in the gates of the daughter of Zion
I may rejoice in your salvation. (9:13, 14)

Ultimately God's deliverance would circle back to praise. David wants
God to rescue him so that he can praise God even more. The "gates" (v. 14) of
the city were a public place where people gathered, the hub of city life. David
wants to sing his praise before all the people of God. As the people heard
David retelling what God had done, they would praise God for themselves.
Contagious praise!

Justice and Providence

David also petitions God to make himself known in the world by bringing
justice in the course of everyday life.

The nations have sunk in the pit that they made;
    in the net that they hid, their own foot has been caught.
The Lord has made himself known; he has executed judgment;
    the wicked are snared in the work of their own hands. *Higgaion. Selah*
    (9:15, 16)

God's providence is his rule in the ordinary events of life. God does not
save his judgment to pour it all out at the end of time. He weaves his justice
in the fabric of everyday life. Those who dig a pit to trap others fall into it
themselves. God is not mocked: sin carries its own punishment. Violent men
tend to die by violence. The greedy suffer the discontent that comes with their
greed. Those who view pornography ruin their own sex life. Gossips tear
down their own character—as they spread stories, others think less of them.

God's providence weaves justice into ordinary human life. God makes
himself known through the natural consequences of our sin.

Put Man in His Place

Finally, David petitions God to put man in his place.

The wicked shall return to Sheol,
    all the nations that forget God.

For the needy shall not always be forgotten,
    and the hope of the poor shall not perish forever.

Arise, O Lord! Let not man prevail;
    let the nations be judged before you!

> Put them in fear, O Lord!
> Let the nations know that they are but men! *Selah* (9:17–20)

An earlier psalm tells us that God created man "a little lower than the heavenly beings" (Psalm 8:5). Yet our sinful nature is to lift ourselves up and take the place of God.

In 1905 Harvard built Emerson Hall to be the new building for the philosophy department. The design included an inscription on the north facade over the main doorway.

The Department of Philosophy decided that this inscription should read, "Man is the measure of all things." This is a quote from the philosopher Protagoras, one of the earliest statements of relativism. In many ways it summarizes man's rejection of God. The faculty instructed the architect to carve this quote above the door.

The president of Harvard University, Charles William Eliot, quietly decided otherwise. "When the professors returned from the summer vacation they found the building essentially complete, and cut into the stone were the words: 'What is man that Thou art mindful of him?'"[13] The inscription still stands there today, a witness to generations of students.

This conflict between President Eliot and the faculty captures the heart of our rebellion against God. The human heart says, "It's all about me. There is no one above me." David calls on God to humble us with his overwhelming power and glory. "Put them in fear, O Lord! Let the nations know that they are but men!" (v. 20).

Closing Thoughts

Do you know that you are just a man, just a woman? Have you lifted up your eyes to see God for who he is? God brings himself glory by ruling and judging the world with justice. Solomon in his wisdom cannot hold a candle to the searchlight of God's judgment.

If you see him, your heart will leap to praise him. May you open your eyes to see God. May everything within you praise him.

10

God, Where Are You?

PSALM 10

KING AHAB has come down to us as the most wicked king of Israel, worse than all who came before him. But his wife Jezebel was more evil yet. She was a coiled snake. The Scriptures leave us with a chilling commentary on their lives.

> There was none who sold himself to do what was evil in the sight of the LORD like Ahab, whom Jezebel his wife incited. (1 Kings 21:25)

At one point Ahab wanted to buy a vineyard near the palace. The owner, a man named Naboth, wouldn't sell it, so Ahab was depressed. Queen Jezebel knew just what to do. She wrote a letter to the elders of Naboth's village in the king's name, ordering them to frame Naboth for blasphemy and treason. She even planned for two liars to testify against him. The plan went exactly as she hoped: Naboth was stoned to death by his own people in his own hometown. And Ahab confiscated the vineyard (1 Kings 21:1–16).

What a perverse and wicked thing to do! She corrupted the village elders. They were the guardians of justice in that village. They had probably known Naboth since he was a boy. Now his blood was on their hands. In fact, she corrupted his whole village because the community had betrayed their neighbor. She dishonored God by using his Word as part of her sinful plot. And when she took Naboth's life, she stole his family's inheritance. This was a multigenerational sin; if Naboth had a wife and children, Jezebel left them destitute.

This terrible injustice happened during the monarchy in Israel, but it could have been in our newspapers today. Human nature has not changed in three thousand years. Greed still drives men and women to do great wrongs.

On September 4, 2008 Tulsa business owner Neal Sweeney was shot in the head at his business, Retail Fuels Marketing. As investigators examined the case, they uncovered a conspiracy. A gas station owner who hadn't paid his bills was upset when Sweeney wouldn't deliver more fuel to his station. So he arranged to have Sweeney killed.

My friends Tim and Suzanne sold their home to buy a new house for their growing family. After the closing, they were shocked to discover that their old mortgage had not been paid off. The owner of the title company had taken the money from several closings and disappeared, leaving several families holding two mortgages.

Injustice happens in families. One couple I know slogged through eight years of medical school and residency in Dallas. This young wife postponed having children and worked full-time through her twenties to support them both and get him launched in a successful career. A few weeks after he finished his residency, he served her with divorce papers. They weren't compatible now, he said. He used her to get through school, and now he didn't need her anymore.

Where is God when this happens? This is the question that grips the psalmist in the opening verse of Psalm 10.

> Why, O LORD, do you stand far away?
> Why do you hide yourself in times of trouble?

We may go through terrible injustice and yet God seems distant and detached. Where is he? Psalm 10 is one of the few psalms in Book 1 that does not have a heading linking this song with an author or specific situation in history. As a result the psalmist's question feels like a timeless question. Every generation asks, "God, where are you?"

This is an especially penetrating question because the previous psalm, Psalm 9, teaches us that God is the great Judge of all the world. "[H]e has established his throne for justice" (Psalm 9:7b). He hears the cry of the weak and afflicted and avenges them (Psalm 9:12). So why do the wicked still succeed? Where is the God of justice?

As the psalmist appeals to God, he describes the wicked (10:2–11), he calls God to action (10:12–15), and he ends with new confidence in God's justice (10:16–18). There is hope in this world. God is a God of justice.

The Character of the Wicked

The psalmist describes two sides of the character of the wicked in verses 2–11. Structurally each description is five verses long and ends with the inner thoughts of the unjust oppressor, "He says in his heart"[1] (10:6, 11). Two words summarize these wicked oppressors: arrogant and aggressive. Their pride and violence spell disaster for anyone who stands in their way.

Arrogant

First, the wicked oppressors are arrogant. The trouble they cause flows out of self-importance.

> In arrogance the wicked hotly pursue the poor;
>   let them be caught in the schemes that they have devised. (10:2)

Where does this abusive pride come from? For one thing they forget that the rich and poor were both created by God. We did not make ourselves. We did not choose which family we were born into and the opportunities we were given. We did not decide how intelligent we would be, how wise we would be, how self-motivated we would be. All this is from God's hand. The writer of Proverbs says, "The rich and the poor meet together; the LORD is the maker of them all" (Proverbs 22:2). The wicked forget this. They like to view themselves as self-made men, like sharks made to swim at the top of the food chain. This pride is Darwinian at its core—a survival of the fittest that grinds the poor into the dirt. And in their arrogance they think God will never do anything. They have nothing but contempt for God and laugh at any idea of judgment.

In fact, they do not worship God. They worship themselves.

> For the wicked boasts of the desires of his soul,
>   and the one greedy for gain curses and renounces the LORD.
> In the pride of his face the wicked does not seek him;
>   all his thoughts are, "There is no God." (10:3, 4)

The word "for" (v. 3) tells us why the wicked pursue the poor. They turn on the poor and the helpless because they first turned against God.

What does it mean to boast in your desires? That is an unusual phrase. The wicked are proud of their desires. Their cravings are a virtue. After all, didn't they succeed because of their will to win? Their greed got them where they are.

One of the most powerful illustrations of this came from the 1987 Oliver Stone movie *Wall Street*. The main character, Gordon Gekko, was modeled after high-powered traders who ran the financial markets like masters of the universe. In one famous scene Gekko delivers a speech to the nervous shareholders of Teldar Paper Corporation.

Greed, for lack of a better word, is good. Greed is right. Greed works. Greed clarifies, cuts through, and captures, the essence of the evolutionary spirit. Greed, in all of its forms; greed for life, for money, for love, knowledge, has marked the upward surge of mankind and greed, you mark my words, will not only save Teldar Paper, but that other malfunctioning corporation called the U.S.A.[2]

This quote struck a chord because it hit so close to home. The spirit of American materialism declares that greed is a virtue, that in fact greed is the foundation of success. This is the mind-set of the man or woman who boasts of the desires of his or her soul. They boast because they believe it is a good thing never to be content, never to be satisfied, always to want more. And in their greed they grind the poor into the ground to get what they want.

It is sobering to notice that these wicked men and women renounce God by his personal name, Yahweh ("the LORD," v. 3). This implies that these oppressors are not foreigners; they are Israelites who knowingly reject the God of Israel. In their greed they loved money and possessions more than God. In their pride they did not look for him. Finally they denied that God even exists.

Greed and pride can turn your heart away from God today too. You may have grown up knowing the Bible, but you are living for yourself. Jesus said, "What does it profit a man to gain the whole world and forfeit his soul?" (Mark 8:36). The wicked boast in their desires, but the Scriptures say, "Let the one who boasts, boast in the Lord" (1 Corinthians 1:31).

You might assume that someone who openly rejects God would be struck down by lightning. But atheists often prosper. People who give themselves to gathering money often get rich. And because they have laughed at God and have still been successful, their arrogance grows. They assume that they must be invincible.

His ways prosper at all times;
    your judgments are on high, out of his sight;
    as for all his foes, he puffs at them. (10:5)

Because he is affluent, he is convinced that nothing can touch him. He has the latest tech gadgets; he drives a new Aston Martin; he goes on the best vacations; he wears new clothes. Success has blinded his eyes to God's judgment—it is too high for him.

Here is what he thinks in his heart of hearts:

He says in his heart, "I shall not be moved;
    throughout all generations I shall not meet adversity." (10:6)

The wicked man is thoroughly deceived. He thinks that the blessings God reserves for the godly belong to him! It is the blameless man who shall not be moved (Psalm 15:5; 16:8), but the wicked "are like chaff that the wind drives away" (Psalm 1:4). The wicked think they can set up their children to prosper after them. They can put them in the right schools and introduce them to the right people and leave a trust that will provide for them. But the Scriptures say that "the generation of the upright will be blessed" (Psalm 112:2). In his pride the wicked man has believed a lie.

Aggressive

The wicked man is not only arrogant and proud, he is aggressive and violent. This is the second part of the psalmist's description.

First, his words are violent.

> His mouth is filled with cursing and deceit and oppression;
>   under his tongue are mischief and iniquity. (10:7)

In the summer of 2012, northeastern Oklahoma was a tinderbox after weeks of drought and triple digit temperatures. On August 2 a devastating wildfire in Creek County burned 58,500 acres, destroyed 376 homes, and left hundreds of people homeless. As it turned out, the fire was started by a single cigarette. A wicked man's words are like a spark that ignites violence.

In fact, sins of the tongue are the most common kind of violence in the Psalms. C. S. Lewis notes,

> I think that when I began to read it these surprised me a little; I had half expected that in a simpler and more violent age when more evil was done with the knife, the big stick, and the firebrand, less would be done by talk. But in reality the Psalmists mention hardly any kind of evil more often than this one, which the most civilised societies share. . . . It is all over the Psalter. One almost hears the incessant whispering, tattling, lying, scolding, flattery, and circulation of rumours. No historical readjustments are here required, we are in the world we know.[3]

Evil shows itself most often in verbal violence. In fact, the Apostle Paul quotes Psalm 10:7 to show that everyone, Jews and Gentiles alike, are under the power of sin (Romans 3:14). And James says,

> And the tongue is a fire, a world of unrighteousness. The tongue is set among our members, staining the whole body, setting on fire the entire course of life, and set on fire by hell. (James 3:6)

And from a violent heart come violent actions.

> He sits in ambush in the villages;
>   in hiding places he murders the innocent.
> His eyes stealthily watch for the helpless;
>   he lurks in ambush like a lion in his thicket;
> he lurks that he may seize the poor;
>   he seizes the poor when he draws him into his net.
> The helpless are crushed, sink down,
>   and fall by his might. (10:8–10)

The wicked man is treacherous. He ambushes the unsuspecting. He doesn't do his work in cities where he might get caught but rather hunts in the villages where people trust each other and don't lock their doors at night. His eyes shift around stealthily, watching for his victims. He lurks. He hides his net. God help the man he catches because not only is he treacherous, he is also merciless. He cares nothing about the people he attacks, whether they are good or bad or whether they have families depending on them.

Why does he attack the poor? For one thing, his heart is bad. Jesus said, "out of the abundance of the heart the mouth speaks" (Matthew 12:34). His words are full of "cursing and . . . oppression" (10:7) because his heart is full of cursing and oppression. His very nature is to use whatever power he has to use and exploit others.

The poor are also easy victims. A poor man doesn't have connections; who will go to bat for him? A poor man may not know his rights. If he is an immigrant, he might be ashamed that he can't speak English well, and he might not have the confidence to stand up for himself. A poor woman can probably be frightened and silenced. If she gets pregnant, you might be able to intimidate her into having an abortion. The poor can't hire a lawyer, especially not one who can fight the legal department of a large company. A poor man doesn't have the clout at City Hall that comes from owning a business and providing jobs in the community. The poor are easy prey for the wicked. This is why the Scriptures command us to "defend the rights of the poor and needy" (Proverbs 31:9).

Ultimately he oppresses the poor because he thinks no one will call him to account. Verse 11 tells us his thoughts.

> He says in his heart, "God has forgotten,
>   he has hidden his face, he will never see it."

"The arrogance of the wicked expresses itself in injustice, but their root problem is their utter disregard for the Lord."[4] They no longer sense any accountability to God. They decide that God has not stepped in to stop them because he doesn't know or he doesn't care. So the wicked give free rein to the violence in their heart.

In fact, they have badly mistaken God's silence. God is not forgetful, and he is not negligent. Instead God is patient and kind with sinners, giving them every opportunity to turn away from their sin and repent. The Scriptures warn us not to draw the wrong conclusion when God is patient with our sin.

> Or do you presume on the riches of his kindness and forbearance and patience, not knowing that God's kindness is meant to lead you to repentance? But because of your hard and impenitent heart you are storing up wrath for yourself on the day of wrath when God's righteous judgment will be revealed. (Romans 2:4, 5)

If God doesn't stop you or strike you down when you sin, don't think this means he doesn't know or doesn't care. God is kind and patient, and he offers you every opportunity to turn away from your sin. The wicked mistake God's patience for negligence. The godly recognize God's kindness and run to him.

Calling God to Act

God will judge the world. He stores up judgment for the future, and he judges sin and oppression today as well. After describing the wicked, the psalmist calls God to action.

A Prayer for Action

First, he pleads with God to intervene.

> Arise, O Lord; O God, lift up your hand;
>   forget not the afflicted. (10:12)

Many times God does not seem to act. It is agonizing to watch injustice unfold like a slow-motion train wreck. We can't understand why God would allow this to happen. The right response is to turn to God in prayer and ask him to step in and intervene. This is a prayer of faith, believing that God is concerned and can deliver and rescue the needy.

The phrase "lift up your hand" (v. 12) suggests a warrior raising his arm in battle. The psalmist wants God to step forward with power on behalf of the weak and the helpless. They need a champion to stand against the wicked.

If you are a Christian, he may use you to answer this prayer! You may be part of his solution. When William Wilberforce saw the horrors of the slave trade, he could have simply prayed for God to end it. Instead Wilberforce took action. He gave his first major speech against slavery in Parliament on May 12, 1789. In 1791 he joined the Society for Effecting the Abolition of the Slave Trade to work formally with others who were committed to the same goal. After eighteen years of work, the Slave Trade Act was passed in 1807, outlawing the sale and transportation of slaves. But slavery itself was not abolished in the British Empire until August 1834. Wilberforce died in 1833, only three days after learning that the Slavery Abolition Act was guaranteed to be passed. He worked for forty-four years to see the end of slavery. Soon after his death over eight hundred thousand African slaves were set free.

Who is weak and helpless today? Is God calling you to do something?

You Do See!

We can pray and take action because we know God is the Judge of all the earth and he is at work today.

> Why does the wicked renounce God
>   and say in his heart, "You will not call to account"?
> But you do see, for you note mischief and vexation,
>   that you may take it into your hands;
> to you the helpless commits himself;
>   you have been the helper of the fatherless. (10:13, 14)

The helpless and the fatherless are the most vulnerable and most easily taken advantage of. God cares passionately about the way we treat the poor and vulnerable among us. In the Law of Moses, God promised to protect the weakest among the people and warned that he would take up their case.

> You shall not wrong a sojourner or oppress him, for you were sojourners
> in the land of Egypt. You shall not mistreat any widow or fatherless child.
> If you do mistreat them, and they cry out to me, I will surely hear their cry,
> and my wrath will burn, and I will kill you with the sword, and your wives
> shall become widows and your children fatherless. (Exodus 22:21–24)

As the psalmist looked around, he saw Israelites who thought God would never keep his promise to defend the poor. So he calls on God to be true to his word and act decisively against the violence and oppression all around.

> Break the arm of the wicked and evildoer;
>   call his wickedness to account till you find none. (10:15)

Breaking their arm symbolizes breaking their power. But we shouldn't sanitize this and think that God would never be violent. God does bring violence on the wicked in this life.

After Ahab took possession of Naboth's vineyard, God sent the prophet Elijah to confront him with God's judgment.

> Behold, I will bring disaster upon you. I will utterly burn you up, and will cut off from Ahab every male, bond or free, in Israel. . . . And of Jezebel the LORD also said, "The dogs shall eat Jezebel within the walls of Jezreel." Anyone belonging to Ahab who dies in the city the dogs shall eat, and anyone of his who dies in the open country the birds of the heavens shall eat. (1 Kings 21:21, 23, 24)

Gruesome words! And they came true. Ahab died in battle, and all his male descendants died. Jezebel was thrown from an upper window and died on the street. God does indeed defend the weak and the powerless. He brings judgment on oppressors today, and he stores up wrath for them on the final day.

New Confidence in God

The psalm ends with new confidence in God.

> The LORD is king forever and ever;
>   the nations perish from his land.
> O LORD, you hear the desire of the afflicted;
>   you will strengthen their heart; you will incline your ear
> to do justice to the fatherless and the oppressed,
>   so that man who is of the earth may strike terror no more. (10:16–18)

We don't know whether the psalmist ever saw the answer to his prayer. God's timing is not our timing. You and I may go to our graves without seeing justice done. But we know that God is King. He defends his people. He stands up for the weak.

May he strengthen your heart by faith. If you trust him, you will be able to live joyfully even in times of trouble. You will be able to endure injustice with quiet confidence. You will be able to take action and defend the weak. You will be able to rest in him.

11

Faith or Flight?

PSALM 11

IN PSALM 11 David declares his confidence in God while the world seems to be falling apart. David's friends looked around in fear and told him he should run away. After all, they reasoned, "if the foundations are destroyed, what can the righteous do?" (11:3).

Many Christians today are asking the same fearful question as David's anxious friends. "If the foundations are destroyed, what can the righteous do?" What can we do when same-sex marriage is rising like a storm surge to flood our nation? The 2012 election marked a new high-water mark. *The New York Times* reported:

> Gay rights advocates savored multiple victories on Wednesday, with the first election victories for same-sex marriage in Maine, Maryland and Minnesota, the election in Wisconsin of the nation's first openly gay senator and the re-election of President Obama, who had taken a risk by endorsing same-sex marriage.
>
> "It truly was a milestone year," said Chad Griffin, the president of the Human Rights Campaign, which raised millions of dollars for this year's campaigns. "We had success across the board and across the country."[1]

Christians don't see much to celebrate in these so-called victories. We know from Scripture that God created heterosexual marriage to reflect his committed love for his people. Heterosexual marriage is one of the basic building blocks God established for human society. Many are asking today, "if the foundations are destroyed, what can the righteous do?" (v. 3).

What can we do when murdering children in the womb is called "health care"? Obamacare forces Americans to participate in the barbaric spread of abortion. The U.S. Conference of Catholic Bishops recently released their analysis of the new health care law.

> Through their tax dollars all taxpayers will be forced to subsidize over-all health plans that cover elective abortions, contrary to the policy of the Hyde amendment and every other major federal program . . . Many of these Americans will also be forced to pay directly for other people's abortions.[2]

The courts have not been friendly to Christians who are forced to violate their conscience. Several dozen Christian groups sued the Department of Health and Human Services because the law requires them to provide insurance coverage for the "morning after" pill. A federal judge threw out their lawsuit. Children will continue to be killed in our land in the name of health care and women's rights. What about caring for the health of unborn women? If we follow our present trajectory, outright infanticide is not far behind. "If the foundations are destroyed, what can the righteous do?"

We could go on. Voters in Washington and Colorado approved ballot initiatives to legalize recreational marijuana. NPR was very supportive in its post-election coverage. Pornography is all over the Internet, corrupting grade-school and junior high boys along with adult men. You may be surprised to learn that viewing pornography is also on the rise among women. At one time it was considered shameful to have a baby out of wedlock. As of 2012, more than half of the children born to women under 30 occur outside marriage.[3] "If the foundations are destroyed, what can the righteous do?"

Christians can be tempted to give in to fear. Psalm 11 is David's answer to the panic that gripped his friends when the foundations of their society seemed to be crumbling. God's people have a choice between flight and faith. David's response was to take refuge in God and keep doing what is right. This needs to be our response too as we apply Psalm 11 to ourselves. We'll look at David's temptation (vv. 1–3) and David's foundation (vv. 4–7).

David's Temptation

Psalm 11 opens with an account of David's temptation to doubt God in a time of turmoil.

We're not sure when David wrote this psalm. Some think it was when he was serving in King Saul's court and the king was plotting to murder him. The uncertainty and intrigue of this time certainly fits. Others think David wrote this when Saul was chasing him in the wilderness. At one point Saul murdered Ahimelech the priest, along with his entire family and village, eighty-five priests with their families. This sent shock waves throughout Israel and shook the foundations of the nation. Others think this was written during Absalom's rebellion.

None of these situations seem to fit well with Psalm 11. One obvious difference is that in each of these cases David did flee when his life was threatened, while he refuses to flee in Psalm 11. Not only so, but the mountains were generally places of danger for him, not safety. Jerusalem is in the mountains, and Saul's capital, Gibeah, was also in the mountains three miles north of Jerusalem.[4] David hid mostly in the wilderness (1 Samuel 24:1; 26:2) because fleeing to the mountains would be suicide, not security.

This suggests that this psalm is not talking about physically running away. We are supposed to read this more broadly as a temptation to abandon the place God has appointed for us because of the onslaught of evil.[5] God had anointed David to be king. His friends counseled him to forget his calling and save himself. "Fly like a bird," they said. In the same way God has given us a role in this world. We are the salt of the earth and the light of the world (Matthew 5:14–16). Jesus commanded us to make disciples of all nations, including our own (Matthew 28:19, 20). The temptation to fly away means abandoning the work and the calling God has given us.

Confident Refusal

David met this temptation with a confident refusal. He couldn't believe they were suggesting this! Derek Kidner calls this psalm "a spirited retort to some demoralizing advice."[6] He is indignant from the opening line.

> In the LORD I take refuge;
> how can you say to my soul,
>   "Flee like a bird to your mountain . . . (11:1)

The verb "flee" is plural, as is the pronoun "your" (v. 1). This advice was being given to all God's people. A rising tide of fear and despair was sweeping through Israel. So this was like a hurricane evacuation. *Everybody run to your place of refuge, "your mountain"* (v. 1).

But God is the refuge for his people. His presence is better than strong walls around us. When our children were younger, we often carried them in a backpack child-carrier. We brought them to all sorts of places in that backpack, some of them very dangerous for a baby on her own. We hiked with them on mountain trails in Washington and Oregon. We carried them through crowds of strangers at the state fair. We bundled them up in snowsuits and took them on walks in the Minnesota winter. We walked at night when the wind was blowing and the sky was threatening to storm. Our children could have been terrified in any one of those places, but they weren't. Why not? They were with mom and dad; we were right there with them. We were their refuge in a strange and dangerous world.

David chose to take refuge in God. By faith he knew that God was near, a strong wall to protect him and care for him. He would not surrender to unbelief. He would not deny God by giving in to panic and running away from the place God had called him to as his anointed king.

The Counsel of Despair

We shouldn't think this was an easy decision. David felt this temptation deeply, in his soul. It tugged at him where he was vulnerable. To make it even more tempting, the people counseling him to flee were probably his friends. Their advice appealed to his deepest needs, desires, and hopes.[7] On the surface what they said made sense.

> [F]or behold, the wicked bend the bow;
>   they have fitted their arrow to the string
>   to shoot in the dark at the upright in heart. (11:2)

The godly were in clear and present danger. David's friends described the danger in graphic terms. If an archer has nocked an arrow on the string, he is ready to shoot. Once he bends his bow, he can only hold the string so long before his arm shakes and his fingers give way. The godly are in imminent danger from the violence of the wicked. Like assassins, evil men are hiding in the shadows, ready to strike when God's people can't see it coming.

Their treachery was destroying the very structures of society. David's friends concluded that there is nothing left to do but throw in the towel and concede defeat.

> [I]f the foundations are destroyed,
>   what can the righteous do? (11:3)

This is the counsel of despair. The godly are helpless, they say. There is nothing anyone can do. Whatever we had is gone. Why waste your life in a hopeless crusade? Why build on sand? Why try to plow the sea? Better to give up and run away.

Timeless Temptation

This is a timeless temptation. Jesus was tempted with the same advice to run away from the danger God appointed for his life. Some Pharisees came up to him and said, "Get away from here, for Herod wants to kill you" (Luke 13:31). Jesus would not be moved. He answered,

> Go and tell that fox, "Behold, I cast out demons and perform cures today and tomorrow, and the third day I finish my course . . . for it cannot be that a prophet should perish away from Jerusalem." (vv. 32–34)

Even Jesus' disciples advised him to turn away from the work God had for him to do. When Jesus set off for Bethany to raise Lazarus from the dead, "[t]he disciples said to him, 'Rabbi, the Jews were just now seeking to stone you, and are you going there again?'" (John 11:7, 8). Later when Jesus told his disciples clearly that he must be killed and rise again, Peter tried to speak some sense to him: "Far be it from you, Lord! This shall never happen to you." Jesus rebuked him, saying, "Get behind me, Satan!" (Matthew 16:22, 23).

If Jesus had followed the counsel of despair, he would have left the path God laid out for him and would not have died as our Savior. Humanly speaking, what good could come from his death? But he trusted God, and through his faithful obedience we were saved.

Those who follow Christ today hear the same counsel of despair. We are told to abandon the work God has given us because the situation seems hopeless. The foundations are destroyed, they say. You can't hold back the tide. Don't waste your time. Get yourself and your family out of danger.

How do people "flee like a bird" today (Psalm 11:1)?[8] Some are spiritual survivalists who flee physically and move away from civilization. They live off the grid, moving to remote areas to get away from a world that seems to be falling apart at the seams. The problem is that you can't be the light of the world when you cut yourself off from the world (Matthew 5:14).

Some people isolate themselves culturally. They might live in our neighborhoods or subdivisions, but they maintain a separate cultural identity. They reject changes in culture that have nothing to do with godliness or the gospel. New styles and developments are guilty by association in their minds. An extreme example are Hasidic Jews who walk through the streets of New York City in black hats and clothes like those their ancestors brought from Eastern Europe. One of the problems with this approach is that you become known more for your old-fashioned ways than for Jesus Christ and the gospel.

Some withdraw emotionally. They stop caring for the world around us.

When they see a man suffering the consequences of his sin, they say to themselves, "It serves him right. He is getting what he deserves." They forget that God does not give us what our sins deserve (Psalm 103:10). They forget the beatitude that says, "Blessed are the merciful, for they shall receive mercy" (Matthew 5:7). Emotional withdrawal is not an option for someone who has been touched by the grace of God.

Some people flee through nostalgia. They long for a gentler time when the world was supposedly less evil. Their hearts live in a Photoshopped version of the past, often an airbrushed nineteenth-century America. They imagine a golden age that never existed, a nation without slavery, the Trail of Tears, Jayhawkers, the Civil War, tuberculosis, smallpox, infant mortality, or the financial panics of 1819, 1837, 1857, 1873, and 1893. Sin has been in the world since the garden of Eden. Evil men triumphed in David's day and in Christ's day. The world was wicked in the 1950s; the world is wicked today. In his sovereignty God appointed us to be born in this place and time to serve him here and now. We can't live in the past.

These are some of the ways Christians are tempted to flee when the foundations are shaken. These withdrawals seem to offer an escape, but they come at the expense of the Great Commission and our influence for the gospel. Worse, they imply that God is not able to protect us. Flight is a form of unbelief if it is a substitute for trusting God.

David's Foundation

David rejected the counsel of despair. From David's temptation we turn to David's foundation.

David's friends had made a serious mistake. The foundation that supports God's people was not destroyed. God is the foundation of his people and is their security forever. Moses, the man of God, said it well in Psalm 90.

> Lord, you have been our dwelling place
>   in all generations.
> Before the mountains were brought forth,
>   or ever you had formed the earth and the world,
>   from everlasting to everlasting you are God. (Psalm 90:1, 2)

David focuses his eyes on God in the second half of Psalm 11. God's personal name, Yahweh, is repeated emphatically four times in these verses. David's unflinching courage comes from knowing Yahweh, the Lord, and taking refuge in him.

God Rules

First, David affirms that God rules. He is the sovereign King over Heaven and earth. "The LORD is in his holy temple; the LORD's throne is in heaven" (11:4a).

When we see the word *temple*, we automatically think of Solomon's temple or Herod's magnificent temple that stood in Jerusalem during the time of Christ. But David is not referring to an earthly temple. For one thing, Solomon's temple had not been built yet. The second half of this verse also makes it clear that the throne room David is thinking of is in Heaven. In fact, the Hebrew word for *temple* is the same word as *palace*. God's palace is in Heaven, far above our puny courts and government buildings. His throne is a symbol of his authority to rule and to judge. No matter what is happening on earth, God is still in control.

When the foundations seem to be shaking, God is not frightened. Nothing happens in Heaven above, on the earth around, or even in Hell below that he does not ordain and overrule.

God Sees

From his throne the Lord carefully watches the world of men. ". . . his eyes see, his eyelids test the children of man" (11:4b).

The word "see" (v. 4) can be translated "gaze" or "scrutinize." God is paying attention. To paint a picture in our minds, David says his "eyelids test" us. That's an interesting expression. On the one hand, this could suggest that God's attention never wavers. Even if his eyes seem closed, he is so perceptive that his eyelids still search the heart and minds of men and women. Or David could be picturing God with his eyes narrowed like an appraiser carefully scrutinizing and evaluating an antique. The writer of Proverbs says, "The eyes of the LORD are in every place, keeping watch on the evil and the good" (Proverbs 15:3).

When it seems like God is not doing anything, you can rest assured that he is carefully watching and evaluating the life of every human being. He gives all men and women ample time to show who they are by their actions. Character is what you do in the dark, when no one is watching. The wicked think they can shoot unseen from the shadows and get away with it. God sees us late at night and in secret. He watches our lives, and he knows our hearts.

Jesus himself looked into the heart of man during his earthly life. John writes that Jesus "needed no one to bear witness about man, for he himself knew what was in man" (John 2:25). And when John saw Christ exalted in his heavenly glory, he reports, "His eyes were like a flame of fire" (Revelation 1:14). All hearts are open before Christ, and all desires are known to him. When we stand before Jesus, we stand before the God who sees.

God Judges

From his throne, God judges the evil and the good. The righteous are not exempt from God's judgment: "The LORD tests the righteous" (11:5a). But God's examination is for their good. The verb "tests" or "examines" (v. 5 NIV) refers to the process of proving or assaying precious metal. God "tests the righteous" (v. 5) to demonstrate to the world that they are genuine (1 Peter 1:6, 7). This is the kind of testing that Job endured when God proved that Job truly loved him. This test is related to the activity of a goldsmith purifying gold or silver. He heats it up and melts it to remove the impurities and refine it, making it even more precious than it was.[9] God refines the righteous with trouble and afflictions because he loves them and wants to purify them and give them more of himself.

The testing fire of God's judgment is devastating for the wicked, though.

> [B]ut his [God's] soul hates the wicked and the one who loves violence.
> Let him rain coals on the wicked;
> fire and sulfur and a scorching wind shall be the portion of their cup.
> (11:5b, 6)

God's innermost being detests the wicked and the violent. He is adamantly and eternally angry with everyone who does evil. We shouldn't be surprised to read about God's anger. His wrath is a natural and necessary part of his love. If God loves that which is good, beautiful, and pure, he must hate everything that is set against it. If you love your wife, you will hate an intruder who enters your house to harm her while you're gone. If you are not furious at someone who hurts her, you obviously don't love her. In the same way, God's love for the righteous must be matched by his hatred for the wicked. For this reason, it is God's glory to hate sin. He would be less than God if he was not a God of wrath. His love for his people would be a fraud without an equally passionate hatred for the wicked.

God's judgment is not fantasy or fiction. God has already rained down coals of fire and sulfur in human history when he destroyed Sodom and Gomorrah (Genesis 19:24). The Scriptures say that fiery judgment is coming again. The Apostle Peter writes that "the heavens and earth that now exist are stored up for fire, being kept until the day of judgment and destruction of the ungodly" (2 Peter 3:7). God's judgment is delayed as he watches and weighs the world of men, but it is coming.

God Rewards

David ends with God's reward for those who are faithful to him.

> For the LORD is righteous;
> he loves righteous deeds;
>   the upright shall behold his face. (11:7)

As the world shakes around us, we need to be sure that we continue to act justly because the Lord "loves righteous deeds" (v. 7). If we flee, we lose our Christian influence in this world. The opposite danger is to become so much like the world that we lose our distinctive identity as Christians. We must remain people who reflect God's character in our hearts and in our actions. "The LORD is righteous; he loves righteous deeds" (v. 7). His reward is for those who faithfully do what is right.

God promises that those who trust him will see "his face" (v. 7). This will not be attractive to you if you do not love him. There is no motivation in seeing God if you do not delight in him and treasure him. But this is the greatest reward possible if your heart says to God, "Your steadfast love is better than life" (Psalm 63:3). On our wedding day Lisa and I were apart from each other getting ready with our friends. We took pictures before the service, though, and I remember walking into the Fireside Room at our church and seeing her waiting for me across the room. I treasured the moment I saw her face because I love her. So it is with those who love God. We long to see his face because he is the desire of our hearts.

Not long ago my nephew and his wife lost their little baby. It was a tragic time for our family. My mother came to the hospital too and grieved the loss of her great-grandson. It was especially poignant because they named him Arthur after my father, who died several years ago. This little life carried a double sorrow for her, the loss of the baby and the loss of her husband. As we drove home, I mentioned to her how comforting it was to know that Dad was there in Heaven to welcome his great-grandson, his namesake. She said to me, "Yes, that's true, but when we get to Heaven, we are going to see Jesus. The most wonderful thing will be to see him." My mother had it right—we will see believers who have gone there before us, but our great reward is to "behold his face" (v. 7).

Is this wishful thinking as the world crumbles around us? Not at all. Jesus said, "I will come again and will take you to myself, that where I am you may be also" (John 14:3). And the Apostle John promised, "we know that when he appears we shall be like him, because we shall see him as he is" (1 John 3:2).

If this is our confidence and hope, we can stand firm. As the world goes from bad to worse, we will not give in to the counsel of despair. God is the firm foundation for his people.

> Therefore let us be grateful for receiving a kingdom that cannot be shaken, and thus let us offer to God acceptable worship, with reverence and awe, for our God is a consuming fire. (Hebrews 12:28, 29)

12

Deliver Us from Deception

PSALM 12

HAVE YOU EVER FELT ALL ALONE? Really alone?

I have never felt more alone than when I walked into a hotel lobby in Budapest, Hungary in April 1999. I had been visiting missionaries in Eastern Europe and was spending the night in Budapest before flying home.

That spring American and NATO warplanes were bombing Yugoslavia to prevent ethnic cleansing in Kosovo. Many Yugoslavian Serbs fled with their families to escape the bombing. A large number ended up in neighboring countries like Hungary and Romania.

As we pulled into our small hotel, I noticed that all the cars in the parking lot had Yugoslavian license plates! Sure enough, the lobby was filled with families who had fled to Hungary for safety. I was one American surrounded by almost a hundred Serbians—and we were bombing their country. I have never felt so vulnerable and so alone.

David felt alone as he wrote Psalm 12. He looked around and saw only enemies. In Psalm 11 the wicked were destroying the foundations of society. Now it seems like they have succeeded in wiping out the godly with their lies and deception.

David may have written this psalm as Saul was trying to kill him. Saul lied about David to manipulate his leaders. In return people lied to Saul (1 Samuel 24:9). David may also have written this during his son Absalom's rebellion. Absalom seduced Israel with his lies, and his military coup was marked by espionage, betrayal, misdirection, and intrigue. Whenever this was written, David felt utterly alone.

Our Lord Jesus was even more alone as he walked through this world. He was the only Son of God. He is the only man in history who always spoke the truth. In the end even his closest friends abandoned him, and he walked to the cross alone. David's sense of isolation in Psalm 12 points forward to Christ, the son of David.

David entrusted this psalm "to the choirmaster" so that future generations would hear these words sung in the temple, take them to heart, and learn to love the truth. Unfortunately, they didn't listen. Years later the prophets Hosea, Isaiah, Jeremiah, and Micah condemned Israel for the same wicked culture of lies (Hosea 11:12—12:1; Isaiah 59:4; Micah 6:12; Jeremiah 5:1, 2).

If this is how things are among God's people, what must the Gentile world be like? David extrapolates from what was happening in Israel to conclude that all humanity is depraved. The psalm begins and ends globally with David's comment on all human beings. In verse 1 David says, "the faithful have vanished from among the children of man." Verse 8 tells us, "vileness is exalted among the children of man." When God's people are corrupt, what must the rest of the world be like—people who have never known God or heard his Word?

This is the world in which we live. This is the world that is set against Jesus Christ, God's King (Psalm 2). If you are a Christian, what should you do when you feel alone in a society soaked in lies? David's response in Psalm 12 is our example. David prays for help as wickedness prevails (12:1–4). Then David trusts God's promise to protect his people (12:5–8).

David Prays for Help as Sin Prevails

As the psalm opens, David has nowhere to look but upward to God. He could have retreated, but instead he lifts his prayer up to the God of Heaven. There are Christians today who spend more time complaining about the sinfulness of the world than they do in prayer. Some Christians spend more time getting stirred up by talk radio than they spend talking to God. David starts with the right instincts. He looks up to God and calls out to him for help.

God Save!

David's first words are a short prayer that shoots up to Heaven like an arrow: "Save, O Lord." This could also be translated "Help, O Lord." David fills out his prayer for help with an explanation.

> Save, O Lord, for the godly one is gone;
> for the faithful have vanished from among the children of man. (12:1)

When we think of faithfulness, we tend to think of maintaining sound doctrine and remaining faithful to the truth. This is certainly important. The Scriptures tell us to "contend for the faith that was once for all delivered to the saints" (Jude 3). But "faithful" in this context refers to faithful living that pleases God (Psalm 12:1). Faithful ones steadfastly keep their commitments.[1] They honor their covenant with God by trusting him and serving him from the heart. They honor their relationships with others through their loyalty, trustworthiness, integrity, and dependability.

David saw many people who said all the right things. He didn't see many people whose lives matched their words. It's the same for us today. You can be orthodox in your theology while your life is far from God. At a recent Annual Meeting of the Evangelical Theological Society, a friend mentioned to me that he had just seen someone he knew from seminary. This other man is doing very well as a scholar. He has a good teaching position and is publishing books and articles like a machine. But as they met, he introduced my friend to his new wife—his fourth wife in fact. This man signed a doctrinal statement, but he broke faith with the first three women he married. David saw men like him. They offered sacrifices and observed the religious festivals, but their lives denied what their lips said. So he concludes, "the faithful have vanished from among the children of man."

David zeros in on their wicked speech as the essence of their evil.

Everyone utters lies to his neighbor;
   with flattering lips and a double heart they speak. (12:2)

Lying, fake compliments, and proud boasting had destroyed faithful living. The word "everyone" (v. 2) emphasizes the breadth of the problem. The phrase "to his neighbor" (v. 2) emphasizes the depth of the problem. Young and old, rich and poor, male and female—every segment of Israel's society was deceitful. The fabric of society was torn since neighbor was lying to neighbor.

As a church, nothing will destroy our relationships more quickly than lies. When Christians are dishonest with each other, they tear apart the Body of Christ. Deceit breeds distrust. Distrust leads to division. This is why the Scriptures clearly say, "Therefore, having put away falsehood, let each one of you speak the truth with his neighbor, for we are members one of another" (Ephesians 4:25). If we want to live together in love and unity, we must be people of truth.

What our lips say comes from who we are inside. Jesus said, "Out of

the abundance of the heart the mouth speaks" (Matthew 12:34). We think of
the heart as the seat of emotions and affections—we cut out paper hearts for
Valentine's Day. But in the Hebrew way of thinking, the heart was the seat
of thought, your true self. In fact, in the Scriptures the heart is usually closer
to what we think of as the intellect or the mind. The double-hearted man is
thinking two things at the same time: what he wants and what he needs to say
to get what he wants. Truth takes a back seat to selfishness.

The Apostle James gave us the classic description of the power of evil in
the human tongue.

> So also the tongue is a small member, yet it boasts of great things.
> How great a forest is set ablaze by such a small fire! And the tongue is
> a fire, a world of unrighteousness. The tongue is set among our members,
> staining the whole body, setting on fire the entire course of life, and set on
> fire by hell. For every kind of beast and bird, of reptile and sea creature, can
> be tamed and has been tamed by mankind, but no human being can tame
> the tongue. It is a restless evil, full of deadly poison. (James 3:5–8)

How God Will Save

No wonder that David calls on God to take drastic measures. He asks God to
do away with liars.

> May the Lord cut off all flattering lips,
>   the tongue that makes great boasts,
> those who say, "With our tongue we will prevail,
>   our lips are with us; who is master over us?" (12:3, 4)

What does David mean by cutting off lips and slicing out the tongue?
Frankly this sounds grotesque. The parallelism between verses 3 and 4 suggests that this is a figure of speech called synecdoche where parts of the body
refer to the whole person. For instance, when a ship's captain says, "All hands
on deck!" he wants more than just thumbs and fingers. He wants his sailors on
deck—their whole bodies. In the same way, the "lips" and "tongue" in verse
3 refer to the flatterers and boasters themselves as people. David asks God to
cut off their lives.

This may seem like a harsh prayer until you stop to think about the destruction that liars and deceivers do with their tongues. A fourteen-year-old
Christian girl in Pakistan named Rimsha Masih was accused of desecrating
the Koran, a crime punishable by death. It turns out an imam from a local
mosque planted pages from the Koran in a bag of garbage she was taking out

to burn. The police discovered the truth, and Rimsha was freed. Others have not been so lucky; they have been put to death on the basis of false testimony.

Liars and boasters can do far worse damage by perverting the gospel. Those who listen to them will lose more than their lives; they will lose their eternal souls. When Jude warns us that false teachers will creep into the church, he describes them with almost the very words of Psalm 12: "they are loud-mouthed boasters, showing favoritism to gain advantage" (Jude 16). These teachers not only condemn themselves, they drag others into the fires of Hell along with them. On November 18, 1978 Jim Jones led 914 members of his cult to commit mass suicide in Guyana. He boasted that God had anointed him. He flattered his people, and he betrayed them, body and soul. Most false teachers do not take their followers' lives physically like this, but their false gospel just as surely leads them to eternal punishment in Hell.

When we consider the damage that deceivers can do with the tongue, David's harsh words make more sense. The stakes are so high that the punishment must fit the crime.

Good talkers think they can win with their words. Karl Marx said, "Give me twenty-six lead soldiers and I'll conquer the world." The soldiers he was referring to were the twenty-six letters of the alphabet. The closing words of his *Communist Manifesto* are a powerful slogan: "Working men of all countries, unite!" These six words have mobilized and motivated millions of people. But in a demonstration in Moscow on the seventy-second anniversary of Communism in Russia, people carried signs that said, "Workers of the world, we're sorry" and "72 years leading nowhere."[2] Boastful words may succeed for a season, but ultimately they will fail.

We can't just apply this to others without looking at ourselves. Our own lips are sometimes deceitful. According to James, your tongue and mine is a restless evil that makes great boasts. When David says, "May the LORD cut off all flattering lips, the tongue that makes great boasts" (v. 3), he is talking about you and me too. We all deserve to be judged for our words. If we are honest, we know that we have hurt and deceived others with our tongues.

So where does that leave us? There has only been one man who never flattered or boasted, never deceived in the slightest. The Bible says that Jesus "committed no sin, neither was deceit found in his mouth" (1 Peter 2:22). Jesus Christ is the one man who never sinned with his words. The good news of the gospel is that although you and I should be condemned for our words, our sins can be forgiven—wiped away—and we can be credited with his sinless mouth and spotless obedience. This is why the Bible says,

He himself bore our sins in his body on the tree, that we might die to sin and live to righteousness. By his wounds you have been healed. (1 Peter 2:24)

When we come to Jesus, he turns us into faithful people who speak the truth from the heart. The Holy Spirit who lives inside us is called "the Spirit of truth" (John 14:17). God's truth now lives in us (2 John 2). It's not enough just to be like Jiminy Cricket and try never to tell a lie. Our tongue is a restless evil. Even if we never utter another deceitful word, we are guilty for the things we have already said. We need our guilt taken away and a new power inside us that is strong enough to control our tongue. We need to be forgiven through Jesus' death and resurrection. We need the power of God's Spirit inside us. We need to be saved.

People who trust their ability to speak think they will never be held accountable; they ask, "Who is master over us?" The answer is easy: God is our master, and he will judge. And now it is time for this God to speak.

God Promises Help to Protect His People

In the second half of Psalm 12, God's Word confronts the words of the wicked. Man's words seem powerful, but they are weak. God's words may seem weak, but they are living and powerful.

God's Promise

This is the first psalm that contains a direct answer from God to the psalmist's prayer. It is only the second psalm to quote God's direct words (Psalm 2:6 was the first). A direct answer to prayer stands out because it is rare in the Psalms.

"Because the poor are plundered, because the needy groan,
  I will now arise," says the LORD;
  "I will place him in the safety for which he longs." (12:5)

The weak and helpless are the first victims of a deceitful society. Because they are powerless, the poor and needy are vulnerable. Sometimes the needy are actively plundered. Scammers take advantage of them with cheap products—cheap furniture that falls apart, used cars that were written off in a flood, or food that has almost no nutritional value. Since they don't have a financial cushion, it is easier to rip them off with credit scams and payday loans. Brewers and distillers often target low-income communities with billboards. They promise a man he'll have a good time and be popular if he drinks their beer. In return for his money, they give his family a drunken man for a husband and father. But God sees when the poor are plundered.

He also hears when the needy quietly groan from neglect. In a deceitful society, neighbors do not trust each other or care for one another as they should. No one bothers to lift the load from the widow's shoulders. No one stands up for the immigrant who is paid less than he is worth. No one thinks to feed children who are hungry over the weekend. But God hears them moan when no one else cares.

In the context of these psalms, the godly are by and large the poor and oppressed. The wicked shoot at them from the shadows (Psalm 11:2) and have been so successful that the godly seem to have disappeared from the land. David numbers himself among the poor and needy by using the pronoun "us" in 12:7. So while David speaks of the poor in general, he is particularly thinking about God's people who are often trampled and abused in this world. God sees, and he hears the cries of his people.

And God takes action. Like a warrior standing up to do battle, God says, "I will now arise" (v. 5).[3] He is a champion for his people. God is at work every day through divine providence, but the word "now" implies a specific moment in time when God takes action.

This decisive moment came when God sent his Son, Jesus Christ, into the world. When Christ began his earthly ministry, Jesus himself defined his ministry as announcing good news to the poor as he taught in the synagogue.

He unrolled the scroll and found the place where it was written,

> "The Spirit of the Lord is upon me,
>   because he has anointed me
>   to proclaim good news to the poor.
> He has sent me to proclaim liberty to the captives
>   and recovering of sight to the blind,
>   to set at liberty those who are oppressed,
> to proclaim the year of the Lord's favor."

And he rolled up the scroll and gave it back to the attendant and sat down. And the eyes of all in the synagogue were fixed on him. And he began to say to them, "Today this Scripture has been fulfilled in your hearing." (Luke 4:17–21)

Throughout history the gospel has especially gone forward among the poor and needy of society. This was true of the churches in the first century. The Apostle Paul wrote,

For consider your calling, brothers: not many of you were wise according to worldly standards, not many were powerful, not many were of noble birth. But God chose what is foolish in the world to shame the wise; God chose what is weak in the world to shame the strong; God chose what is low and despised in the world, even things that are not, to bring to nothing things that are, so that no human being might boast in the presence of God. (1 Corinthians 1:26–29)

Even today the church is growing most quickly in the majority world of the southern and eastern hemispheres, not the affluent West. God took action decisively through Jesus Christ, and more often than not it has been the poor who have responded to his call. He places everyone who calls on him in the safety for which they long.

The walls of his kingdom surround us and protect us more securely than shield, armor, or missile defense systems. This does not mean that you will never lose your job because a coworker lies about you. This doesn't mean that you will never be deceived and tricked out of your savings. It does mean that God will only allow things into your life that will be for your good and his glory (Romans 8:28). Even if the worst happens, you know that God is in control and is using even this hardship to bless you. In fact, as painful as it is, this hardship is the best thing that could happen to you. This is the ultimate security anyone could hope for. God is for us.

David's Faith

All this was still far off for David as he wrote Psalm 12. Christ would not come to this earth for another thousand years. We might wait for years and decades before God steps in. You might go to your grave still waiting for God to make things right.

Can we trust God to keep this promise? Yes! David responds to God's Word with a beautiful expression of faith.

> The words of the LORD are pure words,
>   like silver refined in a furnace on the ground,
>   purified seven times. (12:6)

The words of the wicked are corrupt. Every word of God, on the other hand, is precious and "pure" (v. 6). The picture is of a silversmith refining precious metal to remove the impurities.

When I picture this process, my mind goes back to when I was twelve years old. My parents rented a cabin for our family at Honey Rock Camp for a long weekend. One morning I went to the rifle range and collected a can of lead bullets from the sandy hill behind the targets. When I got back to the cabin, I built a fire and melted down the lead. The dirt and sand formed a crust on top of the metal as it cooled. I knocked the crust off, put the lead back on the fire, and repeated the process. After I refined it four times this way, the lead was clean, and I poured it into little ingots.

David compares God's Word to silver refined in a crucible not four times but seven times. Not the slightest impurity remains—the silver is ultra-pure and ultra-precious. This is a picture of the priceless perfection of God's Word.

Today we generally use the word *inerrancy* to describe the purity and truthfulness of God's Word.[4] As the word suggests, inerrancy means that the Scriptures are without error in all they affirm.[5] If we state it positively, inerrancy means the Scriptures are wholly true. Because God inspired the Scriptures by his Holy Spirit, the Scriptures are true and without error whenever they speak about history, geography, science, and archaeology, as well as spiritual truths and matters of salvation.

Spurgeon described the tested purity of God's Word this way:

> So clear and free from all alloy of error or unfaithfulness is the book of the words of the Lord. The Bible has passed through the furnace of persecution, literary criticism, philosophic doubt, and scientific discovery, and has lost nothing but those human interpretations which clung to it as alloy to precious ore. The experience of saints has tried it in every conceivable manner, but not a single doctrine or promise has been consumed in the most excessive heat.[6]

When David heard God's answer to his prayer, he marveled at the brilliant perfection and purity of God's Word. His faith continued as he stood on God's promise and trusted him to protect his life.

> You, O LORD, will keep them;
>   you will guard us from this generation forever.
> On every side the wicked prowl,
>   as vileness is exalted among the children of man. (12:7, 8)

Nothing has changed in David's life. The wicked are still prowling as they were at the beginning of the psalm. If anything, the situation is worse. Not only are the godly still a small remnant, but depravity is exalted among all peoples. But David has changed. He is not crying out to God for help anymore. He has heard God's Word, and he believes it. Whatever man may do, God surrounds him with his presence as with a shield. This was David's confidence. It was the confidence of our Lord Jesus Christ as well as he walked alone in a world of lies and deceit. It needs to be our confidence too.

John Newton described God's protection in a familiar hymn.

Glorious things of thee are spoken, Zion, city of our God!
God, whose Word cannot be broken, formed thee for his own abode.
On the Rock of Ages founded, what can shake thy sure repose?
With salvation's walls surrounded, thou may'st smile at all thy foes.

Do you know God? Do you trust his Word? If you do, you will be able to smile with quiet, Christian confidence at the world around you.

You may feel as alone as I was—an American surrounded by Serbians. But you will know that God has placed you in the safety for which you long. He has surrounded you with the walls of his kingdom.

13

How Long?

PSALM 13

HAVE YOU EVER FELT LIKE GOD HAS FORGOTTEN YOU? As a pastor I have spoken with men and women who feel like God has turned his back on them. "Where is God while my life is falling apart? Why has God abandoned me?"

Some people feel this way, but they would never say so out loud. They have been taught that Christians don't experience such things—a good Christian always experiences abundant life, the victorious Christian life. They're worried that if they say what they are thinking, their Christian friends will look down on them and wonder whether there is unconfessed sin in their lives. Maybe they will question their salvation. So they keep up appearances and keep their questions to themselves. And yet they can't shake the feeling that God has turned away from them.

If that describes you, it's good to know that you are not alone. Charles Spurgeon, the great nineteenth-century preacher, once announced from the pulpit of London's Metropolitan Tabernacle, "I am the subject of depressions of spirit so fearful that I hope none of you ever gets to such extremes of wretchedness as I go to." This was not unusual for him. Ten years earlier, he had been honest and vulnerable as he introduced a sermon on Isaiah 41:14.

> Periodical tornadoes and hurricanes will sweep o'er the Christian; he will be subjected to as many trials in his spirit as trials in his flesh. This much I know, if it be not so with all of you it is so with me. I have to speak to-day to myself; and whilst I shall be endeavoring to encourage those who are distressed and down-hearted, I shall be preaching, I trust to myself, for I need something which shall cheer my heart . . . my soul is cast down within me, I feel as if I had rather die than live. . . . I need your prayers; I need God's Holy Spirit; and I felt that I could not preach to-day, unless I should

preach in such a way as to encourage you and to encourage myself in the good work and labor of the Lord Jesus Christ.[1]

If you have walked many miles with Christ, you know what he means. You have probably felt the same way at times. There are days when my prayers seem empty too, when my Bible is just letters on a page, when I feel like God is nowhere near me.

How good to know that David experienced the same things we do. David is one of the giants of the Old Testament, "a man after [God's] own heart" (1 Samuel 13:14). The prophet Samuel anointed him. He was a king, a general, and an author of Scripture. He is an ancestor of Christ. Yet in Psalm 13 David describes a time when he felt like God had turned away from him. What's more, David was a prophet; in the Psalms he is speaking for Christ. So this is the experience of our Lord Jesus in his humanity too. If David could be honest with us, we should be able to be honest with each other.

Psalm 13 doesn't end with David's questions. If we feel like God has abandoned us, we shouldn't abandon ourselves to discouragement. We need to turn to God in faith like David did to find the joy and peace he experienced in the end. God has given us his great and precious promises. We have an anchor for the soul. We need to encourage our hearts by looking to Jesus.

Psalm 13 begins with David's honest questions (vv. 1, 2) and ends with David's joyful confidence (vv. 5, 6). The hinge at the center of this psalm is David's prayer (vv. 3, 4). David calls out to the very God who seems so far away. And eventually the shadows part and the light shines once again in his heart. We don't know how long the process of Psalm 13 lasted in David's life. Did it take an hour, a day, a month, a year? However long it took, David moved out of darkness as he called out to the very God who seemed to have abandoned him. David wrote this psalm from his personal experience and gave it "to the choirmaster" so that we could follow the same path from darkness to light.

Crisis Questions

David starts by asking God the honest questions that often flare up when we are in a crisis. He feels like God has abandoned him.

How long, O LORD? Will you forget me forever?
  How long will you hide your face from me?
How long must I take counsel in my soul
  and have sorrow in my heart all the day?
How long shall my enemy be exalted over me? (13:1, 2)

How Long?

We notice right away that David repeats the same question four times, "How long?" It feels like this trouble and sorrow is never going to end. Time flies when you're having fun, but the hours crawl by when life is hard. A week in the hospital is longer than a month of good health and exercise.

We can put up with something if we know how long it will last. Trouble can be unbearable when there is no end in sight. Your endurance wears thin like old brake pads. We can usually stand under short, sharp trials. Long-term trials grind us down over time.

To make things worse, David doesn't seem to know why this is happening. There is no confession of sin in Psalm 13, no repentance, no guilt that seems to be hindering God's blessings. For some reason that is hidden to David, it feels like God has turned away from him.[2]

What are some reasons we might feel like God has turned away from us? Sometimes we're just plain tired. Elijah was emotionally exhausted after confronting the prophets of Baal on Mount Carmel. He needed sleep (1 Kings 18:1—19:8). We get tired too. A young mom hasn't had a full night of sleep in weeks; she feels spiritually dry because she is exhausted. You own a business and are worn out because you're not sleeping. Revenues are down, you're facing a lawsuit, or you think your partner is cheating you. You get tired, and God seems far away. You are asking, "How long?"

You may be dealing with a long-term illness, and there is no end in sight. Maybe you have been unemployed for months or years; you want to work, but you can't find a job. You may have a child with special needs, and the stress of caring for her is taking a toll on your marriage. You may be caring for someone with Alzheimer's. Maybe you were transferred into a dead-end branch of the company, and your career is on hold. You might be worried about downsizing. The road is long, and you are asking God, "How long?"

We might feel like God has turned away because of an accident. I know a professional musician who fell from a tree and lost the use of his right arm. He could not perform and struggled spiritually for a time. In such a situation you might be asking, "How long?"

It might be a problem in your family. You were happy when you first got married, but now you don't seem to get along. Why is God not blessing your marriage? Your family was happy when the kids were young, but now a prodigal brings tension whenever you get together. You thought that if you followed the right parenting principles your kids would turn out the way they should, but they haven't. Or you may be single and want so badly to be married. You are saying with David, "How long?" (v. 1).

Four Downward Steps

We can trace four downward steps in this feeling that God has withdrawn his blessing.

First, David complains that God has forgotten him. It feels like God no longer cares enough to pay attention and take special care of him as a beloved child. We think to ourselves, "If he remembered me, he would not have allowed this to happen. And he would certainly not allow this to go on."

Can God forget us? Of course not! The Lord says,

Can a woman forget her nursing child,
    that she should have no compassion on the son of her womb?
Even these may forget,
    yet I will not forget you.
Behold, I have engraved you on the palms of my hands;
    your walls are continually before me. (Isaiah 49:15, 16)

Our hearts may tell us that we have been forgotten. Satan wants us to believe that we are like an orphan on a street corner. Yet we know this cannot be true.

The next step down is that it feels like God has hidden his face. This is worse. This is rejection. If God has only forgotten, then when he remembers me he will do something. But if he has hidden his face, then he knows I am there and is consciously turning away. "The hiding of God's face is an . . . expression for alienation and curse."[3] How terrible to feel like God has turned against us.

This naturally leads to morbid introspection, the third step down. We "take counsel in [our own] soul" (v. 2). As we ask ourselves why this is happening, we might start dredging up past sins. We know that we are saved by grace, but we wonder whether God has really forgiven us. Maybe he is punishing us for what we did. He has decided to take it out of our hide. Our thoughts become dark, and our hearts are full of sorrow.

Finally, at the bottom step, David wonders how long his enemy will triumph over him. David fought against the Philistines his whole life. And he was on the run from King Saul for about eight years. The Ancient Near East was a violent place.

Most of us do not have human enemies trying to kill us, but we all have two great enemies. The Bible says that Satan is "a roaring lion" looking for "someone to devour" (1 Peter 5:8); he is the enemy of our souls. And death is the great enemy of us all. In fact, some scholars think that David is thinking of death as his enemy. When darkness descends in our hearts, it can feel like death will swallow us forever.

David felt like he was about to collapse under the weight of this unrelenting burden. We might feel the same way. But ultimately this psalm is about Christ. It was hard for Christ to endure this world of sin for thirty-three years. At one point in his ministry Jesus said, "O faithless generation, *how long* am I to be with you? *How long* am I to bear with you?" (Mark 9:19). In the Garden of Gethsemane, Jesus' heart was in such anguish that he sweat drops of blood—enormous strain and inner turmoil. And ultimately God did hide his face from Christ. Jesus called out on the cross, "My God, my God, why have you forsaken me?" (Matthew 27:46). When Christ carried our sin in his own body, God did turn his face away from him. We might feel like God has turned away from us; but if we are believers, we know this cannot be true. Jesus actually was forsaken for us and for our salvation.

Crucial Prayer

Mercifully, David doesn't leave us with these dark questions. He shows us the way out of the darkness into the light. David's prayer in verses 3, 4 is the turning point in this psalm.

David prays to the very God who seems so far away from him, who seems to have abandoned him. Although his heart tells him that God has turned away, David doesn't believe his own feelings. By faith he pleads with God to hear and answer.

> Consider and answer me, O Lord my God;
>   light up my eyes, lest I sleep the sleep of death,
> lest my enemy say, "I have prevailed over him,"
>   lest my foes rejoice because I am shaken. (13:3, 4)

David's faith is tenacious. By faith he holds on to his relationship with God and calls him, "Yahweh my God." He would not be torn from the arms of God.

The word "consider" (v. 3) might be translated "Look!" Every so often my kids want to show me something when I am focused on what I am doing. They will say, "Dad, Dad." And when I don't turn to see what they have, they will take my chin in their hand, physically turn my head, and say, "Look!" That is the picture I have when I read these words. David is saying to God,

"Look! Answer me! Give me light!" Three requests. He prays with the passion and confidence of a man who knows God. The Lord is "my God" (v. 3).

To raise the stakes, he reminds God that if he doesn't turn to him, then the enemies will win (13:3b, 4). God had promised to bless David. David subtly reminds God that if he fell, God would default on his promises. The enemy would see that God had not been faithful to keep his word; so God's character is on the line. God had committed himself to David, and David prayed on the basis of those promises.

God has committed himself to us too. Jesus said, "I am with you always, to the end of the age" (Matthew 28:20). When our hearts are full of questions and we wonder why God has left us, that is the time for tenacious faith. We need to pray like never before.

The temptation is to turn somewhere else besides God. God said to the people of Jeremiah's day,

> my people have committed two evils:
> they have forsaken me,
>   the fountain of living waters,
> and hewed out cisterns for themselves,
>   broken cisterns that can hold no water. (Jeremiah 2:13)

When our hearts tell us that God is far away, we are tempted to take matters into our own hands. *God's way hasn't worked, so I will do things my way. God has not given me a Christian husband, so I will date this nice man at work even though he is not a Christian. God has put me in a dead-end job, so I will betray somebody to get ahead. God left me with a disability—he doesn't care about me, so why should I care about him? I'll do what I want to be happy.*

The first step of faith is to turn to the very God who seems to have abandoned us. When it feels like God is far away, that is when we need to pray the most. The Scriptures encourage us. "Draw near to God, and he will draw near to you" (James 4:8). "You will seek me and find me, when you seek me with all your heart. I will be found by you, declares the LORD" (Jeremiah 29:13, 14). Jesus promises, "Ask, and it will be given to you; seek, and you will find; knock, and it will be opened to you. For everyone who asks receives, and the one who seeks finds, and to the one who knocks it will be opened" (Matthew 7:7, 8).

Our Lord Jesus strengthened his heart through prayer. He prayed all night several times during his ministry. He prayed in the garden before his arrest.

He prayed on the cross, "Father, into your hands I commit my spirit" (Luke 23:46). The writer of Hebrews describes his passionate prayer this way:

> In the days of his flesh, Jesus offered up prayers and supplications, with loud cries and tears, to him who was able to save him from death, and he was heard because of his reverence. (Hebrews 5:7)

We need to follow in Jesus' footsteps. Turn to God. Pour out your heart to him. If you are a Christian and it feels like God has abandoned you, don't believe your heart. Say to God, "You are my God." And pray, knowing and believing that he knows, he cares, and he loves you.

Confident Joy

As David settled his heart through prayer, the Lord gave him light. David's prayer turns to confident joy.

Trust God

David declares his confidence in God's character: "But I have trusted in your steadfast love" (13:5a).

The grammar shows that he trusted God at a specific point in time.[4] I picture this like setting a stake in the ground. David could point to a moment in time when he said, "Lord, I do trust you. No matter what is happening, I am deciding right now that I believe you are good and you care for me." David made a conscious decision to hope in God.

"Steadfast love" (v. 13) is the Hebrew word *chesed*. It is not love in the sense of warm fuzzies. "Steadfast love" means God's loyalty to his promises and commitment to his people. It is covenant love. When a husband vows to love his wife "until death do us part," this is *chesed*, steadfast love. He will not always feel warm fuzzies for her; he might even be angry at her sometimes. But if he is a good man he will be committed to her and faithful to her and will care for her and love her. God has committed himself by covenant to his people like a husband to his bride. David trusts in God's committed love.

Hope in God

And because he trusts in God, David also hopes in God. Looking to the future, he says, "my heart shall rejoice in your salvation" (v. 5).

"Salvation" in this sense means complete well-being. God will meet every need. David means more than knowing that his sins are forgiven, as wonderful as that is. He means complete salvation: comfort for his heart, quiet for his mind, healing for his body, complete safety, perfect peace.[5] God is not just saving our souls: he is saving us body, mind, heart, soul, spirit, senses, eyes, hands, feet, thoughts, emotions, relationships—everything we are! God says, "Behold, I am making all things new" (Revelation 21:5).

David had not yet received what God had promised. He looked forward and rejoiced to see God's salvation in the distance. This is the way it has always been for God's people. We look forward by faith for blessings that are to come. Peter puts it this way:

> [P]reparing your minds for action, and being sober-minded, set your hope fully on the grace that will be brought to you at the revelation of Jesus Christ. (1 Peter 1:13)

Real hope—hope that sees the future—will give you joy, even in the worst trouble. God's promises are so real and so big that having them changes everything. How does this work? Mark and Cindy Hill won the Powerball lottery in Missouri in December 2012. Before they received a single dime, Cindy told a newspaper, "I think I'm going to have a heart attack!" She knew what those numbers meant, she knew that the lottery would pay out like they promised, and her heart started racing even though she had not received anything yet.

I am not encouraging anyone to play the lottery! Here is the point: God's promises are more reliable than a winning lottery ticket. Our hearts should start racing when we read what he has promised because we know it is going to happen. Christians who believe God's Word should say, "I think I'm going to have a heart attack!" God has such a great future for his children that we should feel like we are going to burst sometimes. The Bible says,

> our citizenship is in heaven, and from it we await a Savior, the Lord Jesus Christ, who will transform our lowly body to be like his glorious body, by the power that enables him even to subject all things to himself. (Philippians 3:20, 21)

Just think—these bodies will be raised in glory to be like Christ! And again,

> For this light momentary affliction is preparing for us an eternal weight of glory beyond all comparison, as we look not to the things that are seen but to the things that are unseen. For the things that are seen are transient, but the things that are unseen are eternal. (2 Corinthians 4:17, 18)

So hope in God. God may not change your circumstances, but if you believe that his Word is true, you will be filled with joy at what is to come. This is cross time; that will be crown time. You need to look beyond your trouble today to see the great future God has for you tomorrow.

This was Christ's experience. Our Lord Jesus looked beyond today to see tomorrow. He set his hope on God, believed God's promises, and trusted him to save.

> . . . Jesus, the founder and perfecter of our faith . . . for the joy that was set before him endured the cross, despising the shame, and is seated at the right hand of the throne of God. (Hebrews 12:2)

Jesus, the author of our faith, set his hope on what is to come. If we are following him, we need to look ahead to the joy God has for everyone who loves him. Psalm 13 is not just the pathway that David walked from darkness to light—it is the pathway that our Lord Jesus followed during his earthly life. And it is our pathway too.

Sing to God

When the clouds had lifted, David saw the blessings that had been there all along.

> I will sing to the LORD,
>   because he has dealt bountifully with me. (13:6)

God's bounty is nothing less than all his generosity that he pours out day by day. When his heart was heavy and his eyes were dark, David was blind to the good things God was doing today and the good things he has stored for tomorrow. He was blind to God's blessings. When he turned to God in prayer and fixed his hope on God, he sang for joy at God's generosity.

If you are a Christian and you feel like God has abandoned you, I can't tell you when the emotional darkness will lift. But I can tell you that you are not alone. You are following the footsteps of godly men and women who have gone before you. David felt abandoned by God. Our Lord Jesus truly was forsaken by God.

When the clouds lift and the light shines on you again, you will see his face, and you will know that he has been right beside you all along. For now you need to call out to God in prayer, the very God who seems so far away. You need to hope in him. His promises are true, his Word is sure, and he will save you.

14

I Am the Problem

PSALM 14

IN 1908 *The Times* asked a number of authors to write on the topic, "What is wrong with the world?" G. K. Chesterton's answer was the shortest one submitted. He simply wrote:

> Dear Sirs,
>
> I am.
>
> Sincerely yours,
> G. K. Chesterton

Chesterton did not mean that he had committed every crime on earth, of course. His point is that what is wrong with the world is that we human beings are sinners. It's no use pointing my finger at everyone else. Since I am a sinner, I am the problem.

Psalm 14 is a key passage of Scripture that teaches us all humanity is ruined by sin. Our entire species—each and every one of us—has rebelled against God. That is the bad news. But there is good news in the Psalms too. Psalm 8 teaches our glory as human beings—we are "crowned . . . with glory and honor" (8:5). God created us in his image. Psalms 8 and 14 are like bookends for a short section of the Psalms that describes the nature of humanity.[1] We are at once glorious and fallen. We carry both the honor of bearing God's image and the shame of our sin. Psalm 14 ends this section with the hard news of our disobedience. Like Chesterton, we need the honesty and courage to say, "I am the problem."

Most of us would rather ignore this diagnosis. Sometimes a patient will block out what a doctor has told him because it is so hard to hear. The Scriptures repeat Psalm 14 two more times to make sure we are listening. Psalm 53 quotes Psalm 14 in its entirety with only a few minor changes. In Romans 3:10–12 Paul quotes Psalm 14 to show that everyone, Jew and Gentile alike, is under sin. When God speaks once, we should listen. When he speaks twice, we should be sure to remember. When God speaks three times, we should study his words, take them to heart, ponder them, and never let them go.

Psalm 14 also ends the first short section of the Psalms, which includes Psalms 3—14. You have probably noticed that Psalms 3—13 are full of danger and sorrow. Time and again David calls out for God to rescue him. In this context Psalm 14 teaches that David is experiencing these problems because of the sin that infects humanity. Matthew Henry put it this way:

> In all the psalms from the 3d to this . . . David had been complaining of those that hated and persecuted him, insulted and abused him; now here he traces all those bitter streams to the fountain, the general corruption of nature, and sees that not his enemies only, but all the children of men, were thus corrupted.[2]

David's experience points forward to Jesus Christ and the hatred he endured in his life. If we read Psalm 14 with an eye to Christ, we reject Jesus and his rightful authority as our king because we are sinners. The world is set against Christ (2:1–7) because the world is ruined by sin.

We need to understand the awful truth of our sin before we are ready to welcome Jesus as a Savior. Psalm 14 ends with David's hope and prayer, "Oh, that salvation for Israel would come out of Zion!" (14:7). We will not long for a Savior like David did until we see our sin like David did. So this can be a moment of grace for you today. As we walk through Psalm 14, you may see your need for Christ for the first time. For the first time you may realize that you are a sinner who needs to be forgiven through Jesus. You will never love Jesus and be desperate for his help until you can say, "I am a sinner. I am the problem."

The outline of this psalm hangs on four words: rejection (14:1), inspection (14:2, 3), miscalculation (14:4–6), and salvation (14:7). May this be a moment of grace.

Man's Rejection

We start with man's rejection. David describes ungodliness and its consequences.

The fool says in his heart, "There is no God."
  They are corrupt, they do abominable deeds,
  there is none who does good. (14:1)

Foolish Thinking

There is a thought process behind sin. The word "fool" (v. 1) does not mean someone who is dumb or stupid. As the word is used in the Bible, a fool may be quite intelligent and well-educated, but he or she is morally flawed. The word implies aggressive perversity.[3] A fool breaks his relationships with others and with God to serve himself. As a result, a fool brings trouble on himself and those around him. The opposite of folly is steadfast love, having the wisdom to honor our relationships with God and with others.[4]

When the fool speaks to himself "in his heart" (v. 1), this is not an emotional reaction. In the Bible the heart is not our emotions but rather the thinking part of who we are, the part that makes decisions and defines us as persons. The fool is not a helpless victim—he knowingly and consciously commits himself to a life that denies God. The Apostle Paul described this thought process in Romans 1:18–23.

> For the wrath of God is revealed from heaven against all ungodliness and unrighteousness of men, who by their unrighteousness suppress the truth. For what can be known about God is plain to them, because God has shown it to them. For his invisible attributes, namely, his eternal power and divine nature, have been clearly perceived, ever since the creation of the world, in the things that have been made. So they are without excuse. For although they knew God, they did not honor him as God or give thanks to him, but they became futile in their thinking, and their foolish hearts were darkened. Claiming to be wise, they became fools, and exchanged the glory of the immortal God for images resembling mortal man and birds and animals and creeping things.

The wicked see God's majesty in the world he created, but they suppress the evidence. They are fools because they refuse to honor God even though they know him. They make a deliberate choice to block out the truth.

Practical Atheism

When someone today says, "There is no God" (v. 1), we call him an atheist. What he means is that he does not believe that God exists or that there is spiritual life beyond this physical, material world. In recent years you may have heard of more vocal atheists such as Christopher Hitchens and Richard Dawkins. And in fact atheists are becoming more mainstream in our society.

After the Newtown Massacre, Susan Jacoby published an article in the *New York Times* titled "The Blessings of Atheism," in which she argued that atheists were in a better position to comfort the parents who lost their children.[5]

David is probably not talking about the sort of atheists we know today. For one thing, the pagan world around Israel believed in many gods. When Jews went astray, they didn't become philosophical atheists like Hitchens or Dawkins—they turned their back on the true God to worship idols that are no gods at all, gods they could manipulate and control with the right sacrifices. They were religious, but they denied the true God and ran life their own way. So in the deepest sense of the word they were atheists.

Job describes this sort of practical atheism perfectly. As he suffered and questioned God, he wondered why the wicked seemed to have such good lives while they denied God.

> They spend their days in prosperity,
>   and in peace they go down to Sheol.
> They say to God, "Depart from us!
>   We do not desire the knowledge of your ways.
> What is the Almighty, that we should serve him?
>   And what profit do we get if we pray to him?"
> Behold, is not their prosperity in their hand? (Job 21:13–16a)

This describes men and women today too. Human nature has not changed. We think to ourselves, "Who needs God? I run my business without him. I have a family without him. I pay my mortgage without him. I can do life my own way." And so we deny God any meaningful place in our lives. We deny God any meaningful place in our plans and decisions. God is not relevant to real life. Functionally we deny that God exists.

When we read 14:1 our first instinct might be to apply these words to outspoken atheists like Hitchens, Dawkins, and Jacoby. But this is really describing you and me apart from Christ. We are the fools who say, "There is no God." To be honest, each of can and must say, "I am the problem."

Depravity

When we surrender the knowledge of God, we open the door to all sorts of depravity. David lists three dimensions of wickedness.

First, "they are corrupt" (v. 1). This is the inner effect of denying God. The word "corrupt" means to spoil or ruin or to act ruinously. Their corruption is infectious; not only are they perverse, but they pervert others too. If you have a bag of apples and one of those apples is bad, the rot will spread to the others. When men and women turn their backs on God, their corruption spreads to others.

Then David describes the actions that flow from their wicked hearts: "they do abominable deeds" (v. 1). Fools refuse to accept the fact that they are accountable to God. As a result, they do all sorts of perverse things. *No one will judge me—why not do what I want?* In December 1989 the cover of *The Atlantic* asked the question, "Can We Be Good Without God?" The point of this article is that while Christians are not perfect, the ethics and morality we value in western civilization come from the Bible. As our society becomes secular, we will lose the foundation for ethics and morality. "If Christianity declines and dies in coming decades, our moral universe and also the relatively humane political universe that it supports will be in peril."[6] The underlying principle is that the way we behave is ultimately rooted in what we believe about God. Without God there is nothing to hold us back from plunging into all sorts of horrors. Without God we do "abominable deeds."

In case you think David is talking about someone else, he says, "there is none who does good" (v. 1). The Russian poet Turgenev once said, "I do not know what the heart of a bad man is like, but I do know what the heart of a good man is like, and it is terrible."

Sometimes someone will say to me, "Pastor, will you get up and share your heart?" I know what they mean, of course, but I want to answer, "You don't want me to share my heart." Why not? Because the Bible says, "The heart is deceitful above all things, and desperately sick" (Jeremiah 17:9). The Apostle Paul himself says, "I know that nothing good dwells in me" (Romans 7:18). So when a pastor gets up to speak, you don't want him to share his heart. You want him to open God's Word and point you to Christ. "There is none who does good" (v. 1). The best things the best of us do are still tainted by selfishness and sin.

God's Inspection

Can this be true? That seems a bit pessimistic. Is it possible that all humanity denies God and is corrupted by sin?

God Looks

Actually this is not David's idea—it is God's conclusion after his thorough inspection of humanity.

> The LORD looks down from heaven on the children of man,
>   to see if there are any who understand,
>   who seek after God. (14:2)

When we deny God, that doesn't make him any less real. No matter what we small humans say and think, God still examines our lives. He doesn't have to look down or come down literally from Heaven to know our hearts. God is omniscient; he already knows everything. This is a figure of speech for us to visualize God's careful inspection of our world and our lives. He doesn't look up as if he is beneath us. He doesn't look over as if he is beside us as our peer. He looks down because he is exalted high above us.

The word "man" (v. 2) in Hebrew is *adam*. Depending on the context, *adam* can mean human beings in general or the first man God created, Eve's husband. Here it means human beings, but it still carries a subtle echo of creation and the fall. "The children of man" (v. 2) could be translated "the children of Adam," a reminder of our father, Adam, who sinned. As his children, we are sinners after him.

What is God looking for? He wants to see if anyone has the sense to seek him. He made us. He gives us everything: life and breath, brains and brawn, homes and health, friends and family, sunrises and sunsets, grass and golf, groceries and gravity. Will we snub this God who gives us everything? Will we bother to send him a thank you note? He has told us how to live so that we can find joy and satisfaction in his world. Will we listen, or are we fools who break the good things he has given us?

God's Findings

Verse 3 tells us what God finds when he inspects our world.

> They have all turned aside; together they have become corrupt;
>   there is none who does good,
>   not even one. (14:3)

Notice the words "all," "together," "none." God's findings are all-inclusive. He is not talking about just a few especially bad people but every man and woman on earth. Verse 3 confirms what we saw earlier. "The fool is not a rare subspecies within the human race; all human beings are fools apart from the wisdom of God."[7]

The problem is not that there is not enough religion in the world. Many people are religious, but they do not want the God of the Bible, the true God. Many people reject the real God by multiplying false gods. You might meet someone who offers incense on four or five small altars in his home. He might seem spiritually sincere, but he is an atheist in the truest sense of the word—he has rejected the true God.

Religious activity that does not come to God through Jesus Christ is an active denial of God and, by definition, the essence of atheism.[8] The opposite of atheism is not religion. The opposite of atheism is true Christianity, believing the gospel of Jesus Christ. Anyone who does not believe in Jesus Christ does not believe in God (1 John 2:22) and is therefore an atheist in the truest sense of the word.

An Ominous Problem

Significantly, this is not the first time that the Bible talks about God looking down to see sin. In the book of Genesis, God looked down to inspect humanity three separate times.[9] Psalm 14 sounds like the beginning of the flood in Genesis 6. The same word "corrupt" (14:1, 3) occurs three times in Genesis 6:11–13.

> Now the earth was *corrupt* in God's sight, and the earth was filled with violence. And God saw the earth, and behold, it was *corrupt*, for all flesh had *corrupted* their way on the earth. And God said to Noah, "I have determined to make an end of all flesh. . . . Behold, I will destroy them with the earth."

God also looked down and saw humanity's sin before he divided the world at the Tower of Babel (Genesis 11:5–7). And God came down to investigate the sin of Sodom and Gomorrah before he destroyed those cities with fire and sulfur (Genesis 18:21). God's investigation is ominous indeed. When God looks down to see that the earth is full of sin, this is the beginning of judgment.

Amazing Miscalculation

But the sinful world is blind to the judgment that is hanging over its head. They pretend nothing is going to happen. Verses 4–6 show an amazing miscalculation.

Amazing Ignorance

This amazing miscalculation starts with amazing ignorance.

> Have they no knowledge, all the evildoers
>   who eat up my people as they eat bread
>   and do not call upon the LORD? (14:4)

The wicked do not have even basic knowledge of God. They turn their back on the true God and do not seek him. As a result, they do not know him and are lost in ignorance. To "call upon the Lord" (v. 4) is another way of describing a relationship with him. It means appealing to God for help or asking for his presence in worship. The wicked do not want God, seek God, or know God.

The words "my people" (v. 4) should surprise us. If we have been tracking with the psalm to this point, we might not expect that God has people on this earth. When God looked down on our world, he saw that "all have turned aside . . . there is none who does good, not even one" (v. 3). So where did God's people come from? Obviously they were not seeking him on their own; they had "turned aside" too. Rather, in this psalm we see God's rich and eternal purposes in saving unworthy sinners. He forms his people from the very men and women who have rejected him and were not looking for him. This is what the Apostle Paul is talking about when he says,

> For while we were still weak, at the right time Christ died for the ungodly.
> . . . God shows his love for us in that while we were still sinners, Christ died
> for us. (Romans 5:6, 8)

Through Christ, God turns atheists into worshipers. When you and I are ready to admit, "I am the problem," we are ready to become one of God's people. Jesus died to save sinners like you and me.

Becoming one of God's people does not mean your life will suddenly be easy. The world devours God's people. The two great commandments—love God and love your neighbor—are foreign to them. The picture of eating bread is particularly graphic. Bread is a staple; we eat it every day. The world devours the righteous daily and constantly. Eating bread is also normal. We don't write postcards or tweet about eating a slice of bread; it is totally unremarkable. For the wicked, devouring God's people is a casual thing, an everyday occurrence.

Terrifying Miscalculation

In their ignorance they never realize that they are touching the apple of God's eye. One consequence of their sin is gripping fear.

> There they are in great terror,
>   for God is with the generation of the righteous.
> You would shame the plans of the poor,
>   but the Lord is his refuge. (14:5, 6)

There is fear today and fear tomorrow for the wicked. On the one hand they live with the constant anxiety that comes from knowing in our heart of hearts that God will indeed judge each of us for the things we do in this life. The Scriptures say, "For we must all appear before the judgment seat of Christ, so that each one may receive what is due for what he has done in the body, whether good or evil" (2 Corinthians 5:10). No matter how we might argue otherwise, instinctively we know this is true. In the still of the night, guilt terrifies the wicked. Toby Mac says it this way.

> You can go on playin' like you're all rock and roll,
> But guilt does a job on each and every man's soul.
> And when your head hits the pillow at the nightfall
> You can bet your life that there's gonna be a fight, y'all.[10]

The guilt of unforgiven sin will weigh heavy on our conscience and terrify us when we are all alone with our thoughts. This present fear will give way to even greater terror when Christ returns and we stand before him.

The presence of God terrifies the wicked, but he is unspeakable joy and comfort to his people. If you're held hostage in a bank robbery, you will be happy to see the SWAT team when they come through the door. But the robbers will be terrified to see those very same men. This is how it is with God's face too. C. S. Lewis said, "In the end that Face which is the delight or the terror of the universe must be turned on each one of us . . . either conferring glory inexpressible or inflicting shame that can never be cured or disguised."[11]

Longing for Salvation

Those who know God long to see him. We long for salvation. David looked around and saw the misery of a world that denies God and lives in moral chaos. He ends the psalm with a fervent prayer of hope and longing.

> Oh, that salvation for Israel would come out of Zion!
>   When the LORD restores the fortunes of his people,
>   let Jacob rejoice, let Israel be glad. (14:7)

Zion is God's holy hill, the place where God has established his King (Psalm 2:6). When David prays for salvation from Zion, he is longing for the Messiah, the King whom God has set over all the nations.

The word "salvation" (v. 7) is the Hebrew word *yeshua*. The name Jesus comes from this very word. When Christ was born, he was given this name Jesus, "salvation," because he would save his people from their sins (Matthew 1:21). I can't help but think that when Jesus read Psalm 14 during his life, he said, "Yes, I have come. I am salvation. I am the Savior of my people." Jesus is the ultimate answer to David's prayer.

Jesus is the answer to the folly of turning away from God. The Apostle Paul writes in 1 Corinthians 1:30, "Christ Jesus . . . became to us wisdom from God, righteousness and sanctification and redemption." When we were foolish enough to say "There is no God" (v. 1), God reached out to us and gave us his Son to make us wise.

You will not be ready to welcome Jesus until you have the courage and honesty to say, "I am the problem." When you admit your sin, when you grieve over what you have done, when you feel the weight of God's judgment, then you will be ready to pray with David, "Oh, that salvation . . . would come out of Zion!" You will be ready to say, "Come, Lord Jesus. Come into my heart. Wash away my sin. Take control of my life. Save me from myself. Make me new."

I am the problem. Jesus is the answer.

15

The Ultimate Question

PSALM 15

WHEN WE ARE YOUNG, we want to have all the answers. As we get older, we learn that it is more important to ask the right questions. The right answer to the wrong question is the wrong answer.

Asking the right question makes all the difference. If you're hiring someone, you need to ask the right questions. If you're buying a car, the salesman will make it sound wonderful, but you need to ask the right questions. If you are helping your parents transition to a retirement home, you need someone to help you ask the right questions. If you have a good friend, she knows to ask the right questions so you can share your heart. If you are wondering where to go to college, you need to ask why you are going to college and what kind of education you want. If you are falling in love and think this might be "The One," your parents and friends will help you ask the right questions. Yes, she is pretty, but will she be a godly mother and a faithful companion? In ten years that will be much more important than the way her hair glistens in the moonlight. Asking the right questions is a key part of wisdom.

The Ultimate Question

Of all the right questions to ask, 15:1 is the most important.

> O Lord, who shall sojourn in your tent?
>   Who shall dwell on your holy hill?

This is the ultimate question. Who can live in God's presence? Who is qualified to stand before him? Who can know him face-to-face now and forever? Who can go to Heaven?[1]

David is not just asking a superficial question about who may enter Jerusalem or worship in the tabernacle. The words "sojourn" and "dwell" (v. 1) point to more than a visit to the tabernacle.[2] A sojourner is a resident alien.[3] Abraham sojourned in the promised land; Israel sojourned in Egypt for four hundred years (Genesis 15:13; 23:4). It is hard to imagine that a pilgrim would ask to "sojourn" in God's tent when they visited Jerusalem—the tabernacle was the dwelling place of God.

David is asking a bigger question: What kind of people can live in God's presence? In Psalm 14:5 we saw that although all humanity is ruined by sin, God has reserved for himself "the generation of the righteous." Psalm 15 now tells us who God's people are.[4] Psalm 15 describes God's righteous people.

Is there any more important question you can ask? This is more important than asking how you are going to pay for your mortgage or plan for retirement. This is more important than whom you date or even whom you are going to marry. This is more important than what school you go to or what career you choose. In a hundred years those questions will not matter anymore. But this question will matter for all eternity. Who can live with God in his Heaven? This is the ultimate question.

The Ultimate Answer

The ultimate question requires the ultimate answer. In the rest of the psalm David speaks for God as a prophet to answer his opening question. Verses 2–5 lay out eleven requirements for anyone who wants to live in God's presence in Heaven. They are structured in parallel form so that we have to read them with each other and not as independent tasks to be done. Taken together, these requirements represent a full-bodied life of godliness.

Notice that not one of the qualifications in this list is religious. Ceremonies and sacrifices are not the answer. These requirements are more penetrating because they have to do with our everyday lives. This is not about what we do on Sunday; these qualifications are about what we do during the week. God's people are known by the way they live when they are not at church.

These qualifications are arranged into four main categories: Personal, Relationships, Heart, and Money.

Personal

God's answer begins with the personal character of the man or woman who can live in his presence. As the first set of qualifications, this verse is the starting point for all the rest. In fact, some think that verse 2 is the answer and the rest of the psalm simply fills out verse 2 in more detail.

> He who walks blamelessly and does what is right
> and speaks truth in his heart. (15:2)

God points to three aspects of a man or woman's personal character. First, he "walks blamelessly" (v. 2). Our lifestyle has pride of place as the first qualification. The word "blamelessly" does not mean sinless perfection but carries the sense of wholeness, honesty, integrity. This man is genuine, the real deal. He consistently walks in the way of the Lord because what he is on the outside comes from who he is on the inside.[5] He is both whole and holy. In the Bible Noah was "blameless in his generation" (Genesis 6:9). God told Abraham to "walk before me, and be blameless" (Genesis 17:1). A lifestyle of genuine integrity is one of the defining marks of the great men and women of the Old Testament.

Integrity is in short supply in every age, even today. I received a call this week from a friend who needs someone to speak at an event next month. The pastor who was supposed to speak just resigned from his church because of a moral indiscretion. We need to be genuine in our walk with the Lord. Being blameless means that we walk with God on the inside where only he can see. Road engineers will sometimes take a core sample of an asphalt road to see what lies below the surface. With that core laid out on the workbench, the engineer can see the quality of the materials all the way through the pavement. What would a core sample of our hearts show? Are we solid on the surface but crumbling inside where no one can see? A blameless man is a man of integrity.

The second personal quality is that this person "does what is right" (v. 2). This shifts the focus more specifically to actions. The righteous person does what is right; he or she lives up to God's standards.

In 1929 Marion Wade started ServiceMaster as a moth-proofing company. Then in 1947 he branched out into carpet cleaning with his partners. ServiceMaster has become a Fortune 1000 company with almost sixty thousand corporate and franchise employees, one of the largest privately held companies in the world. Marion Wade was a committed Christian, known for his personal integrity and character, and his values have shaped the company. One of his sayings has stuck with me: "If you don't live it, you don't believe it." No matter what we say, we will always do what we really believe.

This describes a man who "does what is right" (v. 2). His actions show what he believes in his heart. James, the brother of our Lord Jesus, describes the same connection between what we do and what we truly believe.

> What good is it, my brothers, if someone says he has faith but does not have works? Can that faith save him? If a brother or sister is poorly clothed and lacking in daily food, and one of you says to them, "Go in peace, be warmed and filled," without giving them the things needed for the body, what good is that? So also faith by itself, if it does not have works, is dead. (James 2:14–17)

God is looking for actions to back up our words.

The third qualification is that he "speaks truth in his heart" (Psalm 15:2). The fool lies to himself in his heart and says, "There is no God" (14:1). The godly man doesn't lie to himself; he doesn't push down the truth.

The godly man speaks the truth to himself about God. He keeps himself from being deceived by carefully reading the Scriptures and lining up his thinking with God's Word. He has the courage to change his mind when he sees that his ideas do not line up with the Bible like he thought they did. The godly man speaks the truth to himself about others too. He does not allow a critical spirit to blind him. And he speaks the truth in his heart about himself. He doesn't flatter himself and become conceited; he doesn't run himself down and get depressed. He is balanced.

We can summarize these three personal qualifications with three words: integrity, activity, honesty. Together they represent the personal, individual character God requires.

Relationships

As a prophet speaking for God, David moves to the second category, the godly man or woman's relationships.

> [W]ho does not slander with his tongue
> and does no evil to his neighbor,
> nor takes up a reproach against his friend. (15:3)

The qualifications in verse 3 are horizontal, focusing on my dealings with others. All three of these qualifications are negative, describing what not to do. In fact, these negative descriptions are specific applications of the positive command in Leviticus 19:18 that "you shall love your neighbor as yourself."

The godly do not slander others. The Hebrew word for "slander" usually means "to spy" and by extension "to backbite or slander." Like spying, slander is not out in the open. It means saying bad things about others behind their back.

The church is no place for friendly-fire casualties. James says, "Do not speak evil against one another, brothers" (James 4:11). Gossip and slander have done untold damage to fellow believers over the centuries. We have enough trouble from a sinful world to waste our time telling each other what is wrong with a fellow believer. Slander focuses on people's warts and pimples, but "love covers a multitude of sins" (1 Peter 4:8).

With the fifth qualification, David expands from damaging words to damage in general. He "does no evil to his neighbor" (v. 3). There is a natural progression from evil words to evil actions. Who is my neighbor? Jesus answered this question with the Parable of the Good Samaritan. Your neighbor is whoever comes in contact with you throughout the day. When we consider the national evil of abortion on demand, a pregnant woman's closest neighbor is the little one she is carrying in her womb. This unborn baby is a unique human being who depends on her for everything. How terrible to do evil to that little neighbor. How terrible for a doctor to welcome this mother into his clinic and harm this little neighbor in her womb.

We protect our neighbor in lesser ways too. A woman should not have to worry about leaving her purse in her shopping cart because you're around. Your boss should not feel like he has to watch his back because of you. Your employee should not worry that you are going to take advantage of him. My friends Bill and Donna came home from vacation once, and their neighbor had hired a tree service to cut down several trees on their property. They were shading her patio, she complained. People should not worry about what we will do when they leave for vacation.

Instead the opposite should be true. When we bought our first house, we met an older couple across the street, Uncle Bill and Auntie Beth. A month after we moved in, we had to go on a three-week trip, and we entrusted them with a key to the house. When we got home after a long international flight, they had stocked our fridge with milk, orange juice, and a few other staples. They had checked the thermostat every day and replaced a burned-out light bulb. We have known them now for fifteen years, and they have done us no evil—they have always been a blessing to us. We gave our third daughter the middle name Elizabeth after our dear neighbor Auntie Beth.

The sixth qualification is that he does not take "up a reproach against his friend." He is loyal and does not betray his friends. Friendship and loyalty are important in the psalms, and they are important to God. One of the deep pains Christ endured was his betrayal by Judas. David spoke about this in Psalm 55.

> For it is not an enemy who taunts me—
>   then I could bear it;
> it is not an adversary who deals insolently with me—
>   then I could hide from him.
> But it is you, a man, my equal,
>   my companion, my familiar friend. (Psalm 55:12, 13)

The people God welcomes as his own are loyal to their friends. We need to honor the relationships God has given us.

Heart

The third category deals with the heart.

> [I]n whose eyes a vile person is despised,
>   but who honors those who fear the LORD;
> who swears to his own hurt and does not change. (15:4)

All eleven of the qualifications in this psalm are tied one with another, but the seventh and eighth are particularly close. Despising a vile person and honoring those who fear the Lord are two sides of one coin. It means loving what God loves and hating what God hates.

The "vile person" (v. 4) is literally a "rejected person." We can take this to mean that this person has been rejected by God.[6] When a godly man or woman despises "a vile person," their feelings and attitudes are aligned with God's. They agree with God's evaluation on an emotional level. They are thinking God's thoughts after him and feeling God's feelings after him. David says in Psalm 139,

> Do I not hate those who hate you, O LORD?
>   And do I not loathe those who rise up against you?
> I hate them with complete hatred;
>   I count them my enemies. (Psalm 139:21, 22)

A key aspect of godliness is to hate sin and be revolted by evil. This is why James says, "friendship with the world is enmity with God" (James 4:4). A godly man doe not laugh with someone who tells off-color jokes. A godly man does not look up to a man who boasts and swaggers. Instead we love the things that God loves. If your heart is aligned with God's heart, you will honor those who fear the Lord.

The people you admire say a lot about you. We had a number of hydrangeas around our home in Minnesota. One of the wonderful things about hydrangeas is the way they react to the acidity of the soil. If the pH of the soil is below 6, the flowers will tend to be blue. If the pH is high, the flowers of a hydrangea will tend to be pink. If you are wondering about the chemistry of your soil, the color of the flower is as accurate as a litmus test. It is the same with our hearts. If you want to know the soil of someone's heart, notice who they admire. Be careful with your heroes. Your affections will tell you whether your heart is aligned with God. If you love him, you will love the things he loves. If you love the world, the love of the Father is not in you (1 John 2:15).

The ninth qualification expands on the godly man or woman's heart: "who swears to his own hurt and does not change" (v. 4). This means keeping our word even when it is to our disadvantage. No one has a problem keeping his word when he benefits. But how about when things have changed and you will take a loss by doing what you promised? That is the test of integrity. Does your word mean anything? The godly keep their word, no matter what.

Money

The fourth category of qualifications has to do with money.

> [W]ho does not put out his money at interest
> and does not take a bribe against the innocent. (15:5)

These tenth and eleventh qualifications have to do with materialism and the love of money—classic American sins. For the godly, people are more important than money.

Some people have taken the first part of the verse to mean that Christians should never charge interest. I don't think that is what David means. In the Law of Moses, God forbids interest among Israelites specifically to protect the poor. "If you lend money to any of my people with you who is poor, you shall not be like a moneylender to him, and you shall not exact interest from him" (Exodus 22:25; cf. Leviticus 25:35–37). Those who needed loans were usually in distress.[7] This wasn't consumer lending; they weren't borrowing for a new iPhone. In that context they were borrowing because the crops failed and their clan was desperate. The rich were not to take advantage of their fellow Israelites when they were over a barrel and had to borrow money.

The Law of Moses does allow charging interest from Gentiles. "You may charge a foreigner interest, but you may not charge your brother interest" (Deuteronomy 23:20). With that in mind, we can conclude that Psalm 15 is talking about financial dealings between Israelites and not about all lending in general. We should also realize that this instruction was written in the law for Israel with its tribal society and agrarian culture. The principle is that a godly man doesn't use the power of his money to take advantage of a fellow Israelite. He lends without charge to honor their relationship. He puts people before money.

He puts people before money by not perverting the truth as well. He "does not take a bribe against the innocent" (v. 5). Taking bribes is not only an offense against the victim, it is an offense against justice that perverts the courts. The godly man cares about where his money comes from. You can't pay him to say he saw something he didn't see. You can't pay him to rule against the evidence. To return to the topic of abortion, you can't pay him to harm an innocent child. He won't perform an elective abortion to help fund his family's ski trip or to pay off the loan on his boat. He will not accept money at the expense of another person or the good of society. He puts people before money.

David closes these qualifications with a promise. "He who does these things shall never be moved" (v. 5). He is secure because he dwells in God's presence. The God of Jacob is his fortress.

The Ultimate Man

How do you feel when you read these qualifications? As I read this psalm, my heart sinks because I know I fall far short. Do I walk blamelessly? Do I do what is right? Do I always speak truth in my heart? God knows me inside and out. He knows my thoughts. David says to God in Psalm 143:2, "Enter not into judgment with your servant, for no one living is righteous before you." If you and I are honest with ourselves, we don't live up to this psalm.

So where does that leave us? We are asking the right question, the most important question, but the answer is terrible. None of us are the kind of people who qualify to live in God's presence.

Only one man has ever fulfilled this psalm. Jesus Christ is the only man who ever lived a blameless life, who did what is right, who spoke truth in his heart. The Bible says, "He committed no sin, neither was deceit found in his mouth" (1 Peter 2:22). He did no evil to his neighbors; instead he laid down his life for his enemies. He swore to obey the Father and did not change even though it cost him his life. And he was not moved. He set his face toward the cross and has been exalted to the right hand of God.

Only Christ measures up. He was accepted by God because of his blameless life. Psalm 15 begin a new section in the psalms that focuses on Jesus' welcome in God's presence. Much of Psalm 15 is repeated again in Psalm

24, the end of this section. Together Psalms 15 and 24 are like bookends for this section that deals with Christ coming into God's presence. Psalm 15 introduces some of the key themes that run through this section such as David's integrity, God's presence, and the security of not being shaken. If you look through the following chapters, you will notice that these themes come up several times.

If we compare this with the previous section, Psalms 3—14 teach us that Christ would be rejected by man, and Psalms 15—24 teach us that he would be accepted by God. This tension—rejected by man, accepted by God—is rooted in Psalm 2:1–6. The nations rage against God's Anointed, but God sets him as king on Zion, his holy hill. The structure of Book 1 of the Psalms develops the reign and rule of God's anointed king that was introduced in Psalm 2.

Where does this leave us today? What good is it to us if Jesus fulfilled this psalm and was accepted by God? We are asking the most important question: Who can live in God's Heaven? So far we're still out in the cold.

The good news is that Jesus' perfect obedience and sinless life can be credited to you and me. The Bible says, "by the one man's obedience the many will be made righteous" (Romans 5:19b). And again, "we know that a person is not justified by works of the law but through faith in Jesus Christ" (Galatians 2:16a). Jesus' full obedience as he lived up to Psalm 15 can be counted as yours. This is how we are made right with God.

How can this happen? You need to come to him and follow him as your Lord and Savior. Jesus said,

> Truly, truly, I say to you, whoever hears my word and believes him who sent me has eternal life. He does not come into judgment, but has passed from death to life. (John 5:24)

You need to turn to him today. Psalm 15 is a bar we can never clear. We can't jump high enough. But Jesus has done it for us. His godly life can be counted as yours. And if you follow him, he will make you into this kind of person. He will welcome you into God's presence forever.

16

An Easter Psalm

PSALM 16

PSALM 16 IS FAMOUS BECAUSE the apostles preached Jesus' resurrection in the New Testament from this psalm.

For instance, when Peter preached at Pentecost that Jesus had been raised from the dead, he quoted Psalm 16:8–11.

> For David says concerning him,
>
> > "I saw the Lord always before me,
> >   for he is at my right hand that I may not be shaken;
> > therefore my heart was glad, and my tongue rejoiced;
> >   my flesh also will dwell in hope.
> > For you will not abandon my soul to Hades,
> >   or let your Holy One see corruption.
> > You have made known to me the paths of life;
> >   you will make me full of gladness with your presence."
> >   (Acts 2:25–28)

Peter argues that David could not have been talking about himself. Why? Because David was still dead—his body did "see corruption" (v. 27); his muscles, skin, and tissues rotted away and turned to dust over the centuries. So Peter concludes that David must have been speaking on behalf of Christ, who did not stay in the tomb and did not decay.

> Being therefore a prophet, and knowing that God had sworn with an oath to him that he would set one of his descendants on his throne, he foresaw and spoke about the resurrection of the Christ, that he was not abandoned to Hades, nor did his flesh see corruption. This Jesus God raised up, and of that we all are witnesses. (Acts 2:30–32)

As Peter applied Psalm 16 to Jesus, the crowds in Jerusalem heard him, and three thousand people believed.

The Apostle Paul also preached Jesus' resurrection from this same psalm. Speaking to Jews in Antioch, Paul says,

> And we bring you the good news that what God promised to the fathers, this he has fulfilled to us their children by raising Jesus.
> . . . he says also in another psalm,
>
> "You will not let your Holy One see corruption."
>
> For David, after he had served the purpose of God in his own generation, fell asleep and was laid with his fathers and saw corruption, but he whom God raised up did not see corruption. (Acts 13:32, 33, 35–37)

Paul read Psalm 16 the same way Peter did. Both apostles followed the same path of logic. David could not have been talking about himself because he died and his body rotted in the grave.[1] But Jesus rose again before the process of decay could set in. Since David was a prophet, he must have been speaking for Jesus.

This fits with the message of the New Testament as a whole. The apostles were convinced that Jesus' death and resurrection was prophesied in the Old Testament.

> For I delivered to you as of first importance what I also received: that Christ died for our sins in accordance with the Scriptures, that he was buried, that he was raised on the third day in accordance with the Scriptures. (1 Corinthians 15:3, 4)

Psalm 16 is one of the passages the apostles used to teach Jesus' resurrection "in accordance with the Scriptures" (vv. 3, 4). This is an Easter Psalm.[2]

Since David was speaking for Christ, Psalm 16 gives us a window into Jesus' heart. When David says "me" and "I" in this psalm, he is speaking for Jesus, the great Son of David. Psalm 16 records Jesus' thoughts as he lived his earthly life and walked the hard road to the cross.

When we read the Gospels, Jesus' courage as he faced death—his sheer guts—are absolutely amazing. He was a real human, like we are—how could he have been so brave as he was about to be killed? What was going on in his heart? What was he praying when no one else was around? How could he be sure he would rise again? Jesus was fully human; he had thoughts and emotions just like you and me. Psalm 16 gives us a window into his soul. This is how the real man, Jesus, strengthened his soul as he faced the cross.

The Holy Spirit inspired this Easter Psalm so we could strengthen our souls in Christ. We may be facing some trouble or hardship that shakes us to the core. Jesus' thoughts need to be our thoughts. His feelings need to become our feelings.

As David speaks for Christ, this psalm expresses his commitment (vv. 1–3), his contentment (vv. 4–8), and his confidence (vv. 9–11). It seems to me that these are in order. Commitment to God brings contentment in God that leads to confidence in God.

Commitment

David first commits himself fully to God. He trusts God to protect him like the Secret Service protects the President. He trusts God to provide every good thing. There is no Plan B in this kind of commitment. If God does not come through for him, he is finished. This sort of commitment is where faith begins.

Refuge

He commits himself to God for physical protection: "Preserve me, O God, for in you I take refuge" (16:1).

The word "preserve" (v. 1) means "to keep or to watch over." As a shepherd, David watched over his sheep; he preserved his flock from danger (1 Samuel 17:34–36). David is asking God to watch over him with the care and concern of a shepherd. This is the only petition he makes in this psalm; he doesn't make any other requests.

David expected God to care for him because he took "refuge" (v. 1) in God. Like a soldier crouching behind his shield, David crouches behind God. Like children running to their parents' room at night, David runs to God. Psalm 15:5 promises that the godly man will never be shaken. David is banking that God will keep this promise. God will wrap his arms around him and be his refuge.

It is striking that David runs to God like this because he was a strong man. As a teenager David faced Goliath with a sling and a stone. When he was an officer in Saul's army, the people had chanted, "Saul has struck down his thousands, and David his ten thousands" (1 Samuel 18:7). David led a guerrilla war for several years; his army in the desert of Judea was like our Special Forces. On the throne David was a shrewd diplomat. If there ever was a man who could take care of himself, it was David.

Trusting God is a manly thing to do. Taking refuge in God is not the last option for weak men and sissies, a coward's way to avoid responsibility. The

American ideal is that real men take care of themselves. We're taught to be self-reliant—only weak men turn to God first. But just the opposite is true! It takes immense courage and strong faith to trust God and say, "Preserve me, O God, for in you I take refuge" (v. 1). This warrior and statesman banked everything on God's protection.

All Good Is in You

David committed himself to God because he was convinced that God is good. Even more, there is nothing good that is not from God.

> I say to the LORD, "You are my Lord;
> I have no good apart from you." (16:2)

It is important for every Christian to be convinced that the God we serve is good. And what's more—*only* God is good. We can't let ourselves imagine that there is even a slight sliver of good apart from God and his will for our lives. This is why James says,

> Do not be deceived, my beloved brothers. *Every* good gift and every perfect gift is from above, coming down from the Father of lights with whom there is no variation or shadow due to change. (James 1:16, 17)

There is no good gift that doesn't come from God. Not one. Satan tempts us to think we can find something good and satisfying that is not from God. The essence of sin is looking for good outside of God's provision and his will.

A young woman thinks she will find love and security if she gives in to her boyfriend. What is she doing? She is looking for a good thing—namely, love and security—apart from God and his will for her life. A man indulges himself in pornography or an office romance. He is looking for a good thing—namely, sexual pleasure—but he is looking for it apart from God. God's way is through monogamous, heterosexual marriage. A woman tells her friends the latest gossip to make herself feel significant. What is she doing? She wants a good thing; she wants to feel like she matters and is important. She should feel precious because God created her in his image and Christ died to redeem her. But instead she bases her significance on having the latest juicy news. She is looking for good apart from God. An unforgiving man craves justice—a good thing. But he takes revenge into his own hands. God says, "Vengeance is mine" (Deuteronomy 32:35). A greedy person clings to possessions for security instead of taking refuge in God.

When I dig beneath the surface of any sin in my life, I am trying to achieve something good apart from God and his ways. That good thing might be pleasure, security, significance, justice, some physical need, etc. In the end it is idolatry. I am serving someone or something other than God to satisfy my needs or desires.

John Calvin put it this way:

> . . . it will not suffice simply to hold that there is one whom all ought to honor and adore, unless we are also persuaded that he is the fountain of every good, and that we must seek nothing elsewhere than in him. . . . For until men recognize that they owe everything to God, that they are nourished by his fatherly care, that he is the Author of their every good, that they should seek nothing beyond him—they will never yield him willing service. Nay, unless they establish their complete happiness in him, they will never give themselves truly and sincerely to him.[3]

You cannot commit yourself to God unless you believe that God is good and that *only* God is good. This was David's commitment. This was Jesus' commitment. It needs to be our commitment too.

I Love Your People

David's commitment continued with his love for God's people.

> As for the saints in the land, they are the excellent ones,
>   in whom is all my delight. (16:3)

This follows the spirit of Psalm 15:4 where we read that the godly man "honors those who fear the LORD." If we love God, we will love his people. John writes, "[E]veryone who loves the Father loves whoever has been born of him" (1 John 5:1). I think of a high school girl I know who pretended to be good when she was at church and laughed about Christians when she was alone with her friends. She didn't "delight" in God's people (v. 3).

When I was at a church in northern Illinois, Ken was one of the men in our Evangelism Explosion class. I remember Ken because he was a rough guy who had been in a motorcycle gang for many years. You would not have wanted to meet him before he became a Christian. Yet he had come to know the Lord and was one of the sweetest men I have ever met. He would pull up to church on his Harley, and a smile would break out on my face. Ken was a delight. He loved God's people, and we loved him.

The towering faith of Psalm 16 starts with David's commitment to God and to his people.

Contentment

David's commitment is followed by his contentment. Trusting God is not a life sentence of misery. Rather if you hope in God, you are choosing life and joy! David could not be more delighted with the way God cared for him and blessed him with his presence.

A Great Refusal

His contentment starts with a refusal.

> The sorrows of those who run after another god shall multiply;
>   their drink offerings of blood I will not pour out
>   or take their names on my lips. (16:4)

Being happy in God starts with saying no. You cannot be happy and satisfied in God if you are riding the fence. Some people wonder why they cannot find joy in Christ, but they have a foot in each world. They want God to bless them, but they are living for themselves too. They hedge their bets.

David knows better. He will have nothing to do with pagan sacrifices. He will not worship by pouring out the blood of their sacrifices, and he will not pray to their gods. Finding joy and satisfaction in God starts by saying no.

Content in God Himself

Instead David says yes to God. David would not take the names of other gods on his lips because he does take Yahweh's name on his lips.

> The LORD is my chosen portion and my cup;
>   you hold my lot.
> The lines have fallen for me in pleasant places;
>   indeed, I have a beautiful inheritance. (16:5, 6)

David's contentment was in God himself. His blessings hang on four words that stand out in these verses: "portion," "lot," "lines," and "inheritance" (vv. 5, 6). These four words point back to the time when Joshua divided the land between the twelve tribes after the conquest of Canaan.[4] Each tribe was given its *portion* of the land by *lot* with clear *boundary lines* demarking the borders of their land. This land was their *inheritance* to be passed down through the generations.

One tribe did not receive a portion of land. God said to the Levites, "You shall have no inheritance in their land, neither shall you have any portion among them. I am your portion and your inheritance among the people of

Israel" (Numbers 18:20). The priests and Levites did not have the security of their own tribal area but had to rely on God for their safety.

David is claiming the same close relationship with God. True safety and security does not come from property and possessions but from knowing God and living in his presence.

And what a heritage! He is blessed with God himself—God himself is David's inheritance. God gives many precious blessings to his people, but what makes them truly good is having God himself. David says in Psalm 27:4,

> One thing have I asked of the LORD,
>   that will I seek after:
> that I may dwell in the house of the LORD
>   all the days of my life,
> to gaze upon the beauty of the LORD
>   and to inquire in his temple.

Asaph says in Psalm 73:25, 26,

> Whom have I in heaven but you?
>   And there is nothing on earth that I desire besides you.
> My flesh and my heart may fail,
>   but God is the strength of my heart and my portion forever.

The greatest blessing God can give us is himself. And if we do not have God, then no other gift he gives means anything.

If God gave you health but didn't give you himself, would you be satisfied? If God gave you a nice home, nice vacations, and plenty of money but did not give you himself, would you be satisfied? If you went to Heaven and the streets were solid gold; the air was clean and bright; there was no more sin; everyone got along without fighting, arguing, or conflict; but Jesus was not there, would you be satisfied?

God himself is the one great blessing that makes all the other things he gives worthwhile. Think of the great blessings you have as a believer. God has forgiven you. Why is that good news? Forgiveness is good news because God has removed the guilt that separated us from him. Justification is good news because Christ gives us access to the presence of God. Eternal life is good news because it means seeing Jesus and enjoying his presence forever. The great blessing God gives us is himself. David's heart was not set on the gifts God gave him. God was his portion.

Content in God's Blessings

Even though the greatest gift God gives us is himself, we shouldn't look down on his other blessings. One way we love God is by enjoying the good gifts he gives us.

Imagine a goody two-shoes boy at Christmas time. You give him the Airsoft gun he has been dying to have. You expect him to jump up, shout "Yes," pump his fist in the air, and run off to play with it. Instead he sets it aside and comes over and says, "You know, Father, this is a really nice gift. But the thing I want most is you." Then he ignores the Airsoft gun and sits quietly next to you.

Is that what you wanted when you bought him that present? Of course not. You wanted to see him jump up and get all excited. You wanted him to enjoy the gift you gave him because you love him. Your gift is an extension of your love for him. This is how it is with God. He wants us to enjoy the good gifts he gives and praise him as the giver.

David praises God for two great gifts that God's presence brings: God's counsel and God's support.

> I bless the LORD who gives me counsel;
>   in the night also my heart instructs me.
> I have set the LORD always before me;
>   because he is at my right hand, I shall not be shaken. (16:7, 8)

God gives him advice throughout the day and night. This is a reality that is even more real for us under the new covenant than it was for David. God has placed his Holy Spirit inside us and has written his law on our hearts (Jeremiah 31:31–34). James says, "If any of you lacks wisdom, let him ask God, who gives generously to all without reproach, and it will be given him" (James 1:5).

God also stood beside him to strengthen and support him. This is the closing promise of Psalm 16; the godly man or woman will never be shaken. God's support is also a new-covenant reality for every believer. Jesus said, "I am with you always, to the end of the age" (Matthew 28:20). Many Christians have felt God's support as he stood beside them. Paul described it this way:

> At my first defense no one came to stand by me, but all deserted me. May it not be charged against them! But the Lord stood by me and strengthened me, so that through me the message might be fully proclaimed and all the Gentiles might hear it. So I was rescued from the lion's mouth. (2 Timothy 4:16, 17)

Confidence

Commitment and contentment lead to confidence. Faith follows from setting our hearts fully on God and being satisfied in him.

Confidence in the Resurrection

David sings about his confidence in the resurrection.

> Therefore my heart is glad, and my whole being rejoices;
>   my flesh also dwells secure.
> For you will not abandon my soul to Sheol,
>   or let your holy one see corruption. (16:9, 10)

As the apostles preached, this was the faith of our Lord Jesus Christ as he faced the cross. Speaking through David, Jesus saw that he must die but that his body would not remain in the tomb to rot away. Jesus also said to his disciples during his earthly life, "The Son of Man is going to be delivered into the hands of men, and they will kill him. And when he is killed, after three days he will rise" (Mark 9:31).

This is amazing confidence. And better yet, it was true! God did not abandon Jesus to the grave but raised him on the third day. And everyone who is in Christ has the same sort of faith as Jesus did. We trust God in the face of death. We believe on the basis of God's character and his Word that he will not abandon us to the grave. The Scriptures say,

> Behold! I tell you a mystery. We shall not all sleep, but we shall all be changed, in a moment, in the twinkling of an eye, at the last trumpet. For the trumpet will sound, and the dead will be raised imperishable, and we shall be changed. (1 Corinthians 15:51, 52)

If you are a believer, you know that death is not the end. It was not the end for Jesus, and it will not be the end for you.

Confidence in God's Presence

David ends with a positive statement of his confidence. Not only will God deliver him from death, but he will bless him with life in his presence.

> You make known to me the path of life;
>   in your presence there is fullness of joy;
>   at your right hand are pleasures forevermore. (16:11)

This was Jesus' great hope, and it is our hope as well. The path of life leads through death to everlasting joy with God.

God has promised us the greatest blessing—he will give us himself for all eternity! Is there anything better than that?

17

Lord, Hear My Prayer

PSALM 17

HAVE YOU EVER WONDERED whether God hears your prayer?

When my parents were returning to France as missionaries in 1956, they were surprised to find that Harry Truman was on the same ship. On Sunday the captain asked my father to preach. To his surprise, the former President was in the congregation.

After the service was over, my dad stood at the back greeting people as they left. Sure enough, Harry Truman came up to shake his hand. My father explained that they were going to Paris for their second term as missionaries, and he said to Truman, "Pray for me." Truman was genuinely surprised. He shot back, "Me pray for you? No, you pray for me!"

Why would a former President think that God would hear a young missionary but not him? Why would we think God answers the prayers of one man or one woman but not another?

In many ways Psalm 17 is a model prayer. It is urgent, perceptive, honest, and moving. David appeals to God and convinces him to answer and to act. He argues his case, explaining why God should listen to him.

Psalm 17 is closely connected to the psalms around it. Psalms 15, 16, and 17 all call for the protection of God's presence (Psalm 15:1; 16:8, 11; 17:15). All three use the same rare Hebrew word for slipping, being shaken, or being moved (Psalm 15:5; 16:8; 17:5). And if we look at Psalm 15—18, we notice that the godly find refuge in God's presence in each of these four psalms.[1] If you picture Psalms 15, 16, 17, and 18 as the squares of a quilt, these themes are the matching colors they share even though they have different patterns.

Why should God hear David's prayer and be his refuge? There are three sets of appeals in Psalm 17, beginning in verses 1, 6, and 13. David first appeals to God on the basis of his own innocence, then he appeals on the basis of God's love for his people, and finally he appeals on the basis of his own love for God. Since David was a prophet, we will notice at the end that this psalm points us once again to Christ. Ultimately God hears us because of Jesus.

David's Innocence (17:1–5)

First David appeals to God on the basis of his own innocence. Why should God hear him? David claims that his cause is just and his life is above reproach.

His Appeal

David claims to be innocent in his opening statement.

> Hear a just cause, O LORD; attend to my cry!
>   Give ear to my prayer from lips free of deceit!
> From your presence let my vindication come!
>   Let your eyes behold the right! (17:1, 2)

David is not asking God to commit an injustice. David has been wronged, and he is asking God to do what is right. "Just cause" is the English translation of the Hebrew word meaning "righteous." This opening line could be translated, "Hear, O righteous Lord," or "Hear, O Lord, a righteous person," or, "Hear, O Lord, a righteous case." Each of these translations is possible, and each has its own nuance. What they have in common is that David is asking God to do what is right.

When you and I come to God in prayer, we need to examine what we are asking for. Is what I am asking unfair to someone else? Am I asking for something that is against God's Law? Is my prayer angry or selfish or jealous? Am I asking God to help me sin? We need to be able to say with David, "Hear a just cause, O LORD" (v. 1).

David's innocence also comes out in his honesty. His "lips [are] free of deceit" (v. 1). God sees through hypocrisy. He knows our thoughts and the deep secrets of our hearts. We can't fool him by making our prayers sound spiritual. We need to be honest with God.

Since our hearts are deceitful, it is all too easy to baptize our selfish desires into something pious as we pray. As a pastor I might pray, "Lord, bless our church so that more people will hear the gospel." But in reality I might want to feel important because more people are coming to my church. God sees that deceit. A woman might ask God to provide finances so she has more to give. But in reality she is materialistic—she loves money and wants to buy more clothes. A man might pray for a promotion so he can influence his company for Christ. But deep down he loves power and wants to get ahead. God knows deceit when he hears it. God listens to honest prayers.

His Examination

David didn't just say he was innocent. God had examined him and found he was innocent. It's one thing to claim that you have done no wrong. It's another thing for God to search the deepest corners of your heart and not find a single fault.

> You have tried my heart, you have visited me by night,
>   you have tested me, and you will find nothing;
>   I have purposed that my mouth will not transgress.
> With regard to the works of man, by the word of your lips
>   I have avoided the ways of the violent.
> My steps have held fast to your paths;
>   my feet have not slipped. (17:3–5)

This testing is intense. The word "visited" (v. 3) has the sense of an inspection or investigation, a purposeful visit. When an auditor visits your office, he is there to inspect your books and procedures. When a colonel visits the barracks, he is there to inspect the state of his troops. The word "tested" (v. 3) is the same word used for refining gold or smelting metal (see, e.g., Psalm 12:6). The picture is that God has melted down David's heart so that whatever impurity was present would come to the surface.

This testing is also thorough. God went through his whole life with a fine-toothed comb. "Heart" (v. 3) refers not so much to emotions but to David's thoughts and his whole inner being. David also invites God to inspect his words; his "mouth" has not "transgress[ed]" (v. 3). And he has kept himself from violence. So he welcomes God's inspection of his thoughts, words, and deeds—his whole life.

His commitment to avoid violence is a word we need to hear in our culture today. America is becoming an increasingly violent place. Video games allow players to shoot lifelike pictures of fellow human beings. These games are so realistic that a young man can easily become desensitized to killing. The title of a recent Sylvester Stallone movie was *Bullet to the Head*. Our culture glorifies violence, and violent men are our heroes. But God's people should be different. We should consciously turn away from blood and violence on TV, in the movies, in video games, and in everyday life. Jesus said, "Blessed are the peacemakers" (Matthew 5:9). We should love peace. We shouldn't entertain ourselves with killing.

The underlying principle is that God notices the life of a person who comes to him in prayer. Isaiah says, "[Y]our iniquities have made a separation between you and your God, and your sins have hidden his face from you so that he does not hear" (Isaiah 59:2). "Open and unconfessed sin is a great barrier to prayer."[2] But the opposite is also true. A godly life gives you firm footing as you pray. James says, "The prayer of a righteous person has great power . . ." (James 5:16b).

We need to examine ourselves when we come to God. Am I coming to God with "a just cause" (v. 1)? Am I being honest with God? Is there known sin in my life? David appealed to God on the basis of his innocence.

God's Love

David also appealed to God on the basis of God's love for his people (17:6–12). Notice his confidence in this second part of his prayer.

> I call upon you, for you will answer me, O God;
> > incline your ear to me; hear my words. (17:6)

God's Covenant Loyalty

How could David be sure God would hear and answer? The prayers of verses 7–9 refer back to God's faithfulness to Israel in the wilderness and the covenant promise God made with them as his people. God committed himself to Israel, and David knew he could count on him.

> Wondrously show your steadfast love,
> > O Savior of those who seek refuge
> from their adversaries at your right hand.
>
> Keep me as the apple of your eye;
> > hide me in the shadow of your wings,
> from the wicked who do me violence,
> > my deadly enemies who surround me. (17:7–9)

The words "steadfast love" (v. 7) are a translation of the Hebrew word *chesed*. This is God's covenant loyalty, the faithful love he promised when he saved his people. When a husband takes his marriage vows and promises to love his wife, he is pledging his *chesed*, his steadfast love. He will be faithful to her, care for her, and stay with her. When David says, "Wondrously show your steadfast love" (v. 7), he is appealing to God to honor his covenant vows. God will be faithful to love his people (Isaiah 54:5–8).

With this in mind, it's important to notice that verses 7–9 point back to God's faithfulness when he brought Israel out of Egypt and established his covenant with them as a nation. David quotes two songs of Moses from the Pentateuch.[3] God's "right hand" points back to the time when God saved his people from Pharaoh through the Red Sea. As they stood on the shores of the Red Sea with pieces of broken chariots bobbing on the waves, Moses said, "Your right hand, O LORD, glorious in power, your right hand, O LORD, shatters the enemy" (Exodus 15:6).

The phrases "the apple of your eye" and "hide me in the shadow of your wings" (v. 8) are not random pieces of poetry either. David is echoing another great song of Moses that describes the exodus.

> [H]e kept him as the apple of his eye.
> Like an eagle that stirs up its nest,
>   that flutters over its young,
> spreading out its wings, catching them,
>   bearing them on its pinions,
> the LORD alone guided him. (Deuteronomy 32:10–12)

By appealing to God with these words from Moses, David is counting on God's enduring love for his people. God would answer because God will keep the promises he made when he led Israel out of Egypt.

Deadly Danger

David's confidence in God's faithfulness becomes even more clear when we see the danger he was in.

> They close their hearts to pity;
>   with their mouths they speak arrogantly.
> They have now surrounded our steps;
>   they set their eyes to cast us to the ground.
> He is like a lion eager to tear,
>   as a young lion lurking in ambush. (17:10–12)

It's one thing to trust God when the sun is shining. The storms reveal the strength of our faith. David trusted God's enduring love and loyalty when he was surrounded by real violence.

David's Love

David ends this psalm by appealing to God on the basis of his own love for God (17:13–15). The final verses draw a contrast between David and his enemies. His enemies are worldly; their hearts love this created world. But David loves the Creator. Their portion is in this life, while David will not be satisfied by anything less than seeing God in the world to come. They are focused selfishly on the gifts God gives. David loves the Giver.

The Wicked Love Creation

The wicked love this present world, and David asks God to rebuke them. David starts his third set of appeals in verse 13.

> Arise, O Lord! Confront him, subdue him!
>   Deliver my soul from the wicked by your sword,
> from men by your hand, O Lord,
>   from men of the world whose portion is in this life.
> You fill their womb with treasure;
>   they are satisfied with children,
>   and they leave their abundance to their infants. (17:13, 14)

David's enemies are worldly, "men of the world" (v. 14). What does it mean to be worldly? David says their "portion is in this life" (v. 14). They are focused on this world. If you are worldly, you love this present life, and you are not looking for the world to come. You love the gifts God gives—your children and the inheritance you pass down to them. But you do not love God. In fact, you take his generosity for granted.

David talks about outward blessings, but his focus is internal. Since their "portion is in this life" (v. 14), they measure everything by what it means for here and now. *Does it make me more popular now? Will I earn more profit now? Does it give me more power now?*

> It is a man-centred way of thinking; it proposes objectives which demand no radical breach from man's fallen nature; it judges the importance of things by the present and material results; it weighs success by numbers; it covets human esteem and wants no unpopularity; it knows no truth for which it is worth suffering; it declines to be "a fool for Christ's sake." Worldliness is the mindset of the unregenerate.[4]

Worldliness is not a matter of outward behavior. Outward behavior can be evidence of inner worldliness, but the real location of worldliness is internal, in our hearts. The Apostle John says,

For all that is in the world—the desires of the flesh and the desires of the eyes and pride of life—is not from the Father but is from the world. (1 John 2:16)

How does John define worldliness in this verse? He doesn't say that these particular clothes, this way of speaking, this kind of music, or these particular possessions are worldly.

Worldliness is much more penetrating than simple rules for behavior. When John defines "the world," he points to the things we want in our hearts (1 John 2:16). The essence of worldliness is what we love—our desires and our pride, the things that motivate us.[5] We can be worldly by following a strict set of rules or by throwing all the rules out the window. What makes someone worldly is that his or her "portion is in this life" (Psalm 17:14). They live for approval, for respect, for status, for money, for pleasure, for security here and now, in this world, and they are not looking for the world to come.

This is the consistent teaching of the Bible. New Testament scholar Greg Beale points out that in the book of Revelation, John repeatedly refers to unbelieving idolaters as *earth dwellers*. It seems to me that David means the same thing when he refers to those whose "portion is in this life" (v. 14). The term *earth dwellers*

> is reserved for such people because they cannot look beyond this earth for their security, which means that they trust in some part of creation instead of the Creator for their ultimate welfare. . . . Christians instead are exiles in a foreign land and are those who are told to "come out of her [Babylon]," the ungodly earthly system, since their ultimate home is in the coming new cosmos. Believers are "strangers and exiles on the earth," not trusting in the present old earth but "they desire a better home, that is a heavenly one," since God has "prepared a city for them," for which they wait (Heb. 11:13–16). Thus "the ones dwelling on earth" in Revelation have their ultimate identity with the old earth they adore, while believers have their ultimate identity with the God of the coming new cosmos, the God in whom is their ultimate trust.[6]

David Longs for the Creator

David himself is not an earth dweller; his portion is not in this life. Instead God is his reward. He is not in love with this creation; he loves the Creator. In Psalm 16:5 he says, "The Lord is my chosen portion and my cup." He ends Psalm 17 by saying,

> As for me, I shall behold your face in righteousness;
>   when I awake, I shall be satisfied with your likeness. (17:15)

Nothing on earth can satisfy the heart of a man or woman who loves God. Nothing can compare to the beauty and glory of Jesus Christ. The phrase "when I awake" (v. 15) probably refers to the resurrection of the dead when we will see Jesus face-to-face.[7] If you love God, you have a gnawing sense of homesickness wherever you go in the world. The most beautiful rainbow reminds you of someone more beautiful you are waiting to see. The most majestic mountains remind you of a greater majesty to come. You will not be satisfied by anything less than seeing the face of God.

David closes his prayer, this appeal for God to hear his prayer, with a declaration of his genuine love for God himself.

David Points to Christ

As with all the psalms of David, Psalm 17 is ultimately about Jesus Christ. The Old Testament is Christian Scripture, and this prayer is no different. If this psalm is simply a pattern for our prayer, then it is almost useless for us.

Why is it useless? Because which one of us can appeal to God on the basis of his or her innocence like David does in the opening verses? We might be innocent in regard to one thing or another, but the inspection of verses 3–5 goes much further than that. The psalmist claims that his whole life is clean. "You have tested me, and you will find nothing" (v. 3).

As we have seen before, only one man could pray this way—our Lord Jesus Christ. The Scriptures say, "In him there is no sin" (1 John 3:5). Jesus trusted in God's steadfast love when he was surrounded by violent men. And Jesus was not worldly—his portion was not in this life. Instead our Lord had his eyes fixed firmly on the world to come. "[F]or the joy that was set before him [he] endured the cross, despising the shame, and is seated at the right hand of the throne of God" (Hebrews 12:2). Ultimately this psalm is a prophecy waiting for Jesus. This is Jesus' prayer, his appeal for God to hear him.

And when he prayed, he was heard! The writer of Hebrews says,

> In the days of his flesh, Jesus offered up prayers and supplications, with loud cries and tears, to him who was able to save him from death, and he was heard because of his reverence. (Hebrews 5:7)

Although Jesus is fully God, he is also fully human like you and me. God examined his life and accepted his righteous prayer.

And because God heard his prayer, Jesus opened up the way to the throne of God so that your prayers and mine can be heard. The writer of Hebrews goes on to say,

Therefore, brothers, since we have confidence to enter the holy places by the blood of Jesus, by the new and living way that he opened for us through the curtain, that is, through his flesh, and since we have a great priest over the house of God, let us draw near with a true heart in full assurance of faith, with our hearts sprinkled clean from an evil conscience and our bodies washed with pure water. Let us hold fast the confession of our hope without wavering, for he who promised is faithful. (Hebrews 10:19–23)

This means that if Harry Truman was a believer, then he had the same access to God's throne as my father did. God hears the prayers of a missionary or a U.S. President on the same basis—Christ has opened the way to the throne of God.

And ultimately we have someone better than a President or missionary to pray for us. The Holy Spirit, who is the Spirit of Christ, intercedes for us with groanings too deep for words (Romans 8:26). Not only so, but Jesus himself is praying for you and me. "Christ Jesus . . . who died—more than that, who was raised . . . is at the right hand of God . . . interceding for us" (Romans 8:34).

Christian, you have a lawyer pleading your case before God—Jesus Christ, the Righteous One. God hears his prayer. And he hears yours too. He cares for you.

18

The Lord Is My Rock

PSALM 18

ONE OF THE MOST famous pictures from the 1940s is Alfred Eisenstaedt's *VJ Day in Times Square*, sometimes called *The Kiss*.

If you grew up in America, I'm sure you've seen this picture. When the news broke that Japan had surrendered, crowds flooded into the streets all across America. The war was over! In Times Square a young sailor swept a nurse into his arms and planted a kiss on her. And Eisenstaedt was there with his trusty Leica to get the photograph.

I think this picture became part of American culture because it captures the joy and euphoria of that moment. After years of fighting and sacrifice, the killing and dying was over. We had won! Something in that image captures the elation and excitement of victory.

That same sense of joy and euphoria is behind Psalm 18. David sang this song after God gave him victory over all his enemies. His words almost jump from the page.

The superscription gives us the historical setting. This introduction is unusually long—the second longest superscription in the Psalter, just a hair shorter than Psalm 60's.

To the choirmaster. A psalm of David, the servant of the Lord, who addressed the words of this song to the Lord on the day when the Lord rescued him from the hand of all his enemies, and from the hand of Saul.

After decades of fighting, the wars were over. David finally experienced rest from his enemies. He had won! To reinforce this historical background, 2 Samuel 22 contains Psalm 18 almost word for word. This psalm came near the end of David's life. It is the third longest psalm after Psalm 119 and Psalm

193

78. David is reflecting back over a long life of conflict and battles to praise God for a wonderful victory.

The sense of joy and euphoria in Psalm 18 is even greater because the victory of Jesus Christ is bursting through the seams. David himself wants us to realize that he is writing about more than his own victories. He ends with the words,

> Great salvation he brings to his king,
>   and shows steadfast love to his anointed,
>   to David and his offspring forever. (18:50)

God had promised David to set one of his descendants on his throne as an eternal king. God said, "I will establish the throne of his kingdom forever" (2 Samuel 7:13). The "offspring" he mentions in verse 50 refers to Christ, the eternal King. He is the king that we meet in Psalm 2 at the doorway to the Psalter (Psalm 2:6). He will rule forever over all the nations of the earth. David mentions him at the end of this psalm as if to say, "This is not just about me. I am writing about the Christ, 'his anointed,' to come."

In fact, the actual content of Psalm 18 is too big and too full to refer only to David. Like a river that overflows its banks, this psalm overflows the historical events of David's life. There is simply more here than was true of David himself. The light of Christ in Psalm 18 is like a floodlight behind an ice sculpture, shining through and melting the ice with its heat.

The writers of the New Testament certainly saw that this psalm is about Christ. We see this in two places. The writer of Hebrews quotes 18:2 as the word of Christ (Hebrews 2:13). In Romans 15:8, 9 Paul quotes 18:49 as the words of the Lord Jesus to show that salvation was for the Gentiles all along.

> For I tell you that Christ became a servant to the circumcised to show God's truthfulness, in order to confirm the promises given to the patriarchs, and in order that the Gentiles might glorify God for his mercy. As it is written,
>
> > "Therefore I will praise you among the Gentiles,
> >   and sing to your name."

As we read Psalm 18, the triumph of our Lord Jesus Christ shines through David's joy for the victories God gave him. "David was given victory to make possible the greater victories of his Greater Son."[1]

David's Opening Praise

David starts with his opening words of praise (18:1–3).

I love you, O LORD, my strength.
The LORD is my rock and my fortress and my deliverer,
    my God, my rock, in whom I take refuge,
    my shield, and the horn of my salvation, my stronghold.
I call upon the LORD, who is worthy to be praised,
    and I am saved from my enemies. (18:1–3)

The opening words, "I love you, O LORD, my strength" (v. 1), are not found in the parallel song in 2 Samuel 22. They stand out because they have been included in this psalm. As a result this psalm is not simply a catalog of great things God has done for David. It is a response of genuine devotion and affection. David's love identifies him immediately as a man after God's own heart.[2] He loved the God who had rescued him.

Many people do not love God even though God has rescued them from danger. For instance, Judas was in the boat with the rest of the disciples when they were about to drown. He saw the Lord rebuke the wind and calm the sea. Yet he did not love Jesus—he loved money and helped himself to the money bag. Many people today have experienced wonderful answers to prayer when God rescued them, but they still do not love him. They prayed for healing, and God healed. They prayed for a son in Iraq or Afghanistan, and God brought him safely home. They prayed for God to help them make the mortgage, and God provided money unexpectedly. Yet in all this they do not say with David, "I love you, O LORD, my strength" (v. 1).

Loving God is the one unmistakable mark of God's people. God's people not only receive his blessings, they genuinely love him. When someone comes to Christ, it is important that they understand the facts of the gospel— that Christ died for our sins according to the Scriptures and that God raised him up on the third day. Yet knowing these facts is useless unless one comes to him in faith and actually loves him. This is why the Apostle Paul could say, "If anyone has no love for the Lord, let him be accursed" (1 Corinthians 16:22). Love for God is the great dividing line that runs through humanity. God's people love him; those who do not love him are cut off from him.

David then stacks up eight names to say who the Lord is to him: "my strength," "my rock," "my fortress," "my deliverer," "my rock . . . [of] refuge," "my shield," "the horn of my salvation," and "my stronghold" (vv. 1, 2). The pronoun "my" is repeated with each of these names. David claims the Lord as his own God—he has a personal relationship with God. This list also includes almost all the names that focus on God's protection and salvation in the Psalms. No other psalm brings together as many of these names as Psalm

18. David gathers them all in one place to lift up the greatness of the God he loves. He wants us to love him too.

How God Saved Him

David describes how God saved him in 18:4–19.

David's Cry

David's life hung in the balance many times throughout his life. As a shepherd, he was in danger from wild animals. Goliath was the first of many men he fought in combat. Saul almost caught him several times. His own son, Absalom, almost killed him. No wonder that death is David's primary concern in verses 4, 5. He was caught in "the cords of death," "the cords of Sheol," and "the snares of death." This meant that he was about to die. Death is like an octopus dragging him under the waves.

Jesus was not just dragged away to death; he did die. He was bound in graveclothes and was laid in the grave itself. Psalm 16:10 teaches us to expect that God's Holy One would die but would rise before his body began to decompose. With that expectation just two psalms earlier, we can see the death of Christ himself in these verses. Jesus called out to God from the grave—and he was heard! What does this mean for you and me? If you belong to Jesus, God will save you from "the cords of death" too (v. 4). The Bible promises that "he who raised the Lord Jesus will raise us also with Jesus" (2 Corinthians 4:14). Your body may die, but you will live.

God Comes in Power

How did God save David? God's answer was a dramatic and overwhelming rescue. When God rose from his throne in Heaven, the earth itself trembled in the presence of its Creator.

> Then the earth reeled and rocked;
> the foundations also of the mountains trembled
> and quaked, because he was angry. (18:7)

God's anger at the way his king is being treated echoes his anger that was introduced in Psalm 2:5, "Then he will speak to them in his wrath, and terrify them in his fury." Psalm 18:7–19 is a fuller description of the same conflict and rebellion against God and his anointed that David has been presenting in the Psalms from the beginning.

David's description is a theophany, an attempt to describe the overwhelming presence of the infinite God in this world. God's presence caused earthquakes, smoke, darkness, wind, hail, fire, and arrows of lightning. As far as we know, David never physically experienced the awesome events of verses 7–15. This is figurative language that the Scriptures use to describe the indescribable. What human words could we use to explain the awesome majesty of almighty God when he steps into this world? These descriptions are meant to give us a sense of the terrifying presence of Yahweh.

David borrowed this language from the awesome displays of God's majesty in the days of Moses and Joshua. Verses 7–11 echo Israel's experience of God's presence at Mount Sinai. When God gave the Ten Commandments, the sky was filled with clouds and lightning, the mountain was surrounded by smoke and clouds of thick darkness, God descended in fire, and the whole mountain trembled (Exodus 19:16–20). Verses 12–14 echo God's fighting on behalf of Israel during the conquest of the land under Joshua. Verse 15 clearly echoes the parting of the Red Sea when the Lord opened a path on dry ground through the waters. Spurgeon says,

> David has in his mind's eye the glorious manifestations of God in Egypt, at Sinai, and on different occasions to Joshua and the judges; and he considers that his own case exhibits the same glory of power and goodness, and that, therefore, he may accommodate the descriptions of former displays of the divine majesty into his own hymn of praise.[3]

What is the point? The same God who rescued Israel from Egypt was powerfully at work in David's life too. The victory God gave to him over his enemies is on a par with these major events in salvation history—the giving of the Law at Sinai, the parting of the Red Sea, and the conquest of the land.[4]

Why was David's victory on a scale with a great Old Testament event like the exodus? When God rescued David, this pointed forward to God's rescue of our Lord Jesus Christ. When Jesus cried out to God, the earth shook, darkness descended on the land, and God drew him up from death because he was his beloved Son. Man rejected Christ, but God delighted in him.

Why God Saved Him

David was part of the larger drama of God's salvation through Jesus Christ (18:20–29). This is more clear when we see why God saved him.

David's Integrity

David insists that God rescued him because of his integrity.

The Lord dealt with me according to my righteousness;
  according to the cleanness of my hands he rewarded me. (18:20)

David claims to be righteous because of his clean hands; this means he did not have blood on his hands.[5] He also kept the Law of Moses with its "rules" and "statutes" (18:22). To make this claim of innocence even bigger, David says, "I was blameless" (18:23). In this psalm his "blameless" character mirrors that of God himself. Verse 30 uses the same word to describe God's conduct: "This God—his way is perfect [blameless]; the word of the Lord proves true." David claims absolute purity and integrity.

David was indeed a man after God's own heart. Throughout the book of 1 Kings, David is the yardstick—the gold standard—against whom the rest of the kings of Israel are measured. Yet David was not without sin. First Kings 15:5 remembers David's great flaw.

David did what was right in the eyes of the Lord and did not turn aside from anything that he commanded him all the days of his life, except in the matter of Uriah the Hittite.

When David sinned with Bathsheba, Uriah's wife, he started by breaking the tenth commandment—he coveted another man's wife. Then he broke the seventh commandment by committing adultery and the sixth commandment by having Uriah killed. This was stealing (the eighth commandment), and he lied too (the ninth commandment). The affair dishonored his parents (the fifth commandment) and brought shame on the name of God (the third commandment).

When David claims that he is "blameless" (Psalm 18:23), he cannot be talking about himself. David himself says in Psalm 14:3, "[T]here is none who does good, not even one." But David was a prophet, and he foresaw and spoke about the absolute innocence and purity of Christ.[6] God answered the Lord Jesus and delivered him from death precisely because of his sinless life. Jesus could say, "The Lord dealt with me according to my righteousness" (v. 33).

Reciprocity

David states a fundamental principle for our relationship with God.

With the merciful you show yourself merciful;
  with the blameless man you show yourself blameless;
with the purified you show yourself pure;
  and with the crooked you make yourself seem tortuous. (18:25, 26)

God responds to us in kind. He reveals himself as good to those with good hearts. He hides his goodness from those who hide from him. We can't fool God or manipulate him; he can throw curveballs with the best of us. In the Old Testament Jacob was a schemer. He tricked Esau out of his birthright and tricked Laban out of his flocks. How did God save scheming Jacob? God had a scheme of his own. He let him think his son Joseph was dead and surprised him with grace. God knows how to deal with tricky people. In the book of Job, Elihu says, "For according to the work of a man he [God] will repay him, and according to his ways he will make it befall him" (Job 34:11).

The good news is that God is gracious to the humble. David says, "[Y]ou save a humble people" (18:27). If you belong to Christ, his goodness and purity are given to you so that when God looks at your life, he sees the blameless obedience of Jesus. Your heart is like an onion, and Jesus is like Saran Wrap. When God picks you up to smell you, he smells the goodness of Jesus covering you. His plans and purposes for you are good. He will order all the events of your life to bless you and make you more like Christ.

How God Strengthened Him

David's heart continues to sing as he looks back over his career as a warrior, a general, a king. God had been more than faithful and good to him. David describes how God strengthened him (18:30–45).

God's Equipping

He begins with God's equipping. "God . . . equipped me with strength and made my way blameless" (18:32). When a soldier goes off to boot camp, the Army begins to train him for combat, issues him equipment, and prepares him to serve in the military. Verses 33–36 describe God's boot camp for David. God gave David speed and agility, making his "feet like the feet of a deer" (v. 33). God trained him in the use of weapons. If "a bow of bronze" (v. 34) refers to a physical bow that David used, it may have been a wooden bow with bronze decoration or a bow with bronze-tipped arrows. But this is probably a poetic way to describe the enormous strength God gave him for combat—it was as if he could bend solid bronze.[7] God also provided him with armor—salvation like a "shield" (v. 35). And like the Army Corps of Engineers, God cleared a road for his feet.

David's experience of God's equipment for battle is a wonderful description of our Lord Jesus too. Jesus came as a warrior to fight spiritual battles against Satan and this fallen world. Demons could not stand before him; his enemies could not refute his wisdom; he completed his conquest by his obedience to death, even death on a cross.

If you are a believer, you have spiritual weapons and equipment through Jesus Christ for the battle before you. The Scriptures say,

> For we do not wrestle against flesh and blood, but against the rulers, against the authorities, against the cosmic powers over this present darkness, against the spiritual forces of evil in the heavenly places. Therefore take up the whole armor of God, that you may be able to withstand in the evil day, and having done all, to stand firm. Stand therefore, having fastened on the belt of truth, and having put on the breastplate of righteousness, and, as shoes for your feet, having put on the readiness given by the gospel of peace. In all circumstances take up the shield of faith, with which you can extinguish all the flaming darts of the evil one; and take the helmet of salvation, and the sword of the Spirit, which is the word of God, praying at all times in the Spirit, with all prayer and supplication. (Ephesians 6:12–18)

God equips us for battle through the Lord Jesus Christ. Are you wearing the armor of God? Is truth your belt? Are your vitals protected by Christ's righteousness? Do you have the agility—the feet of a deer—from the gospel of peace? Are you holding the shield of faith in front of you? When you begin to doubt God's goodness or his care for you, you need to lift up your shield and tell yourself to believe what you believe.

David's Victory

David describes his victories in verses 37–45. Interestingly, David's enemies include both foreigners and fellow Jews.

> You delivered me from strife with the people;
>   you made me the head of the nations;
>   people whom I had not known served me. (18:43)

Here "the people" refers to Israel. And it's true—to the end of his life, much of David's conflict was with fellow Jews. It took seven years for the northern tribes to accept him as king after Saul died, and they were quick to turn against him and follow Absalom. David also conquered surrounding nations, of course, and some foreigners did submit to him when they heard word of his victories (see 2 Samuel 8:9).[8]

David's victory points forward to the greater victories of his descendant, Jesus Christ. As the Son of David, Jesus experienced conflict with his fellow Jews. How did God deliver Jesus from his strife with the Jewish people? God allowed Jesus to be put to death by the hands of sinful men—then God raised him up! They rejected him, but God vindicated him and delivered him from "the cords of death" (18:4). We foreigners hear about the victory of this risen Messiah, and we obey him.

Jesus not only defeated human enemies, he crushed our greatest enemies: death and the devil. On the cross Jesus destroyed "the one who has the power of death, that is, the devil" (Hebrews 2:14). He won this victory over Satan for all his people—for you and me as believers. His victory is our victory.

Even more, through his conquering death, Jesus conquered death. The Scriptures say,

> For he must reign until he has put all his enemies under his feet. The last enemy to be destroyed is death. For "God has put all things in subjection under his feet." (1 Corinthians 15:25–27)

God established David's kingdom as a scale model of the greater kingdom of Jesus Christ. God is not absent from this world but is very present, giving his Son Jesus victory in this world. He is not distant; he is near. He is not weak; he is mighty. With the eyes of faith we see the earth tremble and the mountains smoke as the gospel goes forward across this world.

David ends Psalm 18 as a prophet, praising God that Jesus, his offspring, would experience salvation like he had.

> For this I will praise you, O LORD, among the nations,
>   and sing to your name.
> Great salvation he brings to his king,
>   and shows steadfast love to his anointed,
>   to David and his offspring forever. (18:49, 50)

One day Christ's victory will be complete. We will hear a voice from Heaven saying, "The kingdom of the world has become the kingdom of our Lord and of his Christ, and he shall reign forever and ever" (Revelation 11:15). We will celebrate with joy and euphoria that makes VJ Day seem like nothing.

19

The Skies and the Scriptures

PSALM 19

ONE OF THE FIRST THINGS we learn in the Bible is that God talks. He is a speaking God. Genesis 1:3 says, "And God said, 'Let there be light.'" God is not silent. He talks to us.

So how does God speak? Psalm 19 describes how God communicates with human beings. The first half of Psalm 19 teaches us that God speaks through nature—the heavens reveal God's glory. This is what we call general revelation—God reveals his power and greatness through nature to all people everywhere. The second half of Psalm 19 tells us that God speaks through his Word, the Bible. This is special revelation—God speaks to anyone who picks up and reads the words of this Book.

God speaks to us through the skies and the Scriptures. The message of Psalm 19 is that the glory of God displayed in the heavens points us to the grace of God displayed in the Bible.[1]

Psalm 19 doesn't stand alone like a tree in the middle of a field. It fits in the context of the surrounding psalms. The theme of Psalms 3—14 seems to be that God's king is rejected by man; Psalms 15—24 teach that the king is accepted by God. David's closing prayer in 19:14 places this psalm in this larger context: "Let the words of my mouth and the meditation of my heart be acceptable in your sight." The king is accepted by God because he hears God's voice in the skies and the Scripture, and he obeys.

To develop this thought, we should notice that Psalm 19 is closely connected with Psalm 18 before it. One of the names for God, "my rock," occurs three times in Psalm 18. David starts Psalm 18:2 by saying, "The Lord is my rock," and he repeats that name two more times at important transition points (Psalm 18:31, 46). Psalm 19 ends with this same name for God, "O Lord, my rock and my redeemer" (19:14). David also calls himself God's "servant" twice in Psalm 19 (19:11, 13). This is significant because David is called "the servant of the LORD" only two places in the Old Testament (in the superscriptions for Psalms 18 and 36).

There are more connections we should notice between Psalms 18 and 19. Both celebrate God's power in the heavens (Psalm 18:9–15; 19:1–6). Both celebrate the perfection of God's Word (Psalm 18:30; 19:7–9). Both celebrate the blessings of obeying his commandments (Psalm 18:20–24; 19:11–14)—there is a *great reward* for those who keep his Word.[2] So the two main points of Psalm 19—the glory of God in the sky and the grace of God in the Scriptures—actually start in Psalm 18.

Both psalms also focus on the blameless perfection of Jesus Christ, God's servant. In Psalm 18 David speaks for Christ as he looks back on his life, saying, "I was blameless" before God (Psalm 18:23) and again "God . . . made my way blameless" (Psalm 18:32). In Psalm 19 David asks God to keep him from willful sins so that he will be "blameless" (19:13). So Psalm 19 is looking forward, asking for the blameless life of Psalm 18.

We all see the glory of God in the sky. We have the Word of God in the Scriptures. We ought to obey them perfectly, but we don't. Jesus was the one man who did. Jesus Christ is the great Servant who was "blameless, and innocent of great transgression" (19:13). He could appeal to God with complete confidence and say, "Declare me innocent from hidden faults" (19:12). The words of his mouth and the meditations of his heart were acceptable in God's sight.[3] Psalm 19 is a window into the heart of our Lord Jesus Christ.

The Holy Spirit inspired Psalm 19 so you could strengthen your heart in Christ today and learn to obey. You need to see God's glory in the heavens for yourself. You need to love his Word. This is the example Jesus left so you could follow in his steps. The sky and the Scriptures teach God's servants to obey him.

The Eloquence of the Skies

I can picture David staring up at the night sky in verse 1.

> The heavens declare the glory of God,
>   and the sky above proclaims his handiwork.

Creation has a message for those who notice and think about what they see every day. God has surrounded this world with a giant Omnimax screen running a full-length feature on an endless loop. Any time you lift your eyes, you see God's glory in the sky above.

I was in Southern California a few years ago, and late one afternoon we went down to the pier and joined a crowd of people to watch the sunset. The sun glowed bright orange, then red, purple, and pink as it sank into the wide waters of the Pacific—beautiful! As the last light faded away, a man in shorts and a T-shirt started clapping, and soon everyone was clapping. In the beauty of that sunset, we saw something of the beauty of God. If the sky is glorious, the God who made it must be even more glorious.

The more we discover in the heavens, the more clearly we see God's power. The magnetosphere is a magnetic field surrounding the earth, reaching 36,000 miles into space. It deflects most of the damaging particles of the solar wind into radiation belts around our planet. Some of these particles funnel down to the North and South Poles where they create the aurora borealis and aurora australis, the northern and southern lights. God is an amazing electrical engineer who designed this magnetosphere to make the skies beautiful as it protects our planet.

On February 27, 2013 a team of astronomers published data on a super-massive black hole at the center of galaxy NGC 1365. Based on data from two X-ray telescopes, they calculated that the black hole was 3,000,000 kilometers across, and its outer edges were spinning near the speed of light.[4] The pull of a black hole this size is so powerful it can disrupt an entire galaxy. How much more powerful is the God who created it?

We should be impressed when we see the power and majesty of God in the universe he has made. The word "glory" has the sense of being weighty or important. Glory is "that asset which makes people or individuals, and even objects, impressive."[5] God has revealed how important he is through his glory in creation.

Universal Witness

Every human being sees this display of God's glory. The skies above are a constant and consistent witness across time.

> Day to day pours out speech,
>   and night to night reveals knowledge. (19:2)

Literally every day gushes out speech, like a fire hydrant. Where one day leaves off, the next day picks up. And where the days end, the night takes over. Day and night, this witness to God's glory has been constant since the beginning of time.

This witness is also comprehensive, spanning the globe.

> There is no speech, nor are there words,
>   whose voice is not heard.
> Their voice goes out through all the earth,
>   and their words to the end of the world. (19:3, 4a)

Language and culture are not a barrier. Distance is not a barrier either. The voice of the heavens reaches the farthest corner of the globe. A woman in New Guinea looks up and sees the Southern Cross. A man in Finland looks up to see the Big Dipper. Men and women in every age and every place have seen God's glory in the heavens.

A Case Study

David gives us a case study to illustrate his point.

> In them he has set a tent for the sun,
>   which comes out like a bridegroom leaving his chamber,
>   and, like a strong man, runs its course with joy.
> Its rising is from the end of the heavens,
>   and its circuit to the end of them,
>   and there is nothing hidden from its heat. (19:4b–6)

Is there anyone who doesn't see the light of the sun? It shines on every corner of the globe with such power that we can't look at it.

The earth receives 120,000 terawatts of energy from the sun every day. How much is that? Picture Niagara Falls flowing at full force. Now multiply the height of the falls by 20—a kilometer of falling water. Now multiply the flow by 10—instead of 30 tons of water falling over each meter of the falls every second, picture 300 tons of water per meter. Finally, widen the falls. Stretch them until they span a continent, with trillions of tons of water falling over them every second. And don't stop there—widen them until they stretch all around the equator: a kilometer-high wall of water thundering down incessantly, cutting the world in half. That is what 120,000 terawatts looks like.[6] That is what the sun constantly pours out on our planet every day. And God created it!

If you are a believer, God has surrounded you with a hymnbook. Wherever you are, day or night, you can look up and see the majesty and power of your God. And you can praise him.

If you are not a believer, you are responsible for what the skies above have been telling you since the day you were born. You ought to worship God. The Apostle Paul writes in Romans 1:20, his invisible attributes, namely, his eternal power and divine nature, have been clearly perceived, ever since the creation of the world, in the things that have been made. So they are without excuse.

You may say to yourself, "I don't hear creation telling me about God." But think about it this way. If you shout at someone standing five feet away from you and he doesn't respond, he is either deaf or he is ignoring you. If you don't see God's glory in the universe he made, you need the courage and honesty to ask yourself, *Could it be that I am deaf? Or could it be that I am ignoring God, turning my back on him?* The Bible says, "The heavens declare the glory of God."

The Clarity of the Scriptures

The sky eloquently declares God's glory, but we cannot truly know God without the clarity of the Scriptures. We can see the power of God by looking at the universe he created, but we can only know him personally through his written Word.

If you go to the Gilcrease Museum in Tulsa, you can spend hours enjoying Frederick Remington's bronzes. As a sculptor, he catches a horse floating in mid-gallop with its mane whipping in the wind. You can feel the weariness of his "Mountain Man" leaning back in the saddle. He catches the energy of four young cowhands in "Coming Through the Rye." All this is enough to convince you that Remington was a true master. But it doesn't tell you anything about Remington as a man—what kind of person he was. Where was he born? What is his middle name? In the same way we can see the glory of God in the universe—his power, majesty, and wisdom—but we cannot know him personally and be saved without his Word.

God's name is mentioned only once in the first half of the psalm—David uses the general name *El* in verse 1. In the second half of the psalm, David uses God's name, Yahweh, six times in verses 7–9 and a seventh time in verse 14. God's name Yahweh is often connected with his covenant and with redeeming his people. God revealed himself to Moses as Yahweh at the burning bush when he came to save Israel from the Egyptians. By shifting to the name Yahweh, David is saying that while the heavens teach us there is a glorious Creator, the Scriptures introduce us to God as Redeemer.

The Character of God's Word

Verses 7–9 describe the perfections of God's Word and its effects on God's people. The five synonyms for the Scriptures in these verses also occur in the opening verses of Psalm 119, in the same order: "law," "testimony," "precepts," "commandment," and "rules."

First, "[t]he law of the LORD is perfect, reviving the soul" (v. 7). The word "law" is the Hebrew word *torah*. Sometimes this refers specifically to the Law of Moses, but here it refers to all Scripture.[7] God's Word is perfect, complete, blameless, and without blemish. There is nothing missing from God's Word—it is completely sufficient (2 Timothy 3:16, 17). There is not the slightest error in God's Word—it is wholly true in every detail.

God's perfect Word brings life to the human heart, "reviving the soul" (v. 7). There is some breadth to this expression. On the one hand, the Scriptures convert us. God uses his Word to give us life when we are dead in our sins, restoring us and returning us to our Creator. This phrase "reviving the soul" is also used for food that restores strength and vitality. There is the sense here that the Law of the Lord is our spiritual food.[8] This was true for Jesus, of course. When he was tempted in the wilderness, he quoted the Scriptures. For example: "Man shall not live by bread alone, but by every word that comes from the mouth of God" (Matthew 4:4). The Scriptures were bread and meat for Christ. And the Scriptures are bread and meat for Christians. God's Word is our life.

God's Word also teaches us: "the testimony of the LORD is sure, making wise the simple" (v. 7). The word "simple" doesn't mean a fool but someone who is uninstructed. The Bible makes us wise and teaches us how to live.

When my mother was a senior at Wheaton College, she took a class from Dr. Lois LeBar called "Christian Education in the Family." On the last day of class, Dr. LeBar tried an experiment. She asked, "How many of you think your parents followed the principles we've discussed in this class in your family?" My mother raised her hand. She thought her parents had followed what she learned in class, and she expected the other students at this Christian college would feel the same way.

She was shocked to see only one other girl out of forty students raise her hand. After a long train ride from Chicago to Brooklyn for Christmas, she found some time alone with my grandfather. She asked him, "Dad, you never made it past eighth grade. How did you learn all these principles of Christian parenting I'm only learning as a senior in college?" My grandfather didn't say a word. He was sitting in his favorite chair. Right next to him was his Bible. He picked up his Bible, looked at it, looked at her, and set his Bible down again. She knew what he meant. She knew the place God's Word had in his life and in their home. "[T]he testimony of the LORD is sure, making wise the simple" (v. 7).

Also "the precepts of the LORD are right, rejoicing the heart" (v. 8). Notice the progression here. God makes us alive through his Word, makes us wise, and makes us glad. And to joy is added discernment: "the commandment of the LORD is pure, enlightening the eyes" (v. 8). Without God's Word, we are in the dark. We stumble through life, walking into walls and falling into one ditch after another. With the light of Scripture, we see ourselves and we see the world. The psalmist says, "Your word is a lamp to my feet and a light to my path" (Psalm 119:105).

In verse 9 David shifts to focus on the relationship between God and his people: "the fear of the LORD is clean, enduring forever." The word "clean" often has the sense of being ritually pure. "The fear of the LORD" (v. 9) purifies God's people. This lasting blessing endures forever, qualifying us to be in his presence for eternity.[9]

Those who are made alive and made wise by God's Word do learn to fear him. Our instinct is to domesticate God and make him manageable. But the Bible teaches us that God is a genuinely frightening God. When Isaiah saw the Lord seated on the throne, with the train of his robe filling the temple, he cried out, "Woe is me! For I am lost" (Isaiah 6:5). When the Apostle John saw the risen Christ in his glory, his knees buckled, and he "fell at his feet as though dead" (Revelation 1:17). The great prophets and apostles were terrified when they came face-to-face with the living God. God is truly fearsome, but he is good. If you know the God of the Bible, you love him and serve him with deep respect and reverence. You can't play games with the Lord God of Israel. His glory is overwhelming. He takes your breath away. He is truly awesome.

David ends with this section with a final word: "the rules of the LORD are true, and righteous altogether" (v. 9).

The Value of God's Word

After rehearsing these six perfections of Scripture, it's no wonder that David sings about the priceless value of God's Word.

> More to be desired are they than gold,
>   even much fine gold;
> sweeter also than honey
>   and drippings of the honeycomb. (19:10)

God's Word is the greatest treasure for those who love him. We love the Bible more than we love money, more than fine gold. God's Word is our greatest pleasure. Sweet honey represents the pleasure of the senses—the finest tasting food, the best-smelling perfume, the most fashionable clothes, the fastest cars, the best new songs. The Bible is better.

Do you feel that way? Do you love the Bible and treasure it? If you know God, his Word will be your treasure and your delight.

The Obedience of the Servant

The final four verses focus our attention on the obedience of God's servant. He has seen the glory of God in the sky; he treasures the Word of God and obeys it.

God's Servant Is Innocent of Hidden Sins

> Moreover, by them [God's rules] is your servant warned;
>> in keeping them there is great reward.
>
> Who can discern his[10] errors?
>> Declare me innocent from hidden faults. (19:11, 12)

I learned Psalm 19 in the King James Version when I was a boy. The KJV says in verse 12, "cleanse thou me from secret faults." But this verse does not say anything about cleansing.[11] John Goldingay writes,

> The verb is not one meaning "cleanse" but . . . "acquit." The OT makes a number of references to acquitting the guilty, but always to affirm that God does not do so and that human beings should not . . . acquitting the guilty is an immoral act.[12]

David is not asking God to forgive his sin. Forgiveness is not mentioned in these verses at all. David is asking God to review his inner life and declare him innocent. As God examines him, a fair review of the evidence will lead to his acquittal.

None of us could say that. Our secret sins are no secret to God. Only Jesus alone obeyed God faithfully in the depths of his heart; as a prophet, David spoke for him. If we have hidden sins, and we do, we need a Savior like Jesus who obeyed with every thought and every glance of his eyes. He can forgive our sin and teach us to obey from the heart.

God's Servant Is Innocent of Willful Sins

God's servant is also innocent of intentional sins. It would be nice if we could say that our sins are all just accidents, that we didn't mean to disobey. But that is not true. We decide to sin more often than we care to admit. David refers to these willful sins.

> Keep back your servant also from presumptuous sins;
>   let them not have dominion over me!
> Then I shall be blameless,
>   and innocent of great transgression. (19:13)

David appeals to God for strength to obey, and he asks to be kept "blameless" (v. 13). As a prophet, David is again speaking for Christ. Jesus was fully God, and he was also fully man, a human being like you and me. As a man he prayed to the Father for strength not to sin during his earthly life. The triumphant words of Psalm 18:32 tell us that this prayer was answered: "God . . . made my way blameless."

The word "blameless" in 19:13 is the same word that describes God's Word in Psalm 19:7, "The law of the LORD is perfect [blameless]." In other words, the servant in Psalm 19 has the same blameless, complete, perfect character as God's Word itself![13] Jesus is in fact the Word of God incarnate, "the radiance of the glory of God and the exact imprint of his nature" (Hebrews 1:3a). After speaking through the Law and the Prophets, God spoke his final word through his Son. Psalm 19 anticipates this stunning reality as the servant shares the same blameless character as the Word of God.

Psalm 19 ends with the servant's closing prayer.

> Let the words of my mouth and the meditation of my heart
>   be acceptable in your sight,
>   O LORD, my rock and my redeemer. (19:14)

Since Jesus was acceptable in God's sight, we can be saved. Since he was innocent, he could die for sinners like you and me. God vindicated Jesus and declared that he is innocent by raising him from the dead.

We need to turn to him and be forgiven. We need to follow him. Jesus left us an example so we could follow in his steps. The sky and the Scriptures teach God's servants to obey him. The skies and the Scripture point us to Christ, the one man who truly obeyed God.

20

The Faith of Israel

PSALM 20

HOW WERE PEOPLE SAVED in the Old Testament? Psalm 20 fills out our picture of Israel's faith in the Messiah centuries before Jesus was born.

To explore this question, we will start with a big picture, looking at faith in the Messiah in the Old Testament as a whole. Then we will narrow the focus to look at Psalm 20 as a whole. After we build this picture frame, we will walk through the details of Psalm 20 to see what this psalm teaches us about Christ.

Faith in the Messiah in the Old Testament

How were people saved in the Old Testament? God's people have always been saved by faith in Christ. The Old Testament contains the Law of Moses, but it does not teach that we are saved by keeping the Law. The writer of Hebrews says plainly, "Without faith it is impossible to please him" (Hebrews 11:6). God's people have always been saved by trusting him.

Peter

What did people in the Old Testament know and believe? More specifically, what did they know about Christ? This is a complex issue, of course, but a number of places in the New Testament tell us what Old Testament believers believed. One of the clearest is 1 Peter 1:10–12.

> Concerning this salvation, the prophets who prophesied about the grace that was to be yours searched and inquired carefully, inquiring what person or time the Spirit of Christ in them was indicating when he predicted the sufferings of Christ and the subsequent glories. It was revealed to them that they were serving not themselves but you, in the things that have now been

announced to you through those who preached the good news to you by the Holy Spirit sent from heaven, things into which angels long to look.

God's people knew that the Messiah would suffer and be glorified. The predictions of Christ's sufferings begin in Genesis 3:15, the first mention of the gospel in the Bible. This is sometimes called the *protoevangelium*, the first gospel. God gave Adam and Eve a ray of hope after sin entered the world. Speaking to the serpent, God said,

> I will put enmity between you and the woman,
>   and between your offspring and her offspring;
> he shall bruise your head,
>   and you shall bruise his heel. (Genesis 3:15)

We see here the first word of Christ's suffering: the serpent would bruise his heel. The predictions of Christ's sufferings then grow throughout the rest of the Old Testament in various ways. For instance, Isaiah 53 comes quickly to mind.[1] The predictions of Christ's glory also begin here: he would triumph by bruising the serpent's head. These predictions of his victory also grow throughout the Old Testament.[2]

What didn't Old Testament believers know? According to the Apostle Peter, they did not know who the Christ would be or when he would come.[3] They knew what would happen to him because they studied their Scriptures. But they did not know his name (his person) or the timing of God's plan. The big message of the New Testament is that the Christ is Jesus of Nazareth. He was born of the Virgin Mary, and he suffered, died, and rose again under Pontius Pilate.

Paul

What does the Apostle Paul have to say about this? In 2 Timothy 3:14, 15 Paul also teaches that the Old Testament teaches faith in Christ. Timothy learned the Old Testament Scriptures from his Jewish mother and grandmother. Paul says to him,

> But as for you, continue in what you have learned and have firmly believed, knowing from whom you learned it and how from childhood you have been acquainted with the sacred writings, which are able to make you wise for salvation through faith in Christ Jesus.

The Scriptures that Timothy had from infancy are the books of the Old Testament. The New Testament had not yet been written. But according to

Paul the Old Testament teaches salvation by faith! And the object of this Old Testament faith is Christ Jesus.

Jesus

Jesus himself said that the Old Testament taught about his own suffering and glory as the Christ. Luke 24 records some of Jesus' last words with his disciples.

> Then he said to them, "These are my words that I spoke to you while I was still with you, that everything written about me in the Law of Moses and the Prophets and the Psalms must be fulfilled." Then he opened their minds to understand the Scriptures, and said to them, "Thus it is written, that the Christ should suffer and on the third day rise from the dead, and that repentance and forgiveness of sins should be proclaimed in his name to all nations, beginning from Jerusalem." (Luke 24:44–47)

The Law and the Prophets are the two main sections of the Old Testament. Grammatically, Jesus' words here include the Psalms as a part of the Prophets. According to Jesus, each part of the Old Testament Scriptures testifies about his suffering, death, and glory.

Abraham

The first time faith is mentioned in the Bible, it is centered on the Messiah. God had promised Abram that he would bless all the nations of the world through him and his Descendant or Seed (Genesis 12:1–3; 13:16). But Abram was childless; it seemed like God could not keep his promise.

> After these things the word of the LORD came to Abram in a vision: "Fear not, Abram, I am your shield; your reward shall be very great." But Abram said, "O Lord GOD, what will you give me, for I continue childless, and the heir of my house is Eliezer of Damascus?" And Abram said, "Behold, you have given me no offspring, and a member of my household will be my heir." And behold, the word of the LORD came to him: "This man shall not be your heir; your very own son shall be your heir." And he brought him outside and said, "Look toward heaven, and number the stars, if you are able to number them." Then he said to him, "So shall your offspring be." And he believed the LORD, and he counted it to him as righteousness. (Genesis 15:1–6)

This is one of the landmarks of the Old Testament, a text that is the taproot for salvation by faith. Abram was declared righteous on the basis of his faith. Abram's faith looked forward to the Messiah. His one Offspring (or

Seed) would become as numerous as the stars of the heavens, and all nations would be blessed through him. Walter Kaiser makes this comment about Genesis 15:6:

> And what Abram placed his faith in was the content of the promise made originally in Gen 12:2–3, which focused on the Seed, or the Messiah who was to come. As a result, God added this up and credited this belief to Abram's account as one who was "righteousness" (Gen 15:6b).[4]

Abram's faith is the same as the justifying faith of New Testament believers. This Old Testament "faith may not possess full understanding of the details of redemptive work and the atoning sacrifice. Yet in essence it is trust in the Savior sent by God."[5]

All this helps us begin to put together a picture of what God's people believed before Jesus was born. The Scriptures prophesied the suffering and glory of the Messiah from the opening chapters of Genesis on. The details became progressively clearer, of course. As they read and studied the Scriptures, Old Testament believers put their hope in the Messiah, the man God would raise up to defeat Satan and bless the nations of the world.

Faith in the Messiah in Psalm 20

Understanding the faith of Israel helps us to understand Psalm 20. This psalm was given to the choirmaster to teach the people to hope in the Messiah. The heart of Psalm 20 is the confidence that God will save "his anointed" and give him victory (20:6).[6]

What King?

Who is this anointed king? Some think this psalm was a worship liturgy before the kings of Israel went out to war.[7] But the introduction does not give us much background for the psalm. In the end we simply don't know when or why it was written. This could have been used when a king went out to war, but there is no reason why it could not have been written as a prophecy of events far in the future. Calvin concludes,

> The object, therefore which David had expressly in view was, to exhort all the children of God to cherish such a holy solicitude about the kingdom of Christ, as would stir them up to continual prayer in its behalf.[8]

The book of Psalms itself gives us the context for reading Psalm 20. Psalms 1, 2 are the introduction for the whole book of Psalms and set the stage for the psalms that follow. Psalm 2 introduces us to Christ, the King God has anointed and set on the throne of Heaven. God rescued him, and he rules the nations with a rod of iron. In a real sense the rest of the book of Psalms is about this king, his kingdom, and his people. The promise of a king in Psalm 2 is a key for understanding the whole book of Psalms.[9] When we read about a king in Psalm 20, we should remember Psalm 2 and have this eternal King in mind.[10]

Psalm 20 also fits together closely with the more immediate context of the psalms that come right before and after it.

> The Psalm has a number of verbal links with Ps. 18, so that we might reckon that the psalms have been (almost) juxtaposed so as to suggest that Ps. 18 offers testimony that the blessings of Ps. 20 have come about, or that Ps. 20 promises that God will do again what Ps. 18 testifies to.[11]

In Psalm 18:6 the king calls to God in his trouble or distress; in Psalm 20 the people pray for the king in his "day of trouble" (20:1).[12] In both psalms God answers the king from Heaven, supports him, and saves him (Psalm 18:9,13, 35, 50; 20:2, 6). Psalm 20 is looking at the victory of Psalm 18 from a different angle. In Psalm 20 we hear the voice of the people praying for the King and trusting in him.

David's King

The introduction tells us that this is "A PSALM OF DAVID." The preposition "of" has a range of meanings. In Hebrew it could mean that this psalm is about David, written for David, written to David, or written by David. When Jesus quoted Psalm 110 in the temple (Matthew 22:43–45), he understood the phrase "of David" to mean "written by David." Following Jesus' example, it seems best to assume that when a psalm is introduced by the words "of David," it means David wrote it unless there is good reason to think otherwise.

If King David wrote Psalm 20, then he is writing about another king— his descendant, Christ the Messiah. He mentions this coming King in Psalm 18:50, "Great salvation he brings to his king, and shows steadfast love to his anointed, to David and his offspring forever." Here in Psalm 20 he is speaking to this other King, "May the LORD answer *you* in the day of trouble" (20:1).

David is writing about Christ. King David and all the people put their faith in him. David prays for Christ, his great Son who would be born one thousand years later. David hopes in Christ, "Now I know that the LORD saves his anointed" (20:6a). And verse 9 tells us that David submits to Christ: "O Lord, save the king! May he answer us when we call."

God will answer the King, and the King in turn will answer the people. With that word "we," King David includes himself with the rest of the people to say that he will call on this greater King. A king does not appeal to someone lesser than himself—he commands them to do what he wants. A king only appeals to someone greater, a greater king. With that word "we," David includes himself with the people who call on this King. David recognized that his Offspring would be greater than he.

This is the point that Jesus made clearly when he quoted Psalm 110 in the temple. The beginning of Psalm 110 reads, "A PSALM OF DAVID. The LORD says to my Lord: 'Sit at my right hand, until I make your enemies your footstool'" (Psalm 110 introduction, v. 1). David himself calls the Messiah "my Lord," submitting to him and recognizing his superior greatness.

So at the heart of the Old Testament great King David put his trust in a greater King. In Psalm 20 David submits to Christ and looks forward to his kingdom.

The Specific Faith of Psalm 20

We have seen that Old Testament believers were saved by faith in Christ. We have looked at faith in Christ in Psalm 20 as a whole. This brings us to our last question. What do we learn more specifically about the Messiah in Psalm 20? Based on Psalm 20, what did God's people know about Christ before he was born? How does Psalm 20 fill out what we know about Jesus ourselves?

Psalm 20 is the people's prayer for their King. Strictly speaking, the people are speaking to the King, not to God; so as a prayer it is an indirect prayer. The people are telling the anointed King what they want God to do for him. It may seem strange to think about praying for Christ—after all, Jesus is our High Priest who prays for us. But Jesus was a human being like we are. As a man he came to walk the hardest road any man ever walked. You can be sure that Mary prayed for him when he was a baby. And for a thousand years before he was born, faithful Jews prayed for him when they sang this psalm.

A Prayer for the King's Protection

Psalm 20 starts with a prayer for the King's protection.

> May the LORD answer you in the day of trouble!
> May the name of the God of Jacob protect you!
> May he send you help from the sanctuary

> and give you support from Zion!
> May he remember all your offerings
>   and regard with favor your burnt sacrifices! *Selah* (20:1–3)

The Messiah would have a hard and troubled life. As the people prayed for Christ with the words of this psalm, they should have learned that the coming King would be pressed so hard that he would need God to intervene and send help from Heaven.[13] The Messiah of the Psalms is a suffering Messiah.

In fact, Jesus' life was full of hardship. He was a refugee; his parents fled to Egypt shortly after he was born. The U.N. recently announced that more than a million refugees fled Syria in the months just prior to this writing. When you see pictures of families who have lost everything and left home, think of Christ. This was the pattern of his life. Isaiah said of him, "He was despised and rejected by men; a man of sorrows, and acquainted with grief" (Isaiah 53:3).

Psalm 20 tells us Jesus would respond to this trouble by turning to God in prayer. When the people say, "May the LORD answer you" (v. 1), this implies that Christ called out to God for help. Jesus was known as a man of prayer. He rose early to pray; he prayed through the night on occasion. In the Garden of Gethsemane he sweat drops of blood. Although Jesus was alone at that moment, the prayers of God's people had come up to the Father for centuries on his behalf in the words of Psalm 20. Andrew Bonar put it this way:

> This Psalm is the prayer which the church might be supposed offering up, had all the redeemed stood by the cross, or in Gethsemane, in full consciousness of what he was doing there. Messiah, in reading these words, would know that he had elsewhere the sympathy he longed for, when he said to the three disciples, "Tarry ye here, and watch with me.[14]

Peter, James, and John fell asleep in the garden, but millions of Old Testament believers had already prayed for him in the words of Psalm 20, asking God to hear his agonized cries and respond.

The King's Success Brings Joy to His People

Psalm 20 continues with the confidence and joy God's people have in their Messiah.

> May he grant you your heart's desire
>   and fulfill all your plans!
> May we shout for joy over your salvation,
>   and in the name of our God set up our banners!
> May the LORD fulfill all your petitions! (20:4, 5)

Why would the people celebrate when God saved their anointed King? The King represents the people, and their life is bound up in his. If a king wins a great battle, the nation has won a great battle. If the king loses, the whole nation is defeated. So by rescuing the King, God is rescuing and blessing the people as a whole. Psalm 20 taught men and women in Old Testament times that their lives were bound up in the life of the Messiah. He would be their representative. His victory would be their victory. His "salvation" would be their "joy" (v. 5).

This was fulfilled in the life of Jesus, of course. When Jesus was preparing his disciples for his death he said to them, "I will see you again, and your hearts will rejoice, and no one will take your joy from you" (John 16:22). After the Resurrection they were filled with joy (Luke 24:52). And everyone who comes to Christ finds joy; joy is the emotion of salvation. We sing for joy because God saved our King, and we are saved with him.

The bond of love between the Messiah and his people is so close that they trust him completely. We do not trust our leaders. Our system of government in the United States is set up with checks and balances to keep our leaders under control. Lord Acton, the British historian, said, "Power tends to corrupt, and absolute power corrupts absolutely. Great men are almost always bad men." History has proved him right time and again.

But this Messiah is a leader we can trust. The people give the King a blank check, asking God to "fulfill all your plans" and "fulfill all your petitions" (vv. 4, 5). What kind of man is he if every plan and purpose of his heart can be trusted! He is a good man; he is a perfect man; he is a godly man. He is God become man; he is our Savior.

Christian, Jesus' plans and his thoughts for you are nothing but good all the time. He thinks about you constantly and prays for you in Heaven. The Bible says that "Christ Jesus . . . is at the right hand of God . . . interceding for us" (Romans 8:34). You can trust him. You can rest and relax. Your King has your best in mind, even in hard things and days of trouble. Novelist Ann Tatlock tells this story:

> There was a rabbi who lived in Poland a long time ago. I think hundreds of years ago. And one day he was out with his students having a picnic or something up on a big hill that overlooked the town. While they were there, a bunch of people came riding into town—people who hated the Jews— and started killing everyone, even the women and children. And here was the rabbi and his students looking down from the hill and seeing it all happen. Well, of course they were horrified. And the rabbi said, "If only I were God." And one of his students said, "If you were God, what would you do

differently?" And the rabbi said, "If I were God, I wouldn't do anything differently. If I were God, I would understand."[15]

Someday, when we are with God, we will understand his plans for us. In the meantime we can trust Jesus with our life. As Jesus prays for us, we can say with Psalm 20, "May the LORD fulfill all your petitions!" (20:5b). There has never been a sliver of a second when Jesus wanted anything second best for us. And since he is God, he is able to work out all things for our good and his glory.

Faith in the Messiah's Deliverance

Psalm 20 ends with David's great confidence in God's plans for his Son, the great King who was to come.

> Now I know that the LORD saves his anointed;
>   he will answer him from his holy heaven
>   with the saving might of his right hand.
> Some trust in chariots and some in horses,
>   but we trust in the name of the LORD our God.
> They collapse and fall,
>   but we rise and stand upright.
>
> O LORD, save the king!
>   May he answer us when we call. (20:6–9)

As a prophet, David looked forward with the eyes of faith to see the day when God would save his Christ. Did he understand the details of the Messiah's life? Did he know when he would come? Did he even know his name? He didn't know any of these things. But he did know that God would raise up one of his descendants to be the Messiah and sit on his throne. He knew this King would suffer and that God would rescue him. He prayed for his great Son; he hoped in his great Son; he trusted his great Son; he submitted to his great Son.

We know his name, and we know when he came. His name is Jesus of Nazareth. He was crucified under Pontius Pilate, but God raised him from the dead as King and Lord. The New Testament fills out the picture of his life.

Do you trust him? God's people have always been saved by faith in Christ. You need to believe in him today.

21

Jesus' Joy

THE NATION OF ISRAEL faces danger from almost every direction. Hezbollah threatens from their strongholds in southern Lebanon. To the northwest, Syria resents Israel's seizure of the Golan Heights. To the east, Jordan has a peace treaty with Israel, but the West Bank simmers with hostility. Militants in Gaza fire rockets into Israel. Hamas is to the south. Farther south, the ongoing unrest in Egypt has allowed militants to gain power in the Sinai.

These dangers are not new. In fact what we see today is a repetition of what David and the other kings of Israel faced for centuries. Israel is situated at the hub of three continents—Asia, Europe, and Africa—and sits on the major trade routes between Egypt and Mesopotamia. The kings of Israel faced pressure from every side. Warfare was a way of life in ancient times.

This history of war is the general historical context behind Psalm 21. The people of Israel lived in a dangerous world and praised God for saving their king. Why? Because as the king goes, so go the people. The king trusted God, God answered him with power, and through his salvation the whole nation was saved.

You may have noticed that Psalm 21 echoes the last words of Psalm 20, "O LORD, save the king!" These two psalms are paired together; they match like two candlesticks. In Psalm 20 the people asked God to save the king. In Psalm 21 the people praise God because he has saved the king.[1]

God did rescue David many times. But Psalm 21 quickly points us forward to Jesus. King David is writing about another King. Many Jews near the time of Christ understood that Psalm 21 points to the Messiah. In fact, the word "king" in verse 1 is translated as *king messiah* in two ancient Jewish sources—the Targum[2] and the Talmud. Around AD 1100 a prominent rabbi named Rashi suggested that this translation be dropped, saying, "Our old doctors interpreted this psalm of King Messiah, but in order to meet the Schismatics [that is, the Christians] it is better to understand it of David himself."[3]

During the Reformation John Calvin wrote,

> But, above all, it was the design of the Holy Spirit here to direct the minds of the faithful to Christ, who was the end and perfection of this kingdom, and to teach them that they could not be saved except under the head which God himself had appointed over them.[4]

We should hear Jesus our King speaking in Psalm 21. Christ rejoices in the way God saved him. Psalm 21 begins and ends with praise for God's saving power.

> O LORD, in your strength the king rejoices,
>   and in your salvation how greatly he exults!
> You have given him his heart's desire
>   and have not withheld the request of his lips. *Selah* (21:1, 2)

In verse 13 we read,

> Be exalted, O LORD, in your strength!
>   We will sing and praise your power.

These brackets set the tone for the psalm—a celebration of God's strength in saving the King. The trajectory of the psalm moves from Christ's joy to our joy. When God saved Christ, he saved us. Our lives are bound up in his. His victory is our victory. The King's joy is our joy. The rest of the psalm fills this out. God's strength blesses the King (21:3–7), and God's strength fights for the King (21:8–12).

God's Strength Blesses the King

Verse 3 introduces the blessings God poured out on Christ.

> For you meet him with rich blessings;
>   you set a crown of fine gold upon his head.

The word for the "crown" God sets on his head is not a king's royal crown. This crown or wreath is a gift to honor visiting dignitaries or guests at a banquet. They were made out of leaves, flowers, or precious metal. This is not a royal crown, although he certainly does rule. The point here is that God publicly honored the king and showed his love for him. "This rich gift, then, is a sign of the honor bestowed on the king by God—an open sign of divine approval for all to see."[5]

How did God honor him? David lists three ways God blessed the Messiah with his mighty power.

Life

First, God blessed the King with eternal life.

> He asked life of you; you gave it to him,
>   length of days forever and ever. (21:4)

The first half of this verse could refer to David. He was a warrior-king, and his life was in danger many times as he went into battle. The second half of the verse, though, can only refer to Christ, the Messiah who was to come. "Length of days" (v. 4) by itself already means a long life. By adding the phrase "forever and ever" (v. 4), David takes this beyond the lifespan of a human king.[6]

God had promised David that his great Son, the Messiah, would be an eternal King. In 2 Samuel God promised to David, "I will establish the throne of his kingdom forever," and again, "Your throne shall be established forever" (2 Samuel 7:13, 16).[7] David referred to this promise as he wrote Psalm 21. The Scriptures say that "Christ, being raised from the dead, will never die again; death no longer has dominion over him" (Romans 6:9). Through the resurrection, God has given "length of days forever and ever" to Jesus Christ (v. 4). So he will always be King. He will reign and rule over the universe for all eternity, and his kingdom will never end.

Glory

Secondly, God also gave him exalted glory.

> His glory is great through your salvation;
>   splendor and majesty you bestow on him. (21:5)

The word "glory" means "to be heavy" and by extension "to be important." Glory is "that asset which makes people or individuals, and even objects, impressive."[8] God has made Christ impressive, important, weighty, glorious in this world. You can't avoid him.

Verse 5 tells us how God gave Jesus great glory. David says, "His glory is great *through* your salvation." In other words, the way God made Jesus Christ great was by saving him. For God to save him, Jesus first had to suffer. Then God gave Jesus a magnitude of glory that he could not have had unless God had saved him. Because of the cross and resurrection, Jesus is more famous, more impressive, more important, more glorious than if he had lived his life in peace. He is more glorious than if his disciples had rescued him. He is more glorious than if he had been a successful general.[9]

It is no accident that Psalm 22, with its description of Jesus' agony, comes right after this one in the Psalter. God made Christ great by allowing him to suffer at the hands of evil men, even unto death, and rescuing him. "His glory is great *through* your salvation."

Why is Jesus more glorious because of the cross and resurrection? Through the cross God displayed Jesus' perfect obedience. A true son obeys his father, and Jesus obeyed to the point of death, even death on a cross (Philippians 2:6–8). Through his resurrection he was declared to be the Son of God with power (Romans 1:4). Jesus is more glorious because he is now the firstborn from the dead, a second Adam, the founder of a new race of human beings. This glory would not have been possible if God had not allowed him to suffer and die and then saved him with his power.

God works the same way in our lives too. God gives glory to those who belong to Christ by saving us through his power, not through our own strength. God allows suffering in our lives so that his power can be clearly displayed in us. God brings us to a dead end so that the answer will obviously be from him and not from our own planning. God will allow hard things into our lives to make it clear that we follow him because we truly love him, not because he has bought our obedience with his blessings. He honors us by saving us in times of trouble.

Presence

Thirdly, God blessed his King with his presence.

> For you make him most blessed forever;
> you make him glad with the joy of your presence. (21:6)

God's presence does not seem like a great blessing to those who do not love him. It is like receiving a fruitcake at Christmas—can I save this to regift next year? They love the things God gives but not God himself. They want God to provide for them, to forgive them, to protect their children, to heal them, and to give them countless other blessings, but they do not want God himself. So they are not excited at the thought of being in God's presence. They wouldn't be happy in Heaven because being with God is the joy of Heaven.

But God's people love him. They are thankful for the good things he gives, but their hearts are set on God himself. Would you be happy if you went to Heaven and it was cooler than you could have ever imagined? You saw a city that took your breath away. You met scientists like Isaac Newton and artists like Michelangelo. You saw your grandparents. You walked on streets of gold—you kicked huge nuggets like gravel. There's only one catch—God wasn't there. You had everything good you could imagine but not him. Would you be happy?

God himself is the greatest blessing for which we can hope. Without him the best things we can imagine are nothing. But to be in his presence is to be "most blessed forever" (v. 6): life, joy, delight, satisfaction. As a man, Jesus loved his Father and longed to return to his presence. The universe was created through him. He could have had anything he wanted, yet his great joy was to be in his Father's presence. And it is our joy too if we belong to him.

When God commanded the priests to bless the people of Israel, he told them to bless Israel with his presence, the greatest blessing.

> The LORD spoke to Moses, saying, "Speak to Aaron and his sons, saying, Thus you shall bless the people of Israel: you shall say to them,
>
> > The LORD bless you and keep you;
> > the LORD make his face to shine upon you and be gracious to you;
> > the LORD lift up his countenance upon you and give you peace.
>
> So shall they put my name upon the people of Israel, and I will bless them." (Numbers 6:22–27)

David says later in the Psalms,

> One thing have I asked of the LORD,
> that will I seek after:
> that I may dwell in the house of the LORD
> all the days of my life,
> to gaze upon the beauty of the LORD
> and to inquire in his temple. (Psalm 27:4)

If we love God and long to see him, we have a strong weapon in the fight against sin. When we are tempted to sin, Satan is baiting us with something we want. It's no use pretending that we don't want to sin. You do—you fight against your own real desires. That is why sin is tempting. How do we fight against something we want? How do we go beyond modifying behavior to dealing with sin in our heart? We fight this wrong desire with something we want even more.

Jesus said in the Beatitudes, "Blessed are the pure in heart, for they shall see God" (Matthew 5:8). If we love God and get excited about the thought of being in his presence, we can quote this verse to ourselves and say, "I want to see God. I want to see God more than I want this bike I could steal, more than I want this relationship with a married man, more than I want to watch porn on my iPod, more than I want another drink, more than I want guys to look at me, more than I want to text the gossip I just heard. I want to be pure in heart because I want to see God." The Apostle John writes, "We know that when he appears we shall be like him, because we shall see him as he is. And everyone who thus hopes in him purifies himself as he is pure" (1 John 3:2, 3).

One of our goals in worship in our local churches is to see Jesus more clearly so that he is more beautiful and desirable to us. If we have a small, dinky Jesus, we will not want him more than we want the temptations that are pulling at us. When we come together, we need to have our eyes opened to see the beauty and majesty and glory of Christ more and more clearly. Wrong desires are real, and we won't defeat them with a small thumbnail view of Christ. We need a 50 megapixel view of Christ so we can expand the picture to fill our vision. We can learn techniques to manage sin—where not to look, where not to go—and this is important. But until we fight our sinful desires with a greater desire, we will not win the battle in our hearts. Christ was blessed with the joy of God's presence. This joy is set before us, too, and it is a powerful weapon against sin.

In verse 7 David gives the reason these three great blessings were given to the King, the Messiah.

> For the king trusts in the LORD,
>   and through the steadfast love of the Most High he shall not be moved.

This verse describes a mutual faithfulness. On the one hand, "the king trusts in the LORD" (v. 7). God answered Christ because of his faith. He placed his life in God's hands, trusted God's strength, and believed that God would save him. In return, "steadfast love" (v. 7) is God's loyalty to his covenant. Christ trusted God, and he was not moved because God is trustworthy.

God's Strength Fights for the King

Up to this point David described the blessings God gives to Christ. Now the psalm focuses on the way God fights on Christ's behalf. God establishes his kingdom by crushing his enemies. We first saw this in Psalm 2 when God terrifies the King's enemies.

The violence of these verses might catch us by surprise. We are not used to thinking about God's wrath as one of the ways he blesses Christ and his people. But this is part of God's full salvation. Not only did he crown Jesus with honor, he takes up his cause by destroying his enemies.

No nation can be safe and secure when it has strong enemies. For instance, South Korea has emerged over the last fifty years with a vibrant economy and strong political role in the Pacific Rim and beyond. But in spite of all these advances South Korea will never be safe as long as North Korea has the fourth largest army in the world. God makes the kingdom of Christ safe by destroying his enemies. His great power protects the King and his people.

The gospel means both salvation to God's people and judgment on his enemies. Martin Luther saw this as he taught on the Lord's Prayer. When we pray, "Your kingdom come, your will be done," we "must put all the opposition to this in one pile and say: 'Curses, maledictions and disgrace upon every other name and every other kingdom. May they be ruined and torn apart and may all their schemes and wisdom and plans run aground.'"[10] If we pray for the kingdom of God to grow in this world, by definition we are praying for the kingdom of Satan to be destroyed. We cannot love Christ and at the same time wish his enemies well. Victory for the church means utter defeat for Satan and the kingdom of darkness.

David mentions three stages to God's judgment: discovery, destruction, and defeat.

Discovery

First, God searches out and discovers the enemies of Christ.

> Your hand will find out all your enemies;
>   your right hand will find out those who hate you. (21:8)

The word "find" appears twice in this one verse. If you are against Jesus Christ, you cannot stay hidden from God.

God takes the way we treat his Messiah personally. These enemies are not just Christ's enemies. David is speaking to God, and he says they are "your enemies" (v. 8). God so completely identifies with his Christ that those who are against him are his enemies.

Don't fool yourself. If you are against Jesus, you are against God. Some people like to think of themselves as "spiritual." They believe that God exists, but they don't want to follow Jesus. If you don't want to obey Jesus, you don't want to obey God. If you have a problem with serving Jesus, you have a problem with God. God searches out and finds those who are against him. There is no hiding and no mistaken identity. He knows who you are.

Destruction

The second stage of God's judgment is destruction.

> You will make them as a blazing oven
>   when you appear.
> The LORD will swallow them up in his wrath,
>   and fire will consume them. (21:9)

This is a dreadful judgment. It was meant to be a sober warning to God's people as they sang this song. Everyone who reads these words should examine their hearts to be sure they are not numbered among the enemies of God. If you are a believer, these words should teach you the fear of the Lord, to have a healthy respect for his holiness and the power of his anger. This is not just an Old Testament idea—this is the message of the whole Bible.

> Therefore let us be grateful for receiving a kingdom that cannot be shaken, and thus let us offer to God acceptable worship, with reverence and awe, for our God is a consuming fire. (Hebrews 12:28, 29)

Not only does God destroy his enemies, he destroys their descendants too.

> You will destroy their descendants from the earth,
>   and their offspring from among the children of man. (21:10)

The idea here is that the offspring are like the parents. The children are just as guilty as the fathers because they too rebel against God. God does not indiscriminately sweep away the innocent with the guilty.[11] Unless God's grace steps in, they will be just like their parents.

God is at work destroying the enemies of Christ in our lifetimes. Many of us remember how God answered millions of prayers in 1989 to overthrow Nicolae Ceausescu, the dictator of Romania who persecuted the church.

> Another persecutor of the Church who challenged God was Samora Machel, the first dictator of Marxist Mozambique. . . . Thousands of churches in Mozambique were closed, confiscated, "nationalized," claimed and padlocked, burnt down or boarded up. Missionaries were expelled. . . . Evangelism was forbidden. Bibles were ceremonially burnt and tens of thousands of Christians, including many pastors and elders, were shipped off to concentration camps—most were never seen again.

. . . On 19 October 1986, while several churches were specifically praying for God to stop persecution in Mozambique, Machel's Soviet Tupelov aircraft crashed in a violent thunderstorm.[12]

Defeat

The third stage of God's judgment is that his enemy's plans will be completely defeated.

> Though they plan evil against you,
>   though they devise mischief, they will not succeed.
> For you will put them to flight;
>   you will aim at their faces with your bows. (21:11, 12)

No matter how well they plan, God's enemies will fail. God's great power will defend his King and utterly defeat them.

This happened literally with Samora Machel as he died.

> The plane crashed 200 metres within South Africa's boundary with Mozambique. Amidst the wreckage the marxist plans for overthrowing the government of Malawi were discovered and published. Not only had God judged a blasphemer and a persecutor, but He had also saved a country from persecution.[13]

David ends where he began, celebrating God's great strength.

> Be exalted, O LORD, in your strength!
>   We will sing and praise your power. (21:13)

God's great power saved and exalted Christ. His power gives joy for his people and judges his enemies. Does that make your heart sing? I pray that it does.

22

The Psalm of the Cross

PSALM 22

PSALM 22 stands out as perhaps the clearest and most compelling picture of Jesus' death and resurrection in the Old Testament. As Charles Spurgeon said, "This is beyond all others The Psalm of the Cross."[1]

We should make several points by way of introduction. First, Christ himself connected his death and resurrection to this psalm. Jesus prayed the first words of Psalm 22 from the cross: "My God, my God, why have you forsaken me?" (Matthew 27:46). Jesus was not only saying that God had abandoned him, he quoted these words in particular so we would understand his suffering and death in the light of Psalm 22. It is also possible that Christ's last words on the cross echo the last words of this psalm as well. The words "It is finished" (John 19:30) could be an allusion or loose quotation of Psalm 22:31, "he has done it."[2] If that is the case, then Jesus was saying that everything God promised in the second half of this psalm was as good as done. His suffering would save the world, and the nations would turn to God.

Psalm 22 is prophetic. In the words of the Apostle Peter, this psalm foretells "the sufferings of Christ and the subsequent glories" (1 Peter 1:11). David is the human author, of course, but nothing we know about David's life can account for the agony and victory of this psalm.[3] And in fact the writer of Hebrews quotes Psalm 22 as the words of Jesus himself (Hebrews 2:12). So David is writing as prophet, describing the agony of Christ's suffering and the victory that followed.

Psalm 22 is also emotional. This is one of the most intimate and personal connections we have with Jesus as he suffered for our sins. The Gospels tell us what happened to Jesus physically; they also give us his seven last words from the cross.[4] But through the prophet David, the Holy Spirit tells us what Jesus was thinking and feeling inside as a human being like us. He felt abandoned, surrounded, desperate, and overwhelmed; then his heart rocketed up in joy as God answered. Our Lord Jesus opens up his heart to us in this psalm. We are standing on holy ground.

The shape of this psalm is straightforward. The first half is Jesus' cry for help (22:1–21); the second half is Jesus' song of praise (22:22–31). The center point or hinge is at the end of verse 21, "you have rescued [ESV margin, answered] me." God did not abandon Christ to the grave. After Calvary comes Easter.

Jesus' Cry for Help

Christ calls out to God for help in the first half of Psalm 22. As a human being, he was stretched to the limit, pushed beyond the red line.

This description of Jesus' suffering is powerful because he is one of us. We can identify with his agony because these are the thoughts and feelings of a person like you and me.

Anguish

There were two parts to Jesus' anguish: he was abandoned by God, and he was mocked by man.

> My God, my God, why have you forsaken me?
>   Why are you so far from saving me, from the words of my groaning?
> O my God, I cry by day, but you do not answer,
>   and by night, but I find no rest. (22:1, 2)

Jesus felt that God had abandoned him. But even so, he still held on to God. Three times in these opening verses he calls out to "my God." God is his God. God seemed to have turned his back. But by faith Jesus still called out to God, even as he died.

Have you ever felt like God has abandoned you? When I was growing up, I used to lie awake in bed at night, terrified that my family would abandon me. I don't know why I thought that—I grew up in a warm, loving home. Maybe this is a normal childhood fear; maybe this happened because my parents were missionaries and we moved a lot. But for whatever reason I would wake up terrified and sneak to my parents' room to make sure they were still there. I can still remember the absolute horror that gripped my heart when I thought I might be left all alone.

How much worse for Jesus! He had enjoyed perfect unity and love with his Father for all eternity up to that point. "I and the Father are one," Jesus said (John 10:30). He had never known a shadow of separation or spiritual distance from his Father. Now he called out to God, but there was no answer.

The idea that Jesus was truly abandoned by God is so disturbing that people have suggested various theories to explain what this means. Some think that Jesus was just calling attention to Psalm 22 as an example of the sort of anguish he was in. Others suggest that Jesus felt alone but was not truly alone.[5] But Jesus was utterly alone as he carried our sins. The Scriptures say that God is too pure to look upon evil (Habakkuk 1:13). Jesus drank down the sewage of all our sin and our guilt—he actually became sin for us (2 Corinthians 5:21). At that moment God the Father truly turned his back on him, forsaking him. It is an eternal mystery how this could happen. The perfect unity of the Trinity was broken for a moment as God the Father turned away from God the Son. This cannot be! Yet for a moment it was so. The Father turned away from him.

Jesus was truly forsaken so that you and I would never be forsaken. We may feel like God has turned his back on us, like our prayers are bouncing off the ceiling, but if we belong to Christ we have his promise, "I am with you always" (Matthew 28:20). Jesus was truly alone so we would never have to be. We need to believe his promise.

Jesus strengthened his faith by remembering God's faithfulness.

> Yet you are holy,
>   enthroned on the praises of Israel.
> In you our fathers trusted;
>   they trusted, and you delivered them.
> To you they cried and were rescued;
>   in you they trusted and were not put to shame. (22:3–5)

The word "trusted" is repeated three times in these verses. The fathers trusted, trusted, and continued to trust God—and God delivered them. When Jesus was in his darkest hour, he strengthened his heart by remembering the way God had been faithful to those who had gone before.

Jesus is our example here. When we feel like God has abandoned us, we can remember how God has been faithful to others. He was faithful to the fathers, to Abraham, Isaac, and Jacob. He was faithful to Paul, and to Peter, James, and John. Lisa and I can remember God's faithfulness to people in our lives. When I was in high school, my brother was in a truck that was hit by a train; the accident left him in a coma for five days. Last fall my brother and his wife welcomed their first grandchild into the family—God has been faithful to him. On the other hand, God also carries us when things don't turn out the way we want. He was faithful to our friends Marc and Lori when they lost their little boy, Gabriel. He has also been faithful to our friend, Anne, through her very sad divorce. Whatever our circumstances, we can look back to the way God has cared for others and take courage. He is faithful.

The second part of Jesus' anguish was the mocking he endured. God may have been silent, but his enemies were not.

> All who see me mock me;
>   they make mouths at me; they wag their heads;
> "He trusts in the LORD; let him deliver him;
>   let him rescue him, for he delights in him!" (Psalm 22:7, 8)

This is exactly what happened when Jesus hung on the cross. The Gospels tell us that "those who passed by hurled insults at him" (Matthew 27:39, NIV). Jesus wasn't bulletproof. As a man these insults hurt. He felt it. Jesus was silent on the cross and didn't respond, but David tells us here what these insults did to him inside. They made him feel subhuman. "I am a worm and not a man" (22:6). If you have been insulted for the sake of Christ, even to the point where you get deeply depressed, it is a great encouragement to know that Jesus has felt that way too.

As he wrestled with his thoughts and feelings, Jesus strengthened himself again with what he knew about God. "[Y]ou are he who took me from the womb," he says (22:9). God had been with him since birth. This God would continue to care for him even now.

Appeal

After the anguish of God's silence and man's scorn, Christ appeals to God.

In verses 11–18 we are looking down from the cross with Jesus. Through the Spirit, David describes the vicious torture that completed Jesus' sacrifice, the suffering he went through because he loves you and me. He did not pray for escape even though he could have called ten thousand angels to ride on the wings of the wind and set him free. Instead Jesus begged God to be near him: "Be not far from me" (22:11). The psalmist says elsewhere, "[Y]our steadfast love is better than life" (Psalm 63:3). Jesus lived this out on the cross where he treasured God's presence more than anything else.

Notice also that Christ was surrounded.

> Many bulls encompass me;
>   strong bulls of Bashan surround me;

they open wide their mouths at me,
  like a ravening and roaring lion. (22:12, 13)

As Jesus looked down from the cross, the men around him were like violent beasts. Bashan is known today as the Golan Heights. Because of the topography of Israel, this area receives more rain and provides better grazing for cattle. So bulls of Bashan were bigger and stronger than others—and more dangerous.[6] These men will trample him like bulls or tear him apart like a lion.

And Jesus was powerless.

I am poured out like water,
  and all my bones are out of joint;
my heart is like wax;
  it is melted within my breast;
my strength is dried up like a potsherd,
  and my tongue sticks to my jaws;
  you lay me in the dust of death. (22:14, 15)

Think of this! The one who holds all things together (Colossians 1:17) had every joint dislocated. The one who gives living water (John 4:10–15) was dried up like a broken clay pot. And this is God's doing. Speaking in the Spirit, David says, "[Y]ou lay me in the dust of death" (v. 15). His God has done this to him. And Isaiah says, "It was the will of the LORD to crush him" (Isaiah 53:10).

And in God's will, he was still surrounded.

For dogs encompass me;
  a company of evildoers encircles me;
they have pierced my hands and feet—
I can count all my bones—
they stare and gloat over me;
they divide my garments among them,
  and for my clothing they cast lots. (22:16–18)

The piercing of Jesus' hands and feet points to the exact method of his death on a cross.[7] As he hung there, suspended between the earth and sky, he could count his bones as his skin was stretched over the dislocated joints. Artists who paint the scene at Calvary usually put a modest towel around Jesus' waist. But he was naked and could not cover himself. People laughed and stared and gloated. The soldiers who had his clothes gambled for them—after all, he would never need them again.

So what does this mean for us? In the Psalms we have seen that the life of the people is bound up in the life of the king. The people are blessed through him. The people are saved through his salvation. Christ suffered this way for you and me. What do we say to such love?

> Alas! and did my Savior bleed
> And did my Sovereign die?
> Would He devote that sacred head
> For such a worm as I?
>
> Was it for crimes that I had done
> He groaned upon the tree?
> Amazing pity! grace unknown!
> And love beyond degree!
>
> But drops of grief can ne'er repay
> The debt of love I owe:
> Here, Lord, I give myself away
> 'Tis all that I can do.[8]

Jesus' Song of Praise

The turning point of Psalm 22 comes in verse 21. Jesus breaks into a song of praise.

If we sharpen our translations, verse 21 should read,

> Save me from the mouth of the lion and from the horns of the wild oxen—
> you have heard me!

In the middle of his prayer, he knows that God has heard him. In Hebrew, verse 21 ends with a one-word shout, "You have heard me!"

After his unspeakable agony, Jesus shouts for joy! And he announces the growth of the gospel around the world and across time. Derek Kidner calls these verses "The Spread of Joy," which is fitting.[9] Jesus announces the good news that God answered him and rescued him. The second half of Psalm 22 describes the ministry of the risen Christ. After the Resurrection, Christ is a preacher and a missionary.

The Risen Christ Is a Preacher

> I will tell of your name to my brothers;
>   in the midst of the congregation I will praise you:
> You who fear the LORD, praise him!
>   All you offspring of Jacob, glorify him,
>   and stand in awe of him, all you offspring of Israel!
> For he has not despised or abhorred

> the affliction of the afflicted,
> and he has not hidden his face from him,
>   but has heard, when he cried to him. (22:22–24)

After God heard him and rescued him, Jesus sets himself to the task of lifting up God's name to God's people. He reveals the Father to us.[10] This is why the text says, "I will tell of your name to my brothers" (v. 22). Whenever the gospel is proclaimed, Jesus himself is speaking and Psalm 22:22 is being fulfilled. Christ is a preacher.

How does this work? How could Jesus speak to us two thousand years after the Resurrection? The New Testament helps us answer this question. When Paul was writing to Gentiles in Ephesus, he said to them that Christ "came and preached peace to you who are far off" (Ephesians 2:17). Jesus himself never went to Ephesus, of course, yet Paul says Jesus preached to them. What does he mean? When Paul preached the gospel to the people in Ephesus, the Spirit of Christ was speaking through him. So Paul could say that Christ preached to them. Jesus preaches today through human preachers.

This means we need to listen carefully and pay close attention whenever God's Word is opened. Assuming that the preacher is opening the Bible, this is not just a man speaking. Jesus himself is speaking through his Word. The risen Christ himself declares God's name to us.

As a preacher, Jesus has committed himself to serve us. Jesus' first words to his Father were for you and me, for his church. He had been forsaken and separated from his Father, but as soon as God answered, Christ was thinking about how he would announce this good news to us. You and I were first on his mind. I remember visiting a man in the hospital who was coming out of surgery. As he came to, his first question was about his wife. "How is she?" he asked me. I marveled at his love for his bride; he thought of her first.

Christian, Jesus' first thought in Psalm 22 is for you! He loves you. And Jesus has not stopped thinking of you. The Scriptures say that our Lord Jesus is now "at the right hand of God . . . interceding for us" (Romans 8:34).

Don't miss that Jesus calls us his "brothers." Every Christian is Jesus' brother (or sister). The writer of Hebrews applies the words of Psalm 22 to all of us.

> For it was fitting that he, for whom and by whom all things exist, in bringing many sons to glory, should make the founder of their salvation perfect through suffering. For he who sanctifies and those who are sanctified all have one source. That is why he is not ashamed to call them brothers, saying,

> "I will tell of your name to my brothers;
> in the midst of the congregation I will sing your praise."
> (Hebrews 2:10–12, quoting Psalm 22:22)

When I was in seventh grade, I remember going down onto the field after one of my brother's college football games. He let me hold his helmet and introduced me to his friends. I was so proud that this was my big brother! Christian, Jesus calls you his brother. If you love Jesus, you are family.

There is a wrinkle in Psalm 22 we need to mention. The word "brothers" in verse 22 is parallel to the phrase, "All you offspring of Jacob" in verse 23. So does this mean that the brothers to whom Jesus preaches are Jews?

I don't think so. Here's why. In the Old Testament, the descendants of Abraham, Isaac, and Jacob always included Gentiles along with ethnic Jews, the nation of Israel. For instance, when God repeated his covenant with Jacob, he said,

> And God said to him, "I am God Almighty: be fruitful and multiply. A nation and a company of nations shall come from you, and kings shall come from your own body. (Genesis 35:11)

Jacob's descendants would be more than one nation in this world, the people of Israel. Rather, God promised that many nations, a company of *goyim*, would be Jacob's descendants.[11] The psalmist says much the same thing in Psalm 47:9, "The princes of the peoples gather as the people of the God of Abraham."

Even in the Old Testament, Gentiles were included among the people of God, the children of Abraham, Isaac, and Jacob.[12] Paul explains this more explicitly in Romans 4 and in Galatians 3:29, which says, "If you are Christ's, then you are Abraham's offspring." In a very real sense we are children of the patriarchs. Abraham, Isaac, and Jacob are our fathers. Jesus calls us his brothers, and he preaches the good news of his resurrection to us.

The Risen Christ is a Missionary

This becomes clearer as we notice the worldwide scope of Jesus' ministry after the Resurrection. The risen Christ is not only a preacher, he is also a missionary. He announces God's name to the nations so that they turn to God.

> All the ends of the earth shall remember
> and turn to the LORD,
> and all the families of the nations
> shall worship before you.

For kingship belongs to the LORD,
    and he rules over the nations.

All the prosperous of the earth eat and worship;
    before him shall bow all who go down to the dust,
        even the one who could not keep himself alive. (22:27–29)

Jesus preaches God's name to the nations. Because Christ suffered and was forsaken, because he prayed to God and was heard, people at the farthest corners of the globe will turn to worship God. His suffering was not pointless—it is powerful. The world has forgotten God and turned away from him. But because of the suffering and salvation of Christ, the nations of the world will remember their Creator and return to God, repenting of their sins. And the nations will worship God, bowing down to serve him as their King. Jesus was comforted and encouraged to know that his death and resurrection would bring the most distant peoples of the world back to God.[13] His suffering was not in vain.

This promise motivates us to be committed to missions and evangelism. We send out missionaries because we want men and women around the world to "turn to the LORD" (v. 27) and worship him. This is Jesus' passion, and it is ours as well. We are committed financially to world evangelism too. Our churches should send a significant portion of our budget outside our walls in outreach. Jesus was rewarded in that the nations of the world would turn to God. We are joining in his joy as we spend ourselves for his kingdom. Christ is a missionary, announcing God's salvation to the world through the men and women he sends to the ends of the earth.

The risen Christ calls people across the centuries.

Posterity shall serve him;
    it shall be told of the Lord to the coming generation;
they shall come and proclaim his righteousness to a people yet unborn,
    that he has done it. (22:30, 31)

Jesus sees the process of one generation telling another about the Lord. After his suffering, Jesus looked far into the future to see people not yet born hearing about the greatness of God through his cross and resurrection. This means that we who are alive today have a responsibility to tell the next generation about God.

When will our work be done? As long as there are children in the world, our job is not complete. About a quarter of the world's population is under fifteen years of age, 1.8 billion young people. Of these, roughly 80 percent, or 1.4 billion, are growing up in places where they will never hear the gospel. Who will tell this new generation about the God who raised our Lord Jesus Christ?

Christ saved the nations of the world through his death and resurrection. Jesus suffered for sinners. He cried out to God, and he was heard. God saved him from death and gave him the nations of the world as his inheritance (Psalm 2:8). As long as children are still being born, Psalm 22 should send us out to the world with this good news.

23

The Lord Is Christ's Shepherd

PSALM 23

PSALM 23 is easily the most famous and most familiar chapter in the Psalms. Millions of people have memorized Psalm 23. As a pastor I have read Psalm 23 in some tragic situations. If the average American knows anything about the Bible, he or she probably knows the opening line of Psalm 23, "The LORD is my shepherd."

Psalm 23 was written by David about Christ for Christians. This is an important place to start if we want to understand this comforting psalm.

Introduction to Psalm 23

Written by David

First, Psalm 23 was written by David. Many of us who love this psalm take the first words to mean, *God cares for me, and I am so glad he does.* We immediately take these as our own words. But when we read the word "my" in verse 1, we should notice that David is speaking. The Bible does say that God's people are all "the sheep of his pasture" (e.g., Psalm 79:13; 95:7). But in Psalm 23 David says that the Lord is *his* Shepherd.

Why does this matter? In the ancient world a king was called the shepherd of his people. Israel certainly thought David was their shepherd. When David became king, the people said to him, "The LORD said to you, 'You shall be shepherd of my people Israel, and you shall be prince over Israel'" (2 Samuel 5:2). And the psalmist says that God "chose David . . . to shepherd Jacob his people" (Psalm 78:70, 71).

David himself was the shepherd of Israel. In Psalm 23 David is also a sheep—the Lord is his Shepherd. A greater Shepherd cares for him.

This helps us understand Psalm 23 historically, what it would have meant to ancient Israelites. The message was that God cared for their king. Why would this have mattered to them? By watching over David, God was watching over all Israel. The life of the people was bound up in their king—when David prospered, the nation prospered. So Psalm 23 is about God caring for his people by caring for their king. Through David, God himself was the true Shepherd and King over all his people.[1]

Written about Christ

This brings us to our second introductory point: this is fundamentally a psalm about Christ. David was not only a king, he was also a prophet. His life and his words point forward to Christ. David spoke for Christ in the opening words of Psalm 22 as he foretold Jesus' words on the cross, "My God, my God, why have you forsaken me?" (Psalm 22:1). He also speaks for Christ in Psalm 23, "The LORD is my shepherd."

Like David, Christ was both a sheep and a shepherd. As the Lamb of God, Christ trusted his Father with his life (1 Peter 2:23). The Lord is Christ's Shepherd. Psalm 23 records Jesus' confidence that God cared for him as he faced death on the cross.

> Even though I walk through the valley of the shadow of death,
>   I will fear no evil,
> for you are with me;
>   your rod and your staff,
>   they comfort me. (23:4)

And in fact God did carry Jesus through death. The word "soul" in verse 3 could also be translated as "life" or "breath." Psalm 23, then, declares Jesus' confidence in the resurrection: "He restores my life."[2] God did restore Jesus' life. Christ rose from the dead and was exalted to the right hand of God the Father where he lives "in the house of the LORD forever" (23:6). God spread a banquet table for the Messiah in the presence of his enemies. The Scriptures say, "Blessed are those who are invited to the marriage supper of the Lamb" (Revelation 19:9). Psalm 23 is a summary of the death, resurrection, and exaltation of Christ.[3]

More specifically, it gives us a window on the inner life of our Lord Jesus as he faced the cross. The Scriptures say,

> like a lamb that is led to the slaughter,
>   and like a sheep that before its shearers is silent,
>   so he opened not his mouth. (Isaiah 53:7b)

How could he be silent before Pilate? How could he keep from insulting those who insulted him? As the Lamb of God, Jesus trusted his Shepherd to carry him through death into eternal life.

Christ is not only a sheep, he is also our Shepherd. God took on flesh to become a Lamb to save us and a King to rule over us. The Scriptures say in Revelation 7:17 that "the Lamb in the midst of the throne will be their shepherd."

Jesus taught that he is our Shepherd in John 10.

> I am the good shepherd. The good shepherd lays down his life for the sheep. He who is a hired hand and not a shepherd, who does not own the sheep, sees the wolf coming and leaves the sheep and flees, and the wolf snatches them and scatters them. He flees because he is a hired hand and cares nothing for the sheep. I am the good shepherd. I know my own and my own know me, just as the Father knows me and I know the Father; and I lay down my life for the sheep. . . .
>
> My sheep hear my voice, and I know them, and they follow me. (John 10:11–15, 27)

Written for Christians

The third point of this introduction is that Psalm 23 is for Christians. How do you know if Jesus is your Shepherd? There are two tests. Jesus says, "My sheep hear my voice" (v. 27). Do you listen to his Word? And Jesus also said, "they follow me" (v. 27). Do you do what he says?[4]

Many people have taken false comfort from Psalm 23. They want to believe that God is their Shepherd, but they do not listen to Christ or follow him. None of God's blessings come to us except though Jesus Christ. Christ is the great Shepherd for God's people. If you do not belong to Jesus, God is not your Shepherd. If you know Jesus and love him, Psalm 23 is for you.

So Psalm 23 is by David about Christ for Christians. David describes God's care for us in Christ with two main pictures. Jesus cares for you as a shepherd (vv. 1–4) and as a host (vv. 5, 6).

The Lord Is My Shepherd

It is amazing that Jesus should stoop to be our Shepherd. In the ancient world, being a shepherd was one of the lowest jobs. If a family had sheep, the youngest son was the shepherd—none of the older brothers would want to do it. When Samuel went to anoint David, David was the youngest of eight sons; they had to call him in from tending the sheep. Being a shepherd was a twenty-four-hour job. Summer and winter, rain or shine, you lived with the dirty, smelly sheep in the heat of the day and the cold of the night. No one in his right mind would want to be a shepherd.

Yet God loves us so much that he chose to be our Shepherd. And he is a good Shepherd. When we read, "I shall not want" (v. 1), some people think that means God gives us everything we desire. But the idea is not that God gives us everything we ask for; rather, he cares for us by giving us everything we need. Sheep are helpless animals; left to themselves they lack everything. A good shepherd knows what they need. If the God of the universe is your Shepherd, you will lack nothing.

Abundant Life

How does our Good Shepherd provide for us? David paints a picture of abundant life. First:

> He makes me lie down in green pastures.
> He leads me beside still waters. (23:2)

Philip Keller worked as a shepherd for eight years and recorded his insights in his book *A Shepherd Looks at Psalm 23*. When sheep lie down, Keller says, it is because they are safe and satisfied.

> It is almost impossible for them to be made to lie down unless four requirements are met. Owing to their timidity they refuse to lie down unless they are free of all fear. Because of their social behavior within a flock, sheep will not lie down unless they are free from friction with others of their kind. If tormented by flies or parasites, sheep will not lie down. Only when free of these pests can they relax. Lastly, sheep will not lie down as long as they feel in need of finding food. They must be free from hunger.[5]

So lying down implies that sheep are free from fear, friction, flies, and hunger. Their shepherd cares for them physically, medically, socially, and emotionally.

Finding green pastures where sheep can prosper like this is easier said than done. Even if you have never been to Israel, you may know from pictures that the land is a "dry, rocky set of rolling hills covered with sparse and tough grass."[6] The only time the pastures are truly green like this is in the late winter and spring—come summer, the grass withers and the fields turn brown in the heat. So this is a picture of springtime. The still waters are wells and springs where the sheep can drink without being rushed or swept away by the strong current.

Our Good Shepherd cares for us like this. He provides for our physical needs, and he taught us to pray, "Give us this day our daily bread" (Matthew 6:11). God knows what we need, and he has committed himself to provide for us. Even more, he satisfies our souls and meets our deepest needs. Jesus said, "I came that they may have life and have it abundantly" (John 10:10b). He feeds us with the bread of Heaven. Jesus said, "I am the bread of life; whoever comes to me shall not hunger, and whoever believes in me shall never thirst" (John 6:35). Our Shepherd also said,

> Come to me, all who labor and are heavy laden, and I will give you rest. Take my yoke upon you, and learn from me, for I am gentle and lowly in heart, and you will find rest for your souls. For my yoke is easy, and my burden is light. (Matthew 11:28–30)

David continues this picture of abundant life: "He restores my soul" (v. 3). The sense of the word "restore" is to return or to bring back. As a Shepherd, Jesus brings his sheep back to God. This is another way of describing the ministry of the risen Christ in Psalm 22:27 where the same verb is used for those who return to the Lord.

> All the ends of the earth shall remember
>   and turn to the LORD,
> and all the families of the nations
>   shall worship before you.

One of the most beautiful descriptions of Jesus' shepherding work to restore his people is found in the Gospel of Luke, where we read Jesus' Parable of the Lost Sheep.

> What man of you, having a hundred sheep, if he has lost one of them, does not leave the ninety-nine in the open country, and go after the one that is lost, until he finds it? And when he has found it, he lays it on his shoulders, rejoicing. And when he comes home, he calls together his friends and his neighbors, saying to them, "Rejoice with me, for I have found my sheep that was lost." Just so, I tell you, there will be more joy in heaven over one sinner who repents than over ninety-nine righteous persons who need no repentance. (Luke 15:4–7)

Has the Good Shepherd found you? Can you say, "He restores my soul" (v. 3)? You may know in your heart that you have wandered far away. The good news is that you are not alone—someone is looking for you.

And when Jesus finds his sheep, he leads them. They hear his voice and follow him. David says, "He leads me in paths of righteousness for his name's sake" (v. 3). There is some debate over the meaning of the word "righteousness" here. It could mean righteousness in a moral sense—when we follow Jesus as our Shepherd, he teaches us to live righteous, godly lives. The word "righteousness" could also refer to God's righteousness, that he will do right by his sheep as he leads them. So one way of paraphrasing this could be: the Lord "leads me in paths of his righteousness, paths where he fulfills *his* obligations to the psalmist . . . and does so in order to maintain his reputation as a covenant-keeping God."[7] On the other hand, it could mean right paths in the most basic sense. Our Shepherd does not lead us by crooked paths or take wrong turns—he guides us on straight paths, "paths that bring the sheep most directly to their destination."[8]

In fact, we don't need to choose one of these meanings over the other. I think David leaves this phrase, "paths of righteousness" (v. 3), ambiguous because these meanings all overlap in real life. The paths Jesus chooses for us are right in every sense of the word: we are righteous as we follow him, God is righteous as he keeps his Word to us, and the road he leads us on is the best, most direct route from here to our heavenly home. And in this way he is glorified. God's reputation grows as his sheep follow him.

Since water and grass can be hard to find in the land of Israel, shepherds had to be ready to lead their flocks on long migrations from one pasture to another. The sheep would not understand why they left a good place to climb up and down ravines as they walked through the wilderness. *Where are we going? The ground is rough, and there is no water here. And still the shepherd leads on.* The sheep don't know where they are going, but he does. He has good pasture in mind: green grass and still water. Not a single step of this journey is wasted. He leads them by straight paths.

And so it is with our lives. We can look back and say, "Why couldn't we have stayed where we were? Why are you leading me here? I don't like this rough ground. I'm thirsty, and there is no water." And still our Shepherd leads on. He knows where he is going. He leads us in straight paths. We need to trust him.

Secure Life

Nowhere do we need to trust him more than when we are face-to-face with death.

As shepherds led the flocks in search of grass and water, they must pass at times into and through deep rugged wadis—dry streambeds cut through the hills by the winter rains. The air at the bottom of these deep ravines is thick and heavy with the heat of the day; like canyons they are covered in dark shadows as the cliff walls block out the sun.[9] The whole flock had to struggle over rocks and boulders and up the sides of the canyon. If the flock is caught in a wadi during a storm, a flash flood could sweep them away to their deaths. To make it worse, wild animals live in the shelter of the wadi, ready to tear the sheep to shreds.

The shadows of these dangerous canyons are a picture of the terrors and trials of death. Yet even then we trust the Shepherd.

> Even though I walk through the valley of the shadow of death,
>   I will fear no evil,
> for you are with me;
>   your rod and your staff,
>   they comfort me. (23:4)

"[T]he valley of the shadow of death" (v. 4) is as much the Shepherd's right path as the green grass and quiet waters. The Christian life is not always peaceful and easy. God gives us valleys, too, and each one of us will face the deep valley of death at the end of our lives.

One of the greatest problems in the valley is fear. Is God still in control? Is evil going to harm me? Will I be swept away or torn to pieces? The Shepherd's presence is the answer to our fear. Jesus himself trusted God the Father through the valley of death—and God was faithful to him. Jesus, our Shepherd, traveled through the valley of the shadow of death and came out triumphant on the other side. We will not fear because our Shepherd is with us. Up to this point David has been talking about the Lord in the second person—"he makes . . . he leads . . . he restores . . . he leads" (vv. 2, 3). Now to emphasize that God is near, he switches to the third person—"you are with me . . . you prepare . . . you anoint" (vv. 4, 5).

Jesus is never closer to us than at the moment of death. When my grandmother was dying, my uncle came into the room and asked if she wanted to hear her favorite music. "Do you want me to put on the 'Hallelujah Chorus' for you?" he asked. "Oh no," she said. "It will sound so much more beautiful in just a minute."

Eight years ago my wife's brother Todd was a missionary in South Africa. A pastor from Dublin, California named Bill (not his real name) came to visit them with his sons. One day the two men decided to take their boys for a hike in the mountains near their home. As they were climbing, a huge boulder came loose and crashed down onto Bill, crushing his lower body. Todd stayed with him while help came, but there was no way Bill was going to make it. At the end he said, "Tell my family I love them, and tell them I see Jesus." Then he died. "Even though I walk through the valley of the shadow of death, I will fear no evil, for you are with me" (v. 4). Jesus is never closer to us than at the moment of death.

And because he is near, we are safe. Disease and destruction can do its worst—we do not need to fear evil. Our Shepherd is armed. His "rod" (v. 4) is probably a long club, a sort of mace, that a shepherd wore on a thong tied to his belt. His "staff" (v. 4) is a long walking stick. He defends us and walks with us down the roughest road.

We need a Shepherd to care for us because life can get as bad as death. How can I be sure that all will be well? How can I be sure that death is not the end? If you are a Christian, you have a Shepherd who cares for you.

The LORD Is My Host

Jesus is also our host. After passing through death, the picture changes to a man welcoming special guests to his home.

> You prepare a table before me
>   in the presence of my enemies;
> you anoint my head with oil;
>   my cup overflows. (23:5)

This is far better than being a sheep with a shepherd. Jesus welcomes us to sit with him as friends at his table. This is a public honor. God will honor Jesus himself in the presence of his enemies, those who mocked him and taunted him, saying, "He trusts in the LORD; let him deliver him; let him rescue him, for he delights in him" (Psalm 22:8). And he will honor us publicly with him. Jesus described this messianic banquet in Matthew 8:11: "I tell you, many will come from east and west and recline at table with Abraham, Isaac, and Jacob in the kingdom of heaven."

The picture of this meal is even better than just good food though. In the Old Testament world, to eat and drink at someone's table created a bond of loyalty and fellowship.[10] It could even be the final step of sealing a covenant. David is promising us a close, intimate relationship with our Shepherd. Instead of dumb sheep, Jesus calls us friends (John 15:15).

And as his guests, he will welcome us into our eternal home.

> Surely goodness and mercy shall follow me
>   all the days of my life,

and I shall dwell in the house of the Lord
   forever. (23:6)

The blessing of being in "the house of the Lord" (v. 6) is being with the Lord. If you travel for business, you may stay in hotels that have nicer furniture than you have in your house. Managers do their best to make you feel at home, but you never do. Home is where your family is. Take away the people and a house becomes a sad and empty place. The joy of Heaven is not mansions or streets of gold. Jesus is the joy of Heaven. It will be home because he is there. Jesus said, "[I]f I go and prepare a place for you, I will come again and will take you to myself, that where I am you may be also" (John 14:3).

Jesus was a sheep. God cared for him and watched over him through the valley of death. He has walked the road we are traveling. And Jesus is also our Shepherd. He guards and guides us through this life. We shall be his honored guests for all eternity. No wonder we love this psalm so much.

24

The King of Glory

PSALM 24

THE QUESTION THIS PSALM ASKS is one of the most important any man or woman can think about: what does God require of me? If God exists (and he does) and Heaven is real (and it is), what do I need to do to get there?

This is an ultimate issue that everyone faces, a question everyone must answer. The danger with the really big questions of life, of course, is that we seldom stop to think about them. We can live our lives at ninety miles an hour without ever stopping to ask if we are going in the right direction. If you get on Route 66 in Tulsa, you might think you are driving to LA when really you are heading toward Chicago.

With Psalm 24, God has brought us to a place where we need to stop and think about this ultimate issue of what God expects from us. No other question or concern is more important right now than that great question of where we will spend eternity after we die.

Psalm 24 challenges us. We'll also find that Psalm 24 gives us hope. God knows how he made us; he knows our frames, that we are dust; he meets us in our need. So along with an ultimate question, we're going to be talking about an ultimate hope, a hope everyone can experience.

God Owns This World (vv. 1, 2)

God has the right to ask what he wants of you and me because he created us.[1] Since he made us, he owns us. Psalm 24 begins,

> The earth is the LORD's and the fullness thereof,
>   the world and those who dwell therein,
> for he has founded it upon the seas
>   and established it upon the rivers. (24:1, 2)

God owns the world and everything in it. He created the continents and the seas; he invented plate tectonics. Personally, you and I belong to God. This is where we start in order to understand how to live in God's world.

We can see this illustrated in the way the Apostle Paul uses this verse. In 1 Corinthians Paul was writing to help the church with a controversy over eating meat sacrificed to idols. In those times much of the meat sold in the markets was slaughtered in pagan temples. Imagine if most of the meat at your local grocery store had not been slaughtered on a farm or in slaughter-house; when you bought it, you knew it had been butchered as part of a pagan, occult ritual in a temple.

What should you do? Should a Christian eat food that had been offered to an idol? What should you do if you were not sure where the meat came from? Paul first says not to participate in a sacrifice to an idol. Then he gives this instruction:

> Eat whatever is sold in the meat market without raising any question on the ground of conscience. For "the earth is the Lord's, and the fullness thereof." (1 Corinthians 10:25, 26)

What is Paul saying? If you don't know where that ten-ounce fillet came from, go ahead and enjoy it. Why? "The earth is the Lord's" (v. 26). This meat may have been offered to a demon in sacrifice, but God still owns it. He created it; it still belongs to him. The principle is that we do not need to reject things in this world simply because they have been misused. God created this world, and it is good.

Some of us think that God no longer has a claim on our lives. Worse yet, maybe you think he couldn't possibly want you any longer. You might have given yourself to alcohol, and maybe you think God doesn't want you any more. You might be a woman who has given herself to men, looking for their approval, and there came a point where you said, "I've gone too far. God doesn't want me back." Or maybe you've turned away from God and said, "This is my life. I'm going to do what I want."

God created you in his own image, and nothing you can do will ever change that. God made you, and he cares about you. So once again our question is, what does my loving Creator expect from me? How do I need to live to please him so that I can live with him in Heaven?

Who Can Come before God? (vv. 3–6)

David asks that very question.

> Who shall ascend the hill of the LORD?
>   And who shall stand in his holy place? (24:3)

In other words, who can come before God? What kind of men and women will he admit into his presence in Heaven?

Coming before a Holy God

God is a holy God; he is absolutely pure. Those who come into his presence must be holy and pure also. The Scriptures say that "the LORD your God is a consuming fire" (Deuteronomy 4:24).

What does this mean? If you have a cookout after church and spill barbecue sauce on the middle of your white shirt, it will stain. Your shirt is no longer clean. God's holiness, on the other hand, is active, like fire. What happens when that same barbecue sauce drops off a piece of meat onto the coals? Do the coals get dirty? No; the fire burns up the barbecue sauce.

In the same way, when sin and impurity comes into God's presence, does God get dirty, like your shirt? No; his holiness consumes sin like fire. Those who come into God's presence must be holy for their own protection. We must be clean and pure to come before him, or his holiness will consume us in our sin.

Dimensions of Purity

David describes the sort of person who can come before God.

> He who has clean hands and a pure heart,
>   who does not lift up his soul to what is false
>   and does not swear deceitfully. (24:4)

These four qualifications should make us more than a little uncomfortable. First, those who come before God must have "clean hands" (v. 4). This talks about our actions. We cannot come into God's presence with hands stained by wrong things we have done.

Do you remember Shakespeare's Lady Macbeth? She helped her husband murder King Duncan in their home. After the killing, she could not quiet her guilty conscience, and her servant found her sleepwalking, convinced that her hands were stained with blood. In her sleep she scrubbed and scrubbed, but she could not get the bloodstain off her hands. She cried, "Out, damned spot! Out I say! . . . What, will these hands never be clean?"[2]

There is a very real sense in which Lady Macbeth's dream is our reality. Every sin we have ever done has left its stain on our hands. Everything we have ever stolen stains our hands before God. The ink of every false or cruel thing we have ever written stains our hands before God. The print of every doorknob we should not have opened is branded on our palms. Every keystroke or mouse click is tattooed on our fingertips. Our hands are stained with a lifetime of sins. And God says that those who come into his holy place must have "clean hands" (v. 4).

Along with pure hands, we must have "a pure heart" (v. 4). It's not enough to be clean on the outside; we must be clean inside as well. Our thoughts and intentions and motives must be pure. Imagine how horrified we would be if others could see the thoughts that have flashed through our minds even in the hour before reading these words. Yet God does see each thought that passes through our minds. He sorts out our most subtle motives. And this holy God who owns us and made us requires that we be pure inside!

The first two qualifications focus on purity, and the third and fourth requirements focus on truthfulness. We must "not lift up [our] soul to what is false" (v. 4). This has to do with our hearts. The expression "lift up his soul" (v. 4) basically means to trust in something. This is what it means at the beginning of the next psalm. Psalm 25:1, 2 says, "To you, O Lord, I lift up my soul. O my God, in you I trust." When we "lift up [our] soul to what is false," we are trusting in a lie.

How do we trust in lies? We want something, so we trust falsehood to get it. I want people to think I'm godly, so I lie about my Bible reading. If I want a job, I lie on a resumé. We also lie because we don't want to be punished or embarrassed—we trust a lie to shield us from the consequences of what we have done. "I didn't take a cookie from the pantry." "I didn't leave the stock room door unlocked." Or I might decide that something I want is so good that it's okay to lie to get it. Ironically I've known Christians who have lied to help the church. If you have a problem with lying, you need to recognize that it starts with your heart. You are worshiping falsehood, trusting lies to do things for you when you should be worshiping God by trusting him.

The fourth qualification our text mentions is not to "swear deceitfully" (v. 4). This moves from our hearts to our words.

Paul Griffiths wrote,

"Adults who don't lie are more than original: They're almost nonexistent." . . . Perhaps we deceive by holding back the whole truth. So when your spouse asks, "Did you view pornography this afternoon?" you say, "No, I did not." Your statement is technically true, but you used pornography the night before, and that, as you well know, is what the question was intended to discover.

Christians must put away hair-splitting legalisms, ingenious rationalizations, and dubious casuistry. If we want to follow Jesus, then we must retrain ourselves to put away deceit, guile, duplicity, dissembling, misleading, exaggeration, and, yes, outright lying.[3]

This includes our spoken words, our written words, our texted words, our emailed words. God requires that those who enter his holy place be truthful.

When we stack up our lives against these requirements, we have a problem! Who would dare to say that they don't have the slightest stain of sin on their hands—that their thoughts are always pure, that they have never trusted a lie to protect them, and that they always tell the truth? These requirements, if we take them seriously, bring us to the end of ourselves and show us our sin.

If we are believers, we should never allow ourselves to forget our own sinfulness and the fact that we once stood guilty before God. Some years ago I read a quote from J. C. Ryle that took me by surprise.

Above all, let us pray for a deeper sense of our own sinfulness, guilt and undeserving. This, after all, is the true secret of a thankful spirit. It is the man who daily feels his debt to grace, and daily remembers [that] in reality he deserves nothing but hell—this is the man who will be daily blessing and praising God. Thankfulness [is] a flower which will never bloom well excepting upon a root of deep humility.[4]

I had never thought to pray for a deeper sense of my own sin. But Ryle is right: the more we see the depth of our sin, the more we'll see the height of God's love. When we know we've been forgiven much, we'll love him much. Seeing our sin should make us more grateful than ever for the cross.

If you are not a believer, you have now heard what God requires of you. Can you say that your hands are clean and your heart is pure? God knows and you know that you have sinned. What will you do? You can ignore God's requirements today, tomorrow, and until the day you die, but then you will face your Maker, and what will you do? If you are not a believer and you know your sin will keep you from Heaven, you are ready to hear about Jesus Christ.

Christ Our Righteousness

We read in the Bible that Christ was the only man who has completely lived up to God's requirements.

Did he have "clean hands" (v. 4)? The Bible says that Christ committed no sin (Hebrews 4:15). Instead his hands served us, healed us, and were pierced by nails for you and me. "Pure heart" (Psalm 24:4)? The Bible says that he was "full of grace and truth" (John 1:14). Did he trust in God? The

Bible says that he "entrust[ed] himself to [God] who judges justly" (1 Peter 2:23). Truthful? The Bible says that no deceit was ever found in his mouth (1 Peter 2:22).

So Christ alone met these four requirements. And as our text promises, he received "blessing from the LORD and righteousness from the God of his salvation" (Psalm 24:5). The Resurrection was God's great vindication of his sinless Son.

The good news of God's Word is that Jesus Christ did not meet God's requirements just for himself. He came to make you and me qualified to come into God's holy presence. The Scriptures say,

> For our sake [God] made him to be sin who knew no sin, so that in him we might become the righteousness of God. (2 Corinthians 5:21)

Although Jesus Christ was pure, he became sin for us as he carried our sin on the cross. He died and rose again so that our stained, guilty hands could be washed clean and our impure hearts could be purified. How much does our Creator love us? Christ came to wash us and purify us from the guilt that stains us and keeps us from coming before a God who is like a consuming fire.

And when Christ purifies us, he also makes us into what we should be. He transforms us by his Holy Spirit into people who keep God's requirements ourselves, men and women who are self-controlled and godly, eager to do good. This is why verse 6 says,

> Such is the generation of those who seek him,
>   who seek the face of the God of Jacob. (24:6)

What is striking about this verse is that suddenly we are not reading about an individual anymore but about an entire group of people. One man kept God's requirements completely and perfectly, and an entire race of humanity was made like him. Spurgeon said,

> Our Lord Jesus Christ could ascend the Hill of the Lord because his hands were clean and his heart was pure, and if we by faith are conformed to His image we shall enter, too.[5]

We are saved through a relationship with Christ that is so powerful it changes us to become like him. If we have not seen any change or sign of spiritual growth in our lives, we need to examine ourselves to see if we really belong to Christ. We may need to recommit ourselves today to live the way he asks us to. He was made like us so we could be made like him.

The Entrance of the King

These last verses take us to the gates of Heaven to declare the triumph of Christ as he enters Heaven itself, proving that God's requirements have been met and that he is the rightful King of glory.[6] Some interpreters speculate that this is an entrance liturgy used as the ark of the covenant was brought into the temple. But there is no mention of the ark in these verses, and there is no evidence that the ark was ever carried into the temple as part of a worship ceremony.[7]

Psalm 24 ends the section in the psalms that focuses on Jesus' welcome in God's presence. Much of Psalm 24 is an echo of Psalm 15, which starts off this section. Together Psalms 15 and 24 are like bookends for this section, the central focus of which seems to be Christ being welcomed by God into his presence. If we compare this with the previous section, Psalms 3—14 teach us that Christ would be rejected by man. Psalms 15—24 teach us that he would be accepted by God. Christ is introduced as God's King in Psalm 2. The people of this world rage against him, but God sets him on the throne of Heaven. This is the gospel Peter announced at Pentecost: "[K]now for certain that God has made him both Lord and Christ, this Jesus whom you crucified" (Acts 2:36). These larger patterns in the Psalms announced the gospel in advance. We despised and rejected him, but God honored him and raised him up.

The picture in verses 7–10 is Christ ascending Mount Zion, the hill of the Lord, riding up to the gates of the heavenly city as its King.

> Lift up your heads, O gates!
>   And be lifted up, O ancient doors,
>   that the King of glory may come in. (24:7)

These gates are being called to open to Christ as he rides in triumph.

In Revelation 21 we are told that there is an angel assigned to each gate of the New Jerusalem. So with that picture in mind we imagine an angel who responds, "Who is this King of glory?" (24:8a).

And the answer is shouted back, "The LORD, strong and mighty, the LORD, mighty in battle!" (v. 8b).

How is Christ "mighty in battle" (v. 8)? Christ triumphed over death, Hell, and the grave through his cross. And so he rode up to the gates of Heaven as a conqueror; the battle is won.

This exchange is repeated in verses 9, 10. Why are the gates asked to lift up their heads and open a second time? Didn't they open the first time? This could just be part of the poetry or ceremony of the occasion. But it may also be hinting that the King of glory will enter Zion twice.

The first time he entered as the great King, and they shout out that he himself is "mighty in battle" (v. 8); he defeated his enemies by his cross. But notice that the answer in verse 10 is different from that in verse 8. They shout back the second time, "The LORD of hosts, he is the King of glory!" The "hosts" are his army, so this seems to give us a picture of Jesus as a great King with rank upon rank of warriors behind him. This second shout in verse 10 identifies him at the front of his people.[8]

And in fact in Revelation 19:14 we read this description of Jesus at the end of time:

> And the armies of heaven, arrayed in fine linen, white and pure, were following him on white horses.

So this second shout seems to be hinting that our King will ride up to the gates of Zion, the heavenly city, a second time with his hosts, a crowd of his saints following him, victorious in battle. We read about this again in 1 Thessalonians 4:16–18.

> For the Lord himself will descend from heaven with a cry of command, with the voice of an archangel, and with the sound of the trumpet of God. And the dead in Christ will rise first. Then we who are alive, who are left, will be caught up together with them in the clouds to meet the Lord in the air, and so we will always be with the Lord. Therefore encourage one another with these words.

When Christ returns to call us home, he will return to Heaven as the Lord of hosts, with crowds of us following him.

Will you be in that great crowd? Do you know what God asks of you? Do you know that you can never live up to his standard? Do you know for sure that your stained hands have been washed clean, your heart has been purified, and you are living a new life in Christ?

Your Creator cares for you, even if you have given yourself to some of the worst things this world has to offer. He knows you are not fit for Heaven now; so his Son made the way for you. Won't you come to him today? Let him change you.

If you know Jesus, then you will be a part of that crowd—God's Word says so—and Christ himself, your King, will lead you in victory, along with all those who have gone before us in the Lord.

25

He Will Never Let You Down

PSALM 25

IF YOU'RE A FAN OF *Downton Abbey*, you will never forget Lady Edith's wedding day. After years of disappointment, the sun finally shone on her as she got ready to marry Sir Anthony Strallan. Even Lady Mary was happy for her. The great house prepared for the big day, the carriage pulled up to the front door, and she was carried to the church in style.

As she walked down the aisle, Lady Edith seemed truly happy for the first time since we met her. She was the forgotten sister. Mary and Sybil have gotten all the attention. But there she was, standing with Sir Anthony as the minister began, "Dearly beloved, we are gathered here . . ." But suddenly Sir Anthony interrupted the minister, mumbled, "I can't do this!" and left her at the altar. Lisa and I gasped—poor Lady Edith! The rejection and humiliation of that moment is unforgettable.

This sort of public rejection and humiliation is the kind of shame that David is thinking of in the opening lines of Psalm 25.

> To you, O Lord, I lift up my soul.
> O my God, in you I trust;
>   let me not be put to shame;
>   let not my enemies exult over me.
> Indeed, none who wait for you shall be put to shame;
>   they shall be ashamed who are wantonly treacherous. (25:1–3)

Shame in this context is more than just embarrassment or feeling foolish. It is the humiliation that comes from being rejected and abandoned.[1] To make it even worse, it is the humiliation of being rejected and abandoned by God. Imagine putting all your hope in God for this life and the next, only to have him leave you at the altar. This is more than embarrassing; this is devastating.

Why would David be worried that God would humiliate him like this? Two problems are weighing on his mind. First, he sees his sin. *Will God realize what a sinner I have been—and what a sinner I still am? Will he finally see the truth about me and reject me?* Second, David's enemies hate him with a passion. The stakes are high—if God does not stand beside him, David knows he is toast.

David's fears are our fears too. All of us wonder at times, *How could God put up with a sinner like me? Will he see who I really am and drop me like a bad habit?* And we also feel overwhelmed because the world is against us. There are people who hate us because we are Christians. We have a great enemy, the devil, who wants to destroy us. If God turns away from us, we are doomed.

Verse 3 is our great hope: "Indeed, none who wait for you shall be put to shame." God is faithful. He will never leave his people at the altar.

Psalm 25 teaches us what it means to wait for God and hope in him. As a teaching psalm, Psalm 25 is an acrostic. With a few variations, each line starts with the letters of the Hebrew alphabet. This makes for good poetry, of course, and it is easier to memorize—provided you know Hebrew! But even if you speak English, this is a psalm to be learned so we can set our confidence in God.

How does David wait for God? How do we wait for God—how do we trust him with patience and complete confidence? We can see four aspects to David's waiting in Psalm 25. He waits in obedience, in confession, in fear, and in prayer. With this, David holds on to his hope: "none who wait for you shall be put to shame."

We Wait in Obedience

David starts with obedience, asking God to teach him.

> Make me to know your ways, O LORD;
>   teach me your paths.
> Lead me in your truth and teach me,
>   for you are the God of my salvation;
>   for you I wait all the day long. (25:4, 5)

We can't pretend that we are waiting on God if we do not want to do what he says. Jesus says much the same thing. If we say we trust God but we do not obey, we will lose everything.

Why do you call me "Lord, Lord," and not do what I tell you? Everyone who comes to me and hears my words and does them, I will show you what he is like: he is like a man building a house, who dug deep and laid the foundation on the rock. And when a flood arose, the stream broke against that house and could not shake it, because it had been well built. But the one who hears and does not do them is like a man who built a house on the ground without a foundation. When the stream broke against it, immediately it fell, and the ruin of that house was great. (Luke 6:46–49)

So the first step is a commitment to obey the Lord. As David waits on God, he first asks God to teach him. He waits as a disciple, a learner, a man who is committed to follow God. God's "ways" and his "paths" start with specific decisions (Psalm 25:4). One step after another, these decisions turn into a lifestyle, a path that pleases God in this world.

God has to show us how to obey him—notice the verbs David uses: "Make me to know," "teach me," "lead me" (vv. 4, 5). Why do we need God to teach us how to obey? Can't we just let our conscience be our guide? No; we can't assume we can figure out how to obey God on our own without his help. For one thing, there is every chance that our hearts will deceive us. Psalm 14 says we have all become "corrupt"; our hearts are bad (Psalm 14:2, 3; cf. Romans 7:18). We also need to remember how small and limited we really are.

For my thoughts are not your thoughts,
  neither are your ways my ways, declares the Lord.
For as the heavens are higher than the earth,
  so are my ways higher than your ways
  and my thoughts than your thoughts. (Isaiah 55:8, 9)

If we think we can figure out the right path on our own, we don't understand how small we are. If an ant is crawling on a beach ball, it can't see where it is or where it is going. God looks down on this world he created, and he sees how we should live. If we want to follow God and please him, the place to begin is to ask him what he wants. A proud man assumes he knows what God wants; a humble man or woman says, "Lord, teach me."

It is striking that David asks God to teach him even though he was an inspired writer of Scripture. What's more, since David mentions the sins of his youth a few verses later, he probably wrote this psalm near the end of his life. This is not the prayer of an immature man, a boy who's just learning to shave. David had come to know his own heart over the years—he knew what he was capable of doing. And he had wrestled with the complex questions that life throws at us.

If we think we no longer need God to open our eyes, to lead us, to reveal his truth, we are in a dangerous place. If we grew up in the church or if we have been Christians for some time, it is easy to assume that we know what to do—how to please God and live up to his expectations. The older we are in the Lord, the more mature we are in Christ, the more we realize how much we need him to guide us every day. This is a wise, mature David who prays, "Make me to know your ways, O LORD; teach me your paths" (Psalm 25:4). He asks God to help him lead a good and godly life.

God teaches us through his Word, the Bible. Jesus prayed, "Sanctify them in the truth; your word is truth" (John 17:17). The man or woman who wants to obey God wants to understand the Bible so he or she can follow what it says and live in the truth. We can't understand God's Word on our own; we need God to lead us and teach us the truth as we read. Verse 5 is a good prayer for us as we sit down with our Bibles every day: "Lead me in your truth and teach me, for you are the God of my salvation."

We Wait in Confession

We also wait in confession. It is not enough to commit ourselves to obey God. Even if David turned over a new leaf and never sinned again, he still had a past. God knew who he had been and what he had done. God also knew that he would stumble again in the future. So David humbly asks for forgiveness.

Grace

As David confesses his sins, he asks for grace. He asks God both to remember and to forget.

> Remember your mercy, O LORD, and your steadfast love,
>> for they have been from of old.
> Remember not the sins of my youth or my transgressions;
>> according to your steadfast love remember me,
>> for the sake of your goodness, O LORD! (25:6, 7)

First, he focuses on God's character. He asks God to remember how good God is. The word "mercy" is related to the Hebrew word for womb. This mercy is the gentle compassion that a mother has for her baby.[2] God cares for his people with a mother's love.

> Can a woman forget her nursing child,
>> that she should have no compassion on the son of her womb?

> Even these may forget,
>> yet I will not forget you. (Isaiah 49:15)

David also wants God to remember his commitment to his people. "Steadfast love" is God's committed love, his covenant loyalty to his people (Psalm 25:6). If "mercy" points to a mother's love for her child, then "steadfast love" points to a husband's love for his wife (vv. 6, 7). It is covenant love. When a husband vows to love his wife "until death do us part," this is steadfast love. God has committed himself by covenant to his people as a husband to his bride. By asking God to remember his "steadfast love," David is asking God to remember the wedding vows he made to his people when he first called them and chose them to be his very own.

David also wants God to forget—not to remember his past sins. "The sins of my youth" (v. 7) could refer to besetting sins that David struggled with since he was a boy. I have talked to men who were exposed to pornography in grade school, and this sin of their youth has been a battle for them ever since. I know a woman who started lying when she was a girl, and it has almost destroyed her marriage.

"The sins of my youth" (v. 7) could also be things he did when he was young. Many of us blush when we think back to stupid decisions we made in high school or college. If you are young, you need to know that your sins will follow you. Many of us who are older would like nothing more than to have the sins of our youth left in the past. We wish life had a rewind button. We understand exactly what David is feeling. We don't want God to focus on who we have been or what we have done. We need the grace of God's forgetfulness.

If we are Christians, we have received this kind of grace. Harry Ironside once visited a godly man who was ninety years old. The man had sent for Ironside because, as he put it, "Everything seems so dark." Harry Ironside asked him what was the matter.

> Since I have been lying here so weak, my memory keeps bringing up the sins of my youth, and I cannot get them out of my mind. They keep crowding in upon me, and I cannot help thinking of them.

Ironside turned to this psalm and read, "Remember not the sins of my youth . . . according to your steadfast love remember me, for the sake of your goodness, O Lord!" Then he said to the man,

When you came to God seventy years ago you confessed your sin and put your trust in Jesus Christ. . . . Don't you remember that when you confessed your sins God said, "Your sins and iniquities I will remember no more." If God has forgotten them, why should you think about them? The man relaxed and replied, "I am an old fool remembering what God has forgotten."[3]

Christian, you have received the grace of God's forgetfulness.

Instruction

David feels this grace so deeply that he stops his prayer and turns to teach everyone who reads this psalm. He is no longer talking *to* God—he is talking *about* God.

> Good and upright is the LORD;
>   therefore he instructs sinners in the way.
> He leads the humble in what is right,
>   and teaches the humble his way.
> All the paths of the LORD are steadfast love and faithfulness,
>   for those who keep his covenant and his testimonies. (25:8–10)

God teaches sinners who admit their sin and listen to him. God humbles himself to be an instructor. He does not have to do this, of course. Since we are sinners, he would be fully justified in dropping the hammer on us and condemning us for all eternity. But since he is good, since he is upright, he teaches men and women who will humble themselves to listen to him.

This means there is hope for you and me. If you are not a believer, you might have met Christians who wanted nothing to do with you because they were "good people." You figured God must be the same—*since he is good, he won't touch me*. David says just the opposite. God welcomes sinners and teaches them precisely because he is good. The Bible says that Jesus looks for the best in you. "A bruised reed he will not break, and a faintly burning wick he will not quench" (Isaiah 42:3). God is so good that he reclaims sinful men and women. He makes us into what we should be. If we will listen to God's voice and follow him, he will teach us.

Forgiveness

David also asks for forgiveness. He is not satisfied to ask God simply not to remember his sins. He wants the slate wiped clean.

For your name's sake, O LORD,
  pardon my guilt, for it is great. (25:11)

Our tendency is to minimize our sin. If we were writing verse 11, we might say, "Lord pardon my guilt, for it is small." David does not plead the smallness of his sins—he pleads for pardon because of the greatness of his sins! His situation is so desperate that nothing less than full pardon will do. If you feel the overwhelming weight of your sin, you are in a good place. Like David, you can call out to God and say, "Pardon my guilt, for it is great" (v. 11).

How can God pardon great sin? The reason he can forget the sins of our youth and forgive great guilt is because Jesus died and rose again to save sinners. If your sin is a backpack of guilt and shame, Jesus took the backpack from your shoulders and carried it for you on the cross. The Bible says,

> He himself bore our sins in his body on the tree, that we might die to sin and live to righteousness. By his wounds you have been healed. (1 Peter 2:24)

If you minimize your sin, you minimize what Jesus did on the cross. The greater my guilt, the greater his forgiveness and the greater the glory of Jesus who won that forgiveness.

Jesus is glorified in forgiving the greatest sinners in the same way that a doctor is honored when people bring him the hardest cases. Mayo Clinic is famous as a great hospital not because they can cure small things but because people come from around the world with the most desperate diseases. Christ is willing to forgive the greatest sinners because this is how he receives the greatest glory. Since he died to save sinners, he welcomes even the worst. Jesus is like Johns Hopkins or MD Anderson Cancer Center, not the local urgent care clinic. He is not a Savior who can only handle small sinners; his blood has power to save great sinners.[4]

This is a huge comfort if you are worried that God will finally realize what you've done and leave you at the altar like Lady Edith. He forgives the sins of your youth. We are all great sinners, but Christ is a great Savior. His grace is greater than all our sins. When we wait on God and put our trust in him, we wait in confession.

We Wait in Fear

Third, when we put our hope in God, we wait in fear.

How does David move here from forgiveness to fear? This is surprising;

you would think that fear would be the last thing on his mind after speaking of God's forgiveness. In fact, some people think that forgiveness is an excuse not to fear and to sin even more. But that is not what the Bible says.

So how does David move from forgiveness to fear? The power of God is a fearsome thing. When the disciples were about to sink in a storm on the Sea of Galilee, they called out to Jesus, and he stood up and said to the storm, "Peace! Be still!" (Mark 4:39). Immediately the wind stopped, and the sea was calm. When the disciples saw his power, they were terrified (v. 41).

In the same way, the power of God's forgiveness is a fearsome thing. He quiets the wind and the waves of guilt and shame in our hearts. Nothing else could bring peace to our troubled conscience; a sense of awe descends on us as we realize that we have experienced the awesome power of God. This kind of power is at once comforting and unsettling. The forgiveness we experience as we put our hope in God leads us to fear him. The psalmist says,

If you, O Lord, should mark iniquities,
    O Lord, who could stand?
But with you there is forgiveness,
    that you may be feared.

I wait for the Lord, my soul waits,
    and in his word I hope. (Psalm 130:3–5)

The fear of the Lord brings great blessing. After asking God for forgiveness, David turns to us again and teaches us.

Who is the man who fears the Lord?
    Him will he instruct in the way that he should choose.
His soul shall abide in well-being,
    and his offspring shall inherit the land.
The friendship of the Lord is for those who fear him,
    and he makes known to them his covenant.
My eyes are ever toward the Lord,
    for he will pluck my feet out of the net. (25:12–15)

God teaches the man or woman who "fears" him (v. 12). Students and their families are willing to spend tens of thousands of dollars a year to go to the best schools to sit under the best teachers. God himself, the one who created the universe, personally tutors those who fear him.

How does God teach? He teaches us through his Word. Sometimes the Bible gives us direct commands to follow; sometimes the Bible equips us with wisdom to make a good decision. God also teaches us through fellow believers he places in our lives. And sometimes God speaks to our hearts. Charles Spurgeon put it this way: "Those whose hearts are right shall not err for want of heavenly direction. Where God sanctifies the heart he enlightens the head."[5]

And with this God promises his friendship. To be God's friend is more than knowing about him. Friends enjoy each other's company. Friendship is close, personal knowledge. It is one thing for God to teach us which path to take—this is a blessing. For God to make us his friends is almost inconceivable. Apple CEO Tim Cook offered to have coffee for an hour with up to two people. The only catch—it will cost you $210,000. God is not selling you his time—he offers his friendship. He opens his heart to those who fear him and shares his plans and purposes. Do you fear the Lord? This blessing is yours in Christ. Jesus said,

> No longer do I call you servants, for the servant does not know what his master is doing; but I have called you friends, for all that I have heard from my Father I have made known to you. (John 15:15)

God blesses those who fear the Lord.

We Wait in Prayer

Finally, notice that we wait in prayer. David turns once again to call out to God with seven specific petitions.

> Turn to me and be gracious to me,
>   for I am lonely and afflicted.
> The troubles of my heart are enlarged;
>   bring me out of my distresses.
> Consider my affliction and my trouble,
>   and forgive all my sins.
>
> Consider how many are my foes,
>   and with what violent hatred they hate me.
> Oh, guard my soul, and deliver me!
>   Let me not be put to shame, for I take refuge in you.
> May integrity and uprightness preserve me,
>   for I wait for you. (25:16–21)

Will God hear this prayer, or will he leave David standing at the altar? David has already answered this question. "[N]one who wait for you shall be put to shame" (v. 3). God hears the prayers of his people, and he will answer us.

In case we think that this confidence is just for David, verse 22 tells us that he is speaking for all God's people in this psalm.

> Redeem Israel, O God,
> out of all his troubles.

This last line opens the psalm to make it a prayer for all of us who know Christ.[6] We will never know the humiliation of being abandoned and rejected by God. God did redeem Israel by sending Jesus. Nothing can ever separate us from him. If we trust in him, we will never be disappointed.

26

The Man of Integrity

PSALM 26

J. P. HAYES made the national news in 2008 for breaking a rule. Actually it wasn't that he had broken a rule—it was what he did afterward.

Hayes is a middle-of-the-road pro golfer. After a PGA qualifying tournament in Texas, he realized that he had mistakenly used a non-regulation ball for just two strokes. Hayes had a decision to make.

He didn't have to say anything. No one filmed it. No one saw it. No one would ever know about two shots with a prototype golf ball. It wasn't even his fault—his caddy had mistakenly handed him a ball unapproved for competition. "No one would have known, but I knew," he said. "And I have some people looking down on me that would have known, so that was the decision I had to make."[1] Hayes stepped forward and admitted his mistake. His integrity came at a price. Not only was he disqualified from the tournament, he didn't earn a PGA tour card for 2009. So his decision made him ineligible to play full-time for a year.

Hayes's decision made the headlines because it was such a surprise. Integrity is in short supply in our world. In sports Lance Armstrong lied for years about blood doping. School principals have been caught cheating, doctoring their students' test scores. A woman was caught on camera stealing her neighbor's UPS delivery. Parents work the numbers they put on their son's financial aid form for college.

Psalm 26 is about integrity. David begins and ends this psalm with his integrity. He claims "integrity" in verse 1 and commits himself to "integrity" in verse 11. This focus on integrity follows naturally from the penetrating psalms that come before it. Psalm 15 asks,

> O Lord, who shall sojourn in your tent?
> Who shall dwell on your holy hill?
>
> He who walks blamelessly and does what is right
> and speaks truth in his heart. (Psalm 15:1, 2)

Psalm 24 asks almost the same question.

> Who shall ascend the hill of the Lord?
> And who shall stand in his holy place?
> He who has clean hands and a pure heart,
> who does not lift up his soul to what is false
> and does not swear deceitfully. (Psalm 24:3, 4)

God searches our hearts. He is looking for honesty in public and in private. Character is what you do in the dark, when no one is looking—or better, when only God is looking.

In Psalm 26 David claims his integrity and invites God to examine him (vv. 1–3). Then he offers evidence of his integrity through the company he keeps—he doesn't identify with wicked men but loves gathering with God's people for worship (vv. 4–8). Finally, David is confident that God will reward his integrity with redemption (vv. 9–12). We are not sure what trouble David was facing as he asked God to vindicate him. Apparently he could appeal to God with a clean conscience in this particular matter. As we come to the end, we will see that this psalm is bigger than David's integrity in one situation. It points ultimately to the full integrity of Christ.

We will summarize these points under three headings: Nothing to Hide, Nothing in Common, and Nothing to Fear.

Nothing to Hide

David comes to God with confidence because he has nothing to hide. He appeals to God to reward him because of his integrity.

> Vindicate me, O Lord,
> for I have walked in my integrity,
> and I have trusted in the Lord without wavering. (26:1)

The word "vindicate" is literally "judge." The King James Version translates the beginning of verse 1, "Judge me, O Lord [Jehovah]." David willingly walks into the courtroom and asks for God to pass judgment on his life. The word "vindicate" (v. 1) catches the right sense because David is sure that if God takes up his case, he will be vindicated.

God's Approval

David is looking for God's approval. What motivates our honesty and integrity? Some people try to live with integrity because it is good for society. Our city and our nation will prosper when people do what is right, when our word is as strong as a written contract and a handshake seals the deal. This is the "Code of the West," and it's a good thing. But the good of society is not the ultimate motivation. Others try to live with integrity so they don't have to worry about getting caught. It is wise to think about the consequences, but that is not the ultimate motivation.

If you are a Christian, integrity is about God. David's basic motivation is that God will vindicate him and bless him for living a good, upright life. By faith you know that God sees and rewards integrity. The Apostle Paul says,

> He will render to each one according to his works: to those who by patience in well-doing seek for glory and honor and immortality, he will give eternal life; but for those who are self-seeking and do not obey the truth, but obey unrighteousness, there will be wrath and fury. There will be tribulation and distress for every human being who does evil . . . but glory and honor and peace for everyone who does good. . . . For God shows no partiality. (Romans 2:6–11)

God sees, and God rewards. This is the deepest motivation for integrity. If we honor our word and do what is right, society will benefit, and we will not have to worry about getting caught. But the greatest blessing is God's reward. Integrity has everything to do with what we believe about God. By faith we believe that he sees and he acts. So we live for his approval.

Test Me

David has claimed to be a man of integrity, but he does not ask God to take his word for it. He invites God to test him thoroughly, inside and out. David has nothing to hide.

> Prove me, O LORD, and try me;
>   test my heart and my mind.
> For your steadfast love is before my eyes,
>   and I walk in your faithfulness. (26:2, 3)

David submits to God's searching gaze. He invites God to search him with a three-part test: "prove me," "try me," "test [me]" (v. 2). By opening up his "heart" and his "mind" (v. 2),[2] David gives God complete access to poke around in every corner of his inner life.

This threefold testing is thorough. As I went through security at the airport recently, I watched my carry-on bag go through the scanner. First, I saw a general X-ray of the bag—I recognized a black and white image of my laptop and other things I had packed. Then the TSA agent clicked a button, and the image of my bag turned green, red, and orange. This was a different scan, probably to look for liquids or explosives. Then the screen lit up my bag from the top and the side with a third set of colors. When my bag came through, an agent said, "Is this yours?" I had forgotten to take my tiny Swiss Army knife off my keychain. God's threefold testing is more thorough than even airport screening.

The imagery also suggests that God's examination can be painful and purifying.[3] The word "test" (v. 2) refers to the process of melting down metals so the impurities float to the top. God may test your integrity with a trial by fire. You may be honest and upright at room temperature, but what will happen when he turns up the heat?

I remember feeling the heat at tax season several years ago. Our family moved to England for a year so I could finish my doctorate. When I was doing our taxes that next spring, I was painfully tested when I came to the child tax credit. To claim this credit, our family had to have lived in the U.S. for six months. The problem was that we had flown home on the Fourth of July, and no matter how I counted the days, we came up three days short of meeting the residency requirements. But no one would know. And we needed the money. And I was still unemployed—I had finished my doctorate, but we hadn't accepted a call to a church yet. When I did the math, that credit would have given us close to $4,500. It was painful—I felt the heat—but by God's grace I didn't cheat.

God may test your integrity with money—a painful bankruptcy. He may use your reputation—will you still be godly when someone slanders you? Or he may test you with health problems—will you maintain your integrity when your husband has Alzheimer's or your daughter has cancer? Like Job, these tests may be agonizing and painful. But this is how God vindicates his people and proves their character to the world.

Why would anyone ask for this kind of painful, penetrating testing? David has the confidence to lay himself bare before God because he knows who God is. He is focused on God's "steadfast love" (v. 3), his commitment and loyalty to his people. And he is banking on God's "faithfulness" (v. 3). God is good, and you can trust him.

Integrity has everything to do with what we believe about God. We will not live with integrity unless we believe that God rewards. We will not endure the testing of our integrity unless we believe that God loves us and is absolutely faithful.

David has nothing to hide. He wants God's approval on his life, and he opens himself up to God's penetrating, painful testing.

Nothing in Common

David also argues for his integrity based on the company he keeps. He has nothing in common with the wicked but loves to be with God's people.

Nothing in Common with the Wicked

David had turned away from the company of wicked people.

> I do not sit with men of falsehood,
>   nor do I consort with hypocrites.
> I hate the assembly of evildoers,
>   and I will not sit with the wicked. (26:4, 5)

These are the words of a man who is living out Psalm 1.

> Blessed is the man
>   who walks not in the counsel of the wicked,
> nor stands in the way of sinners,
>   nor sits in the seat of scoffers. (Psalm 1:1)

When David says "I do not sit" (26:4), he does not mean that he will never physically sit with them or eat a meal with them. Sitting with "men of falsehood" or "the wicked" (vv. 4, 5) implies belonging with them. You identify with them, want to be like them, count yourself one of them, and choose to spend your time with them.

The company you keep says volumes about your heart. We naturally gravitate to people who are like us. This is why a key measure of godliness starts with the people with whom we identify. Tell me who you like, and I will tell you what you are like. Tell me who you want to be with, and I will tell you who you will be. The Scriptures say, "Do not be deceived: 'Bad company corrupts good morals'" (1 Corinthians 15:33). Many Christians can trace their lost teenage years to the influence of bad people they looked up to.

Having said that, separation is a delicate and difficult matter.[4] Separation is delicate because it can easily lead to pride. We forget that we are great sinners saved by a great Savior. Like the Pharisees, we begin to assume that we are better than the unwashed masses of people who don't go to church. Non-Christians see this superiority from a mile away, and it turns them away from Christ.

Separation is difficult because we can't avoid people. Paul says,

> I wrote to you in my letter not to associate with sexually immoral people—not at all meaning the sexually immoral of this world, or the greedy and swindlers, or idolaters, since then you would need to go out of the world. (1 Corinthians 5:9, 10)

We would have to close ourselves off from the world to avoid bad people. But Jesus has called us to be salt and light in this world. We can't fulfill the Great Commission if we isolate ourselves from non-Christians. Jesus himself welcomed sinners and sat down with them. He didn't want to be like them, of course; he wanted them to become like him. He is a doctor who came to heal sick and sorry sinners (Matthew 9:12, 13). He sat down with sinners like Matthew and Zacchaeus specifically to call them to follow him and enter the kingdom of God.

Christ did not call us to live in a parallel Christian universe; we are called to be in the world but not of it for the sake of the gospel. Aren't you glad for the Christian man or woman whose life touched yours? She came alongside you and shared Christ with you. He sat down with you over lunch and led you to the Lord.

We don't separate from non-believers because we are better than they are. We watch the company we keep because we are not good enough and strong enough to survive in bad company. Jesus had no trouble associating with sinners because he was not one of them. We are sinners, and we do have trouble. Since we are in the world we cannot avoid working with, shopping with, and living with sinners daily. We will build friendships for the sake of the gospel, but we will not identify with the wicked.

These verses can be troubling because David says he "hate[s] the assembly [or congregation] of evildoers." It's not popular to hate anything. We see bumper stickers that say "No h8ters." No one wants to be negative. No one wants to say they hate anything.

The problem with this political correctness is that hatred is a natural and necessary part of love. If you love your daughter, you will hate the intruder who attacks her. If you are not furious at someone who hurts her, you obviously do not love her. The only way to avoid hatred is to be apathetic, simply not to care about anyone or anything. If you love someone, you naturally and necessarily hate anything that hurts or harms that person.

This is why Psalm 11:5 says, "[God's] soul hates the wicked." He is adamantly and eternally angry with everyone who does evil. His wrath is a natural and necessary part of his love. Imagine if God's heart wasn't roused to anger when his people were hurt, mistreated, and abused in this world. He would be like a father who does not care that his child has been abused. God's love for his people must be matched by his hatred for the wicked. For this reason, it is God's glory to hate sinners. He would be less than God if he was not a God of wrath. His forgiveness would mean nothing if his hatred and anger were not real. His love for his people would be a fraud without an equally passionate hatred for the wicked.

In the same way, if you love God, you will hate his enemies. If you love God, you will care when people despise him, say all sorts of evil against him, and shake their fists at him. He is your joy and your delight. You see his beauty and goodness, his glory and splendor. You long for nothing more than to see the light of his face and to live in his presence forever. How can you yawn and be ho-hum when people lie about him and sin against him? This is why the psalmist says,

Do I not hate those who hate you, O LORD?
And do I not loathe those who rise up against you?
I hate them with complete hatred;
I count them my enemies. (Psalm 139:21, 22)

You are defined by what you love and therefore also by what you hate. If you love this sinful world and its wicked ways, you will hate God because he stands over this world as our Judge. This is why the Scriptures say, "Do not love the world or the things in the world. If anyone loves the world, the love of the Father is not in him" (1 John 2:15). If you love God, if he is your joy and delight, you will hate the wicked who turn against him.

This does not mean you will be unkind and spiteful. In the Sermon on the Mount, Jesus taught that our Father in Heaven is good to his enemies. "[H]e makes his sun rise on the evil and on the good, and sends rain on the just and on the unjust" (Matthew 5:45). He does good to the wicked because he is good. And as his children we should do good to everyone too. As Christians, we love our enemies so that we can live as sons and daughters of God in this world. We do good to everyone, wicked and godly alike.

I Love Worshiping with Your People

Since we are defined by our love and hate, David's hatred for the wicked is balanced by his love for worshiping with God's people.

> I wash my hands in innocence
>   and go around your altar, O LORD,
> proclaiming thanksgiving aloud,
>   and telling all your wondrous deeds.
>
> O LORD, I love the habitation of your house
>   and the place where your glory dwells. (26:6–8)

David's offering here is not a sin offering to atone for his transgressions but a thank offering. Thank offerings were not required by the Law. They were given freely to show love for God and devotion to him. These verses may reflect the way Israelites worshiped in the temple, but at the end of the day this historical reconstruction is guesswork.[5]

More importantly, David's love for God and for God's people shines through as a mark of David's integrity. His thank offering and his praise testify to his love for God. In contrast with the assembly of evildoers, he is in the assembly of God's people. Because his heart loved God, he gravitated to the company of those who worshiped God.

When we apply this to ourselves, we need to remember that the church is now the temple of the living God under the new covenant. In Christ we "are being built together into a dwelling place for God by the Spirit" (Ephesians 2:22). So when David says "I love the habitation of your house" (Psalm 26:8), the application for us is to love the church. The church is not a building—the walls and roof are just a rain shelter. The church is God's people gathering around God's Word, wherever they may happen to be. God's glory dwells in us together by his Spirit. It is a marvelous thing to gather together as believers and feel the presence of the Living God himself with us.

If we love God's people, then we will make coming to church a priority. The company we keep says volumes about our heart. Parents, your children are learning your priorities. Show them your love for church by the way you spend your time on Saturday night. Read that Sunday's Scripture together as a family, get your clothes ready, and get to bed at a decent hour so you are not too tired for church the next day. Sports also test our priorities. Our son Andrew played baseball, and he had several tournaments on Sunday mornings. He wasn't able to play in those games because God's people come before his baseball team.

We are defined by what we love. If we love God, we will love being with his people. We will identify with fellow believers, want to be like them, and choose to be with them. This was a mark of David's integrity, and it is a mark of believers today too.

Nothing to Fear

Finally, because of his integrity David had nothing to fear. He could confidently ask God not to judge him along with his enemies. David had separated himself from the wicked in this life. Now he asks God to separate him from them also in the judgment.

> Do not sweep my soul away with sinners,
>   nor my life with bloodthirsty men,
> in whose hands are evil devices,
>   and whose right hands are full of bribes. (26:9, 10)

Instead he was sure that he would come through God's testing with flying colors. David ends with a strong voice.

> But as for me, I shall walk in my integrity;
>   redeem me, and be gracious to me.
> My foot stands on level ground;
>   in the great assembly I will bless the LORD. (26:11, 12)

When we hear David's absolute confidence in these closing verses, it doesn't seem to fit with what we know of his life. He may have been blameless in the specific situation that gave rise to this psalm, but we know that he did not live his whole life with absolute integrity. Even at the end of David's life, he disobeyed the Lord by ordering a census of the people (2 Samuel 24). From what we know about David, this passage could not be about him. This can't be about us either. If we are honest, we will admit that Psalm 26 holds up a standard of integrity we cannot live up to.

David was a prophet; he spoke for Christ. The blameless integrity of Psalm 26 points to the blameless life of Jesus Christ, the true Man of Integrity. Psalm 18 says of him,

> I was blameless before him,
>   and I kept myself from my guilt.
> So the LORD has rewarded me according to my righteousness,
>   according to the cleanness of my hands in his sight. (Psalm 18:23, 24)

The word "blameless" in Psalm 18:23 is the same root as "integrity" in

Psalm 26:1, 11. Psalm 26 continues to fill out the picture of Christ that has been laid out in the Psalms to this point.

If we preach this psalm without Christ, we end up moralizing. All we can do is tell people to try harder, work harder, and do more. But we know we can't possibly be good enough to have the integrity that will survive God's penetrating, painful testing. The psalmist says," If you, O LORD, should mark iniquities, O Lord, who could stand?" (Psalm 130:3). If we apply Psalm 26 without Christ, we load a backpack of religion onto our shoulders that will not bring us any closer to God.

But if we see that Psalm 26 is ultimately about Christ, then we preach the gospel. Jesus is the true Man of Integrity. Jesus is the one man who lived up to Psalm 26 and fulfilled it completely. He had *nothing to hide*—God tested him at the cross, and he was found blameless. Jesus had *nothing in common* with the wicked—he praised God in the congregation of God's people (Psalm 22:22; Hebrews 2:12). He had *nothing to fear*—God did not sweep his life away with the wicked but brought him back from the dead.

If this Jesus is your Savior, then your feet stand on level ground with him. Your life is joined together with his. His blameless integrity is counted as yours. The Spirit of the true Man of Integrity is within you, helping you to obey. His life is within you. You have nothing to fear.

27

My Light and My Salvation

PSALM 27

IN 1812 THE FAMOUS missionary and linguist Henry Martyn finished his translation of the New Testament into Persian. He realized his translation would need the approval of the Shah if it was going to be accepted in Persia (present-day Iran), so Martyn had two beautiful presentation copies prepared with exquisite penmanship. But before he was granted an audience with the Shah, Henry Martyn had to pass through an interview with the Shah's Vizier.

He arrived at court, the only European there, and all eyes were on him. Within minutes the Vizier's officials began arguing with him. For two hours they assaulted Martyn verbally, interrupting him and saying all sorts of lies about him and his book. Henry Martyn stood alone—ten against one. This man seems to have forgotten how to fear—he was a foreigner with no friends in the Persian court.

Finally the Vizier stood up to ask the crucial question. He challenged Martyn to recite the Moslem creed. "Say there is no god but God and Mohammed is his prophet." The court fell silent, and the room crackled with electricity. Henry Martyn writes,

> I said, "God is god" but added, instead of "Mahomet is the prophet of God," "and Jesus is the Son of God." They all rose up as if they would have torn me in pieces, snarling out one of the classic fighting cries of the Moslem world, "He is neither begotten nor begets." "What will you do when your tongue is burnt out for this blasphemy?"[1]

Martyn's beautiful copy of the New Testament was on the floor before the Vizier. Martyn was afraid the men would trample it in their fury. He went in among them and wrapped it carefully in a towel while they glared at him with contempt.

Christ-centered bravery is not just for missionaries two hundred years ago. We need confidence and courage ourselves today. We might be afraid to stand for Christ when we are alone on a business trip with our boss and our colleagues. We might be afraid to stand as a Christian at a family reunion. We might have to trust God with a hard situation in our marriage. We might be terrified as we stand beside a hospital bed, wondering what the future holds.

Psalm 27 is a psalm of confidence and courage. It starts with the question, "whom shall I fear?" It ends with, "Let your heart take courage." The good news of the gospel is that we have an anchor for our souls. We can be calm and confident, courageous and brave. How? Because God gives us himself. And if we have him, we have no need to fear. We will organize this psalm around four words: confidence, presence, deliverance, and patience.

Confidence

David starts by declaring his confidence in God. The word "fear" or "afraid" is repeated three times in the first three verses. This is a reminder that, humanly speaking, David should fear. Verse 12 tells us what the danger might be: "adversaries" and "false witnesses." Even though enemies are lying about him and his life is in danger, he knows God and what God has done for him.

David's Confidence

God is three things to David: his "light," "salvation," and "stronghold."

> The LORD is my light and my salvation;
>   whom shall I fear?
> The LORD is the stronghold of my life;
>   of whom shall I be afraid? (27:1)

David makes a strong braid with these three descriptions. "Light" and "salvation" are parallel to each other and help explain each other. Both of them are then set in parallel with the second phrase, describing God as a "stronghold." Together these three descriptions emphasize God's protection—a cord of three strands that cannot be broken.[2]

Light means security. As a shepherd, David knew the light of a fire was important to protect his sheep through the night. As a soldier, David knew that enemies are dangerous under cover of darkness. If you are walking on a dark trail, you carry a light so you don't trip over a rock or fall into a trench.

If you are walking in a dark parking lot, you might carry a flashlight in case someone is waiting for you. When I was a boy, I snuck a flashlight to bed with me because I was afraid of the shadows in my room.

Some of the dangers of darkness are real, but the light exposes them so we can deal with them. Some are imaginary—the light exposes them for what they are. The light of God's presence is David's security. Even if he walks through the valley of the shadow of death, God will be his light in the darkness (Psalm 18:28; 23:4).

Interestingly, this is the only passage in the Old Testament where God himself is described as light. Elsewhere it says that God created light, he gave light, and he shone with light, but nowhere else does the Old Testament identify God *as* light. In the New Testament, James says God is "the Father of lights with whom there is no variation or shadow" (James 1:17). The Apostle John says, "God is light, and in him is no darkness at all" (1 John 1:5).

Most significantly, Jesus Christ is himself light. John says about Jesus, "The light shines in the darkness, and the darkness has not overcome it. . . . The true light, which gives light to everyone, was coming into the world" (John 1:5, 9). Jesus is our light, the very radiance of God himself. And as the light, Jesus is our security. For us on this side of the cross, the confidence and courage of Psalm 27 starts with Jesus, the Light of the world. He protects us from the dangers of darkness.

David also says God is his "salvation" (v. 1). This has to do with deliverance or rescue. If Seal Team 6 is going to rescue you, you have good reason to be confident. God does not merely rescue his people, he himself *is* their rescue, their salvation. This reality is so powerful that David exclaims, "whom shall I fear?" (v. 1). Who indeed? "If God is for us, who can be against us?" (Romans 8:31).

David's confidence continues as he calls God his "stronghold" or "refuge" (Psalm 27:1). Some translations render this word "strength," but in any event the result is the same. God not only protects him, God himself *is* protection.

One of the most important words in this verse is "my." It is a small word—two letters in English and one letter in Hebrew—but it makes all the difference. It is not enough to know that the Lord is light—even the demons know this. You must be able to say, "The LORD is *my* light" (v. 1). It is not enough to know that God is a Savior, a stronghold—the demons know this too. He must be your Savior, your stronghold.

Some people who attend church know about God, but they do not know God. They are like travel agents who get so used to talking about far-off places like Tahiti and Bora Bora that they begin to think they have been there. They can talk about Jesus, but they have never truly met Jesus, and they do not love him. They know about God, but they do not know God. They cannot say with confidence, "The LORD is my light . . . my salvation . . . [my] stronghold" (v. 1). If Psalm 27 is going to be yours, you need to be his.

No Fear

David matches the three descriptions of God in verse 1 with four descriptions of his enemies in verses 2, 3. This subtle detail shows that God is not outmatched no matter how many are against us.

> When evildoers assail me
> > to eat up my flesh,
> my adversaries and foes,
> > it is they who stumble and fall.
>
> Though an army encamp against me,
> > my heart shall not fear;
> though war arise against me,
> > yet I will be confident. (27:2, 3)

Since the "evildoers" want to "eat [his] flesh" (v. 2), you might think that he is talking about cannibalism. It's more likely that this is a figure of speech comparing them to wild animals. In Psalm 22 it is prophesied that men would surround the Messiah like ravenous beasts.

> [T]hey open wide their mouths at me,
> > like a ravening and roaring lion . . .
>
> dogs encompass me;
> > a company of evildoers encircles me. (Psalm 22:13, 16)

The language of Psalm 27 and Psalm 22 is so similar at this point that it suggests David is talking about the same thing. In the context of the psalms, David is not only speaking for himself in Psalm 27; he speaks as a prophet foretelling the confidence of our Lord Jesus Christ. This is hugely encouraging because it reminds us that as a man who was as fully human as we are, Jesus trusted God. The Son of God was rescued by God the Father from his enemies. Jesus was truly alone as he walked to the cross—even his closest disciples ran away from him. Yet his heart did not fear, and he was confident when the armies of darkness surrounded him. And if the Spirit of Jesus is living inside us, he can give us his confidence.

Our ultimate options are faith or fear. When we face death, our final enemy, either we know the living God or we do not. As the atheist philosopher Bertrand Russell, advanced in years, said, "The older I get, the more nervous I become."[3] What a contrast with the end of Jonathan Edwards's life. Minutes before he died, Edwards looked about and said, "Now where is Jesus of Nazareth, my true and never-failing friend?" He closed his eyes and those at his bedside thought he was gone. They were surprised when he suddenly uttered a final sentence, "Trust in God, and you need not fear."[4]

Presence

David's confidence is rooted in God's presence. Those who trust God love God and long to be with him.

One Desire

David is literally obsessed with living in God's presence—this is his one desire. Is God our desire?

In the book of Esther, King Ahasuerus was so taken with Queen Esther that he offered to give her whatever she wanted—up to half his kingdom (Esther 5:3, 6). Ahasuerus ruled from India to Ethiopia, an enormous empire with vast riches, and she could have anything her heart desired. What an offer! Imagine if someone said that to us.

If God offered to give you whatever you asked for, what would it be? What is the *one thing* that means the most to you? What would you choose? Pay off your student loans or your mortgage? Marry a certain person? Feel secure for retirement? Would you ask for healing? Maybe you're facing a problem, and you want to know what to do; you would ask for wisdom. What is the one thing you would ask for?

David knows what he wants.

> One thing have I asked of the LORD,
>   that will I seek after:
> that I may dwell in the house of the LORD
>   all the days of my life,
> to gaze upon the beauty of the LORD
>   and to inquire in his temple. (27:4)

God himself is David's great ambition. Living in "the house of the LORD" (v. 4) is a picture of enjoying God's presence constantly.[5] God himself is the greatest gift for which we could ask. He reveals his beauty in his generous goodness to his people. There is nothing better than he, bigger than he, greater than he, grander than he, more satisfying than he, more enjoyable than he, more dependable than he, more fun than he, more lasting than he, or more rewarding than God is himself. We would be fools to ask for anything less than God.

The best and final gift of God's love is the joy of having God himself. David says,

> I say to the LORD, "You are my Lord;
>   I have no good apart from you." . . .
>
> You make known to me the path of life;
>   in your presence there is fullness of joy;
>   at your right hand are pleasures forevermore. (Psalm 16:2, 11)

And again,

> Out of Zion, the perfection of beauty,
>   God shines forth. (Psalm 50:2)

And again,

> A day in your courts is better
>   than a thousand elsewhere. (Psalm 84:10)

David is empty and dry when God is not near. He cannot be satisfied by anything less than the reality of God himself.

> O God, you are my God; earnestly I seek you;
>   my soul thirsts for you;
> my flesh faints for you,
>   as in a dry and weary land where there is no water.
> So I have looked upon you in the sanctuary,
>   beholding your power and glory.
> Because your steadfast love is better than life,
>   my lips will praise you. (Psalm 63:1–3)

The best, most glorious gift you could ask for is to have God himself, to wonder at his beauty and praise him with all your heart.

We might wonder how making much of God could be good for us. Why ask to see him, "to gaze upon the beauty of the LORD" (27:4)? After all, wouldn't we be happier if God made much of us instead?

Think of it this way. Suppose you were to drive to the Grand Canyon. When you get there, you get out of the car on the South Rim and walk to an observation point, and the view takes your breath away. The Canyon is enormous—you can't see it all from one spot. The Canyon is ever changing. As the sun crosses the sky, the stones change color, and the formations stand out against the shadows as the light shifts across the rock formations. The overwhelming vastness leaves you in awe. The joy and attractiveness of the Grand Canyon comes from seeing a wonder that is big and beautiful and beyond yourself. You are willing to drive a thousand miles or more to see this amazing sight. It is a real pleasure and joy to gaze at the beauty of the Grand Canyon.

The greatest joy comes from gazing at a God who is big and beautiful and infinitely beyond ourselves. God is so wonderful that we will gaze at him for all eternity. He captures our attention and fills our heart more than any mountain range or work of art. We will not want to pull our eyes away from him for a moment.

What if having God himself doesn't seem very appealing? If that's the case, then there is something wrong with you. When a man has no appetite, you assume that he is not feeling well, there is something wrong with his body. When a man has no appetite "to gaze upon the beauty of the LORD" (v. 4), there is something wrong with his soul. David had an appetite for God.

If we are Christians, we have already begun gazing at the Lord. With spiritual sight we see the glory of God in the Lord Jesus Christ, who is the image of God. The Scriptures say, "And we all, with unveiled face, beholding the glory of the Lord, are being transformed into the same image from one degree of glory to another" (2 Corinthians 3:18). We hunger and thirst for Christ. We will gaze on him for all eternity.

> The best and final gift of the gospel is that we gain Christ. "I count everything as loss because of the surpassing worth of knowing Christ Jesus my Lord. For his sake I have suffered the loss of all things and count them as rubbish, in order that I may gain Christ" (Phil. 3:8). This is the all-encompassing gift of God's love through the gospel—to see and savor the glory of Christ forever.[6]

One Shelter

Without God we have nothing. But when we have God we have everything. David lists the blessings of God's protection that come from knowing God and living in his presence.

For he will hide me in his shelter
    in the day of trouble;
he will conceal me under the cover of his tent;
    he will lift me high upon a rock.

And now my head shall be lifted up
    above my enemies all around me,
and I will offer in his tent
    sacrifices with shouts of joy;
I will sing and make melody to the LORD. (27:5, 6)

The three words of protection in verse 5 emphasize complete care: God "will hide me," "conceal me," "lift me." The three results in verse 6 emphasize the results of God's care. David is honored as his head is "lifted up." He worships God by "offer[ing] . . . sacrifices." He "will sing" to God in praise. These are the dynamics of experiencing God's presence, the blessings that come to those who know him.

Deliverance

Following David's confidence and his longing for God's presence, David cries out for deliverance. Up to this point David has been talking to himself or to us. Now his meditation turns to conversation. His faith turns into active prayer.

Hear, O LORD, when I cry aloud;
    be gracious to me and answer me!
You have said, "Seek my face."
My heart says to you,
    "Your face, LORD, do I seek."
    Hide not your face from me.
Turn not your servant away in anger,
    O you who have been my help.
Cast me not off; forsake me not,
    O God of my salvation!
For my father and my mother have forsaken me,
    but the LORD will take me in.

Teach me your way, O LORD,
    and lead me on a level path
    because of my enemies.
Give me not up to the will of my adversaries;
    for false witnesses have risen against me,
    and they breathe out violence. (27:7–12)

David's prayer shows us the reality of his suffering in spite of his strong faith. You do not call out to God like this if he has already saved you from your enemies. He is still in the heat of the battle. But by faith David knows he is accepted and God will not abandon him. And so he prays passionately for God to intervene.

There is almost nothing more crushing and devastating than being rejected by your own parents. Many orphans are driven to know why their parents let them go. A woman might work for decades to unlock sealed court records because she needs to know that her mother had no choice. Some boys and girls grow up with rejection. Many years ago a friend shared in his testimony that his mother had rejected him. From their earliest years she told him and his brothers clearly that she did not want them and wished they were not in her life. She lived in the home, but she was cold to them and did not care for them in any way. As a grown man he cried openly in front of one hundred people as he shared his story. Some children experience ultimate rejection. In many Muslim settings if you become a Christian, your family will cut you off and maybe kill you to preserve the family honor.

To people who have felt the pain of a parent's rejection, verse 10 is comforting beyond words: "[M]y father and my mother have forsaken me, but the LORD will take me in." God loves you more than any human mother or father. He wraps his arms around you and holds you close. He hears you. He teaches you. He gives you advice. He protects you. He will always welcome you, no matter what hour of the day or night.

Patience

David returns to the quiet confidence he had at the beginning of this psalm. He waits with patience.

His patience is marked by faith.

I believe that I shall look upon the goodness of the LORD
   in the land of the living! (27:13)

This may mean that David expects God to rescue him during his lifetime. God certainly did step into David's life at various times to save him from death.

On the other hand, this also could mean that David knew God would save him through death, that he would live again to see the goodness of God after the resurrection. In Psalm 23:6, for instance, David expects to experience

God's goodness after death for eternity. In fact, the resurrection was a vital part of Old Testament faith. Job says,

> For I know that my Redeemer lives,
>   and at the last he will stand upon the earth.
> And after my skin has been thus destroyed,
>   yet in my flesh I shall see God,
> whom I shall see for myself,
>   and my eyes shall behold, and not another. (Job 19:25–27)

With this kind of faith in the resurrection, there is no need to fear. You will see the goodness and beauty of God forever—not in these shadowlands, but in the true land of the living.

David ends with his final challenge.

> Wait for the LORD;
>   be strong, and let your heart take courage;
>   wait for the LORD! (27:14)

Don't just wait—"wait . . . be strong"! "Take courage," stand firm, and wait.

Christian, you have asked for the greatest thing—for God himself. With God, you have everything. He is your light, your salvation, your stronghold. "[W]hom shall I fear?" (v. 1).

28

My Strength and My Shield

PSALM 28

HAVE YOU EVER FELT like God did not hear your prayer? You poured out your heart to him—maybe at night, maybe with tears—and a hopeless fear gripped your heart that maybe God was not listening. God might have turned away from you, and you began to panic as a cold sense of despair rose like floodwaters in your soul.

Most of us have had this sort of desperate feeling at one point. It is comforting to know that David experienced this too. The specific thing David is praying about is in verses 3–5. He is afraid that God will number him with the wicked and drag him off to judgment. What could be worse than that? An IRS audit strikes fear because the agent has the power to charge you as a criminal and ruin your life. But imagine if God files you with the wicked and has you dragged away from his presence. That is terrifying indeed.

But while Psalm 28 begins as a passionate prayer, it ends with passionate praise. God does hear and answer him. In verse 2 David says, "Hear the voice of my pleas for mercy." He repeats almost the exact same words in verse 6 because God answered him. "Blessed be the LORD! For he *has* heard the voice of my pleas for mercy." So we meet David at the beginning of this psalm in the dark of midnight. As he prays, the sun rises, and we end with songs of joy.

Hear!

As he began to pray, David cried out for God to hear.

> To you, O LORD, I call;
>   my rock, be not deaf to me,
> lest, if you be silent to me,
>   I become like those who go down to the pit.

Hear the voice of my pleas for mercy,
  when I cry to you for help,
when I lift up my hands
  toward your most holy sanctuary. (28:1, 2)

God hears every whisper, and he knows our words before they reach our tongue (Psalm 139:4). David is not talking about literal deafness. He is talking about God's disposition to him. He is worried that God will give him the cold shoulder and ignore him. He pleads with God to be favorable. The word "mercy" (v. 2) should probably be translated as "grace" or "favor,"[1] God's kindness to him.

Psalm 27:14 says, "Wait for the LORD," and evidently David had waited so long it felt like God would not answer. Jesus told the parable of the persistent widow to show that we should always pray and never give up. Night and day she bothered the judge until he finally gave in and heard her case. David showed this same kind of persistence. The word "pleas" (v. 2) is plural, showing that he prayed and prayed again. If God has not heard our prayer, we must not give up! We need to keep praying. This is one of the ways God builds endurance in his children and strengthens our faith.

Judge!

The heart of Psalm 28 is in verses 3–5 as David lays out the substance of his prayer, asking God to judge rightly. In his prayer he asks God to judge with discernment, to judge by works, and to judge for unbelief.

Judge with Discernment

David asks God to judge with discernment. David's fear was that he would be swept away as one of the wicked.[2]

Do not drag me off with the wicked,
  with the workers of evil,
who speak peace with their neighbors
  while evil is in their hearts. (28:3)

We don't know what David was going through when he prayed this. Why would he have been particularly worried that God would drag him off with the wicked? He knew he was a sinner, of course, and there were times when his conscience condemned him. But Psalm 28 does not give us enough historical information to pin it to one event in David's life.

When we look forward to Christ, though, we can see clearly how this psalm points to him. As a human being, Jesus had good reason to plead with God, "Do not drag me off with the wicked" (v. 3). Jesus was publicly accused of being evil himself; many lumped him together with the wicked. Jesus counted on God to see through the spin and the smears to judge rightly, to clear his name, and to show the difference between him and the wicked.

Think of the false accusations that were leveled at Jesus during his life. He was accused of being a glutton and an alcoholic, a friend of tax collectors and prostitutes (Luke 7:34–39). The Pharisees accused him of being demon-possessed (Mark 3:22). When he was arrested, they came looking for him with swords and clubs as if he were a robber (Matthew 26:55). At his trial they accused him of blasphemy and beat him as a heretic. When they turned him over to Pilate, they charged him with rebellion.

These false accusations came to a head at the cross. The cross was such a gruesome means of execution that the word *cross* itself was vulgar, something like a swear word in Latin. They would use euphemisms like "Hang him on the tree." To be crucified was unspeakably shameful—clear evidence that you were a criminal and a danger to society. If there was any doubt, Jesus was crucified between two insurgents or terrorists. Imagine the optics if you were sentenced to be executed with Dzhokhar Tsarnaev, the Boston Bomber—people would assume that you were a violent criminal yourself.

To make matters even worse, the Law of Moses placed a curse on anyone who was crucified. Deuteronomy declares that anyone hung on a tree is "cursed by God" (Deuteronomy 21:23; cf. Galatians 3:13). Jesus was not only accused by Jews and Romans—God made him a curse through the Law of Moses.

As Jesus was slandered and falsely accused, he appealed to God to judge with justice and not to drag him off with the wicked. And Jesus was heard! God was his strength and shield, a refuge for his Anointed, the Messiah.

Christians are falsely accused just like Jesus was. Paul was thrown in jail for disturbing the city of Philippi (Acts 16:20–23). He was wrongfully accused of bringing a Gentile into the temple (Acts 21:27ff.). A Roman tribune assumed he was a rebel leader with four thousand assassins under his command (Acts 21:38). In the early days of the church, Christians were accused of cannibalism, incest, and other crimes. Nero accused Christians of burning down Rome.

Christians are accused of all sorts of evils today. Recently a pro-life woman quoted Washington, D.C. abortionist Dr. Cesare F. Santangelo as saying he would make sure the baby died if the little one was born alive. How did he respond when confronted with the evidence that he planned to murder a newborn? He accused the pro-life worker of being a terrorist.[3]

There is more on the way. If you believe the Bible is God's Word, many academics, journalists, and politicians will label you a fundamentalist. As a fundamentalist, you are then tarred with the same brush as fundamentalist Muslims and other dangerous groups. We can expect to experience more and more false accusations in the coming years.

How will we handle it? Ultimately we lift up the same prayer as our Lord Jesus Christ in Psalm 28, "Do not drag me off with the wicked" (v. 3a). *Lord, they may accuse, but you judge with discernment. I am not an evildoer. You know how to rescue the godly and clear their name; you know how to reward and punish the wicked* (cf. 2 Peter 2:9).

Judge by Works

Next David asked God to judge by works.

> Give to them according to their work
>   and according to the evil of their deeds;
> give to them according to the work of their hands;
>   render them their due reward. (28:4)

God will judge each man and woman according to what he or she has done. This is not just an Old Testament teaching. Jesus said,

> For the Son of Man is going to come with his angels in the glory of his Father, and then he will repay each person according to what he has done. (Matthew 16:27)

The Apostle Paul teaches the same thing in Romans 2:6–11.

> He will render to each one according to his works: to those who by patience in well-doing seek for glory and honor and immortality, he will give eternal life; but for those who are self-seeking and do not obey the truth, but obey unrighteousness, there will be wrath and fury. . . . For God shows no partiality. (Romans 2:6–8, 11)

As evangelicals we downplay this clear teaching of Scripture because it sounds like salvation by works. Paul says elsewhere in Romans that we are justified—made right with God—"by faith apart from works" (Romans 3:28). But he sees no contradiction between salvation by faith and judgment according to works.

Would it be a contradiction with the gospel of free and sovereign grace if that Gospel were powerful enough that all who truly believed it were radically changed by it and came to heaven on the path of persevering obedience?[4]

The old saying is true: "We are saved by faith alone, but saving faith is never alone." If you belong to God, you will persevere in doing good. You will not be perfect, but you will persevere with patience. The path to Heaven is really the path of obedience, and God's judgment really does line up with our works.

In Psalm 28 David is not a worker of evil. He can confidently ask God to repay the wicked "according to their work," knowing that he is not one of them. He asks God to judge them by their works. The Apostle Paul writes,

> But God's firm foundation stands, bearing this seal: "The Lord knows those who are his," and, "Let everyone who names the name of the Lord depart from iniquity." (2 Timothy 2:19)

Judge for Unbelief

Ultimately their evil actions come from evil hearts that refuse to love God and worship him.[5] David asks God to judge them for their unbelief.

> Because they do not regard the works of the LORD
>   or the work of his hands,
> he will tear them down and build them up no more. (28:5)

These wicked men seem to be Israelites. They have God's Word, but they have not seen God in his Word. "The works of the LORD" here are especially his work in creation and his work in bringing Israel out of Egypt. He revealed himself to Israel by showing his power and glory through these events. But the wicked refuse to understand who God is and give him the glory he deserves.

In the same way, many today have God's Word, but "they do not regard the works of the LORD" (v. 5). The frightening message is that God judges this unbelief. God will bulldoze them to the ground.

Blessed Be the LORD!

The wonderful conclusion of this psalm is that God did hear David's prayer. He heard Christ's prayer. Christian, he hears your prayer.

> Blessed be the LORD!
>   For he has heard the voice of my pleas for mercy.

The LORD is my strength and my shield;
   in him my heart trusts, and I am helped;
my heart exults,
   and with my song I give thanks to him. (28:6, 7)

The great fear on David's heart was that God no longer cared for him and would treat him as one of the wicked. We don't know how the answer came, but now he knows that God heard his prayer and still cares for him. This is a prayer of faith—David does not say that God rescued him from the situation he was in. But he knows God is on his side, and God himself is his "strength and . . . shield" (v. 7). He trusts in God, which means that he is still walking by faith, not by sight—and by faith he sings for joy.

Since David was the king, the blessing expands to the nation.

The LORD is the strength of his people;
   he is the saving refuge of his anointed.
Oh, save your people and bless your heritage!
   Be their shepherd and carry them forever. (28:8, 9)

God strengthens his people by saving his Messiah, his Anointed One. Indeed, God's power is for us through the resurrection of Christ from the dead. Our great hope is that the same power that raised Jesus is at work in us.

If you are a believer, he is your Shepherd. Don't stop praying—he hears you. His arms never get tired. He will carry you forever.

29

The Lord of the Storm

PSALM 29

ON THE AFTERNOON OF MAY 20, 2013, a violent tornado tore through Moore, Oklahoma. It is hard to imagine the destruction. The tornado was 1.3 miles wide; it was on the ground for over forty minutes; it churned on a seventeen-mile path through a suburb of Oklahoma City. Within minutes entire neighborhoods were flattened. The amount of energy in a storm like that is staggering. Some estimated that this EF5 tornado was up to six hundred times more powerful than the atom bomb that was dropped on Hiroshima.

Psalm 29 describes the power of God like a raging storm. Charles Spurgeon writes, "This Psalm is meant to express the glory of God as heard in the pealing thunder, and seen in . . . [a] tornado. . . . The verses march to the tune of thunderbolts."[1] God reveals his majesty, power, and glory in the furious wind, pelting rain, blinding flashes of lightning, and deafening thunder of a violent tempest.

Frankly, this picture of God's power is disturbing. Why would David compare the voice of God to a violent and destructive storm? The fact is, the God we serve is not a tame God, a god we can lead around on a leash. He is not a puny God. Rather, "the God of glory thunders" (29:3). Even in our modern world we fear the power of a storm. That visceral fear helps us learn the fear of the Lord.

Notice the context. Immediately before this, Psalm 28:8 says, "The LORD is the strength of his people; he is the saving refuge of his anointed." In spite of this, Israel was tempted to worship other gods and to look for strength in the idols that their neighbors worshiped. Psalm 29 was a wake-up call—a reminder that the Lord, the God of Israel, is the one true and mighty God. *This God whose voice breaks the cedars is your strength. This mighty God saves and protects the coming Messiah, the Anointed One.* So following immediately after Psalm 28, Psalm 29 taught Israel to trust in God alone and to hope in Christ.

We need to see God's mighty power for ourselves today too. If our God is a puny god, we will have puny faith. If our God is mighty, the door is open for us to have mighty faith. The untamed power of God is like the tempest—and *he* is our strength. This graphic description of the unchained power of God teaches us to trust in God and hope in Christ. This God whose voice breaks the cedars will break every enemy who lifts himself up against Jesus Christ. And through Christ, God will bless us with peace.

At its core Psalm 29 is about God. David uses the personal name Yahweh, translated "the Lord," eighteen times in these eleven verses. We will organize Psalm 29 under three headings: the call before the storm (vv. 1, 2), the power of the storm (vv. 3–9), and the calm after the storm (vv. 10, 11).

The Call before the Storm

David begins with a call to worship. David repeats the word "ascribe" three times to specify who, what, and why he issues this call. Since we know a storm is coming, verses 1, 2 are something like a tornado siren. This is the call before the storm.

> Ascribe to the Lord, O heavenly beings,
>   ascribe to the Lord glory and strength.
> Ascribe to the Lord the glory due his name;
>   worship the Lord in the splendor of holiness. (29:1, 2)

Calling the Gods to Worship

Interestingly, David issues this call to spiritual beings, to gods. The phrase "heavenly beings" (v. 1) is literally "sons of gods." This is sometimes translated "sons of the mighty," but the original reference was to pagan gods, the idols worshiped by Israel's neighbors.[2] David calls these foreign gods to bow down and worship Yahweh, the God of Israel. David puts these foreign gods in their place.

A few years before David was born, foreign gods did bow down to the Lord. When the prophet Samuel was a boy, the ark of the covenant was captured by the Philistines, and they placed it in the temple of their god, Dagon. When they came back in the morning, the idol had fallen down on its face before the ark of the Lord. They propped him back up, but when they came in the next morning, the statue had fallen again—and this time his head and hands were broken off and lying on the threshold (1 Samuel 5:1–5). The gods of the nations cannot stand before Yahweh, the God of Israel.

Although David is calling these idols to worship, he is really calling Israel to worship God. The people of Israel were tempted to worship idols again and again. Why turn to idols when these foreign gods were forced to recognize the greatness and overwhelming majesty of the Lord? By urging these gods to worship Yahweh, "the LORD" (Psalm 29:1, 2), David is speaking to wayward, idolatrous Israel.[3]

This background in Israel's idolatry is reinforced by the language and form of this psalm. Psalm 29 is very similar to ancient Canaanite poems about their gods. For instance, Baal is often described as riding on the clouds, and he is pictured with a lightning bolt in his hand.[4] David uses the language and forms of Canaanite worship to show that Yahweh is superior to these gods, turning their own poetry against them. Peter Craigie writes,

> The general storm image of battle has been subtly transformed into a taunt-like psalm; the praise of the Lord, by virtue of being expressed in the language and imagery associated with the Canaanite weather-god, Baal, taunts the weak deity of the defeated foes, namely the Canaanites. Thus the poet has deliberately utilized Canaanite-type language and imagery in order to emphasize the Lord's strength and victory, in contrast to the weakness of . . . Baal.[5]

As William Booth led the Salvation Army in the late nineteenth century, he did much the same thing with the popular music of his day.[6] One famous example is when the Salvation Army took a song that was wildly popular on the streets of London, "Champagne Charlie," and turned it into one of their favorite hymns, "Bless His Name, He Sets Me Free." Booth reasoned that all music belongs to God anyway—after all, "[t]he earth is the LORD's and the fullness thereof" (Psalm 24:1). So it is right to reclaim songs for his glory. Booth said, "It is like taking the enemy's guns and turning them against him."[7]

Glory and Strength

David is speaking to Israel by addressing foreign gods in the style of Canaanite poetry. What does he call them to do? They must announce the "glory and strength" of Yahweh (29:1).

The word "glory" means "to be heavy" and by extension "to be important." Glory is "that asset which makes people or individuals, and even objects, impressive."[8] These false gods wanted glory and worship for themselves, of course. But God says in Isaiah 42:8, "I am the LORD; that is my name; my glory I give to no other, nor my praise to carved idols." With this storm on the horizon, David warns them to acknowledge that Yahweh alone is impressive, important, weighty, glorious.

"The splendor of holiness" (Psalm 29:2) refers to God's holiness, not the holiness of these idols who bow before Yahweh. Derek Kidner translates this, "worship the LORD for the splendour of his holiness."[9] The splendor of God in his holiness is the visual splendor of a king in his robes. When the Lord appears in power and glory, these pagan gods can only recognize his majesty and bow down in worship.

The Power of the Storm

This sets the stage for God to reveal his majesty and greatness in the power of the storm. David describes the overwhelming glory of God in the tempest.

The Storm Tracker

After the tornado hit Moore, Oklahoma radar showed the storm track in red, orange, and yellow as the storm cells traveled up I–44 toward Tulsa. David writes verses 3–9 like a meteorologist describing the track of a tornado. The picture is of a storm sweeping in from the sea with devastating power.

The storm gathers over the Mediterranean Sea.

> The voice of the LORD is over the waters;
>   the God of glory thunders,
>   the LORD, over many waters.
> The voice of the LORD is powerful;
>   the voice of the LORD is full of majesty. (29:3, 4)

Storms can grow to ferocious power as they feed on moisture. Hurricanes grow over the Atlantic as the sun evaporates surface water and updrafts lift the humid air into the atmosphere. The same process occurs over the Mediterranean as weather systems move across that sea. The phrase "many waters" (v. 3) could be translated "mighty waters," emphasizing the power of the sea.

Beyond the physical picture of this growing storm, though, the voice of God thundering over the waters represents a spiritual victory over the Canaanite gods. "The region of the sea was considered by the Canaanites to be the battleground between Yam, the god of the sea and of chaos, and Baal, the god of fertility and thunderstorms."[10] But David proclaims that Yahweh displays his glory over both of them as his voice thunders in triumph.

Then the storm makes landfall on the coast of Lebanon in the north.

> The voice of the LORD breaks the cedars;
>> the LORD breaks the cedars of Lebanon.
> He makes Lebanon to skip like a calf,
>> and Sirion like a young wild ox. (29:5, 6)

The cedars of Lebanon were known throughout the Ancient Near East as the most spectacular trees in the region. Solomon imported cedars from Lebanon to build his palace and the temple of the Lord in Jerusalem. Even today the Lebanese flag has the outline of a spreading cedar tree in the center. But these tall, majestic trees snap like matchsticks at the sound of God's voice.

In verse 6 "Sirion" is the Sidonian name for Mount Hermon (Deuteronomy 3:9). So "Lebanon" and "Sirion" refer to the two great mountains in the north, Mount Lebanon and Mount Hermon. When God speaks, his voice shakes these majestic mountains. He is not only more powerful and glorious than the waters of the sea—his voice shakes the hills as his lightning strikes the mountaintops.

Once again there is a spiritual victory represented here as well. The forests of Lebanon were considered sacred to the Mesopotamian gods, who used the cedars to build their homes.[11] When God's voice breaks the cedars, he violates their sacred forest and shows that he has power to snap the beams of their houses.

The Canaanites believed that Mount Lebanon and Mount Hermon were the abode of the gods.[12] Yahweh speaks, and these mighty mountains skip like calves. Our family brought some friends to the Will Rogers Stampede in Claremore, Oklahoma so they could see a rodeo. Halfway through the night, they asked all the children ten and under to come down from the stands to try to grab a flag from the tail of a calf. They released three calves, and all fifty children chased these running, skipping calves around the arena. The solid mountains leap like these calves that wouldn't stand still! The Lord displays his glory once again over the idols of the Canaanites.

Finally the storm moves over the wilderness of Kadesh.

> The voice of the LORD flashes forth flames of fire.
> The voice of the LORD shakes the wilderness;
>> the LORD shakes the wilderness of Kadesh.

> The voice of the LORD makes the deer give birth
>> and strips the forests bare,
>> and in his temple all cry, "Glory!" (29:7–9)

The phrase "makes the deer give birth" (v. 9) should probably be translated "makes the oaks to shake." Hebrew was originally written with only consonants, as modern Hebrew is today. The Masoretes, Jewish scholars, came up with a system of vowels around AD 1000 for the Old Testament. Their system of vowels is brilliant, and we use their Masoretic Text to this day. But every so often we come across a word where many scholars agree the word should be read with different vowels. This is the case here. If we read the beginning of verse 9 with the vowels of the Masoretic text, God's voice sends deer into premature labor. If we use different vowels, though, verse 9 reads, "The voice of the LORD makes the oaks to shake and strips the forests bare." This translation seems to make more sense in this context.

Kadesh could be one of two places. There is Kadesh-Barnea on the southern border of Israel, an oasis in the desert. Israel camped there in the exodus, and Moses sent out the spies to report on the land. There is another Kadesh to the north, on the Orontes River in Syria, between Damascus and Aleppo.

David could be referring to either place. If it is the southern Kadesh, this storm makes landfall in Lebanon and sweeps down the length of Israel with its destructive power. I think he means the northern Kadesh, though, because he mentions "forests" in verse 9. There are no forests in the far south, but there are forests in Lebanon and Syria. David seems to be watching this storm come in off the sea to the north of Israel and devastate the forests as it travels inland to Syria.

When I was in college, we had football practice in the rain early one morning. Football coaches do not usually cancel practice for a little rain. They yelled into the locker room as we got ready, "Come on, boys, you're not going to rust!" So out we went. The rain began to pick up, and we saw lightning in the distance. The thunder started getting closer, but none of us paid any attention. Then, without warning, a bolt of lightning shot down and split one of the trees on the edge of the practice field! I had always pictured lightning as being narrow, like a laser beam. This lightning bolt was more like a freight train, and the thunderclap literally shook the field.

Instantly all of us hit the deck, one hundred football players with their faces in the mud. One of our coaches was on crutches, and as I was dropping to the ground, I saw him fling his metal crutches as far away from him as possible. As we ran inside, we said to each other, "Wow, did you see that? Did you feel that thunderclap?" I have always enjoyed watching lightning flashing in the clouds at a distance. But I will never think of lightning the same way again. I have seen its uncontrolled power with the ability to destroy.

This is the sense of verse 9 when David says, "In his temple all cry,

'Glory!'" When we read this psalm, we are supposed to say, "Wow!" at the awesome display of God's power. God reveals his impressive, overwhelming power as his lightning splits the trees of the forest and his thunder shakes the mountains. God is not a puny god. He is not a tame god we can lead around on a leash. Amos says, "The LORD roars from Zion" (Amos 1:2).

Israel needed to see this awesome picture of God so they would not turn to idols—and so do we. We can become so used to talking about God as our friend that we forget he is truly fearsome. The God who saves us rules with uncontrolled power and has the ability to destroy. He hates sin and evil. He saves up wrath and fury for his enemies. This storm devastated the foreign nations and humiliated their gods. The Lord will devastate those who do not know him and humiliate the things we are tempted to worship.

The Voice of the Lord

The phrase "the voice of the LORD" occurs seven times in these verses, repeating like the sweep of a radar beam. For an Israelite who knew his Bible, this sevenfold repetition of God's voice would have reminded him of the repeated power of God's word at creation. Six times Genesis 1 says, "And God said," once for each day of creation. God spoke the entire universe into existence. The power of God's voice brought order out of chaos. Genesis 1 tells us he spoke with creative power. Psalm 29 tells us he can speak also with destructive power.

The terrifying power of God's voice also recalls the covenant that God spoke at Mount Sinai. When God came down to give the Law, the people were overwhelmed when they heard the voice of the Lord that spoke to them. Moses writes,

> Then Moses brought the people out of the camp to meet God, and they took their stand at the foot of the mountain. Now Mount Sinai was wrapped in smoke because the LORD had descended on it in fire. The smoke of it went up like the smoke of a kiln, and the whole mountain trembled greatly. And as the sound of the trumpet grew louder and louder, Moses spoke, and God answered him in thunder. (Exodus 19:17–19)

Israel's experience of God's presence in Psalm 29 is similar to the experience at Sinai: fire, thunder, and an earthquake that shook the mountain. The experience was so overwhelming that they begged not to hear the voice of the Lord anymore.

> Now when all the people saw the thunder and the flashes of lightning and the sound of the trumpet and the mountain smoking, the people were afraid

and trembled, and they stood far off and said to Moses, "You speak to us, and we will listen; but do not let God speak to us, lest we die." (Exodus 20:18, 19)

No other nation had heard God speak to them like this. Then he spoke the covenant with a terrifying voice. In Psalm 29 he speaks judgment on the false gods of the nations.

The powerful voice of the Lord points forward to Jesus Christ, who is himself the Word of God. When Jesus came into the world, the Apostle John says, "[T]he Word became flesh and dwelt among us" (John 1:14). God spoke to us powerfully through Jesus Christ. The writer of Hebrews says,

> Long ago, at many times and in many ways, God spoke to our fathers by the prophets, but in these last days he has spoken to us by his Son, whom he appointed the heir of all things, through whom also he created the world. He is the radiance of the glory of God and the exact imprint of his nature, and he upholds the universe by the word of his power. (Hebrews 1:1–3)

As the Word of God, Jesus spoke with power in this world. He healed the sick, calmed the sea, and cast out demons by the command of his voice. Jesus is not a tame God though, someone we keep like a pet to help us when we need him. We should never forget that the power of his word is truly fearsome. He not only creates and heals with his word, he destroys his enemies with the tornadic fury of his word.

In the end, Jesus will crush his enemies with his voice. The voice of the Lord Jesus Christ will humiliate Satan and his armies. The Apostle John saw this in his vision of the end of time.

> Then I saw heaven opened, and behold, a white horse! The one sitting on it is called Faithful and True, and in righteousness he judges and makes war. His eyes are like a flame of fire, and on his head are many diadems, and he has a name written that no one knows but himself. He is clothed in a robe dipped in blood, and the name by which he is called is The Word of God. And the armies of heaven, arrayed in fine linen, white and pure, were following him on white horses. From his mouth comes a sharp sword with which to strike down the nations, and he will rule them with a rod of iron. He will tread the winepress of the fury of the wrath of God the Almighty. On his robe and on his thigh he has a name written, King of kings and Lord of lords. (Revelation 19:11–16)

The voice of the Lord will thunder from the mouth of Jesus!

The Calm after the Storm

David closes with the calm after the storm.

> The Lord sits enthroned over the flood;
>   the Lord sits enthroned as king forever.
> May the Lord give strength to his people!
>   May the Lord bless his people with peace! (29:10, 11)

When the clouds pass and the skies clear, God is on the throne. The storm did not mean that God had lost control. Rather, God rules over the wind, the rain, the flashing lightning, and the earthshaking thunder.

God reveals his glory in judgment. The only other place this word "flood" (v. 10) is used in the entire Old Testament is in the flood account in Genesis (twelve times) when God judged the world. David is connecting the destructive power of the storm he witnessed with the flood that came on the earth in the days of Noah. God sat in judgment on the wind, rain, and storms of the Genesis flood, and he rules over every storm. This does not mean that a particular storm in our day is a sign of God's judgment on the people in its path, of course. But every violent storm reminds us that a final storm of judgment is coming.

This God is the "strength" of "his people" (v. 11)! Who can compare to him? Why look for anyone besides him? And this God brings "peace" to "his people" (v. 11). He will not let his enemies stand forever. The storm of his judgment will bring peace as all his enemies are defeated.

In 2011 I went to Joplin with a team from our church to help with the cleanup from the EF5 tornado there. We worked on a house that had been ripped in two—the roof and the entire front half of the house had literally been torn away. The ceilings, front walls, and living room were completely gone, along with the wall to the kitchen. Standing on the street, we were looking at the kitchen counters and cabinets on the back wall of the house—exposed and open to the sky.

There was a shelf on one of the walls that was still standing. This shelf had held the wife's small collection of glass hummingbirds. When the family came to see the wreckage the next day, the little birds had not moved an inch! Wind raging at 200 miles an hour had torn off the whole front of the house, but somehow the storm did not touch those fragile glass hummingbirds!

God rages like a storm and leaves his fragile people untouched. God knows how to uproot his enemies and preserve his people. The psalmist says,

> A thousand may fall at your side,
>   ten thousand at your right hand,
>   but it will not come near you.
> You will only look with your eyes
>   and see the recompense of the wicked. (Psalm 91:7, 8)

And Peter writes,

> [T]he Lord knows how to rescue the godly from trials, and to keep the unrighteous under punishment until the day of judgment. (2 Peter 2:9)

His awesome power is minutely focused and exquisitely precise. We may lose everything in this life—we may lose life itself—but we will find that by God's power we have lost nothing.

Do you know this great, untamable, uncontrollable God? He is indeed fearsome—make no mistake—but he is good. You can trust him. He knows what he is about. He "bless[es] his people with peace" (Psalm 29:11).

30

Resurrection Song

PSALM 30

ABOUT TEN YEARS AGO, I stopped by Central Dupage Hospital in Winfield, Illinois to visit a man from our church. Willis was a kind and gentle man. I had first met him fifteen years earlier; he was one of the leaders who trained me in Evangelism Explosion. Now Willis was in the last stages of cancer. As I stepped into his room that evening, the look in his wife Carol's eyes told me I was supposed to be there right then.

Willis was at a point where there was nothing the doctors could do. He slipped in and out of consciousness as Carol and I sat by the bed praying, reading Scripture out loud, and singing hymns from memory. At one point I read the last several paragraphs of 1 Corinthians 15, that great chapter on the resurrection. When I finished reading, Carol said quietly, "He's gone." There was no one else in the room, so I gently took off Willis's glasses and closed his eyes.

Even today that moment gives me chills. The last thing Willis heard on earth was the promise of the resurrection!

> I tell you this, brothers: flesh and blood cannot inherit the kingdom of God, nor does the perishable inherit the imperishable. Behold! I tell you a mystery. We shall not all sleep, but we shall all be changed, in a moment, in the twinkling of an eye, at the last trumpet. For the trumpet will sound, and the dead will be raised imperishable, and we shall be changed. . . . then shall come to pass the saying that is written:
>
> > "Death is swallowed up in victory."
> > "O death, where is your victory?
> > > O death, where is your sting?" (1 Corinthians 15:50–55)

The promise of the resurrection is one of the most precious and glorious gifts God gives us in his Word. In the words of Psalm 30:5, "Weeping may tarry for the night, but joy comes with the morning."

Psalm 30 is a song that celebrates the resurrection. More specifically, it is Jesus' song of joy at his own resurrection. This is a psalm of David, which we take to mean that David is the author.[1] But as we will see, this psalm could not refer simply to him. David was a prophet who spoke of Christ (cf. Acts 2:30, 31), and ultimately this psalm points forward to Jesus Christ, the Son of David.

Reading Psalm 30 in light of Jesus' resurrection helps explain the historical note in the superscription, "A SONG AT THE DEDICATION OF THE TEMPLE." This is interesting because even though David wrote this psalm, the temple wasn't built in David's lifetime. Solomon built it several years after David died.

There are several possible explanations. We know that David prepared for the construction of the temple by gathering many of the materials Solomon would need (1 Chronicles 22). As he was gathering gold, silver, bronze, and lumber, David could have written this psalm to prepare for the dedication as well. In later years Psalm 30 was in fact recited at Hanukkah, the feast commemorating the dedication of the temple. From another angle, the word "temple" can also be translated "house." So many scholars think David wrote this when he finished building his palace. David praises God for showing him favor after years of turmoil.

But as a Christian it is hard to read this superscription without remembering that Jesus described his own body as the temple. Jesus said to the Jews, "Destroy this temple, and in three days I will raise it up" (John 2:19). They thought he was talking about Herod's temple, a huge, magnificent building. But John clarifies that Jesus "was speaking about the temple of his body" (John 2:21). So when we read Psalm 30 in the light of the New Testament, this song celebrates the dedication of Jesus' own body on the cross. Jesus is the temple, the place where we meet God. When God the Father raised him from the dead, God the Son sang for joy.

Death was not the end for Jesus, and death is not the end for anyone who belongs to him. There is joy in the morning. The light of God's presence welcomes us on the other side of the valley of the shadow of death. We have not been raised bodily with Christ yet, but by faith his joy is ours today. Our hearts can fly with the hope of the resurrection!

As David speaks for Christ in Psalm 30, he praises God for the resurrection (vv. 1–5) and prays for the resurrection (vv. 6–11).

Praise for the Resurrection

The very first word of Psalm 30 is praise. Literally David writes, "I will exalt you" or "I will lift you up." This is interesting because God is already exalted. How could David lift God up when God is already lifted up? The answer, of course, is that he is lifting up—exalting—God in the eyes of everyone who reads this psalm.

This is similar to Psalm 29:1 where David writes, "[A]scribe to the LORD glory and strength." God is already strong and glorious. The point is that we need to recognize who he already is. When we read about the resurrection in Psalm 30, God should be exalted higher in our eyes. Even if you have been a Christian for many years, you should see the greatness and glory of God more clearly as you meditate again on the wonder of his power and grace that raised Jesus from the dead.

Christ's Praise

Christ explains why he is praising God. He exalts God because God has exalted him.

> I will extol you, O LORD, for you have drawn me up
>   and have not let my foes rejoice over me. (30:1)

Here the words "drawn me up" describe drawing water from a well. It is the same verb used in Exodus when Moses drew water for the flocks of Jethro, the priest of Midian (Exodus 2:16, 19). A man drops a bucket below the surface, then draws it up again into the light of day. In the same way God drew Christ up like a bucket from deep in a well. And in return Christ lifted up the Father with his praise.

This is the pattern we follow too. We were like a bucket in a well, caught in the dark depths of sin, powerless to lift ourselves, when God reached down and pulled us up. The Apostle Paul describes our salvation this way,

> But God, being rich in mercy, because of the great love with which he loved us, even when we were dead in our trespasses, made us alive together with Christ—by grace you have been saved—and raised us up with him and seated us with him in the heavenly places in Christ Jesus, so that in the coming ages he might show the immeasurable riches of his grace in kindness toward us in Christ Jesus. For by grace you have been saved through faith. (Ephesians 2:4–8)

God lifted us up, made us dearly loved children, and seated us with Christ in Heaven. So we lift up the name of God because he has lifted us up above the stars.[2] Now we praise him by faith, but someday we will see the full reality of what God has done.

Sometimes people wonder if we will get tired of praising God in Heaven. After ten years, or ten thousand years, won't it get old? We think this way because we don't understand how amazing his grace is, how high he has lifted us when we did not deserve it. When we are in Heaven and our eyes are finally cleared from the selfishness of sin, we will see how huge God's grace is, and we will not want to stop praising him. We will want to lift him up forever because he lifted us up.

Verses 2, 3 go on to describe how God drew him up. Up to this point David could have been talking about being lifted from a sickbed or some other trouble. Now it becomes clear that he is talking about being raised from the dead.

> O Lord my God, I cried to you for help,
>   and you have healed me.
> O Lord, you have brought up my soul from Sheol;
>   you restored me to life from among those who go down to the pit.
>   (30:2, 3)

God answered his prayer with an ultimate healing. Sheol is the place of the dead, the netherworld.[3] Christ was in Sheol, in the grave, when God brought him back from the dead. This sounds very similar to what David wrote in Psalm 16:10 about the resurrection of Christ:[4] "For you will not abandon my soul to Sheol, or let your holy one see corruption." We know from Acts 2:30, 31 that Psalm 16 is a prophecy about Christ. Since these psalms say much the same thing, it seems reasonable to interpret Psalm 30 as a prophecy of Christ's resurrection too.

Over the years a number of scholars have not been comfortable with the idea that David is talking about resurrection from the dead in these verses. They interpret verse 3 as a metaphor to mean that David was so sick he was as good as dead, that he had one foot in the grave. This explanation sounds to me a bit like that '80s movie *The Princess Bride*. Billy Crystal plays Miracle Max, a washed-up magician. At a key point in the movie, when everything seems hopeless, he says that Westley, the hero of the story, is not really dead, he is "only mostly dead." And Miracle Max gives him a big pill that brings him back from the brink of the grave.

Is that what David is saying here, that he was "only mostly dead?" If we did not know that David was a prophet who looked forward and spoke about Christ, we might think so. But the plain meaning of his words seems clear. Jesus' soul was in Sheol when God brought him out.

The rest of verse 3 clarifies that David is talking about being raised from the dead. "[Y]ou restored me to life from among those who go down to the pit." The word "pit" here is often used as a parallel to "Sheol," the grave,[5] and means much the same thing. The word "restored" is a word that describes raising someone from the dead. It is the same word used in 2 Kings 8:5 to describe how Elisha raised a boy back to life.

> Now the king was talking with Gehazi the servant of the man of God, saying, "Tell me all the great things that Elisha has done." And while he was telling the king how Elisha had restored the dead to life, behold, the woman whose son he had restored to life appealed to the king for her house and her land. And Gehazi said, "My lord, O king, here is the woman, and here is her son whom Elisha restored to life." (2 Kings 8:4, 5)

In Psalm 30 Christ was not asking for God to save his life—it was too late for that.[6] He was dead, and God had to restore his life, bring him back.[7] He was standing in Sheol with other dead people, in line with those entering the pit, when God drew him out like a man draws a bucket of water from a well. God lifted Christ up, and Christ lifted the Father's name in praise.

Before we move on from these verses, notice that David says this resurrection was God's healing. God "healed" Christ by raising him from the dead, and he will heal all who are in Christ by raising them from the dead too. This is important because we usually think that death and healing are opposites. We pray for someone, and if they die we say, "Well, God chose not to heal him." Some people give God a mulligan when they pray for someone but that person dies anyway. They think to themselves, "Maybe next time."

God heals everyone who belongs to him. His plan is to heal us completely by raising these weak bodies from death. God does give lesser healings in this life. I have seen God cure a man from cancer when the elders of the church prayed over him. He came back a month later to announce that the disease was completely gone. My father used to tell how God healed his broken ankle. He broke it when he was a young missionary in Paris working with French teenagers. Two days before he was supposed to lead a ski trip with two dozen students he fell, and an X-ray confirmed that his ankle was broken. Most of the students were not Christians, and my dad didn't know what to do—he certainly could not lead a ski trip with his leg in a cast. But as he prayed, my dad felt a warm glow spread through his body and focus on that ankle. When he finished praying, he got up, the swelling was gone, and his ankle was normal again. A follow-up X-ray showed no sign that the ankle had ever been broken.

As wonderful as these miracles are, God has a greater healing for those who love him. At Willis's bedside, we read that these "perishable bodies" will be raised "imperishable" and these "mortal bodies" will be raised immortal (1 Corinthians 15:53). Never diminish God's healing through death as if it was second best. The ultimate healing comes when God raises his loved ones from the dead, just like he raised Christ our Lord.

This is your hope and comfort if you have laid a loved one in the arms of Jesus. You prayed for God to heal him or her, and he will! The same God who healed my father's ankle will heal him from Alzheimer's when he raises him from the dead. He will heal your husband, your wife, your son, your daughter, your mother, your father—everyone who belongs to Christ.

The Christian's Praise

As Christ sings his praise to God the Father, he invites us to join in and praise God ourselves.

> Sing praises to the LORD, O you his saints,
>   and give thanks to his holy name.
> For his anger is but for a moment,
>   and his favor is for a lifetime.
> Weeping may tarry for the night,
>   but joy comes with the morning. (30:4, 5)

Christ did endure God's anger for a moment as he hung on the cross. He carried our sins, and for a short time the Father turned his face away. He bore that moment of anger so that you and I would not have to endure the wrath of God ourselves. After Christ endured God's anger for us, he experienced God's favor again. Verse 5 literally says, "his favor is life." God was pleased with Christ's sacrifice for sins, and his favor meant life for Jesus.

Jesus' resurrection started with tears on Good Friday but ended with joy on Easter morning. It is the same for us if we are in Christ. There are tears when a believer dies, but there is joy in the morning! We need to look ahead and wait for that sunrise!

Prayer for the Resurrection

As David continues to speak for Christ, he tells the story of the resurrection again, this time focusing on his personal experience, especially his prayer from the grave.

Verses 6–12 move from a crisis to a cry to a celebration.

The Crisis

As he praises God a second time, Christ describes the crisis that led to the resurrection.

> As for me, I said in my prosperity,
> "I shall never be moved."
> By your favor, O Lord,
> you made my mountain stand strong;
> you hid your face;
> I was dismayed. (30:6, 7)

Verse 6 describes his well-being as he trusted God. Some see an attitude of complacency here, as if David was overconfident and lazy. But since he trusted in God's favor, it's better to read this as his deep confidence in God. He felt secure in God's ongoing strength and support. God made him like a strong mountain. This is, of course, especially true of Jesus.

Then came that terrible moment on the cross when the Father hid his face. Jesus cried out in the words of Psalm 22, "My God, my God, why have you forsaken me?" As a real human being, this was the great crisis of Jesus' life.

The Cry

This crisis led to Jesus' cry: "To you, O Lord, I cry, and to the Lord I plead for mercy" (30:8).

The word "mercy" seems to imply that David has sinned and is asking for forgiveness. We often point out the difference between grace and mercy: grace is getting what you don't deserve, while mercy is not getting what you do deserve. For that reason, "mercy" might not be the best translation for this word—the Hebrew word means grace or favor.[8]

These verses are fascinating because they give us a window into the mind of Christ as he reasoned with the Father in prayer.

> What profit is there in my death,
> if I go down to the pit?
> Will the dust praise you?
> Will it tell of your faithfulness?
> Hear, O Lord, and be merciful to me!
> O Lord, be my helper! (30:9, 10)

We need to sharpen our translation of two important words here by noting the footnotes in the ESV. The word "death" is actually "blood." So verse 9 literally reads, "What profit is there in my blood?" Along with this, the word "pit" can be translated "corruption." This is how the same word is translated in Psalm 16:10, "For you will not abandon my soul to Sheol, or let your holy one see corruption."

With this in mind, in essence Christ asks in verse 9, "What will you gain from my blood if I go down to decay?" What would the Father gain if Jesus died a violent death and turned to dust in the grave? There would have been no gain in Jesus' death without his resurrection. If Christ had stayed in the grave, the cross would have been a loss.

Without the resurrection, Jesus could not have been our Savior. Without the resurrection, we would still be in our sin. Without the resurrection, Christ would not have triumphed over Satan and crushed the serpent's head. Without the resurrection, God would not have displayed his glory and wisdom to powers of the universe. Without the resurrection, God would have betrayed his Son in his hour of need. Without the resurrection, God would not have saved a people for his name's sake. Without the resurrection, the cross would have been a loss.

The Celebration

But God did raise Jesus! And so, speaking for Christ, David says,

> You have turned for me my mourning into dancing;
>   you have loosed my sackcloth
>   and clothed me with gladness,
> that my glory may sing your praise and not be silent.
>   O Lord my God, I will give thanks to you forever! (30:11, 12)

This psalm is full of contrasts, but these final verses are the greatest reversals of all. God turned Jesus' "mourning into dancing" (v. 11). God turned a funeral into a wedding. He turned Good Friday into Easter morning.

Sackcloth is rough, scratchy burlap. People wore sackcloth as a sign of grief and mourning. God himself removed Jesus' sackcloth in this great reversal! When our children were young, Lisa used to go to church early on Wednesday mornings for a Women's Bible Study leaders' meeting. At the time we only had our three girls, and I would wake them up and get them dressed. They would lift up their little arms, and I would pull their nightgowns over their heads. Then I would put on their cute clothes for the day and bring them to church. When God loosed Christ's sackcloth and clothed him with gladness, it was like a parent undressing a child and putting on new clothes.[9] The Father took off Christ's mourning and clothed him with joy!

This joy is for you if you belong to Christ. You have already been raised with Christ to "walk in newness of life" (Romans 6:4). You have new joy, new hope, new life because you are joined with Christ in his resurrection. And one day your body will rise with him. The Bible says that the Lord Jesus "will transform our lowly body to be like his glorious body" (Philippians 3:21).

Christ died and rose again. Because he lives, we too shall live. My friend Willis died with these words in his ears, and we live with these words in our ears: "Weeping may tarry for the night, but joy comes with the morning" (Psalm 30:5).

31

Be Strong and Wait for the Lord

PSALM 31

THE AIM OF THIS CHAPTER is for you to be strong. This was David's aim as he wrote Psalm 31. He wants you to be strong. We can see this in verses 23, 24, which is the main application.

> Love the LORD, all you his saints!
> The LORD preserves the faithful
> but abundantly repays the one who acts in pride.
> Be strong, and let your heart take courage,
> all you who wait for the LORD!

We are talking about a specific kind of strength. This is the inner, spiritual strength of trusting God and waiting patiently for him when life turns against you.

In Psalm 31 David is confident that God loves him and is protecting him even though he is in deep trouble. David is facing a staggering list of dangers and hardships: combat, hidden traps, betrayal, psychological depression, friends rejecting him, threats on his life, persecution, lies, plots against him, and being caught in a siege.[1] He was so terrified that he felt like God did not see him anymore; he cried out, "I am cut off from your sight" (31:22).

And yet the end of the story is that "The LORD preserves the faithful" (v. 23). This is the strength that David is talking about—to see and to know that God is doing good to us when we are facing the worst. By faith we love this God who cares for us, even when we can't see him or understand what he is doing.

One night a house caught fire, and a young boy was forced to flee to the roof. His father stood on the ground below him with his arms outstretched, calling to his son, "Jump! I'll catch you." The boy had to jump to save his life. But all the boy could see was flame, smoke, and blackness, so he was afraid to leave the roof. His father kept yelling, "Jump, son! I will catch you." But the boy yelled, "I don't want to, Daddy—I can't see you." His father called back, "Just jump, son, you don't have to see me—I can see you!"

If you are a Christian, you need to trust God in times of trouble. Godly people do suffer in this world. Some people think that if you really have faith you won't have trouble. Not so! David says in Psalm 34:19, "*Many* are the afflictions of the righteous, but the LORD delivers him out of them all." You can count on having many afflictions if you follow Christ, along with the promise that God will recue you. You need to be strong as you wait for him. He sees you; he knows you; he preserves you; he cares for you.

Psalm 31 is quoted in several other places in Scripture. The prophet Jeremiah quotes the phrase "terror on every side" (v. 13) no less than six times to describe the dangers he was in. Psalm 31 must have been meaningful to him. Jonah quotes Psalm 31:6 from the belly of the fish. The author of Psalm 71 quotes the opening lines of Psalm 31. And, of course, our Lord Jesus quoted Psalm 31:5 from the cross: "Father, into your hands I commit my spirit" (Luke 23:46).[2] Jesus identified with David's experience and trusted God to save him. Psalm 31 points us forward to Christ and calls us to follow in his footsteps.

There are a number of ways we could approach Psalm 31. If we paint with broad strokes, David offers a prayer of faith (vv. 1–8), a prayer for grace (vv. 9–18), and a song of praise (vv. 19–22). Then he closes with his words of application (vv. 23, 24). We need to follow his example today. We need to be strong.

A Prayer of Faith

David begins with a prayer of deep faith as he pleads with God to rescue him.

> In you, O LORD, do I take refuge;
>   let me never be put to shame;
>   in your righteousness deliver me! (31:1)

We usually think of shame as an emotion. It is a private feeling we can hide from others. In the Hebrew context of Psalm 31, though, the idea of being "put to shame" has to do with public disgrace. If you are put to shame, you are disgraced before others as a sign of God's judgment.[3] To be put to shame means humiliation before God and man.

It's hard when people judge you for something you didn't do. David didn't deserve this public shame and disgrace because he was faithful to God. He trusted God to rescue him and restore his reputation. Even more, our Lord Jesus didn't deserve shame and disgrace—he was perfectly obedient and pleased God in everything. By quoting this psalm, Jesus trusted God to rescue him and clear his name publicly as well. And God didn't put Jesus to shame—he honored him before all the world by raising him from the dead.

Faith to Believe What You Believe

David's faith comes out clearly as his prayer continues.

> Incline your ear to me;
>   rescue me speedily!
> Be a rock of refuge for me,
>   a strong fortress to save me!
>
> For you are my rock and my fortress;
>   and for your name's sake you lead me and guide me;
> you take me out of the net they have hidden for me,
>   for you are my refuge.
> Into your hand I commit my spirit;
>   you have redeemed me, O Lord, faithful God. (31:2–5)

These verses are interesting because David asks God to be what he already *is*. He asks God to be his rock because he *is* his rock. He asks God to be his fortress because he *is* his fortress. He asks God to be his refuge because he already *is* his refuge. He commits his life to God because God has already redeemed him.

Why does David ask God to be something he already is? David is claiming personally what he knows about God. Charles Spurgeon said we should learn from this that "we may pray to enjoy in experience what we grasp by faith."[4] We need to pray with our hearts what we know in our minds. We know many things about God from the Bible. When we pray with faith, we ask God to be these things to us personally. Do we believe that God is our strength? By faith we ask God to be our strength when we are weak. Do we believe that God works everything together for our good? By faith we ask God to work a car accident for our good, to work an unexpected job transition for our good, to work a tumor, a disease, a cancer for our good. When we don't know where we will get the money for tuition, for a medical bill, for the rent or the mortgage, for groceries, for retirement, we ask God to be our provider. Why do we pray this? Because we know God is our provider. By faith David claims for himself what he already knows about God.

This kind of faith is never more crucial than at the moment of death. The word "spirit" (v. 5) is the very life of a person, the animating force that makes us alive.[5] Since David entrusts his "spirit" to God, he is convinced that God is able to continue life even after his body dies.[6] This is why Jesus quoted these words as he hung on the cross—it is a powerful declaration of his belief in the resurrection! The previous psalm, Psalm 30, is a resurrection psalm. The hope of the resurrection is at the heart of Psalm 31 as well. Life does not end at death. God's promises extend beyond the grave.

Martin Luther said, "Blessed are they who die not only for the Lord, as martyrs, not only in the Lord, as all believers, but likewise with the Lord, as breathing forth their lives with these words, 'Into thine hands I commit my spirit.'"[7]

John Hus was one of the early lights of the Protestant Reformation. He lived about one hundred years before Martin Luther and was put to death by the Council of Constance. As he was condemned to death, the bishop who conducted the ceremony ended with the chilling words, "And now we commit thy soul to the devil." Hus replied calmly, "I commit my spirit into thy hands, Lord Jesus Christ; unto thee I commit my spirit, which thou hast redeemed."

A Prayer from the Heart

David's faith was not just a mental exercise. He trusted in God with his heart, his emotions, his whole being.

> I hate those who pay regard to worthless idols,
>   but I trust in the LORD.
> I will rejoice and be glad in your steadfast love,
>   because you have seen my affliction;
>   you have known the distress of my soul,
> and you have not delivered me into the hand of the enemy;
>   you have set my feet in a broad place. (31:6–8)

David's heart comes out in these verses. He had no patience for people who worshiped other gods. We are tempted to imitate the successful people we see in this world. Sometimes we want their approval. But David wasn't tempted to imitate the ungodly. In fact, "he hated them for hating God."[8] If God has saved you and has become your refuge, there is a sense in which you cannot love those who despise him. They insult the God who has been so good to you! On the other hand, you should love your neighbors as yourself (Mark 12:21). We care for unbelievers; we are good to them; we want the best for them; we pray for their salvation. But we cannot embrace them and identify with them as long as they hate our God.

David sang for joy because God loved him. "Steadfast love" (v. 7) refers to God's covenant loyalty—God has bound himself to his people like a husband to his wife, and he is faithful to keep his promises. So David rejoiced and was glad.

God showed his covenant love for David in four things (31:7, 8). First, God sees. Sarah's maidservant, Hagar, discovered God as a God who sees when she fled into the desert. Second, God also knows—he knows David's "distress." This is more than mental knowledge—God identifies with him in his anguish. Third, God did not hand him over to the enemy and throw him under the bus. Fourth, he set his feet in "a broad place." What does this mean? If you are walking on a narrow balance beam, it is a relief finally to stand on the wide floor again. It's as if David had been walking on a path carved into the side of a cliff; if he stumbled or slipped, he'd fall down to the rocks below. But God led David into "a broad place" of safety and security.

Notice that God had not changed David's circumstances. In the next verse he is still "in distress" (v. 9). [9] But by faith David knows God has seen him and is protecting him, even if God leads him through death. The men and women in the Hall of Faith, Hebrews 11, did not receive the things God promised in this life either—they welcomed them from a distance and waited to receive them in the life to come. David has the same faith. He sings for joy because God loves him even though he has not yet received the things God promised. Christ too looked forward beyond death to the joy set before him.

If you and I are going to be strong, we need to look forward by faith to the good future God has for those who love him. He sees. He knows. He will not hand us over. He has set our feet in a broad place.

A Prayer for Grace

After this prayer of faith, David prays for God's grace and favor.

> Be gracious to me, O LORD, for I am in distress;
>   my eye is wasted from grief;
>   my soul and my body also. (31:9)

This prayer is wonderful because it is realistic. You can pray in faith and still dissolve in a flood of tears. David knows God has delivered him and will deliver him, yet his eyes still weep and waste away. One of the worst things you can say to a Christian brother or sister is not to cry when he or she is going through something really hard. "Have faith," someone will say, "don't get emotional." David trusted God, and his eye still "wasted from grief." Our Lord Jesus trusted his Father, but he wept at Lazarus's tomb even though he knew he would raise Lazarus from the tomb just minutes later. We can believe with all our heart that God will raise our loved one from the grave and still cry because he is gone.

David's Distress

David catalogs his distress in verses 10–13. This is the emotional heart of the psalm. The best way to read these four verses is backwards. David starts with the anguish he feels and moves to the cause. We will understand these verses better if we start with the cause and work backward to his anguish.[10]

David's main problem was that he was surrounded by enemies. They whispered in the corners and behind closed doors as they planned to take his life.

> For I hear the whispering of many—
>   terror on every side!—
> as they scheme together against me,
>   as they plot to take my life. (31:13)

You have seen this sort of thing. You come around the corner and conversation suddenly stops. You begin to wonder who your friends are. Who can I trust? This was not just office politics—for a king, this was life and death. In his younger years David had to flee from King Saul when people whispered about him and planned to kill him. Once his wife left a large idol in his bed to fool them into thinking he was still asleep (1 Samuel 19:13)—it's the oldest trick in the book, but they fell for it. His son Absalom whispered against him and tried to take the throne. Later Sheba and Amasa plotted against him (2 Samuel 20:1–6).

Because of the danger, even his friends turned their backs on him.

> Because of all my adversaries I have become a reproach,
>   especially to my neighbors,
> and an object of dread to my acquaintances;
>   those who see me in the street flee from me.
> I have been forgotten like one who is dead;
>   I have become like a broken vessel. (31:11, 12)

Many people have experienced this. As long as you are rich and successful, you have lots of friends. As long as you can do things for people, they want to know you. They go out of their way to say hello. But these so-called friends melt away when you can't help them anymore. And when it becomes dangerous to know you, they avoid you like the plague.

Our Lord Jesus Christ experienced this, of course. When he fed the crowds, they came flocking to him and wanted to make him king (John 6:15). But when he stood on trial before Pilate, the crowds yelled, "Crucify him!" (19:6). Even his closest disciples ran away and denied they even knew him.

This stress and rejection takes a toll. David almost crumbled under the pressure.

> For my life is spent with sorrow,
>   and my years with sighing;
> my strength fails because of my iniquity,
>   and my bones waste away. (Psalm 31:10)

These words might seem to be an exaggeration, but they describe the real grief many have experienced when they have been betrayed by those closest to them. When grief and stress like this go on for years, it truly is debilitating.

David's experience in his sorrows pointed forward to Jesus, the ultimate man of sorrows. David was betrayed by many of those closest to him, and he felt like he was going to collapse under the pressure. Jesus was betrayed even more wickedly. In the Garden of Gethsemane he sweat drops of blood as he dealt with the agony he experienced.

David's Confidence

And yet neither Christ nor David gave up their faith in God. They stood strong! David continues to call out for grace with confidence that God will hear him.

> But I trust in you, O LORD;
>   I say, "You are my God."
> My times are in your hand;
>   rescue me from the hand of my enemies and from my persecutors!
> Make your face shine on your servant;
>   save me in your steadfast love! (31:14–16)

When David says, "My times are in your hand" (v. 15), he's not shrugging his shoulders like a laid-back surfer. "Whatever, dude." He's not emptying himself of expectations like an eastern mystic. "You are sad because you want and do not get. If you do not want, you will not be sad." And he is not fatalistic like a Muslim who says, "Insha' Allah"—"it's in God's hands."

Rather, this is a towering declaration of trust. David claims his relationship with God: "You are my God" (v. 14). And God will rescue him because of his steadfast love, his covenant loyalty. The point is that David trusts God to do it in his own timing. *Lord, rescue me when you know the time is best. I would like you to rescue me today. But I trust you if I have to wait until tomorrow or next week. I may not receive the email I need for another six months. You may not rescue me in this life—if I go to my grave still waiting for your promise, I trust you. My times are in your hands."*

In many ways, saying "my times are in your hands" (v. 15) is another way of saying, "Into your hands I commit my spirit" (Luke 23:46).[11] God's hands are the safest place in the world. There is no better place to trust our life, and the length of our life.

This is a comfort to us if someone we love was taken away after just a few years. This is a comfort if our child was born with a problem that will shorten his or her life. Ten-year-old Sarah Murnaghan had cystic fibrosis, and eventually she had only weeks to live unless she received a lung transplant. Other parents face the same agony. As a pastor I remember the day I married my friends Judd and Arlene, a wonderful, happy day. Two years later their son Jeremiah was born with his heart backward, left to right. After some amazing surgeries he made a big improvement. But I'm told that realistically he will probably only live to twenty years old. His life will have just begun.

God's hands are the safest place to deposit the treasure of my earthly life. By faith we can say, "Into your hands I commit my spirit." By faith we can say, "My times are in your hands."

And by faith we can trust God to punish those who do wrong. David's confidence leaves judgment in God's hands.

O LORD, let me not be put to shame,
    for I call upon you;
let the wicked be put to shame;
    let them go silently to Sheol.
Let the lying lips be mute,
    which speak insolently against the righteous
    in pride and contempt. (Psalm 31:17, 18)

It seems massively unfair when wicked men or women live a long life, then people celebrate them after they die and name roads and buildings after them. They never experience the public disgrace, the "shame" (v. 17), that they deserve for what they have done. God is not limited by death. He has shame and judgment in store for everyone who speaks against him and his people. The long arm of God's Law reaches beyond the grave to disgrace the wicked forever in the afterlife.

Praise for God's Goodness

Finally David praises God for his goodness.

> Oh, how abundant is your goodness,
>   which you have stored up for those who fear you
> and worked for those who take refuge in you,
>   in the sight of the children of mankind!
> In the cover of your presence you hide them
>   from the plots of men;
> you store them in your shelter
>   from the strife of tongues. (31:19, 20)

God stores up good for his people. If you are a Christian, picture a warehouse that is full with row after row of goodness for you. God has blessing upon blessing waiting for his people, and he will give them to them before the eyes of the world. By faith we believe that the universe will stand in awe of the good things God gives to his beloved. As Christians death is not the end for us—God has goodness stored up for us. And he stores us up, too, in his shelter. He protects us like works of art in a safe-deposit box.

We receive his goodness today too, of course, even in the middle of trouble and anguish. I was overwhelmed when I visited a friend named Charles in the hospital. He was in excruciating pain from his hip surgery. Charles is also battling cancer. But as I sat with him and his wife Betty, they kept on saying, "God has been so good to us!" Such sweet spirits! Such hearts full of faith! They know what is happening—they're not in denial—but they see the unseen. In that hospital room I felt the glow of their faith like sunlight on my face. They were saying with David, "how abundant is your goodness!" (v. 19).

God has not taken David out of his trouble, but David blesses God.

> Blessed be the LORD,
>   for he has wondrously shown his steadfast love to me
>   when I was in a besieged city.
> I had said in my alarm,
>   "I am cut off from your sight."
> But you heard the voice of my pleas for mercy
>   when I cried to you for help. (31:21, 22)

As a man of war David had probably been under siege. The lies that surrounded made him feel like a city under siege. He was so terrified that he thought God could not see through the fog of war, the cloud of accusations and deceit. But God hears and God saves.

This brings us back to the application David has for everyone who reads this psalm.

> Love the LORD, all you his saints!
>> The LORD preserves the faithful
>> but abundantly repays the one who acts in pride.
> Be strong, and let your heart take courage,
>> all you who wait for the LORD! (31:23, 24)

If you are a Christian, you need to trust God in times of trouble. Be strong! Wait for the Lord!

Your times are in his hands. He rescued Christ through death by raising him from the dead. And he will rescue everyone who belongs to Christ. The goodness he has stored up for you will last for all eternity.

32

The Blessing of Forgiveness

PSALM 32

EDWARD SNOWDEN is behind the biggest leak in the history of the National Security Agency. In May 2013 this twenty-nine-year-old caused an uproar by releasing information on the scope of government surveillance. It turns out that the NSA keeps a record of every phone call we make and looks into our lives at a level we had not imagined.

This started a national conversation about privacy because we now know there is no such thing as anonymity. If we want to keep our privacy, we have to go off the grid, pay cash for every purchase, stay off the Internet, and not use a cell phone. Even then cameras will see us, and face recognition software might identify us.

But the best efforts of the NSA are nothing compared to God's complete knowledge. The NSA has only had their technology for several decades. But three thousand years ago the psalmist said, "You know when I sit and when I rise up; you discern my thoughts from afar" (Psalm 139:2).

This is a problem because all of us sin—even if we have been Christians for many years. In fact, as we grow mature in Christ, we begin to see sin in our life that we had never noticed before. The Apostle John writes, "If we say we have no sin, we deceive ourselves, and the truth is not in us" (1 John 1:8). John wrote this when he was an old man near the end of his life. As an apostle in his nineties, we might think that he had gotten to the point where he no longer sinned. But John includes himself when he says, "If *we* say *we* have no sin, *we* deceive *our*selves" (1 John 1:8). And God sees it all.

All of us struggle with sin.

Now Judas don't you come too close
I fear that I might see

That traitor's look upon your face
Might look too much like me
Cause just like you I've sold the Lord
And often for much less
And like a wretched traitor
I betrayed Him with a kiss.[1]

This is why forgiveness is one of the greatest blessings we could imagine. The God who knows all our sin will forgive all our sin. Having your sins forgiven is better than having your student loans paid off. It's better than having a ticket taken off your record. When God forgives you, he wipes the record clean—all of it.

King David tried to hide his sin from God and from others. Many think that Psalm 32 should be read with Psalm 51, his great psalm of repentance after his affair with Bathsheba (2 Samuel 11, 12). While his armies went off to war, David stayed behind in Jerusalem and seduced an officer's wife. When she became pregnant, David arranged for her husband, Uriah, to be killed in battle. David had adultery and murder on his hands.

He hid his sin, but finally the prophet Nathan confronted him. David described his confession in Psalm 51, a passionate, emotional psalm. As part of this confession, David made a promise to God: "Then I will teach transgressors your ways, and sinners will return to you" (Psalm 51:13). Psalm 32 could be the fulfillment of this promise. The title "A Maskil of David" suggests this is a teaching psalm.[2] The word *maskil* comes from a root word that means "to instruct." In Psalm 32 David does teach sinners and turns them back to God. So there is good reason to have David's sin with Bathsheba in the back of our minds as we look at Psalm 32.

What will you do when you sin? Will you try to hide your sin? That is like gluing wallpaper over a moldy wall. Or will you confess your sin? You need to turn to God and admit your sin so you can be forgiven.

The Blessing of Forgiveness

David declares the blessing of forgiveness. This beatitude is the heart of this psalm, so we will spend a large bulk of our time in these first two verses.

Double Blessing

The word "blessed" (32:1) stands out because Psalms 1 and 2, the introduction to the Psalms, begin and end with this same word. In fact, this is the first time this word "blessed" has been used since the first line of the book of Psalms.

There is an important difference though. Psalm 1 declares the blessings of the ideal man who never sins or stands with sinners.

> Blessed is the man
>   who walks not in the counsel of the wicked,
> nor stands in the way of sinners,
>   nor sits in the seat of scoffers. (Psalm 1:1)

This blessing is for someone who constantly walks in God's way, which none of us do. In fact, the tense of the Hebrew verbs in Psalm 1:1 indicate that this man is never involved with anything tainted by evil.[3] The man of Psalm 1 is the perfect man, Jesus Christ. But Psalm 32 declares the blessing of a man who is far from perfect. This man does sin, and God forgives him.

> Blessed is the one whose transgression is forgiven,
>   whose sin is covered.
> Blessed is the man against whom the LORD counts no iniquity,
>   and in whose spirit there is no deceit. (32:1, 2)

David declares a double blessing on those whom God forgives. To emphasize the blessing of forgiveness, David repeats the beatitude in verse 2. What better way to encourage you and me to confess our sins than a double promise of blessing?

This blessing is even more attractive and tempting because a good translation for the word "blessed" is "happy." So we could translate verses 1, 2, "How happy is the one whose transgression is forgiven. . . . How happy is the man against whom the LORD counts no iniquity." This is the joy of knowing that God is for you, that he is kind and forgiving. Everyone wants to be blessed; everyone wants happiness. How happy and blessed are the forgiven!

Full Forgiveness

This blessing comes with full forgiveness. Verses 1, 2 are an example of parallelism as David places four phrases side by side. This is not just flowery language. This parallelism covers the full scope of our sin and the full spectrum of God's forgiveness.

The Bible uses half a dozen words for sin, and David uses three of them here. Each has its own meaning and nuance. The word "transgression" (v. 1) has to do with rebellion. God created us in his image to live on earth as his representatives. Like a father who leaves his son in charge of the house while he is gone, he expects us to take care of the earth and each other. But we don't obey him, do we? We are traitors. We are like an American soldier who joins Al Qaeda and fights against his country in Afghanistan. We defected to the enemy. We ruin our lives and the lives of others. We live in rebellion against God.

The word "sin" (v. 1) has to do with missing the mark. It has the same idea as a Greek word used frequently in the New Testament, *hamartia*. An archer bends her bow and shoots, but the arrow falls short and tears into the grass. A man lines up his stance to hit the ball onto the green, but instead he hooks it off into the trees. This archer and this golfer didn't hit what they were aiming at—they missed the mark. This is a picture of sin. We try to follow Christ, but we still miss the mark.

The third word for sin in these verses, "iniquity" (v. 2), can mean crookedness, perversion, or waywardness. It can also mean guilt and punishment, or even intentional sins. It is sometimes used in a general way to talk about sin as a whole.

Looking at these words is like holding up a black diamond—we see different facets of our sin. The first word describes our relationship to God: we have rebelled against him. The second word describes our relationship to God's Law: we fall short and miss the mark. The third word describes the effect that sin has on us: we are crooked, perverse, and guilty before God.[4] With these three words David describes the human condition. And with these three words he includes every kind of sin.

But the most important thing in these verses is not the nature of sin—it is that all these sins can be forgiven! David matches these three words for sin with three words for pardon. The first word, "forgiven" (v. 1), literally means to lift or carry away. Your transgression was like a boulder pinning you to the ground, but God lifted it and carried it away. The second word, "covered" (v. 1), has to do with the atonement. The blood of a sacrifice covered the sin of the people and restored their relationship with God.

The third word describes what God does not do; he does not "count" (v. 2) iniquities against this blessed man. This is a bookkeeping word—it means to charge something to an account.[5] When God forgives, he does not charge our sin to our account. It's as if you received your credit card statement in the mail, but when you opened it, there were no charges. You know you used the card quite a bit, but your balance is zero, your minimum payment is zero, and your penalties are zero. Our sin is removed from God's ledger, and the spreadsheet is empty.

This is the same accounting word that Moses uses in Genesis 15:6 to describe the righteousness Abraham had by faith: Abraham "believed the LORD, and he counted it to him as righteousness." In God's accounting he leaves sin off the ledger and adds righteousness to the ledger for those he blesses.

This is incredibly important because the Apostle Paul joins Genesis 15:6 and Psalm 32 to teach salvation by faith in the book of Romans.

> For if Abraham was justified by works, he has something to boast about, but not before God. For what does the Scripture say? "Abraham believed God, and it was counted to him as righteousness." Now to the one who works, his wages are not counted as a gift but as his due. And to the one who does not work but believes in him who justifies the ungodly, his faith is counted as righteousness, just as David also speaks of the blessing of the one to whom God counts righteousness apart from works:
>
> > "Blessed are those whose lawless deeds are forgiven,
> >   and whose sins are covered;
> > blessed is the man against whom the Lord will not count his sin."
> >   (Romans 4:2–8)

By not counting sins against us, God declares us to be righteous. This is God's blessing. It is from God's hand—it is not a reward for our good behavior. So Psalm 32 is at the heart of the gospel. God clears the ledger—he deletes the data on your spreadsheet of sin.

Who Receives This Blessing?

Who receives the blessing of forgiveness? The parallelism of these first two verses shifts in the second half of verse 2 to identify the kind of person God forgives: "and in whose spirit there is no deceit."

This "deceit" does not have to do primarily with lying to others. This is about lying to yourself and to God. Again John says, "If we say we have no sin, *we deceive ourselves*, and the truth is not in us" (1 John 1:8). How do we lie to ourselves? We can be so proud and think we have never done anything wrong—when there is tension or conflict in a relationship, it's always someone else's fault. We can lie to ourselves by thinking God does not know about our sin because it happened a long time ago or a long way from home. We can deceive ourselves by comparing ourselves to others. We might say, "I'm not like Fred at work. I'm not like Susie across the street who dresses so provocatively. I'm not like those people in the gay pride parade." We can deceive ourselves by being moral persons. We can deceive ourselves by focusing on externals—"I don't drink or smoke. I go to church. I give money. I vote for the right candidates." We can deceive ourselves by thinking that this psalm is for somebody else. But the blessing of forgiveness is for those who do not lie to themselves.

We can be so self-deceived that we try to deceive God, even though he knows more about us than the NSA does. We ignore our sin, pretend it didn't happen, and try to hide it from him. But down deep we know he sees. And if God loves us, he will let us know that he sees. This is where David turns next as he describes the process of forgiveness.

The Process of Forgiveness

In verses 3–7 David describes his personal experience as God would not let him ignore his sin. He describes how verses 1, 2 were lived out in his own life. His inner turmoil led to confession and forgiveness. And once he had been restored, he taught others.

Stubborn Silence

The process began with David's stubborn silence. He would not confess his sin but kept on going as if nothing was wrong. But God would not let him get away with it.

> For when I kept silent, my bones wasted away
>> through my groaning all day long.
> For day and night your hand was heavy upon me;
>> my strength was dried up as by the heat of summer. *Selah* (32:3, 4)

This is a perfect description of the misery of living with a guilty conscience. If you are a Christian, this describes the way you have felt when you would not confess your sin to God.

Physiologically David's bones "wasted away" (v. 3), and he felt drained—his strength was sapped. Sin and guilt can indeed have an effect on our health and vitality. Psychologically he felt the heavy weight of God's hand. He felt the burden of his guilt all day, and when he laid down, he could not rest.

Reluctant Confession

Finally David gave in to the pressure and confessed his sins.

> I acknowledged my sin to you,
>> and I did not cover my iniquity;
> I said, "I will confess my transgressions to the LORD,"
>> and you forgave the iniquity of my sin. *Selah* (32:5)

If God's hand is heavy on your conscience, you need to know that he loves you and is making you miserable for your own good. We are so stubborn and sinful that God sometimes has to force us to turn to him for healing and forgiveness. He dragged this confession out of David! If the Holy Spirit is making you miserable because of your sin, that is a sign that he cares for you. The time to worry is when you sin and God doesn't bother you. God disciplines those he loves for their good (Hebrews 12:5–7).

The guilt of our sin is forgiven through Jesus Christ. In God's accounting our sin was placed on his ledger, and his innocence was put on our ledger. To pick up the credit card analogy again, Christ received his statement in the mail and saw all sorts of charges he didn't make. But he didn't call the company and complain—he paid those charges for you and me. On the cross Jesus died for sinners and paid for the guilt of everyone who turns to him.

> In the 14th century, Robert Bruce of Scotland was leading his men in a battle to gain independence from England. Near the end of the conflict, the English wanted to capture Bruce to keep him from the Scottish crown. So they put his own bloodhounds on his trail. When the bloodhounds got close, Bruce could hear their baying. His attendant said, "We are done for. They are on your trail, and they will reveal your hiding place." Bruce replied, "It's all right." Then he headed for a stream that flowed through the forest. He plunged in and waded upstream a short distance. When he came out on the other bank, he was in the depths of the forest. Within minutes, the hounds, tracing their master's steps, came to the bank. They went no farther. The English soldiers urged them on, but the trail was broken. The stream had carried the scent away. A short time later, the crown of Scotland rested on the head of Robert Bruce.
>
> The memory of our sins, prodded on by Satan, can be like those baying dogs—but a stream flows, red with the blood of God's own Son. By grace through faith we are safe. No sin-hound can touch us. The trail is broken by the precious blood of Christ.[6]

The Offer of Forgiveness

Because David had experienced God's forgiveness so powerfully, he turns to teach God's people.

> Therefore let everyone who is godly
>   offer prayer to you at a time when you may be found;
> surely in the rush of great waters,
>   they shall not reach him.
> You are a hiding place for me;
>   you preserve me from trouble;
>   you surround me with shouts of deliverance. *Selah* (Psalm 32:6, 7)

The phrase "let everyone who is godly" (v. 6) tells us that David is thinking primarily of believers as he writes this psalm. Nonbelievers often do not

have the slightest twinge of conscience when they sin. God is not correcting
and leading them. I know one family in which it was normal to get dad a pinup
girl calendar for Father's Day. Like the people of Nineveh, many do not know
their right hand from their left, morally (Jonah 4:11).

David is thinking of godly people like him who fall into sin. The temptation is to stay silent. You are ashamed and angry with yourself. You don't
want to face God and admit what you have done. Like Adam and Eve in the
garden of Eden, you run off and hide when you hear God coming, walking in
the cool of the day.

You need to call out to God while you can. If you do not confess your sins
to God now, you might not be able to call out to him tomorrow. Sin is deceitful, and if you do not deal with it, it will harden your heart. A Christian friend
from college was unfaithful to his wife, and after hiding it for years, it finally
came out into the open. I met with him weekly for a while for accountability,
and after we moved away I talked with him on the phone several times. Unfortunately, he dove headfirst back into a life of sexual sin. I'll never forget our
last phone call. He said, "Jim, I know I should feel bad about this, but I don't."
If you hide your sin and refuse to confess, you will get to the point when you
can't confess your sin. Your conscience will be calloused, you will have an
unbelieving heart, and you will fall away from God (Hebrews 3:12–14).

The Result of Forgiveness
Finally David describes the results of forgiveness. These are the blessings that
follow when we confess our sins.

First, God speaks to promise his guidance to David and to us.

> I will instruct you and teach you in the way you should go;
>   I will counsel you with my eye upon you.
> Be not like a horse or a mule, without understanding,
>   which must be curbed with bit and bridle,
>   or it will not stay near you. (Psalm 32:8, 9)

The sort of guidance God is promising here is not what college you
should go to, who you should marry, whether you should take a new job offer,
or some similar decision. In context this guidance concerns godly living. The
Holy Spirit will teach you to obey and walk in the way of the righteous. A
horse or mule will not obey without a bit turning this way and that. In context
that bit is the heavy hand of God that forced David to finally confess his sins.
God wants you to understand his ways and walk in them by your own will.

God promises his enduring love for those who confess their sins.

Many are the sorrows of the wicked,
   but steadfast love surrounds the one who trusts in the LORD. (32:10)

Steadfast love is God's covenant love, his commitment to his people. He is like a father, always hoping his prodigal son will return, always ready to welcome him home. If you trust him to forgive your sins, his love will surround you.

The third result of forgiveness is joy.

Be glad in the LORD, and rejoice, O righteous,
   and shout for joy, all you upright in heart! (32:11)

This is a loud verse! When you fail and God forgives you, it makes you want to stand up and "shout for joy"! The expressions "be glad" and "rejoice" both describe spontaneous shouts of joy. After describing sin with three words in the first verses, David has three shouts of joy at the end for those who are forgiven.

If you are forgiven, you will make some noise. Jesus said that "he who is forgiven little, loves little" (Luke 7:47). If you know what God has done for you, it makes you want to shout. If your heart is not touched, if your emotions are not involved, do you really know you have been forgiven?

God is so good to us! He knows more about us than the NSA does. But he will forgive. Confess your sin to him today. His complete knowledge means complete forgiveness. Praise his name!

33

Shout for Joy!

PSALM 33

WHEN I WAS A BOY, one of my jobs was to light the coals when we grilled hamburgers on our back patio. I was always impatient for the coals to light. I could not walk away and wait for the fire to spread. So I blew and blew on the parts that were glowing red to spread the fire to the rest of the coals. I felt a sense of satisfaction when I saw an orange flame hold steady among the coals.

The psalmist is doing much the same thing in Psalm 33. He is blowing on the coals of our hearts so they will catch fire with worship and praise. Since he is speaking to the righteous and the upright, even godly Christians must need the breath of the Holy Spirit to blow on their hearts so they catch fire. So my aim in this study is to fan our hearts into flame. I want to stir a fire of joy and praise and worship in our hearts.

Psalm 33 is closely connected with Psalm 32. Psalm 32 describes the blessing and joy of those God has forgiven. David ends that psalm with a command.

> Be glad in the LORD, and rejoice, O righteous,
>   and shout for joy, all you upright in heart! (Psalm 32:11)

The first verse of Psalm 33 repeats this command with almost the same words.

> Shout for joy in the LORD, O you righteous!
>   Praise befits the upright.

It is as if Psalm 33 was written as an extension of Psalm 32. The words they share are like stitches that join these psalms together at the seam.

337

Because Psalm 33 does not have a heading, these two are joined together as one psalm in ten Hebrew manuscripts.[1]

Psalm 32 describes the blessing of forgiveness. Psalm 33 follows as a song of joy.[2] So in many ways Psalm 33 is the song of the forgiven, a song of praise for those whose sin God does not count against them. It is a song for you today if you are a Christian.

The psalmist fans our hearts into flame with a call to worship, cause for worship, and confidence from worship.

Call to Worship

Verses 1–3 are an energetic call to worship. The psalmist describes loud, joyful worship with musicians, singers, and worshipers praising God together. There are times to be still before the Lord, but this is not one of those times. If your sins are forgiven, you will want to make some noise!

A Joyful Shout

The call to worship begins with verse 1.

> Shout for joy in the Lord, O you righteous!
>   Praise befits the upright.

A better translation for "shout for joy" here is "yell."[3] It can mean yelling for joy, but it can sometimes mean a yell of anguish or despair. Here it is obviously an excited shout because we are so happy.

Imagine a high school senior waiting for his college acceptance letter. The day finally comes when that letter arrives. He tears it open with trembling fingers and reads the first line, "We are pleased to offer you a place in the freshman class . . ." and he doesn't get any farther. He drops the letter and yells, "Yahoo! Mom, Dad, I got in!" This is the sort of excited, undignified shout in verse 1.

What could cause that sort of joy and excitement? The psalmist commands us to shout for joy "in the Lord" (v. 1). Grammatically God himself is the cause of this commotion.[4] It's all about him! When you have felt the weight of your sin like David describes in Psalm 32:3, 4 and then felt God's forgiveness, your heart sings for joy to this God. His goodness and generosity are beautiful to you. His kindness takes your breath away.

Who else can praise God like this? The unbelieving world certainly can't. The angels can't because they have not sinned and been forgiven. The seraphim around the throne cannot praise God like we can because they have not experienced his goodness like we have. So it is a beautiful thing when God's people get carried away and shout their praise to God.

We need to be clear that there is a difference between godly emotions in our worship and what I will call emotionalism. There are plenty of religious showmen who know how to manipulate people. A friend of mine is a worship pastor who grew up in a church that worked on people's emotions. Since he is from that background, he knows exactly what to do to get people to cheer or to cry at the right moment. The psalmist is not talking about manipulation or emotionalism.

Rather Psalm 33 is talking about an honest emotional reaction to an experience of the greatness and glory of God. If you drive southeast from Seattle on a clear day, you will see Mount Rainier in the distance. As you get closer, you might come to an overlook where you can pull the car over so you can get out and take it in. Mount Rainier is a massive volcano that towers 14,400 feet above sea level. When you stand at the foot of this huge mountain, you might say, "Wow! Will you look at that!" No one has to tell you to say this—it is an honest emotional reaction. In our worship we should present the majesty and glory of God so clearly and so compellingly that men and women naturally praise him with genuine, heartfelt emotions.

Joyful Music

In verses 2, 3 the psalmist calls for loud, joyful music that is proper and fitting for godly, upright people.

> Give thanks to the LORD with the lyre;
>   make melody to him with the harp of ten strings!
> Sing to him a new song;
>   play skillfully on the strings, with loud shouts. (33:2, 3)

Worship should be accompanied by instruments. This is the first time that musical instruments are mentioned in the Psalms. Israel worshiped God with a variety of instruments including strings, winds, and percussion (cf. Psalm 150:3–5). Here the psalmist commands us to use stringed instruments to worship God.

Some Christians believe that it is wrong to use instruments in church. I don't agree with them because the New Testament tells us to speak to one another in "psalms and hymns and spiritual songs" (Ephesians 5:19). If we sing the psalms, we can hardly avoid the many references to musical instruments. It would be strange if Paul wanted us to speak the psalms to each other but not do what they say. Psalm 33 is one of the many psalms that endorse musical instruments for Christian worship.

Worship should also be fresh. This is the idea behind the command, "sing to him a new song" (v. 3). Believers in every generation experience God's grace for themselves, and their musicians should write new songs with creative joy. Those of us in the English-speaking world have inherited a wonderful treasury of great songs and hymns from earlier generations. But if God is at work today, the music we already have is not enough. We need new songs too.

In the sixteenth century Martin Luther wrote new songs as God worked during the Protestant Reformation. In the eighteenth century Isaac Watts and Charles Wesley wrote new songs that fueled worship during the First Great Awakening. In the nineteenth century the blind hymn-writer Fanny Crosby wrote new songs for her generation. God is giving us new songs in the twenty-first century too. Stuart Townend and Keith Getty wrote "In Christ Alone" in 2001. Chris Tomlin wrote "How Great Is Our God" in 2005. Musicians are writing new arrangements for the words of older hymns too. I think of Bob Kauflin from Sovereign Grace, Page CXVI, and Fernando Ortega. When a new generation experiences God's grace, they write new songs to praise him.

This is important for us if we want to teach the next generation to worship. I was driving home with a car full of teenagers several months ago when Matt Redman's song "Ten Thousand Reasons" came on. They had been chattering away until then, but they all stopped and sang along for the rest of the ride home.

> Bless the Lord, O my soul, O my soul
> Worship His holy name.
> Sing like never before, O my soul,
> I'll worship your holy name.[5]

As I listened to them, it occurred to me that these were almost the exact same words that Andrae Crouch put to music forty years ago, in 1973.

> Bless the Lord, O my soul,
> And all that is within me
> Bless his holy name.
> He has done great things. (x3)
> Bless his holy name![6]

These teenagers stopped to sing the Matt Redman song, but they would not have stopped to sing the Andrae Crouch version. The new song spoke to their hearts in a way the older music did not. Our worship music should be fresh.

Worship should also be led with musical excellence. The psalmist calls on the musicians to "play skillfully" (v. 3). We should be thankful for the amount of time our musicians put in to practice and rehearse so they can lead us well in worship. A good goal for Sunday morning is undistracting excellence. The purpose of playing skillfully is not for a musician to show off how good he or she is. The reason for skillful playing is to honor God and help his people praise him without distracting them with wrong notes.

Worship should also be enthusiastic. "Loud shouts" (v. 3) can sometimes mean a war cry or a cry of alarm.[7] When used for praising God, it shows again the energy, emotion, and enthusiasm that is proper and fitting when we are cheering for such a great King. John Piper spoke about this in a letter to his congregation some years ago:

> Two people recently asked me what I would feel like if they said "Amen!" when something moved them. Now the only reason anyone would ask that is if they are getting wrong signals. The answer is: We would feel great! It's the same with lifting your hands in praise. When it is in your heart, *do it!* Anything that helps you express your heart for God and does not hinder other people is OK with us. We want *life* in the sanctuary on Sunday.[8]

Our personalities are all different, of course. For some people, a deep, heartfelt "Hmm" means their heart is really moved. We need to allow others to respond to truth and the beauty of Jesus Christ as God has wired them. Ultimately God is listening to our hearts, and he hears a quiet groan as clearly as a shout.

Cause for Worship

After this *call* to worship, the psalmist gives us *cause* for worship. In verses 4–19 the psalmist fans the coals of our hearts with three main reasons for praising God. He calls us to worship God because of his word, his will, and his watchfulness. It is hard to get excited about nothing. The joy and energy of verses 1–3 are rooted in the truth and theology of verses 4–19. Great worship grows out of great doctrine.

God's Word

The first cause for worship is the character of God we see through his word.

> For the word of the LORD is upright,
>   and all his work is done in faithfulness.
> He loves righteousness and justice;
>   the earth is full of the steadfast love of the LORD.

> By the word of the LORD the heavens were made,
>   and by the breath of his mouth all their host.
> He gathers the waters of the sea as a heap;
>   he puts the deeps in storehouses. (33:4–7)

God's word cannot be separated from God himself. His Spirit is as close to his word as breath is to speech. This means that God's word is "upright" (v. 4) because God himself is upright. The word "upright" means straight and level. Nothing God says is crooked or deceptive—it is always and everywhere true. God's work cannot be separated from God himself either. God works in this world through his word, as he did in the days of creation. His works, then, are an extension of his word and reveal his character as well.

So God's character is reflected in everything he says and does. Since he spoke the world into existence, his glory is reflected in his work of creation. The earth overflows with his steadfast love. The more we study the world around us, the more clearly we see God's character displayed. The order in the universe displays the order of God's character. The beauty in the world displays the goodness of God's heart; he could have made the world an ugly place in which to live, but he made it beautiful for us to enjoy. He designed food chains to nourish entire ecosystems.

Gerard Manley Hopkins said it well.

> The world is charged with the grandeur of God.
> It will flame out, like shining from shook foil;
> It gathers to a greatness, like the ooze of oil
> Crushed. Why do men then now not reck his rod?
> Generations have trod, have trod, have trod;
> And all is seared with trade; bleared, smeared with toil;
> And wears man's smudge and shares man's smell: the soil
> Is bare now, nor can foot feel, being shod.
>
> And for all this, nature is never spent;
> There lives the dearest freshness deep down things;
> And though the last lights off the black West went
> Oh, morning, at the brown brink eastward, springs—
> Because the Holy Ghost over the bent
> World broods with warm breast and with ah! bright wings.[9]

The earth could have been filled with endless terrors, but instead God filled it generously with grace. Men and women live in the sea of God's goodness like a fish lives in the water. Yet many don't see it! Everyone—Jew or Gentile—should worship this God.

Let all the earth fear the LORD;
  let all the inhabitants of the world stand in awe of him!
For he spoke, and it came to be;
  he commanded, and it stood firm. (33:8, 9)

God's Will

The second reason for our worship is God's will.

The LORD brings the counsel of the nations to nothing;
  he frustrates the plans of the peoples.
The counsel of the LORD stands forever,
  the plans of his heart to all generations. (33:10, 11)

This could be referring to some plot to attack Israel as a nation, of course. But in the context of the psalms it seems natural to think of "the counsel of the nations" (v. 10) in terms of Psalm 2. The nations have set themselves against God and Christ, the King. The words are not exactly the same in Hebrew, but the idea is the same.

Why do the nations rage
  and the peoples plot in vain?
The kings of the earth set themselves,
  and the rulers take counsel together,
  against the LORD and against his Anointed, saying,
"Let us burst their bonds apart
  and cast away their cords from us." (2:1–3)

So when Psalm 33:10 says he "brings the counsel of the nations to nothing," I take this ultimately to mean that God blocks the world's opposition to Jesus Christ. All their plotting is pointless. God pops their plans like a balloon. Instead God's will and his purposes will stand forever. His plan for the universe is to set Christ on the throne of the universe and to bring all things under Christ (Psalm 2:5–9; Ephesians 1:10). So we praise him!

God's will is wonderful news for God's people because it means our salvation. God's plan is to honor Christ, and we are blessed because we are in Christ. This is why he says,

Blessed is the nation whose God is the LORD,
  the people whom he has chosen as his heritage! (33:12)

The psalmist is thinking especially of the nation of Israel as he writes this. In the fullness of time, though, the mystery of God's plan would be revealed that God includes Gentiles as natural-born citizens with his people. The Apostle Peter describes Gentile Christians as God's people, his nation.

> But you are a chosen race, a royal priesthood, a holy nation, a people for his own possession, that you may proclaim the excellencies of him who called you out of darkness into his marvelous light. (1 Peter 2:9)

God has chosen believers to be his heritage (Ephesians 1:18). Someday ethnic Israel will turn to Jesus Christ, and this blessing will finally be fulfilled in them too.

God's Watchfulness

The third reason for our worship is God's watchfulness.

> The LORD looks down from heaven;
>   he sees all the children of man;
> from where he sits enthroned he looks out
>   on all the inhabitants of the earth,
> he who fashions the hearts of them all
>   and observes all their deeds. (Psalm 33:13–15)

God's eye is on everyone—male and female, young and old, great and small—and he considers everything we do. The word "observes" (v. 15) has the sense of perceiving or understanding. God does not merely see what we do—he understands what we are doing.

This complete knowledge is terrifying to those who do not know God. But God's complete knowledge is an immense comfort to his people. If God knows everything, he can protect us from everything and provide in every situation.

> The king is not saved by his great army;
>   a warrior is not delivered by his great strength.
> The war horse is a false hope for salvation,
>   and by its great might it cannot rescue.
>
> Behold, the eye of the LORD is on those who fear him,
>   on those who hope in his steadfast love,
> that he may deliver their soul from death
>   and keep them alive in famine. (33:16–19)

Do you fear the Lord? God sees. He understands all the small ways you are trying to honor him and put him first. No one else may understand, but he knows your heart. And since he knows all things, he can protect you and provide for you in every situation. God's complete knowledge means complete care.

The joyful worship of verses 1–3 is fueled by the powerful truths of verses 4–19. The psalmist calls us to worship God for his reliable word, his enduring will, and his watchful protection.

Confidence from Worship

Finally the psalmist describes the faith that comes from heartfelt worship. The psalm began with a shout; it ends with quiet Christian confidence. There is a place for both.

The point of worshiping God with energy and joy is not just to feel good or to have an amazing experience. The end result of true worship is stronger faith. If you worship in spirit and in truth on Sunday, you are strengthening your heart to trust God in the coming week. This is what we all want for ourselves in our churches. We want to strengthen our faith in God together as we worship him together.

> Our soul waits for the LORD;
>   he is our help and our shield.
> For our heart is glad in him,
>   because we trust in his holy name.
> Let your steadfast love, O LORD, be upon us,
>   even as we hope in you. (33:20–22)

These verses are plural throughout because the psalmist still has all God's people in mind. Relationships are vital for our spiritual growth and health. We praise him together because his Word is reliable, his will for us in Christ is unshakable, his watchful care is unwavering. And we wait together—we know he is "our help and our shield" (v. 20). We wait together as Sunday school classes, asking God to answer our prayers. We wait for the Lord with others in small groups. Waiting is group work—we stand together and strengthen each other's faith.

The psalm comes full circle. When we trust God, he gives us a quiet gladness that is like a smoldering coal, ready to burst into flame again with praise. We should praise God with joy and energy as we hope in him.

34

Taste and See

PSALM 34

PSALM 34 is an invitation, a happy, joyful invitation. God rescued David—now David wants you to praise God with him and trust God to rescue you too. He wants you to look, to taste, to see, to enjoy, to fear, to know God for yourself.

Since the Holy Spirit inspired David to write this psalm, this invitation comes from God himself. He wants you to know him, see him, taste his goodness, fear him, and rejoice in him. God is good—he blesses and protects everyone who trusts in him.

David wrote Psalm 34 when God rescued him from one of the most dangerous situations in his life. This is one of only fourteen psalms that come with a historical setting in the life of King David. The superscript says,

> OF DAVID, WHEN HE CHANGED HIS BEHAVIOR BEFORE ABIMELECH, SO THAT HE DROVE HIM OUT, AND HE WENT AWAY.

This refers back to a time in David's life recorded in 1 Samuel 21. David was running for his life from King Saul. Saul had tried to pin David to the wall with a spear three times, then sent a team of assassins after him. David was so desperate that he fled to Gath, one of the five main cities of the Philistines. Gath was Goliath's hometown, the giant he had killed years earlier. Of course they would know who David was. To make matters worse, David was carrying Goliath's sword, which they were sure to recognize. After David hit Goliath between the eyes with a stone, he had taken Goliath's sword and cut off his head. This is the ultimate humiliation for a warrior—to be executed in public with your own weapon. And now David was carrying this famous sword back into Goliath's hometown.

The people of Gath did recognize him, of course, and reported his presence to their king. The king's name was Achish, but our psalm calls him Abimelech, which literally means "my father is king." Abimelech was probably a title the Philistine used for their kings, much like the Egyptians called their kings Pharaoh.

David had fallen out of the frying pan and into the fire. He was at the mercy of his enemy Abimelech, and he was terrified. What could he do? David was so desperate that he pretended he had lost his mind, scratching the doorpost and letting saliva run down his beard. Abimelech fell for it and said to his servants, "Behold, you see the man is mad. Why then have you brought him to me? Do I lack madmen, that you have brought this fellow to behave as a madman in my presence?" (1 Samuel 21:14, 15). So instead of killing David, he kicked him out of the city.

This experience of God's protection made such an impression on David that he wrote two psalms about it. Psalm 56 records David's prayer while he was still a prisoner in Gath. Psalm 34 is the song he sang after he was set free. Psalm 34 is an acrostic psalm; with only two exceptions, each verse begins with the next letter of the Hebrew alphabet[1] so that it is easier to learn. David wanted Israel to learn that God saves his people. If you belong to him, he will rescue you.

We see two main invitations in Psalm 34. In verses 1–10 David invites us to rejoice with him in God's deliverance. In verses 11–22 David invites us to learn from him. The first half is a song; the second half is a sermon. David wants us to "taste and see" God's goodness for ourselves (34:8). He delivers his people from every trouble.

Rejoice with Me

The first half of the psalm is persuasive. David wants to convince us to worship God and experience the joy of trusting him. He is trying to convince us to taste God's goodness for ourselves.

Without being too trite, David does the same thing we might do if we were attempting to convince a friend to try a new restaurant. First, we might rave to our friend about how great it is and invite her to come with us. Then we might explain specifically what we liked about the restaurant and the food we ate there. And finally we push our friend—"try it, you'll like it!"

David follows this same pattern. He praises God and invites us to worship with him (vv. 1–3). Then he gives his testimony to God's deliverance (vv. 4–7). And finally he pushes us to "taste and see" for ourselves (vv. 8–10).

Invitation

So David starts with an invitation.

> I will bless the LORD at all times;
>   his praise shall continually be in my mouth.
> My soul makes its boast in the LORD;
>   let the humble hear and be glad.
> Oh, magnify the LORD with me,
>   and let us exalt his name together! (34:1–3)

Why didn't David just keep this to himself? Why would it matter that we join him? This is because joy is not complete until it is shared. To use the restaurant analogy again, if you are eating an incredible meal, you will want to tell your husband or your friend—whoever is at the table—how good it is. You might say, "Give me your fork, you have to try this!" Why is that? Because you enjoy the experience more when you share it with others. This is why we enjoy watching sports with other people. After a great play, you can turn to your friend and say, "Did you see that?"

Our delight in God and our joy in what he has done grows when we share it with others. If you have experienced God's power and grace in your life, you want to tell others about it so you can enjoy it more yourself. This is why there is joy around the dinner table in a Christian home when we talk about Jesus. Our joy grows as we share our love for him as a family. This is also why it is so important to come to church. We could watch church on the Internet, of course, just like we could watch a football game on TV. But something different happens when we get together live and in person. As we sing and talk and pray together, we are telling each other what God has done, and our joy in God grows. You need the church to complete your joy in Christ!

It is worth noticing how David praises God in these verses: David blesses God and magnifies him. This is surprising. How can a human being bless God? God himself is eternally blessed—how could we add anything to him? He is the source of every blessing, and he is already infinitely exalted above the heavens. How could we magnify him or make him greater than he already is?

The answer, of course, is that when you bless God, you recognize and praise God for who he is. You are not giving him anything as if God was an insecure teenager who needed affirmation. But you are saying, "Lord, you are blessed!" When we magnify God together, we are not making him greater, but we are setting his greatness before our eyes and praising him for it. This means that worship is the most sane and rational thing we can do. We see reality, we see the greatness of God, and we align our hearts with the truth.

This is at the heart of what makes us Christians. The world actively resists God and hates his authority. The world may accept many deities, but it fights the God of the Bible. It does not like or love the God who revealed himself in Jesus Christ. It cannot bless him or magnify him. But God's people see him, love him, and rejoice in his greatness and glory.

David also boasts "in the Lord" (v. 2). What does it mean to brag about God? Our family recently visited our friends Hector and Jodi in Washington, D.C. Hector is a big Steelers fan, but he lives in Baltimore Ravens country. When he wears a Steelers hat around town, people try to give him the business. But Hector can give as good as he gets. "My Steelers have six Super Bowls—how many have the Ravens won? Only two? Call me when you get to five." What is Hector doing? He's boasting in his team. This is exactly what it means to "boast in the Lord" (v. 2). We brag on him. We show how superior he is to every puny thing that competes with him.

Testimony

This boasting is not empty words. David backs up his boasting in the Lord with his own personal testimony.

> I sought the Lord, and he answered me
> and delivered me from all my fears.
> Those who look to him are radiant,
> and their faces shall never be ashamed.
> This poor man cried, and the Lord heard him
> and saved him out of all his troubles.
> The angel of the Lord encamps
> around those who fear him, and delivers them. (34:4–7)

When David says, "I sought the Lord" (v. 4), he does not mean that God was lost or hiding from him. The Hebrew word "sought" in this verse is never used when we don't know where something is.[2] Rather, seeking the Lord here means to ask of God or inquire of him. David is looking for direction from God. And God answered; he rescued David from his fears.

David's experience was not unique and only for him. God answers and protects everyone who loves him. "The angel of the Lord encamps around those who fear him, and delivers them" (v. 7). He watches over and protects his people. There is another story in the Old Testament that illustrates this well. In 2 Kings 6 Elisha and his servant were trapped in the city of Dothan.

During the night the king of Assyria sent his army to surround the city. When they woke up the next morning, Elisha's servant was terrified. "What shall we do?" he cried (2 Kings 6:15). Elisha's answer is famous.

> He said, "Do not be afraid, for those who are with us are more than those who are with them." Then Elisha prayed and said, "O LORD, please open his eyes that he may see." So the LORD opened the eyes of the young man, and he saw, and behold, the mountain was full of horses and chariots of fire all around Elisha. (vv. 16, 17)

God surrounds his people and saves them from every danger. This was David's experience as a prisoner in Goliath's hometown. It is your experience, too, if you love God and fear him.

What fears are you carrying? Not many of us are afraid for our lives like David was. But you may be afraid for your job. You may be afraid for your children. You may be afraid for your marriage. You may be afraid for your retirement. Cast all your cares on the Lord, because he cares for you (1 Peter 5:7).

If you carry around the weight of your fears, it will take a toll on you and affect you physically. You can see worry written in the lines on someone's face. This is why verse 5 is so precious. In many of the ancient versions, verse 5 is a command, not a statement: "Look to the LORD and shine, don't let your face be ashamed!" If you turn to God and look to him for help, the peace and joy he gives will be written on your face. I have seen women in their eighties who shine with a radiance that is more beautiful than any eighteen-year-old. Why? They have learned to look to the Lord.

Taste and See

After the invitation and testimony, David continues his persuasion by urging us—pushing us!—to experience God for ourselves.

> Oh, taste and see that the LORD is good!
>   Blessed is the man who takes refuge in him!
> Oh, fear the LORD, you his saints,
>   for those who fear him have no lack!
> The young lions suffer want and hunger;
>   but those who seek the LORD lack no good thing. (34:8–10)

David could have said, "believe that God is good." We should certainly believe that, of course, but David is not asking us to affirm a point of doctrine. Instead he tells us to "taste and see" (v. 8). What is the difference? I could tell you that honey is sweet. I could describe the molecular structure of honey and how it interacts with your taste buds. I could show videos of chefs using honey to sweeten their food. I could show you a little boy's face light up when his mom puts honey on his toast. After I have done all that, you might *believe* that honey is sweet, but would you *know* that honey is sweet? The only way you are going to know that honey is sweet is actually to taste it for yourself. Anything else is secondhand.

Many Christians have a secondhand experience of God's goodness. They have heard sermons about God's goodness. Their parents have said that God is good. They truly believe that God is good. But they haven't tasted and seen for themselves that God is good.

Why not? Because when they are faced with their fears, they do not turn to God for refuge. They may have trusted God with their minds, but they have not trusted him with their lives. They do not know for themselves what David knows, that God cares for his people and delivers them from every trouble and fear. They will always be splashing in the shallows when they could dive in the oceans of God's goodness. David wants us to act on what we know of God's goodness when we are in trouble. Only then will we taste for ourselves how good he really is.

The Bible promises again and again that God will protect and provide for those who fear him. Lions are great hunters and predators. They are the least likely of all beasts to go hungry. They symbolize power and self-sufficiency, the qualities that make someone great in our world. And yet the self-confident predators of this world, the men of violence, will come up empty. But as Christians we will not lack anything we need. God may not give us everything we want, but he will provide everything we need. And one day he will give us the best thing of all—he will bring us home to Heaven and give us himself, face-to-face, and he will wipe every tear from our eyes (Revelation 21:1–4). On that day we will taste once again and see that the Lord is good in a way we never imagined.

Learn from Me

After inviting us to praise God with him, David asks us to learn from him. The second main invitation of Psalm 34 comes in verse 11.

> Come, O children, listen to me;
> I will teach you the fear of the LORD. (34:11)

David speaks to us like a father speaking to his children or a teacher to his students. If you had a hard relationship with your father growing up, let David adopt you with these words and invite you into his family.

The Fear of the Lord

What does it mean to fear God? Think of a good father and the way his child fears him. Holly Dunn sang about this in her 1986 hit song:

> Daddy's hands were soft and kind when I was cryin'.
> Daddy's hands were hard as steel when I'd done wrong.
> Daddy's hands weren't always gentle,
> But I've come to understand
> There was always love in daddy's hands.[3]

Spurgeon puts it this way:

> Pay to him humble childlike reverence, walk in his laws, have respect to his will, tremble to offend him, hasten to serve him. Fear not the wrath of men, neither be tempted to sin through the virulence of their threats; fear God and fear nothing else.[4]

The great secret is that if you fear God, you will fear nothing else. And if you do not fear God, you will fear everything else.

In Psalm 34 David defines the fear of the Lord more practically. He doesn't define it as an emotion but as obedience. The fear of God is not simply an attitude—it must be an action.

> What man is there who desires life
>   and loves many days, that he may see good?
> Keep your tongue from evil
>   and your lips from speaking deceit.
> Turn away from evil and do good;
>   seek peace and pursue it. (34:12–14)

It's no use saying that we fear God if we do not do what he says. Our life shows our heart. The fear of the Lord means doing what is right. David balances three negatives with three positives. Negatively the fear of the Lord means keeping our tongue from all forms of evil speech and lies. We will be tempted to lie and trust in falsehood to save us. We will be tempted to do wrong in any number of ways. The fear of the Lord teaches us to turn from evil in all its forms.

Positively, the fear of the Lord means doing good in all its forms too. Whatever good things are before us, we should do them. David emphasizes that fearing the Lord means being a peacemaker—not only looking for peace but chasing after it to run it down. This is worth noticing because many Christians do not value peacemaking the way God does. Jesus said, "Blessed are the peacemakers, for they shall be called sons of God" (Matthew 5:9). This is one of the many points of contact between Psalm 34 and the Sermon on the Mount.[5]

Why? God Sees and Hears

Being a peacemaker is hard, especially when someone mistreats us. But if we fear God, we know that God sees and judges the way we act. He rewards us when we do good.

> The eyes of the LORD are toward the righteous
>   and his ears toward their cry.
> The face of the LORD is against those who do evil,
>   to cut off the memory of them from the earth.
> When the righteous cry for help, the LORD hears
>   and delivers them out of all their troubles.
> The LORD is near to the brokenhearted
>   and saves the crushed in spirit. (34:15–18)

The Apostle Peter quotes these verses in 1 Peter 3 to encourage believers not to return evil for evil and insult for insult. God promises to bless us if we do good, even when we have been treated poorly. The only way we will be able to live a godly life in a sinful world is if we fear this God who sees and rewards. God knows the righteous—his eyes see us, his ears hear us, he himself is near us, and he rescues us.

But the opposite is also true, and this judgment is terrible. God hates sin. He sets his face against wickedness in every form. And he will cut off even the memory of those who do evil. When the combines harvest the wheat fields in western Oklahoma, the bits of husks and stalks are blown like dust in the wind across the open prairie. You could not gather the chaff back together again even if you wanted to. So it will be with those who go on sinning—the very memory of them will be swept away (cf. Psalm 1:4).

God does not exempt those who fear him from trouble. In fact, verses 19, 20 teach anyone who follows God to count the cost.

> Many are the afflictions of the righteous,
>   but the LORD delivers him out of them all.
> He keeps all his bones;
>   not one of them is broken.

God's people do not have a few troubles. Instead David tells us that the righteous have "*many* . . . afflictions" (v. 19). This was seen most clearly in the life of our Lord Jesus Christ—he is the ultimate righteous man. He was known as a man of sorrows, and he was afflicted by sinful men. But God saved him by allowing him to die and then raising him from the dead.

In fact, the Apostle John says that verse 20 was fulfilled at Jesus' crucifixion. "[T]hese things took place that the Scripture might be fulfilled: 'Not one of his bones will be broken'" (John 19:36). As David reflected on God's deliverance from his enemy, the king of Gath, he prophesied and spoke of Christ, the Righteous One, who was rescued from the hands of his enemies through the cross and resurrection.

When God rescues us from trouble, he does not always airlift us out of danger. Since this psalm was fulfilled in Christ's death and resurrection, we conclude that God will allow us to go through hard troubles and even die so that he can save us by raising us to resurrection life. If you want to take refuge in him, you need the faith to believe that God gives life to the dead. If he promises to rescue you, he is able to keep his word and save you even after you die.

Two Ways

In the end Psalm 34 is like Psalm 1 in that it leaves us with two ways to live.

> Affliction will slay the wicked,
>   and those who hate the righteous will be condemned.
> The LORD redeems the life of his servants;
>   none of those who take refuge in him will be condemned. (34:21, 22)

"The wicked . . . hate the righteous" in general (v. 22). Most of all, they hate Jesus Christ, the Righteous One. God will find them guilty, and they will be "condemned" (v. 21).

But God himself "redeems" (v. 22) his people, and they will not be condemned. Why not? Because Jesus, the Righteous One, was condemned in our place. Do you know this God? You need to "taste and see" (v. 8) him for yourself.

35

My Savior Will Defend Me

PSALM 35

THE PSALMS are a feast for worship music. Some of our choruses are simply the words of a psalm put to music. Many of the hymns we sing are based on psalms. For instance, Isaac Watts wrote "Joy to The World" by paraphrasing Psalm 98. Originally he wrote his song to be about Christ's second coming, but we use it to celebrate his first coming at Christmas.

We don't sing many songs with the words of Psalm 35 though. This is probably because Psalm 35 is one of a group of psalms called imprecatory psalms. This is an unusual name, but it's easy to understand once you know that the word *imprecation* means a curse. In an imprecatory psalm the author (usually David) curses his enemies. There are at least nine of these imprecatory psalms in the Psalter,[1] most of them written by David.

Christians sometimes have trouble with these psalms because they seem to go against Jesus' teaching. Jesus said, "Love your enemies, do good to those who hate you, bless those who curse you, pray for those who abuse you. To one who strikes you on the cheek, offer the other also" (Luke 6:27–29). On the cross Jesus said, "Father, forgive them, for they know not what they do" (Luke 23:34).

Psalm 35 sounds like just the opposite. "Let them be like chaff before the wind . . . Let their way be dark . . . Let destruction come upon him when he does not know it" (35:5, 6, 8). To make it even more puzzling, David praises God as he curses his enemies! The three main sections of Psalm 35 each end with a word of praise (35:10, 18, 27–28).

So as Christians, how should we read an imprecatory psalm like Psalm 35? We need to think about these imprecatory psalms in general. Then we are going to look specifically at what David says in Psalm 35.

David's Words of Judgment in the Psalms

How should we understand the hard words of judgment in Psalm 35 and others like it?

Wrong Answers

We should start by ruling out some wrong answers. Some people write off Psalm 35 and other imprecatory psalms by saying that David was vindictive and out for revenge. They suggest that David asked God to destroy his enemies because he was human and this was a character flaw. If he had been a better man, they say, he would not have prayed this way.

This answer will not work for at least three reasons. First, it doesn't square with what we know of David. He wasn't a bitter, vindictive man. Time and again David spared Saul's life even though Saul was trying to kill him (1 Samuel 24:1–7; 26:1–12; cf. 2 Samuel 1). Second, David never asks to take vengeance himself on his enemies. He asks God to be his avenger. This is important because God is a righteous judge who never condemns the innocent. David is not praying with a bitter spirit—he is asking God for justice. There is a big difference between vindication and vindictiveness.[2] Third, David was writing under the inspiration of the Holy Spirit (Acts 4:25). This means that Psalm 35 is not just David's words and personal feelings—these are the very words of God. The bottom line is that we can't just write off these imprecatory psalms as David's personal character flaw.

Another wrong answer is to say that the Old Testament is full of judgment while the New is full of forgiveness and grace. Since David was writing before the time of Christ, it is said, we shouldn't expect him to be a forgiving man. How could he have known any better?

The New Testament does reveal the grace of God more fully to us in Christ—that's true. But we can't set the Old and New Testaments against each other. The Bible was inspired by God from beginning to end.

It's a mistake to think the Old Testament only speaks of judgment but not grace. When Jesus taught the second great commandment, he didn't say something new—he quoted what Moses had said in Leviticus: "[Y]ou shall love your neighbor as yourself" (Leviticus 19:18). Deuteronomy commands us not to take revenge (Deuteronomy 32:35). Solomon says in Proverbs, "If your enemy is hungry, give him bread to eat, and if he is thirsty, give him water to drink" (Proverbs 25:21). God sent the prophet Jonah to the Assyrians, his enemies, so they could repent instead of being destroyed. The Old Testament teaches the grace and mercy of God in powerful and beautiful ways.

359 My Savior Will Defend Me

On the flipside, it's also a mistake to think that the New Testament teaches grace but not judgment. John the Baptist said that Christ would burn the wicked like "chaff . . . with unquenchable fire" (Matthew 3:12). Jesus said those who did not receive him would be thrown into "outer darkness" where there is "weeping and gnashing of teeth" (Matthew 8:12; 22:13). The Apostle Peter says false teachers are "accursed" and condemned to "utter darkness" (2 Peter 2:14, 17). And in the book of Revelation, the Apostle John says that God's people will rejoice when God judges this present, evil world.

> After this I heard what seemed to be the loud voice of a great multitude in heaven, crying out,
>
> > "Hallelujah!
> > Salvation and glory and power belong to our God,
> >   for his judgments are true and just;
> > for he has judged the great prostitute
> >   who corrupted the earth with her immorality,
> > and has avenged on her the blood of his servants."
>
> Once more they cried out,
>
> > "Hallelujah!
> > The smoke from her goes up forever and ever." (Revelation 19:1–3)

These are some of the last words of the New Testament. God's people are not embarrassed by his judgment on this wicked world—they worship God for the eternal fire of his vengeance. God would be less glorious, less great, less good, less than God if he allowed evil to continue without destroying the wicked.

How can this be? We understand how this works in our own world. If a judge in Tulsa County did not convict and sentence criminals but sent them back to the street, we would vote him or her out of office as soon as we could. A good judge clears the innocent and condemns the guilty. God is a good judge. Should we expect less of him than a judge in our courtrooms?

We cannot write off the imprecatory psalms by saying that the Old Testament is full of judgment while the New Testament is full of grace. The Old and New Testaments are not set against each other. God's grace and judgment run side by side from Genesis through Revelation.

Right Answers

So what should we think? As Christians, what should we make of Psalm 35 and other psalms where David calls for judgment on his enemies? Are we supposed to pray this way ourselves?

The most important thing to notice is that David is not a private citizen like you and me. He is the king of Israel. This matters for several reasons.

As the king, he represents something more than himself—he represents peace and stability for the nation through his leadership. If someone were to kill me, it would only affect my family, my friends, and my church. This is a relatively small group of people. But if someone were to kill the President, that would destabilize the whole country. That is why the Secret Service has such an important job. In the same way, the people who plotted against King David threatened the whole country. For the sake of the nation, he could not ignore someone who wanted to overthrow the government.

His enemies were also hurting innocent people. David mentions that "the poor and needy" were being robbed (35:10) and the quiet people of the land were suffering (35:20). It's one thing for you and me to forgive someone who hurts us—this is what Jesus meant when he said in essence, "turn the other cheek." But if you are the king, you can't turn the other cheek when your people are attacked. God has placed kings in authority to maintain order in society (Romans 13:3, 4). King David was responsible to provide law and justice, peace and security for the citizens of his kingdom—he could not turn a blind eye to evil. "A policeman, judge, governor, or president must deal with the violent differently from how you and I might deal with them."[3]

As the king of Israel, David had also been chosen by God to be his servant. The prophet Samuel had anointed David; everyone knew that God had chosen him to lead Israel (cf., e.g., 2 Samuel 5:1, 2). So when someone attacked David, he was actually attacking God and fighting against God's will. When God rescued David, he would bring glory to his own name. This is why David says in 35:27, "Let those who delight in my righteousness shout for joy and be glad and say evermore, 'Great is the Lord, who delights in the welfare of his servant!'" If God did not defend his servant David, then God's name would be tarnished. So in a profound sense David was motivated by the glory of God.

As a final point to understand the curses in this imprecatory psalm, remember also that David was a prophet and a model for the Messiah, the Son of David. The rejection David experienced points forward to Christ's rejection.

In fact, Jesus quotes 35:19 to explain why many of the Jews hated him. As he prepared his disciples to face persecution, Jesus said,

> Remember the word that I said to you: "A servant is not greater than his master." If they persecuted me, they will also persecute you. . . . Whoever hates me hates my Father also. If I had not done among them the works

that no one else did, they would not be guilty of sin, but now they have seen and hated both me and my Father. But the word that is written in their Law must be fulfilled: "They hated me without a cause." (John 15:20, 23–25)

The rejection David experienced in Psalm 35 was fulfilled when Jesus was hated and rejected by his own people. The judgment David calls for in this psalm points forward to the judgment that is waiting for everyone who rejects Christ. God is patient and opens his arms to welcome sinners. But there comes a point when he condemns the enemies of Christ who do not repent.

God My Savior and Avenger

With that in mind, we're ready to hear David's words in Psalm 35. David's friends turned on him and wanted him dead, and we can identify with the sense of betrayal he felt.

One of the most painful things we can experience is when someone we love or trust turns against us. The wound lasts for years. Many people carry this pain to the grave.

My good friend was betrayed by his wife. She humiliated him and divorced him even though he loved her and was trying to make the marriage work. My friend Jeff was betrayed by a business partner, a man who was supposedly a Christian. He was keeping two sets of books and turned against him. Someone you work with at church might turn against you. On Palm Sunday some years ago a former elder put a letter in my box threatening legal action against the church. He is a lawyer and had served in leadership for many years. When he turned against us, it was devastating to all the men who were then serving as elders. I felt such stress that I got sick, I lost my voice, and I could hardly preach that next week for Easter.

David is facing this kind of pain and betrayal in Psalm 35. His enemies were people with whom he was once close. He fasted when they were sick, but they paid him back with hatred. They hid nets to trip up his feet, working in the shadows, plotting in secret. They were "malicious witnesses" (35:11) who tried to confuse him with their questions. They gathered like wolves and kicked him when he was down. He thought they were friends, but they turned against him. And since David was God's king, this was about more than just him.

David calls on God to save him and avenge him. The first three verses set the stage with an urgent call to action.

Contend, O LORD, with those who contend with me;
fight against those who fight against me!

Take hold of shield and buckler
  and rise for my help!
Draw the spear and javelin
  against my pursuers!
Say to my soul,
  "I am your salvation!" (35:1–3)

David gives two main pictures of what he wants God to do. First, he wants God to defend him as a lawyer. The word "contend" (v. 1) is a legal word that suggests a defense lawyer arguing for his client. David asks God to plead his case in a courtroom. Second, David calls God to defend him as a soldier—he calls on God to fight for him. The "buckler" (v. 2) was a larger, rectangular shield that covered the whole body. The "shield and buckler" are for defense, while "the spear and javelin" are for offense (v. 2, 3). Above the noise of the battle, he longed to hear God say, "I am your salvation!" (v. 3).

After this introduction, the first section (vv. 4–10) continues the picture of the battle. The second section (vv. 11–18) picks up the picture of the courtroom again. In the third section the enemies seem to be celebrating already because they think they have already won (vv. 19–28).[4] These sections each contain a prayer, a complaint, and a promise.

The Battle

In the first section David calls on God to fight for him. His prayer is in verses 4–6.

Let them be put to shame and dishonor
  who seek after my life!
Let them be turned back and disappointed
  who devise evil against me!
Let them be like chaff before the wind,
  with the angel of the LORD driving them away!
Let their way be dark and slippery,
  with the angel of the LORD pursuing them!

David's enemies were trying to kill him even though he was God's anointed king—"[they] seek . . . my life," he says (v. 4). David calls down four curses or imprecations on them that represent complete defeat. The "shame," "dishonor," turning back, and disappointment of verse 4 represent defeat in battle. If an army is "turned back," it does not achieve its objective. When Hitler's armies were turned back at the edge of Moscow, it was the turning point of World War II.

And as they retreat, David also asks God to chase them as an avenging angel. David mentions "the angel of the LORD" in the previous psalm (Psalm 34:7) and again twice in these verses. It's worth noticing that these are the only references to "the angel of the LORD" in all the psalms. Who is this "angel of the LORD"? He appears at various times in the Old Testament as the special protector of God's people. We should not think of "the angel of the LORD" as an ordinary angel, though, because at various times "the angel of the LORD" seems to be God himself.

For instance, when Jacob blessed the sons of Joseph, he described the God of his fathers as "the angel who has redeemed me from all evil" (Genesis 48:15, 16). When Israel crossed the Red Sea, Moses said that the Lord was in the cloud and then said it was "the angel of God" (Exodus 13:21; 14:19). There are a number of references like this that lead many Bible teachers to think "the angel of the LORD" is Jesus Christ, the second member of the Trinity, appearing and working before his incarnation. If this is true, and I think it is, then David calls on Christ to curse his enemies and drive them like chaff into darkness. And in fact the same Jesus who is our Shepherd and Savior is also the Messiah of Psalm 2 who breaks his enemies with a rod of iron.

David claims his innocence in verse 7 and again calls down three more curses on his enemy in verse 8. These curses do not embarrass him in the least. In fact he promises to praise God when God carries out this judgment.

> Then my soul will rejoice in the LORD,
>   exulting in his salvation.
> All my bones shall say,
>   "O LORD, who is like you,
> delivering the poor
>   from him who is too strong for him,
>   the poor and needy from him who robs him?" (35:9, 10)

If you have a rose-tinted, Pollyanna view of God—maybe like a nice, white-haired grandfather in Heaven—you will be shocked to hear David praise God for sending destruction. But this is not indiscriminate anger—the people God destroys were robbing the poor. David was the king; he was responsible for the safety of all his people. These enemies were trying to kill him and were terrorizing villages. Do we want them to stop their attacks? Of course. But if they will not stop and they continue their violence, there comes a point when we will praise God for laying them low.

When David says he rejoices in God's judgment on these enemies, it doesn't say what else he might be feeling. When the police catch a criminal, you might feel sorry for the offender even though you are glad he is off the streets. We can praise God for judging an evil person while we are grieved by the sin that controlled him, dragged him down, and destroyed him. It is possible to rejoice and weep over the same event.[5]

The Lawsuit

In the second section David returns to the courtroom.

> Malicious witnesses rise up;
>> they ask me of things that I do not know. (35:11)

In the courtroom dramas we have watched, we have seen what a good lawyer can do to people on the witness stand. Even if they are honest and innocent, he can trip them up. And if other witnesses have already lied about them on the stand, the lawyer can eat them alive. This seems to be what was happening to David.

According to verses 12–16, it was especially painful because the false witnesses used to be his friends. He fasted and prayed for them when they were sick, but they turned against him when he stumbled. Maybe they were simply using him because he was king. When it seemed like he was losing power, they turned against him to get in good with the new administration. But David knew God would rescue him and promises to praise God when he does.[6]

The Plot

In the final section of Psalm 35, David asks God to vindicate him. His enemies are gloating over his downfall. It is hard enough to go through betrayal, but when people laugh about your pain, it's even worse.

> Let not those rejoice over me
>> who are wrongfully my foes,
> and let not those wink the eye
>> who hate me without cause. (35:19)

David uses the word "rejoice" in the sense of gloating three times in these last verses (vv. 19, 24, 26). The worst outcome would be for things to turn out well for the bad guys, for the wicked people who are taking advantage of the people who are "quiet in the land" (v. 20).

Would God allow this injustice to stand? No; when God saves his king, all the people will rejoice.

> Let those who delight in my righteousness
>   shout for joy and be glad
>   and say evermore,
> "Great is the LORD,
>   who delights in the welfare of his servant!"
> Then my tongue shall tell of your righteousness
>   and of your praise all the day long. (35:27, 28)

The good people in Israel were loyal to David, and they rejoiced when God rescued him. All Israel knew that God had chosen David, and the prophet Samuel had anointed him to be king. When God saved the king, he brought blessing to the nation. The faithful in the land praised God for his faithfulness to his servant David.

In the same way, as believers we rejoice at God's faithfulness in saving our Lord Jesus Christ. He is the great Son of David, and ultimately this psalm is about him and the opposition he endured. The leaders of Israel were thrilled when they killed him on the cross. They had their heart's desire. But God raised him from the dead and rescued him. And now Jesus is seated at the right hand of God the Father, waiting for God to place all his enemies beneath his feet (Psalm 110:1).

Christ's enemies hate him still today. I wish they would put down their swords, stop their lies, and worship him, but they will not. And so there is nothing left for them but the judgment God has warned us about in both the Old and New Testaments.

I hope you are not one of them. I hope your heart sings because God has rescued and honored Jesus Christ. I hope you shout for joy because God has given him the name that is above every name.

As it turns out, Isaac Watts wrote two hymns based on Psalm 35. One of them includes these verses:

> They love the road that leads to hell;
> Then let the rebels die,
> Whose malice is implacable
> Against the Lord on high.

> But if thou hast a chosen few
> Amongst that impious race,
> Divide them from the bloody crew,
> By thy surprising grace.

Then will I raise my tuneful voice,
To make thy wonders known;
In their salvation I'll rejoice,
And bless thee for my own.[7]

I pray you are not among Christ's enemies. I pray that you bless him for
your own.

36

God's Steadfast Love

PSALM 36

ON MAY 11, 1960 a team of Israeli Mossad agents kidnapped Nazi war criminal Adolf Eichmann off the streets of Buenos Aires, Argentina and spirited him back to Israel to stand trial. Eichmann had deported millions of Jews to concentration camps. Now he would stand trial before Jews in Israel.

This was the first trial in history to be broadcast on television in its entirety. The eyes of the world were riveted on the courtroom in Jerusalem. The most dramatic moment may have been when Yehiel Dinur, a concentration camp survivor, took the stand.

A film clip shows Dinur walking into the courtroom and stopping as he saw Eichmann. This was the first time Dinur had seen him since Eichmann sent him to Auschwitz eighteen years earlier. Dinur began to sob uncontrollably, then collapsed on the floor as the judge pounded his gavel for order in the crowded courtroom. Mike Wallace later interviewed Dinur and asked about that moment.

> Was Dinur overcome by hatred? Fear? Horrid memories? No; it was none of these. Rather . . . all at once he realized Eichmann was not the god-like army officer who had sent so many to their deaths. This Eichmann was an ordinary man. "I was afraid about myself," said Dinur. ". . . I saw that I am capable to do this. I am . . . exactly like he."

Wallace summed up Dinur's terrible discovery with a terrifying phrase: "Eichmann is in all of us." This horrifying statement captures a central truth about man's nature. Because of the fall, sin is in each of us—not just the susceptibility to sin, but sin itself.[1]

Dinur did not break down and collapse because he saw the horror of sin in one man. He broke down because he saw the horror of sin in humanity. Eichmann is in all of us because all of us are in Adam.[2] Adam and Eve sinned against God, and as their children all of us have inherited their sin nature. We are sinners by birth. The proof of this is that we are so easily tempted to sin.

> We are tempted by theft because we *are* thieves, even though we may not in fact steal. We are tempted to kill because we *are* murderers, even if we do not literally slay our brother. We are tempted to adultery because we *are* adulterers, even though we may not commit adultery. James says, "When tempted, no one should say, 'God is tempting me.' For God cannot be tempted by evil, nor does he tempt anyone; but each one is tempted when, by his own evil desire, he is dragged away and enticed" (James 1:13, 14).[3]

In the words of our psalm, "Transgression speaks to the wicked deep in his heart" (Psalm 36:1). Each one of us hears the voice of sin whispering in our hearts. Eichmann is in all of us.

But there is hope. You and I are sinners, but God is full of steadfast love. This hope is the message of Psalm 36. David contrasts the darkness of our sin with the light of God's steadfast love—his faithful, loving commitment to his people. First, David reveals our darkness (vv. 1–4). Then, in contrast, David reveals God's light (vv. 5–9). David ends with a prayer asking God to keep giving and showing his love to him (vv. 9–11).

God gave us his steadfast love most perfectly and fully by sending his Son, Jesus Christ. We are each so bad that Christ had to die for us. And we are so loved that he wanted to die for us. If we belong to him, he will never let us go.

Revealing Our Sin

Psalm 36 begins with a terrible statement about the human heart.[4]

> Transgression speaks to the wicked
>   deep in his heart;
> there is no fear of God
>   before his eyes. (36:1)

These words are terrible because they show us that the root of evil in this world is not a lack of education. The root of evil is not inequality or injustice, terrible as these are. Evil will not be solved by technology or progress. The problem is that our hearts are bad. Sin speaks to us deep inside, and we listen.

This is not just a problem for the very bad people of the world—the rapists and serial killers. David includes himself. The Hebrew literally says, "Transgression speaks to the wicked deep in *my* heart."[5] David heard the voice of sin whispering inside him even though he was God's anointed, a man who was inspired by the Holy Spirit to write Scripture. You hear the voice of sin inside you too. He is describing the condition of every man and woman.

And because we listen to sin, we do not fear God. The word "fear" (v. 1) is not the word that is normally used in the classic phrase, "the fear of the Lord." David chooses another word that means abject terror, the kind of fear that leaves you trembling. In other words, the voice of sin is so smooth and seductive that we are not terrified of falling into the hands of the living God (Hebrews 10:30, 31).

We should be afraid of God's judgment, of course, and the fact that we are not shows how powerfully sin blinds us to reality. The right fear is a healthy thing. When our children were young, we wanted them to be afraid of the cars that drove down our street. We explained in the gentlest way we could that if a car hit them, it would hurt a lot. They could die, and Mommy and Daddy would be sad—we would cry and cry. If a child or an adult is not afraid of the damage a car can do, that is a real problem.

If you are walking on railroad tracks and a train is coming, your heart should pound. You should be so afraid that you get off the tracks. You should not be on the tracks in the first place, but if you are, the blaring horn of a locomotive should strike fear in your heart and terrify you. The right fear is a healthy thing.

One of the worst effects of sin is that we do not fear God. We do not tremble as his judgment comes thundering down the tracks of history. Jesus said, "[D]o not fear those who kill the body but cannot kill the soul. Rather fear him who can destroy both soul and body in hell" (Matthew 10:28). If Jesus is telling the truth—and he is—then one of the most healthy and rational things we can do is genuinely fear God and his judgment. And one of the worst things that sin can do is blind us and distract us from thinking about this judgment. In Romans 3 Paul describes the sinfulness of humanity by quoting fourteen phrases from six Old Testament sources. As the final word to summarize the deadly power of sin, Paul quotes Psalm 36:1, "[T]here is no fear of God before his eyes."

How do we get to this terrible place where we do not fear God and his judgment? And what does this do to our lives? Verses 2–4 describe humanity's descent into darkness.

We Flatter Ourselves

It starts inwardly with self-deception, lying to ourselves. We flatter ourselves that God will never judge us for what we do.

For he flatters himself in his own eyes
   that his iniquity cannot be found out and hated. (36:2)

It's obvious that people tell themselves they will never be punished. If they didn't, they would be afraid of God's judgment, and the fear of standing before him would make them miserable. So this self-deception is a sort of psychological coping mechanism. The fact that most people go cheerfully about their lives shows that they are blind to the judgment that is to come. Our cities and neighborhoods are full of men and women who pat themselves on the back because they think God will not hold them accountable. We lie to ourselves to avoid dealing with the terrible reality of God's wrath.[6]

How do we flatter ourselves with the idea that we will escape punishment?[7] Many people choose to believe that there is no afterlife, that once you die, that is the end. They tell themselves there is no creator and no judge. In Carl Sagan's famous phrase, we are just "matter grown to consciousness." This is the position of many people who consider themselves to be intelligent, educated, and scientific. They flatter themselves for having minds that lift them above superstition and primitive religious fears.

Others lie to themselves by thinking they will have time to repent later. Death seems a long way off. Their anthem might be, "Tonight we are young, so let's set the world on fire, we can burn brighter than the sun."[8] They assume they will live to an old age and there will be plenty of time to ask forgiveness and turn over a new leaf. They flatter themselves, thinking they can work the system and outsmart God. But no one knows for sure they will be alive tomorrow, or even tonight.

Others think God would never be angry with them because they live orderly, moral lives. "I am a good person," they think. "Could God really be angry with me?" They flatter themselves by thinking that the good things they have done far outweigh any little sins they may have committed.

In a related way, others flatter themselves by remembering some big thing they have done for God. "I gave this large gift. I went on this mission trip. I helped this person. I served in this ministry," they say to themselves. "So God owes it to me to let me into Heaven." They might never say this out loud, of course, but they pat themselves on the back because what they did was such a big help to Almighty God.

Others flatter themselves because they were born in a Christian family. "God will take it easy on me," they say in their hearts, "because I have been in church since I was in the nursery." They think that because God loves their parents, he automatically loves them too. The Jews in Jesus' day thought the same thing. They boasted, "We have Abraham as our Father" (Matthew 3:9).

Others flatter themselves that God will never judge them because they have had a powerful experience of God's presence. Maybe it was a vision or a deep feeling of peace. Maybe it was a prophecy someone spoke about them. They have been holding on to this experience for years and feel good because of it.

Others flatter themselves that they will not face judgment because they have the right doctrine. "I am not like those liberals who water down the Scriptures," they think, "so God likes me." They pat themselves on the back for being orthodox and faithful to the truth. They forget that Satan has good theology himself—the demons believe in God, and they "shudder" at the judgment that is waiting for them (James 2:19).

We Sin against Others

Our descent into darkness starts with self-deception, but it turns outward in our words and actions.

> The words of his mouth are trouble and deceit;
> he has ceased to act wisely and do good.
> He plots trouble while on his bed;
> he sets himself in a way that is not good;
> he does not reject evil. (36:3, 4)

If we are not accountable to God, there is nothing to stop us from going wherever our sinful hearts lead us. Verse 3 is especially sobering because David implies that this person once did "act wisely and do good." But he has "ceased." Sin whispered in his heart, he flattered himself that it would not matter to God, and now he has fallen farther than he could have imagined.

In the end we are no longer able to recognize evil for what it is and reject it. James Stewart put it this way:

> Every time he sins, he is making himself less capable of realizing what sin is, less likely to realize that he is a sinner, for the ugly thing, the really diabolical thing about sin is that it perverts a man's judgment. It stops him from seeing straight.[9]

Revealing God's Steadfast Love

After this sobering look at the terrible reality of our sin, David turns to the glory of God. The good news for sinners like you and me is that we don't have to flatter ourselves that God will not judge us for our sins. We don't have to lie to ourselves—there is another way! We can run to God and find refuge in him.

The choice could not be clearer. We can continue in the darkness, telling ourselves that God will not judge, going from bad to worse. Or we can come into the light of God's love.[10] David sings about God's goodness and love in these next verses to make this choice a no-brainer. Who would not want the blessings of knowing God the way David describes him in verses 5–9? Look at who he is! You should run—not walk—to a God like this.

This Is God!

First, David describes who God is. He mentions five attributes of God that fill the earth and surround us.

> Your steadfast love, O LORD, extends to the heavens,
>   your faithfulness to the clouds.
> Your righteousness is like the mountains of God;
>   your judgments are like the great deep;
>   man and beast you save, O LORD. (36:5, 6)

God's "steadfast love" seems to be the most important attribute of God in this psalm. It is the first attribute David mentions, and he refers to God's "steadfast love" three times in these verses (vv. 5, 7, 10). "Steadfast love" ("lovingkindness" or "unfailing love" in some translations) is God's covenant love. He is faithful and loyal to his people just as a good man loves his wife and is faithful to her.

When David says that God's "steadfast love . . . extends to the heavens" (v. 5), he means there are no limits to his love. One of our children's favorite books was *Guess How Much I Love You?* Little Nutbrown Hare tries to show his daddy how much he loves him—as high as he can reach and as far as he can hop. But Big Nutbrown Hare can reach higher and hop farther, and he loves him back even more.

> "I love you all the way down the lane as far as the river," cried Little Nutbrown Hare.
> "I love you across the river and over the hills," said Big Nutbrown Hare.[11]

Finally Little Nutbrown Hare looked up at the sky and said, "I love you all the way to the moon," and he fell asleep. Big Nutbrown Hare lay down next to him and whispered, "I love you right up to the moon—and back." God's "steadfast love" (v. 5) is even better. He loves us to the moon and beyond! His unfailing love is as vast as the immeasurable vastness of space. There are no limits to his loving commitment to his people.

The second attribute David mentions is God's "faithfulness" (v. 5). Alexander MacLaren argues that this refers to God's Word, the Bible, because only a God who has spoken and given us promises can be thought of as faithful.[12] You can count on God to keep his Word. God promises, "[T]hough your sins are like scarlet, they shall be as white as snow" (Isaiah 1:18). And again the Scriptures say, "[A]s far as the east is from the west, so far does he remove our transgressions from us" (Psalm 103:12). God is faithful to his Word.

Thirdly, David sings that God's "righteousness" (36:6) is like the highest mountains. God will do what is right in every situation. He is always fair and always just. "The mountains of God" (v. 6) is probably a way of saying high mountains. So picture the Rocky Mountains with their granite faces. God's righteousness is strong and unmoving like these. This is good news for those who love him because it means he will do right by them.

The fourth attribute David mentions is God's "judgments" (v. 6). They are as deep as the ocean. God doesn't make shallow decisions or shortsighted plans. God sees to the bottom of every question. He sees to the bottom of every human heart. His judgments are deep.

The fifth thing David wants us to know about God is that he is a Savior. "[M]an and beast you save, O LORD" (v. 6). I take this to mean that it is in God's nature to save his creation. Sin has ruined us—it has destroyed both humanity and nature. But God is a saving God. You may ask yourself, "Why would God bother with me? I've made a mess of my life." You need to know that it is in God's nature to save people. He takes broken lives and rebuilds them. He rebuilds broken families. His plans are even bigger than you or me—he is restoring and rebuilding this entire created world that is ruined by sin.

These Are God's Blessings

David has listed five attributes of God. Now he lists five blessings for those who know him.

The first blessing is protection.

> How precious is your steadfast love, O God!
> The children of mankind take refuge in the shadow of your wings. (36:7)

God's "steadfast love" is "precious" because it means that we belong to him and he is committed to us. If we take refuge beneath his wings, God will protect us.

The picture here is that of a hen hiding her chicks from danger under her feathers. She will shelter her chick, even if she dies in the process. After napalm was dropped on Hiroshima, Nobuo Hayashi returned home to find a hen scorched to death with her chicks still tucked safely beneath her wing.[13] He was amazed to find they were still alive. In the same way, God sacrifices himself to save us.

This is what God has done for us through Jesus Christ. We deserved to die because of our sins. But God took on flesh and became a human being like you and me, the man Jesus Christ. Jesus had never sinned, and he did not deserve to die. But he went to the cross and died in our place. He took the punishment that we deserve, to shield us and protect us. Will you run to him for shelter or will you stay outside and die?

The second blessing is satisfaction. "They feast on the abundance of your house" (v. 8). Literally, those who come into God's house are "satisfied" by its "fullness."[14] Even more literally, the word "abundance" means "fat," which means rich food and not meager rations. Many are like the prodigal son, so hungry they are ready to eat pig slop if they could just go home and be welcomed at the table. God has abundance in his house to satisfy us in Jesus Christ forever.

The third blessing is joy. "[Y]ou give them drink from the river of your delights" (v. 8). What could this river be? The joy God gives his people is the joy of God himself.[15] David says elsewhere,

> You make known to me the path of life;
>   in your presence there is fullness of joy;
>   at your right hand are pleasures forevermore. (Psalm 16:11)

God will be for us an ever-flowing river of joy and delight. Our joy in him begins now, in this life, as we come to know him and his Spirit fills our hearts. But in Heaven we will see him face-to-face—we will be with him, enjoy him, worship him, and our hearts will delight in him forever.

The fourth and fifth blessings are life and light.

> For with you is the fountain of life;
>   in your light do we see light. (36:9)

It is hard to read this verse without thinking of the way the Apostle John described Jesus at the beginning of his gospel: "In him was life, and the life was the light of men" (John 1:4). Jesus Christ is the source of all spiritual and physical life. He shines in the world to reveal truth and reality to us. Without him we only hear the voice of sin whispering in our hearts. The things we thought were truth were really only darkness. But God struck a match by sending his Son into the world. When we recognize "the glory of God in the face of Jesus Christ" (2 Corinthians 4:6), when we realize that this man is God and he died for sinners, his light shines in our hearts, and we see reality for the first time. He is light and life for you and me.

The world will never look the same once God's light is in our hearts. When I was in seminary, I led a mission trip of college students to Ostrava, Czechoslovakia. We met an old man named Josef Rymanek who wanted very much to show me his cabin in the mountains. So one day Josef drove me high into the mountains outside town where we sat and talked for a few hours. I shared the gospel with him and asked him if he wanted to follow Christ. He said yes, so we prayed together as we sat on an old, wooden bench outside his cabin.

When we finished praying, he took my hands in his old, wrinkled palms. Then he looked around us and said, "I will never forget this day, with the green grass and blue sky, the mountains and the trees. Thank you for telling me about God." I was reminded of the old hymn that says, "Heav'n above is softer blue, earth around is sweeter green; something lives in every hue Christless eyes have never seen."[16] When you know your Creator, you see the world with different eyes. "In your light do we see light."

Closing Thought

David leaves us with a choice. There is a stark contrast between those who know God and those who continue in sin.

> Oh, continue your steadfast love to those who know you,
>   and your righteousness to the upright of heart!
> Let not the foot of arrogance come upon me,
>   nor the hand of the wicked drive me away.
> There the evildoers lie fallen;
>   they are thrust down, unable to rise. (36:10–12)

Eichmann is in all of us. Will you continue in your sin, pretending that God will not punish you? Or will you run to Jesus for shelter? Will you stay in darkness or will you come into the light? Will you choose lies or will you choose God's love?

Choose life. Come to Jesus today.

37

Don't Envy the Wicked

PSALM 37

THE MAIN APPLICATION FOR Psalm 37 is in the first verse.

> Fret not yourself because of evildoers;
>   be not envious of wrongdoers.

When wicked people seem to be doing well and getting ahead, don't let it get under your skin. And don't be tempted to be like them.

This Temptation Is Real

This is a real temptation because bad people sometimes look happy and successful. We secretly wish we could be like them. We obey God and follow him, and we may be asking ourselves, "Where has this gotten me? My friends who do whatever they want are better off than I am." Being a Christian doesn't seem to be paying off. And we are envious of wrongdoers.

Teenage girls sometimes feel this sort of envy. They see other girls show lots of skin, and the boys are interested. But they dress modestly, and no one pays them that kind of attention. "They're popular," they think, "so maybe I should be like them." They wish they were not so sheltered or that their parents were not so strict. What is going on in their heart? They are "envious of wrongdoers" (v. 1).

As adults we might feel this sort of envy at work. We see a coworker who has gotten ahead by being deceitful. Maybe he plays with the numbers or maybe he's a master at office politics, and he is climbing the ladder faster than we are. It's hard to admit, but we're a little jealous. We are wondering whether we should start playing that game too. We are "envious of wrongdoers."

Maybe you're retired, and your friend isn't a believer, never goes to church, has lived for himself, and seems to be doing better than you. His 401(k) is bigger. His kids and grandkids seem better off. As you look back, you wonder if following God was worth it. You are "envious of wrongdoers."

Maybe you're a man who is wondering whether it is worth it to stay in your marriage. Your college roommate divorced his wife (without Biblical grounds) and married a beautiful younger woman. He seems happier than you are. You are "envious of wrongdoers."

Or consider a single woman who wants to get married. Her friend snagged the perfect guy by sleeping with him. She is telling this woman that she needs to get out and play the field more. She's beginning to think her friend is right. She is "envious of wrongdoers."

Or consider a married woman who is struggling with respecting her husband. Her friend or sister is sassy and assertive in her marriage. She's worked hard at honoring God by submitting to her husband, but her friend seems happier than she is. She's wondering whether she's made a mistake. She is "envious of wrongdoers."

I have given you these examples to show you that being envious of the wicked is a real issue. This is not a hypothetical question or a theoretical exercise. Lives are on the line. Marriages are on the line. The temptation is real. Psalm 37 is important.

How to Fight This Temptation

How can we fight the temptation to envy the wicked? David's answer in Psalm 37 is to lift up our eyes and look ahead to the future. God has a glorious future for the godly. But the wicked will "fade like the grass" (v. 2). They may seem to be thriving today, but God will uproot them like a gardener pulling weeds.

Psalm 37 teaches us to look ahead to the future that God has in store for those who love him. We can see this when we notice the theme David repeats five times in this psalm: "those who wait for the LORD shall inherit the land" (37:9, 11, 22, 29, 34). How does this look to the future? This phrase "inherit the land" goes back to the time when Moses led the people to the promised land. God gave them the land of Israel as their inheritance (see Numbers 26:52–56; Joshua 11:23).

Joshua led the people into the land four hundred years before David wrote this psalm. As a nation they had *already* received their inheritance. David was not thinking of an earthly inheritance because the people were already in the promised land. He is thinking about a better land, an inheritance in Heaven.

The writer of Hebrews says that Abraham was looking for an inheritance beyond this world too. Abraham and Sarah were waiting for "a better country, that is, a heavenly one. Therefore God is not ashamed to be called their God, for he has prepared for them a city" (Hebrews 11:16).

If you are a Christian, you are looking beyond this world for your inheritance. The Apostle Peter opens his first letter this way:

> Blessed be the God and Father of our Lord Jesus Christ! According to his great mercy, he has caused us to be born again to a living hope through the resurrection of Jesus Christ from the dead, to an inheritance that is imperishable, undefiled, and unfading, kept in heaven for you. (1 Peter 1:3, 4)

When Psalm 37:9 says, "those who wait for the LORD shall inherit the land," I don't think this refers to real estate. David is looking forward to Heaven.

Ultimately you will not be able to fight the temptation to envy the wicked unless you are looking forward to Heaven too. If you are only living for good things in this world, you will be powerless to fight this sin. Our Lord Jesus looked ahead to the blessings God had promised him. "[F]or the joy that was set before him [he] endured the cross, despising the shame, and is seated at the right hand of the throne of God" (Hebrews 12:2). Christ looked ahead when the wicked seemed to be winning. He is our example.

As a teaching psalm, Psalm 37 contains a number of proverbs that could stand alone. It is also an acrostic poem; it has twenty-two units that begin with the letters of the Hebrew alphabet in order. David marks the main transition points between the sections of the psalm by repeating his theme: the wicked will be "cut off," while the faithful will "inherit the land" (37:9, 22, 28–29, 34). This divides the psalm into five main sections.[1] With these sections David gives us five main strategies to fight this temptation to envy the wicked.

Look to God

First, in verses 3–9 David tells us to look to God. These verses contain over a dozen commands that center our hearts on God. Four of these commands directly refer to "the LORD" and appear to be main headings for this section.

Trust in the Lord

David tells us to trust in the Lord.

> Trust in the LORD, and do good;
>   dwell in the land and befriend faithfulness. (37:3)

Trust is faith, believing that God's promises are true and that he will keep his word. He will never, ever let us down.

When we lived in Minnesota, I enjoyed driving across the frozen lakes in the winter. They plow roads across some of the bigger lakes, and you can sometimes cut a mile or more off your trip. It was always nerve-wracking, though, when I first pulled onto the ice. Would it really hold? I knew in my head that the ice was two feet thick. I saw cars and SUVs out on the ice, but I still felt nervous when I drove onto the lake for myself. I had to trust that the ice would hold. Similarly, we need to trust God, that his word will hold.

Do you trust in the Lord? Jeremiah says,

> "For I know the plans I have for you," declares the LORD, "plans for welfare and not for evil, to give you a future and a hope." (Jeremiah 29:11)

Do you trust in the Lord? Isaiah says,

> From of old no one has heard
>   or perceived by the ear,
> no eye has seen a God besides you,
>   who acts for those who wait for him. (Isaiah 64:4)

Do you trust in the Lord? Paul says,

> I consider that the sufferings of this present time are not worth comparing with the glory that is to be revealed to us. (Romans 8:18)

Do you trust in the Lord? You need to believe his promises and put your weight on them. He will never ever let you down. And if you trust him, you will have the strength to obey him and do good.

Delight Yourself in the Lord

David also tells us to delight in God.

> Delight yourself in the LORD,
>   and he will give you the desires of your heart. (37:4)

What does this mean? Before we are converted, we don't think much of God. He is not beautiful and precious to us. We don't find him satisfying. But when we are saved, God opens our eyes to see his beauty and glory. Suddenly we see for ourselves that God himself is the most attractive and beautiful being in the universe. We are overwhelmed by his kindness and goodness, his power and majesty. We "taste and see that the LORD is good" (Psalm 34:8). This is why David says in Psalm 27:4,

> One thing have I asked of the LORD,
>   that will I seek after:
> that I may dwell in the house of the LORD
>   all the days of my life,
> to gaze upon the beauty of the LORD
>   and to inquire in his temple.

God becomes our one thing. If we have him, we have everything. And nothing on earth compares to him (Psalm 73:25). We need to delight ourselves in the Lord so that we learn to love and long for the best thing of all—namely, God himself.

We often focus on the second half of this verse, the part about "the desires of your heart" (37:4). But if we truly delight in the Lord, then the one thing we want above all else is God. God gives us himself, and this is the best of all. If he gave us the whole world but not himself, we would have nothing. But with him we have everything.

When we envy the wicked, the problem is not that we want things too much. Our eyes wander away from God, and we try to find our joy in cheap substitutes. We are jealous of the wicked because we do not delight in the Lord. Instead we delight in a car or a promotion or a phone call from a boyfriend or a bigger bank account. C. S. Lewis put it this way.

> It would seem that Our Lord finds our desires not too strong, but too weak. We are half-hearted creatures, fooling about with drink and sex and ambition when infinite joy is offered us, like an ignorant child who wants to go on making mud pies in a slum because he cannot imagine what is meant by the offer of a holiday at the sea. We are far too easily pleased.[2]

We need to open our eyes and see the beauty and glory, the kindness and majesty of God. He is far and away the best and most satisfying thing we could desire. If the God of the universe gives us himself, the whole world is ours along with him.

Commit Your Way to the Lord

David also tells us to "commit your way to the LORD" (v. 5). The word "commit" literally means "to roll." "Roll the burden of life upon the Lord."[3] Let him carry your worries and anxiety. Let him worry about your reputation. "Cast all your anxiety on him because he cares for you" (1 Peter 5:7 NIV).

Be Still before the Lord

To close this opening section, David tells us to be still. "Be still before the LORD and wait patiently for him" (37:7).

Some people try to start with this verse, and they cannot understand why they find it hard to quiet their hearts and find peace. We can only get to this place by following the path David has led us down in these verses. We need first to decide that we will trust God and believe his promises. We must delight in him. We must commit our plans to him and let him carry our cares and concerns. Then we will be able to be still.

David tells us not to fret twice in verses 3–9. It is easy to get angry when we see a wicked man or woman who seems happy and successful. We need to "be still" and "refrain from anger" (vv. 7, 8).

There is practical wisdom in David's words. An angry man or woman is vulnerable. Anger "tends only to evil" (v. 8). Norm Evans was an all-pro tackle for the Miami Dolphins. He was on the famous 1972 team that went 14–0, the only perfect record in NFL history. He learned how important it is to keep your cool.

> It's really dangerous for a pro football player to get angry. In fact, that's when linemen sustain their most serious injuries. Anger is so harmful in football that if I can get an opposing lineman or end angry at me, he will concentrate on beating me and forget to attack the quarterback—and that's my job, protecting the quarterback.[4]

In the same way, a wide receiver might try to get a defensive back angry. If he gets into the DB's head, he can fool him on the next play. Satan will try to get in our head. He will tempt us to get angry when we see a godless person with something we want. Then he can trick us and catch us.

Be still. Wait patiently. Don't get angry. This is not the end of the story. God is in control. David ends this first section with a variation of his theme verse. "[T]he evildoers shall be cut off, but those who wait for the LORD shall inherit the land" (v. 9).

Remember the Fate of the Wicked

The second strategy is to remember the fate of the wicked. David presents this in verses 10–22 through a series of contrasts between the faithless and the faithful.

The opening verse of this section sets the tone. It may seem like the ungodly are getting ahead and God's people are getting the short end of the stick. But with the eyes of faith we know better.

In just a little while, the wicked will be no more;
   though you look carefully at his place, he will not be there.
But the meek shall inherit the land
   and delight themselves in abundant peace. (37:10, 11)

Jesus quotes verse 11 as one of the Beatitudes, "Blessed are the meek, for they shall inherit the earth" (Matthew 5:5). In the context of Psalm 37, the meek are patiently waiting by faith for God to remove the wicked. Being meek does not mean being weak. It takes strength to wait for God to act. But when he does, he will remove every trace of the wicked from the earth, and "the meek shall inherit the land."

What are the wicked doing while we wait for God to act? The wicked "plot against the righteous" (37:12). They lay their plans to destroy God's people, but God only "laughs" at them (v. 13). The wicked draw their weapons to attack: "the wicked draw the sword" (v. 14). But God uses their own weapons against them; "their sword" pierces "their own heart" (v. 15). If you remember the story of the book of Esther, Haman planned to kill Mordecai on the gallows he had constructed and destroy all the Jews. Instead Haman died on his own gallows.

In verses 16–20 the wicked seem to be wealthy and powerful. They have an abundance; they seem secure and strong. But "the LORD knows the days of the blameless" (37:18). He is not simply mentally aware of the days of his people like an impartial observer. God fights their battles and provides for them. When trouble comes, the faithful will have an abundance, but the faithless will vanish; like smoke they will simply disappear.

If you do not look ahead to see the fate of the wicked, you could easily be tempted to envy them. Many seem so successful and secure. But "in just a little while, the wicked will be no more" (37:10). David ends this section with a variation on his theme: "[T]hose blessed by the LORD shall inherit the land, but those cursed by him shall be cut off" (37:22).

Believe That God Will Bless His People
Third, we need to believe that God will bless those who please him. David summarizes this section in the opening verse. "The steps of a man are established by the LORD, when he delights in his way" (37:23).

How does this happen? David gives an example from his personal experience. As a mature man he has witnessed God's hand.

I have been young, and now am old,
   yet I have not seen the righteous forsaken
   or his children begging for bread. (37:25)

This speaks to one of the ways we are especially vulnerable. Many of us would trust God through all sorts of pain and hardship. But we worry about our children. We wonder, will God take care of them?

I remember when we moved to England for a year so I could finish my doctorate. God stretched my faith tremendously. We left a secure job at our church in Minnesota; we sold our house at a very significant loss. We were living in a new country; we had no idea where God was going to lead us next. I remember walking into the kids' bedroom when they were asleep. They looked so peaceful. I looked down at them and asked myself, *Have I just ruined your lives?* I was ready to step out in faith for myself and Lisa, but did I trust God to care for my children?

I have a note next to verse 26 in my Bible to remind myself that this is an anchor for my soul. "His children become a blessing." Will you trust God for your children? You need to if you want to fight the temptation of being envious of the wicked.

David ends this section with another variation of his theme verse. "[T]he children of the wicked shall be cut off. The righteous shall inherit the land and dwell upon it forever" (37:28b, 29).

Trust God to Defend You

The fourth strategy is to trust God to defend you. It seems to me that the theme of verses 30–34 is believing that God will protect his people.

The righteous man is wise and just; he walks in God's ways. When the wicked come against him, God is with him. The righteous speaks for God because God's word is in his heart. In return God stands up to speak for him and will not allow him to be condemned.

You can count on God to take your side and lift you up. "He will exalt you to inherit the land; you will look on when the wicked are cut off" (37:34).

Consider the Evidence

Fifth, David asks us to consider the evidence. One of the problems when we envy the wicked is that we only see what we want to see. David wants us to think about real life.

He starts with his own personal experience.

I have seen a wicked, ruthless man,
    spreading himself like a green laurel tree.
But he passed away, and behold, he was no more;
    though I sought him, he could not be found. (37:35, 36)

Then he tells us to notice what God does for those who love him.

> Mark the blameless and behold the upright,
>   for there is a future for the man of peace. (37:37)

If you are a Christian, I'm sure you have seen this in people you know. God has a future for the godly.

The one blameless man we should "mark" (v. 37), of course, is our Lord Jesus Christ. He is the only man who never sinned, who was truly blameless. He suffered at the hands of sinners and was killed. But behold this "upright" (v. 37) man now! Behold Christ now! God raised him to life and seated him at his right hand in glory. Jesus was the ultimate "man of peace" (v. 37). God gave him a future, an everlasting kingdom that will never pass away.

Ultimately if you are tempted to envy the wicked, you need to look to Jesus. You need the gospel. You might be a teenager who wants to fit in. You might be single. You might be married. You have been obeying God, but you see someone who looks happy and successful. You are tempted to be like him or her.

You need to look to Christ. Your life is hidden in him. Your future is in him. He is coming to judge the living and the dead. Through him, God has given you an inheritance in Heaven. Don't fall away. Keep following Jesus.

38

A King's Confession

PSALM 38

PSALM 38 is the third of the Penitential Psalms. These are psalms of confession and sorrow for sin. The two before this are Psalms 6 and 32. The ones that follow are Psalms 51, 102, 130, and 143.

These Penitential Psalms are important because they show us how to confess our sin. David puts into words what we are feeling and teaches us how to come to God. When we are overwhelmed with guilt, we can turn to one of these psalms and make its words our own. This may be one reason why Psalm 51 was recited at the end of the daily morning service in the early centuries of the church.

There is an interesting historical note about these seven psalms. In 1633 Galileo was sent to prison for promoting the teachings of Copernicus—namely, that the earth revolved around the sun. As part of his sentence, he was commanded to recite the seven Penitential Psalms every week, presumably to awaken his conscience and make him aware of his guilt.[1] From what we know of the history of science, it doesn't seem to have worked! I suppose the moral of that story is that these Penitential Psalms should not create guilt where there is none.

Penitential Psalms of Christ?

These Penitential Psalms do raise an interesting question. Remember that David was a prophet and the Psalms are about Christ. David speaks about his own experiences in the Psalms, but he also speaks for Christ. Augustine called Jesus *isti cantator psalmorum*, himself the singer of the Psalms.

We seem to run into a problem, though, when we come to Psalm 38. This is a Penitential Psalm, a psalm of confession, yet we know that Christ was without sin. The Scriptures say, "He committed no sin, neither was deceit found in his mouth" (1 Peter 2:22). And again the writer of Hebrews says that Jesus "in every respect has been tempted as we are, yet without sin" (Hebrews 4:15). So how could the words of Psalm 38 be the words of Christ?

Here we see the depth of the union between Christ and his church. He is the Head, and we are the body—the Head and body cannot be separated because they are one being. Christ has joined himself to us so completely that his righteousness becomes our righteousness and our sin becomes his. He did not just wear our sin outside himself like a shirt on the cross—he took our sins into himself and became sin for us. If he had not truly made our sins his own, he could not have paid for them by his death. This is why the Bible says that God "made him *to be sin* who knew no sin, so that in him we might become the righteousness of God" (2 Corinthians 5:21). Christ had no sins of his own to confess, but he is so joined to us that he can call our sins "my sin" (38:3). The Head speaks for the body.

One Flesh with Christ

We can see this from another angle if we think of this in terms of marriage. When a couple is married, they are now one. Jesus himself taught, "they are no longer two but one flesh" (Matthew 19:6). And because of that, many times they speak and act as one. A married couple can file a joint tax return because their income and deductions are viewed as one. And this is true of their larger financial picture too. If she had college debt when they were married, her debts became his. If she had a trust fund, her assets became his. The two have become one.

God placed marriage into human society as an illustration of his oneness with his people. From the beginning of time, marriage has been a picture of the relationship between Christ and his church. The Apostle Paul described this deep oneness in Ephesians 5.

> In the same way husbands should love their wives as their own bodies. He who loves his wife loves himself. For no one ever hated his own flesh, but nourishes and cherishes it, just as Christ does the church, because we are members of his body. "Therefore a man shall leave his father and mother and hold fast to his wife, and the two shall become one flesh." This mystery is profound, and I am saying that it refers to Christ and the church. (Ephesians 5:28–32)

So when we think of Christ and the church, we should think of the deep unity of marriage. We have been made "one flesh" with Christ (v. 31).

We can see this in the way Jesus identifies completely with his people. In Matthew 25 Jesus says,

> I was hungry and you gave me food, I was thirsty and you gave me drink, I was a stranger and you welcomed me, I was naked and you clothed me, I was sick and you visited me, I was in prison and you came to me. (vv. 25:35, 36)

Was Jesus himself in prison or hungry or thirsty? No. Jesus explains, "Truly, I say to you, as you did it to one of the least of these my brothers, you did it to me" (v. 40). Jesus is so joined to his people that he says, "I am hungry" when Christians are hungry. The Head is speaking for the body. On the road to Damascus, Jesus said, "Saul, Saul, why are you persecuting me?" (Acts 9:4). Who was Saul persecuting? He was persecuting Christians. But our suffering is Christ's suffering. Jesus is so joined to his body and bride that Saul was really persecuting him. Since we have been made one with Jesus like this, we should not be surprised to hear our Savior call our sin "my sin" (Psalm 38:3). The Head speaks for the body. He took our sin as his own so he could pay for our guilt on the cross.

This is holy ground. Have you stopped to think that Jesus saved the church by becoming "one flesh" with us (Ephesians 5:31)? If you are a Christian, Christ is so committed to you that he took your sin as his own. Augustine describes the voice of Christ in Psalm 38.

> The Head speaks the words of the Body; whilst you hear at the same time the accents of the Head Itself also. Yet do not either, when you hear the voice of the Body, separate the Head from it; nor the Body, when you hear the voice of the Head: because "they are no more twain, but one flesh."[2]

As we read this Penitential Psalm, David is describing his own experience, of course. David is suffering as a result of his personal sin. He is about to collapse physically and emotionally under the weight of God's anger as he calls out to God for help. This could be describing how he felt after his sin with Bathsheba, but there may have been other times of sin and suffering in David's life that the Scriptures don't tell us about.

And David is also a prophet, speaking for Christ. Jesus identified with us, took our sin as his own, and suffered in our place. The weight of God's wrath and anger crushed Jesus, and he called out to God for help.

We can divide this psalm into three sections, each of which starts with a prayer to God. First, David begs God to be merciful as he disciplines him (38:1–8). Then he confesses his own weakness—no one but God can help him

(38:9–14). And finally David puts all his hope in God—by faith he believes that God will answer him (38:15–22).

God's Discipline

First, David calls out to God for mercy. God's hand is heavy on him, and he begs for relief.

God's Discipline for David

The first verse of Psalm 38 is identical to the opening prayer of Psalm 6.

> O Lord, rebuke me not in your anger,
>   nor discipline me in your wrath.

Does this mean that David does not want to be rebuked or disciplined? Not at all. In the verses that follow, he does not deny that he has sinned but freely admits his guilt.

We should welcome a godly rebuke when it is deserved. David says in Psalm 141:5, "Let a righteous man strike me—it is a kindness; let him rebuke me—it is oil for my head; let my head not refuse it." If the rebuke of a righteous man is "a kindness," how much more kind is a rebuke from God himself? In 38:1 the words "rebuke" and "discipline" describe God more as a teacher than a judge. God is a father who disciplines us as his children for our good to teach us and train us (Hebrews 12:7–10).[3]

The emphasis is on the last words in each phrase, "in your anger" and "in your wrath" (Psalm 38:1). *Don't rebuke me as your enemy; do not discipline me in wrath like those who hate you. Remember that I am your child and your servant. Discipline me, Lord, but discipline me in love for my good. Remember that you are my Father, remember your covenant, remember my weakness, and spare my life.* Spurgeon put it this way:

> Rebuked I must be, for I am an erring child and thou a careful Father, but throw not too much anger into the tones of thy voice; deal gently although I have sinned grievously. The anger of others I can bear, but not thine.[4]

When I was growing up, I got my share of discipline from my dad. Before every spanking he would explain to me why I was being punished. Then afterward he would hold me in his lap, tell me again that he loved me, and give me a kiss. The spanking hurt so much that he knew I might think that he was angry at me or was just being cruel. But he made sure I knew he loved me and that this was for my good. David wants to know that this discipline is for his good.

Why is David worried that God is acting out of anger? This discipline is so painful and seems so harsh that he feels like God has turned against him. David describes the physical and emotional suffering through which he is going.

For your arrows have sunk into me,
    and your hand has come down on me.

There is no soundness in my flesh
    because of your indignation;
there is no health in my bones
    because of my sin.
For my iniquities have gone over my head;
    like a heavy burden, they are too heavy for me.

My wounds stink and fester
    because of my foolishness,
I am utterly bowed down and prostrate;
    all the day I go about mourning.
For my sides are filled with burning,
    and there is no soundness in my flesh.
I am feeble and crushed;
    I groan because of the tumult of my heart. (38:2–8)

There is no doubt that this particular sickness and pain was God's punishment for David's disobedience. We know this because David repeats the words "because of" three times in verses 3 and 5: "because of your indignation," "because of my sin," "because of my foolishness." He suffered physically and emotionally for his sin.

God's Wrath Was on Christ

Since David also spoke for Christ, this was our Lord Jesus' experience too. There was no reason that he should suffer like this. He had no sins of his own for God to rebuke or discipline. But he took our sins as his own and suffered God's punishment in our place. God was indignant at our Lord Jesus because of us. And Jesus was devastated.

Through his suffering and death, Christ turned away God's anger and wrath at our sin. This is what the Bible describes as propitiation. Propitiation means that God was angry and set against us as his enemies, but he loved us so much that he sent Jesus to die in our place and remove his wrath from us.[5] This is what the Apostle John says in 1 John 4:10, "In this is love, not that we have loved God but that he loved us and sent his Son to be the propitiation for our sins."

This is vitally important. If you are a Christian going through some hard trouble or sickness, you can be 100 percent sure that God is not angry with you. How do you know this? Because Jesus is your propitiation. God cannot be angry with you because Jesus made him favorable to you through his death on the cross. By faith you know that God is for you and that everything he does to you and allows in your life is for your good. *Everything* (cf. Romans 8:28).

So you can be confident as you pray with David, "O LORD, rebuke me not in your anger, nor discipline me in your wrath" (Psalm 38:1). God cannot discipline you in wrath because Jesus bore God's wrath. Any discipline he gives you can only come from his love and is for your good.

God's Discipline for Christians

With that in mind, God does discipline us for our sin. Like arrows, his punishments fly silently and swiftly and sink deep to penetrate the spirit. It might seem strange to think that God shoots "arrows" (v. 2) at his own people. This should show us just how terrible and dangerous our sin really is. Sometimes the best thing God can do is to wound us deeply in this life so that he can give us real life, eternal life, in the world to come. I think of a rich, successful man named Greg who was cut down by cancer in his forties. Greg had lived a sinful life and was not walking with God. In the last months of his life, though, he turned to God and was genuinely saved. He said to me at one point, "I am so glad God gave me this cancer. I don't know how else he could have gotten my attention." God's arrows wounded him deeply in this life so that Greg could have eternal life in the world to come.

We need to recognize that sickness or suffering is sometimes God's discipline, but usually it is not.[6] This is important because when we suffer, we can get depressed and ask ourselves, *What did I do?* Satan brings up old sins that have been forgiven, and he is cruel enough to torture us with past sins. At that point if we are Christians we need to believe that we truly have been forgiven; our sins have been removed as far as the east is from the west.

Sometimes, like Job, we suffer precisely because we are obedient. Job was "blameless and upright, one who feared God and turned away from evil" (Job 1:1). I know godly people who have suffered from cancer, genetic diseases, and a variety of painful diseases. I do not think this was a result of sin. God sometimes allows the godly to suffer so that their faith shines like a light in a dark world. In fact, he is honoring them and showcasing the beauty of their godly life. Through sickness and disease, God reveals their faith to a watching world and to a universe of spirits and angels. This is a beautiful and precious thing, and they will receive their reward.

God has other purposes in mind as well. In John 9 Jesus met a man born blind, and his disciples asked who had sinned to cause his blindness, the man or his parents. Jesus answered, "It was not that this man sinned, or his parents, but that the works of God might be displayed in him" (John 9:3). In this case God's purpose was so that Jesus could reveal his glory by healing him.

If you are going through some sickness or suffering, it is possible that God is disciplining you for your sin, just like he did with David. He may be turning up the heat so you will deal with unconfessed sin. Maybe he is pushing you finally to break a pattern of disobedience in your life. If that is the case, I think you can trust the Holy Spirit to make this plain to you. You should examine your heart, but you don't need to become withdrawn and morbidly introspective. If God is dealing with your sin, he wants you to know what he is doing, and he will make it clear.

But remember, your sickness or suffering may have nothing to do with your sin at all. There are any number of good plans he could be working out through the dark threads he weaves in your life. Ultimately you need to trust that God knows what he is doing.

David's Weakness

David moves from God's discipline to his own weakness. As God's hand is heavy on him, he knows that there is no one but God to help him. The point of verses 9–14 is that David has nowhere else to turn but God. There is no one who could possibly rescue him from God's hand.

No Strength

David has no strength in himself.

> O Lord, all my longing is before you;
>   my sighing is not hidden from you.
> My heart throbs; my strength fails me,
>   and the light of my eyes—it also has gone from me. (38:9, 10)

There is no one more lonely than a brokenhearted sinner.[7] But God knows your heart's desire, and he hears your sighs. David longs for everything to be all right again, for life to go back to the way it was. He longs for health and well-being, for this discipline to end. But as he opens his heart to God, he confesses that he is powerless to heal himself. His strength fails.

No Friends

His friends have failed him too. Instead he is surrounded by enemies.

> My friends and companions stand aloof from my plague,
> and my nearest kin stand far off.
>
> Those who seek my life lay their snares;
> those who seek my hurt speak of ruin
> and meditate treachery all day long.
>
> But I am like a deaf man; I do not hear,
> like a mute man who does not open his mouth.
> I have become like a man who does not hear,
> and in whose mouth are no rebukes. (38:11–14)

This is a picture of rejection and isolation. This was fulfilled in Jesus' life when he went to the cross. His disciples all fled, even Peter who vowed he would stay with him. Luke tells us that when Jesus died, all his friends and followers stood at a distance, watching what happened to him (Luke 23:49). He is probably alluding to Psalm 38:11.[8]

We sometimes feel like we have been abandoned too, just when we needed our friends the most. The people we thought we could count on have drifted away. In our better moments we think to ourselves that people simply don't know what to say. But we are alone, and it hurts. It is good to know that David felt this way. And it is good to know that Jesus felt this way too. He was alone, and he will never leave us alone.

If we are Christians, this should remind us not to leave a brother or sister alone when he or she is struggling. We may want to pull back because we don't know what to say; we are uncomfortable. We may want to pull back because we know that this believer is suffering the consequences for his or her sin. We may be worried what people will think or say if we reach out to him or her. Don't be like Job's friends; we don't need to explain why these things have happened—as if we had special access to the mind of God. We just need to be there.

Hope in God

David ends by putting his trust in God.

> But for you, O Lord, do I wait;
> it is you, O Lord my God, who will answer. (38:15)

Waiting is hard to do. Waiting on God is one of the hardest tests of faith there is. Does God know? Does he see? Does he care? Nothing's happening—will he do anything?

David strengthens his faith by giving the reasons why he knows God will act.[9]

> For I said, "Only let them not rejoice over me,
>   who boast against me when my foot slips!"
>
> For I am ready to fall,
>   and my pain is ever before me.
> I confess my iniquity;
>   I am sorry for my sin.
> But my foes are vigorous, they are mighty,
>   and many are those who hate me wrongfully.
> Those who render me evil for good
>   accuse me because I follow after good. (38:16–20)

The word "for" (v. 16) tells us that David is explaining why he knows God will answer. There are five reasons in these verses. First, God will answer because his enemies should not "boast" (v. 16) over him. David was God's anointed. If they gloated over him, they gloated over God who committed himself to David. God's glory is on the line, and David knows God will answer.

Second, David has already slipped, and he is about to "fall" (v. 17). If God waits any longer, it will be too late. Third, he has confessed his sin. He is not hiding anything from God. God's discipline has done what it was supposed to do. Fourth, his enemies are strong. They are many and he is alone. And finally, they hate David because of his "good" (v. 20) and godly life.

David lays these reasons before God to strengthen his faith. He closes with a final prayer.

> Do not forsake me, O LORD!
>   O my God, be not far from me!
> Make haste to help me,
>   O Lord, my salvation! (38:21, 22)

Jesus was forsaken so we would never be forsaken. He was alone so we would never be alone. Since God poured his wrath on him, we know that God is for us (Romans 8:1). He made "haste" to help us before we even knew we needed him. He is our salvation.

39

Waiting in Silence

PSALM 39

WHEN I WAS IN SEMINARY, I was an intern at College Church in Wheaton for two years. It was a great experience as I learned pastoral ministry by watching godly men up close and personally.

I remember walking down the hall one Wednesday evening with Kent Hughes, the senior pastor, when a woman stopped us and began complaining about something. She was pretty upset at him, but Kent listened to her and spoke kindly to her. I was struck by the way he handled this because I knew the rest of the story. He had not done what she thought he had done. Kent was being falsely accused, but he didn't argue with her. He held his peace.

The Terrible Tongue

His silence was impressive because it is so hard to hold our tongues. When someone accuses you, misrepresents you, teases you, makes fun of you, or lies about you, it is almost impossible not to rise up and set the record straight. There is a time and a way to speak the truth and defend yourself. But often we sin by getting angry and saying unkind words in return. Our tongues are hard to control. James says,

> [W]e all stumble in many ways. And if anyone does not stumble in what he says, he is a perfect man, able also to bridle his whole body.
> . . . every kind of beast and bird, of reptile and sea creature, can be tamed and has been tamed by mankind, but no human being can tame the tongue. It is a restless evil, full of deadly poison. (James 3:2, 7, 8)

If you understand the potential for evil in the things you say, you will bite your tongue and think carefully before you speak.

David understood how dangerous his words could be, and he bit his tongue to keep from sinning.

> I said, "I will guard my ways,
>   that I may not sin with my tongue;
> I will guard my mouth with a muzzle,
>   so long as the wicked are in my presence." (39:1)

Why did David have to hold his tongue? We can picture the situation if we look at the rest of the psalm. In verse 8 David prays, "Deliver me from all my transgressions. Do not make me the scorn of the fool!" God laid David low to discipline him for his sins. And as David lay crushed under the weight of God's punishment, wicked people laughed at him.[1]

Notice that David wanted to please God even when God was punishing him. David was suffering for his sin, but he was still resolved not to sin with his words. When God disciplines us, we are tempted to get angry at him. *Why should I obey God when he has done this to me?* Instead of trusting him, we might doubt that he loves us, turn our back to him, and go deeper into sin. God disciplines us to make us more godly, but we sometimes harden our heart and sin even more. One of the signs of Christian maturity is that we want to please God even when we are suffering under his hand. This is faith in action. *I love God through my tears. I believe that even this hard thing is for my good.*

Christ Held His Tongue

David held his tongue to keep from sinning, and his self-control pointed forward to our Lord Jesus Christ. Jesus was silent when he was surrounded by wicked men, too, even as they taunted him. Isaiah foretold that the Messiah would hold his tongue.[2]

> He was oppressed, and he was afflicted,
>   yet he opened not his mouth;
> like a lamb that is led to the slaughter,
>   and like a sheep that before its shearers is silent,
>   so he opened not his mouth. (Isaiah 53:7)

When Jesus stood on trial, Pilate was amazed by his silence.

> [W]hen [Jesus] was accused by the chief priests and elders, he gave no answer. Then Pilate said to him, "Do you not hear how many things they testify against you?" But he gave him no answer, not even to a single charge, so that the governor was greatly amazed. (Matthew 27:12–14)

And the Apostle Peter says,

> When he was reviled, he did not revile in return; when he suffered, he did
> not threaten, but continued entrusting himself to him who judges justly.
> (1 Peter 2:23)

When we read that Jesus was silent during his trial, we should not sanitize and intellectualize this as if he was aloof and above it all. You might picture Jesus like a medieval painting, calm and composed. Or maybe you picture Jesus like a statue of Buddha, detached and serene with a mysterious half-smile on his face.

But Jesus was fully human. His heart surged with questions and emotions just like yours and mine does. Christ had to bite his tongue. David was a prophet; he speaks both for himself and for Jesus as he describes the way his emotions built up pressure like a volcano.

> I was mute and silent;
>   I held my peace to no avail,
> and my distress grew worse.
>   My heart became hot within me. (39:2, 3)

The middle phrase is hard to translate, and our English versions handle it in different ways. The ESV reads, "I held my peace to no avail" (v. 2), and this gives a good sense of what David seems to be saying.[3] I take this to mean that his heart was still churning even though he held his tongue. He was quiet on the outside but shouting on the inside.

How did David resolve this burning fire in his heart? He turned to God in prayer. He did not argue with the wicked who mocked him. He anchored his heart in God. This points forward to the agonized prayers of our Lord Jesus in his passion. It is also an example for you and me when we are biting our tongues, trying not to sin with our words. Spurgeon says with his usual style, "It is well that the vent of his soul was Godward and not towards man. Oh! if my swelling heart must speak, Lord let it speak with thee."[4] I have often wished I could take back an angry word, but I have never wanted to take back a prayer when I asked God for help.

David's prayer in Psalm 39 is surprising. We might expect him to ask God to rise up and defend him; he does this in other psalms. He could have endured by looking ahead to the good things God had in store for him. But in Psalm 39 David asks God to show him that he is nothing, and so his only hope is in God. When people are big and God is small, then it is hard to bite your tongue. David wants to see that people are small but God is big. This will settle the churning of his heart.

There are three parts to this unusual prayer. First, David asks for perspective on his life (39:4–6). Second, he declares his faith in God (39:7–11). And finally David asks for mercy (39:12, 13).

Perspective

David begins by asking God for perspective to see life the way he should. Human beings are small and temporary compared to God. David is small. The wicked who seem so big are actually quite small. All humanity is small. This is the best place to start. We need this perspective too.

The Brevity of Life

David wants to understand how short his life really is.

> O LORD, make me know my end
>   and what is the measure of my days;
>   let me know how fleeting I am. (39:4)

When David asks God to "know" how short his life is, he is obviously not talking about learning new information. He already knows that his life is like vapor because he says this himself in the psalm (39:5). But he wants to know his life is fleeting in a deeper way. He wants truly to understand the nature of human life and take to heart that soon he will die and leave this earth behind.[5]

There is a difference between knowing and *knowing*. A recent college graduate might know that he will retire someday and that the money he sets aside will compound over time. But not many begin to save when they can. Why not? They know about retirement intellectually, but they have not really grasped that truth—in a real sense, they don't know they will retire. That is why so many of us start playing catch-up in our forties when we finally begin to realize that life is short! David wants to know his life is short and take it to heart, specifically in guarding his tongue.

One of the things I admire about older believers is that many of them have learned not to sweat the small stuff. They don't get bent out of shape by words that would rile a man in his twenties or thirties. When you see how quickly the years and decades fly by, it gives you perspective and helps you focus on what matters. You know that life is fleeting in ways that no younger man or woman could. This is part of wisdom and maturity.

If you are younger, this is a wonderful prayer for you to make your own.

Your days are measured by the wise and loving hand of God. You will not live forever on this earth—your life is "fleeting" (v. 4). If you grasp this truth, you'll be able to focus on the things that really matter.

One practical thing you can do is literally to number your days. One of the pastors I work with writes down the number of days he estimates he has left to live every day in his personal calendar. So every day he sees a countdown clock on his life. If the actuarial tables predict that you will live until you are eighty-four, all it takes is a little math to figure out a rough guess for the number of your days. And if you live longer, then your countdown clock can go into reverse in bonus time—think of how you will thank God for each day at that point!

A Humbling Comparison

David emphasizes how small we are by comparing our life to the endless days of God. It is a humbling comparison.

> Behold, you have made my days a few handbreadths,
>   and my lifetime is as nothing before you.
> Surely all mankind stands as a mere breath! *Selah* (39:5)

If you travel to the West Coast, you might stop in Sequoia National Forest to see some famous trees. Sequoias are the biggest trees in the world, and they are absolutely impressive. For one thing, they live for a very long time. The oldest alive today is roughly thirty-five hundred years old—this means it was already five hundred years old when David wrote Psalm 39! The largest ones alive today are almost 280 feet tall, and some were undoubtedly bigger in the past. The widest sequoia is 155 feet around at ground level. The largest branch on a living sequoia has a diameter of 12.8 feet—that's not the tree but just a branch! When we tourists stop to see these giant sequoias, what do we do? We stop and take our picture next to these humongous trees. A six-foot man can stretch to his full height, but he still looks like a shrimp at the base of a sequoia.

The oldest man or woman alive is nothing compared to the days of the eternal God. We take our vitamins, but in spite of our best efforts our lives are fleeting and brief, like a spark from a campfire compared to the sun. A "handbreath" is the width of four fingers, just about three inches. It was one of the smaller units of measure in the ancient world. God doesn't measure our days in miles and certainly not in light-years. We are a few "handbreaths" (v. 5) before him.

Shadowlands

The conclusion of this humbling reflection is to realize that this life is no more solid and lasting than a shadow.

> Surely a man goes about as a shadow!
> Surely for nothing they are in turmoil;
>   man heaps up wealth and does not know who will gather. (39:6)

This is important because the world seems so solid and meaningful. One of the themes that is repeated in the book of Ecclesiastes is "vanity of vanities! All is vanity" (Ecclesiastes 1:2). Some translations use the word "meaning-less." David uses this same word three times in Psalm 39, but our English versions translate it with different words. It is translated "breath" in verses 5 and 11 and "for nothing" in verse 6. C. S. Lewis famously called this world "the shadowlands." This world is as solid and lasting as a soap bubble.

If you don't think your life is a shadow, think about how many years it will be before your name is forgotten. Do you remember your great-grandfather's name? How about his father or mother? Unless they are into genealogies, your great-grandchildren will probably not know your name. And the things you work hard to save up and pass on will go to people you may not know.

My parents were missionaries, and one of their friends was a fellow missionary named Sam. Sadly, his wife died soon after they retired. In a few years Sam remarried. His new wife is a widow whose husband built a mid-sized company from scratch. Needless to say, his new wife was well off. Sam had modest savings when he retired, but he married a wealthy woman. Her first husband "heap[ed] up wealth" (v. 6), and a man he did not know enjoyed them. Sam worked hard in his career, just as hard as, if not harder than, her first husband, but not in a field that paid off as well in this life. What good is saving when you don't know who will spend it? It might go to a foolish child or grandchild. "Vanity of vanity! All is vanity!" (Ecclesiastes 1:2). David says in essence.

This could be rather depressing stuff. What is the point? My life is short, and so is yours. When I am having trouble biting my tongue, I need to remember how small I am. And those who are getting under my skin are small too. With this perspective I don't have to answer them, justify myself to them, or make sure they know I am right. This life is not everything—it is a spark from a campfire compared to the sun. If we do not know this, we will live for this life, and the urge to speak our mind will be almost unbearable. Why? Because if we don't clear our name now, it will not happen.

Our Lord Jesus looked beyond this life to the real life that was before him. He stayed silent before Pilate because he knew this world is short and fleeting. There is a new heaven and new earth waiting for those who love God. As David said in Psalm 37, "[T]hose who wait for the LORD shall inherit the land" (Psalm 37:9). We need this same perspective.

Faith

David moves from the smallness of humanity to the bigness of God. We cannot control our lives, but God is the Judge of all the world. The brevity of life points us to God.[6]

My Hope Is in You

It is foolish to put our trust in ourselves or in another human being. David puts his trust in God. "And now, O Lord, for what do I wait? My hope is in you" (39:7).

The word "Lord" here is not the name Yahweh but could be translated "master." David is speaking to God as a servant to his lord. David was a king, but he looked to God as a higher King. In the ancient Near East, a king might have several lesser kings under his authority. They paid tribute to him, and he was responsible by covenant to rescue them and fight for them against their enemies. David is calling out to God as his master, the one who is responsible for his protection. Is God your master? Have we bent our knee to him and become his servant? If we know how short our life is—we are each a mere breath—then our only hope is for God to be our master.

David's hope is not in anything God will do or give to him—his hope is in God himself. We are shadows, but God is the substance. We are created creatures, but he is the uncreated Creator. He is not part of this universe—he exists by his own power and will continue to be when the farthest stars have run out of nuclear fuel. There is nothing solid in this soap-bubble world we can hold onto. But God is a solid rock to everyone who trusts in him.

Relent

David turns to this God for forgiveness and mercy.

> Deliver me from all my transgressions.
>   Do not make me the scorn of the fool!
> I am mute; I do not open my mouth,
>   for it is you who have done it.
> Remove your stroke from me;
>   I am spent by the hostility of your hand.

When you discipline a man
  with rebukes for sin,
you consume like a moth what is dear to him;
  surely all mankind is a mere breath! *Selah* (39:8–11)

David's confession of sin is a theme in the last four psalms of Book 1, Psalms 38–41.[7] In each of these David waits for God to relent and rescue him from the trouble that has come on him as a punishment for sin. It seems like this is the reason these four psalms have been placed side by side.[8]

David points forward to Christ, who made himself one with us as believers, took our sins, and became sin for us. Christ had no sin of his own for God to punish, but he suffered for the sins of his people. Through David's suffering, we hear the voice of Christ as he suffered for us and for our sin. This is one of the major themes at the end of this first section of the Psalms. Jesus himself said, "For even the Son of Man did not come to be served but to serve, and to give his life as a ransom for many" (Mark 10:45). Psalm 39 reveals how hard it was for Christ to be silent as he carried our sin. He didn't lash out and curse the men who drove the nails into his hands. He said, "Father, forgive them, for they know not what they do" (Luke 23:34). He did not say to his disciples, "I hope you appreciate what I am doing for you!" Instead he loved us all the way to the end. He protected our hearts by biting his tongue.

David begged for God to relent. He did not try to hide his sin but asked God to rescue him from his sin. When God disciplines a man or woman for his or her sin, where else can he or she go? Our only hope is to run to this God whose hand is heavy on us and ask him to forgive us and lift the weight of his hand.

You may feel the weight of God's hand today. You may feel like God has cut you to the heart by taking away the things you love. "Like a moth," he has "consume[d] . . . what is dear" to you (Psalm 39:11). You have a choice today. You can turn your back on God and get angry at him. Or you can come to him and ask for forgiveness. You can come to him humbly as a servant, like David did, and say, "And now, O Lord, for what do I wait? My hope is in you. Deliver me from all my transgressions" (vv. 7, 8).

If you do, you can be sure he will forgive you. Jesus died for sinners like you and me. God rebuked Jesus Christ for the sins of his people. This is why the Scriptures say,

[H]e was pierced for our transgressions;
  he was crushed for our iniquities;

upon him was the chastisement that brought us peace,
   and with his wounds we are healed. (Isaiah 53:5)

If you feel the weight of God's judgment on your sin, you need to turn to him today. He is merciful, and he will forgive you.

Mercy

David ends with his third prayer, a final prayer for mercy.

Hear my prayer, O LORD,
   and give ear to my cry;
   hold not your peace at my tears!
For I am a sojourner with you,
   a guest, like all my fathers.
Look away from me, that I may smile again,
   before I depart and am no more. (39:12, 13)

When David says, "Look away from me" (v. 13), I take this to mean that he wants God to turn his anger away and end this time of discipline.

He wants mercy because this life is so short. As Christians, this world is not our home. We are each "a sojourner," "a guest" (v. 12). We belong in Heaven, the home of righteousness (Philippians 3:20; 2 Peter 3:13). But for now we are strangers and aliens in this world (1 Peter 2:11). This is how it has always been for God's people.

This life is just a short stay in a foreign land. I have gone on quite a few mission trips to various places around the world. Sometimes I slept on hard concrete floors, sometimes I ate food I didn't particularly care for, and sometimes I felt like people looked down on me as an outsider. I could put up with it, though, because that was not my home. In just a few short days I would board a plane and go home where I belonged.

Christian, when you have to bite your tongue, remember that you don't belong here. Life is short. In just a few days you will be going home. God is big, and people are small.

If you know this, you will be able to answer kindly when people say all sorts of things about you. You will be able to hold your peace. And you will inherit a blessing, for Jesus said, "Blessed are the peacemakers, for they shall be called sons of God" (Matthew 5:9).

40

He Set My Feet on a Rock

PSALM 40

A PRINCIPLE that has guided our study of the Psalms is that they are fundamentally about Christ. When David faces enemies in the Psalms, he points forward to Christ, who was rejected and faced his own enemies. When David trusts God in the Psalms, he speaks for Christ, who "entrust[ed] himself to him who judges justly" (1 Peter 2:23).

Tertullian, the great North African theologian, said about David, "He sings to us of Christ, and through his voice Christ indeed also sang concerning Himself."[1] In the Psalms David points forward to Christ the way a model car points to a real car. David is a shadow of the reality that came in Jesus Christ.

This Christ-centered approach to the Psalms is confirmed again when we come to Psalm 40. We could easily conclude that this psalm is simply about David. He was in danger, and God rescued him. This psalm could easily be explained by what we know of David's life without having to look for a fulfillment later in Christ. But the writer of Hebrews quotes Psalm 40:6–8 and says these are the words of Christ.

Consequently, when Christ came into the world, he said,

Sacrifices and offerings you have not desired,
   but a body have you prepared for me;
in burnt offerings and sin offerings
   you have taken no pleasure.
Then I said, "Behold, I have come to do your will, O God,
   as it is written of me in the scroll of the book." (Hebrews 10:5–7)

This psalm that fits David's own life so well is about more than him.[2] David was a prophet, and he spoke for Christ.

407

Psalm 40 is about Jesus' faith that God would raise him up after he laid down his life as a sacrifice for sins. When Christ came into the world, God's will for him was to be the final, perfect sacrifice that would end every sacrifice. Jesus waited patiently for God to lift him up from the pit of death. God did raise him up, and Christ announces his resurrection to all his people.

We can look at Psalm 40 in three roughly equal sections. We hear Christ's testimony in verses 1–5, Christ's mission in verses 6–10, and Christ's prayer in verses 11–17.

Christ's Testimony

Psalm 40 begins with Christ's testimony of God's deliverance. We enjoy hearing people's testimonies of the way God saved them. We enjoy hearing these testimonies at a baptismal service. Or we might share our testimony if we are sitting down with a new Christian friend and are getting to know each other. God's grace never gets old, and the way he touches our lives encourages other people.

Verses 1–5 give Jesus' testimony of the way God saved him. There seem to be four parts to Jesus' thanksgiving in these verses.

Waiting

First, Christ tells us how he waited on God. "I waited patiently for the Lord" (40:1a).

The grammar of this verse highlights the waiting. Literally the first two words read, "waiting I waited." In Hebrew, repeating a verb like this is a way of putting heavy emphasis. It suggests that everything depended on waiting.[3] He did not take matters into his own hands but trusted God and waited for God's timing.

God often asks his people to wait. When Abraham was seventy-five years old, God called him and promised to bless him with children. Fifteen years later Abraham and Sarah were still waiting. Finally when Abraham was one hundred years old, God gave them Isaac, the promised son—after twenty-five years of waiting. David was anointed king as a young man, but he did not take the throne until he was thirty. He could have killed Saul several times, but David refused to take matters into his own hands and harm God's anointed.

The Christian life is a life of patience and perseverance. If you are waiting for God, it might feel like you're not doing anything, and you might be impatient. But waiting is not the same as inactivity. When you are waiting, you are still on the outside, but you are working hard on the inside. In your heart your faith is hard at work as you trust God. You wrestle with your thoughts and emotions to believe that God knows what is happening, that God is wise, that God's plans for you are good, that God is in control of every minute. A duck might look like it is sitting still as it swims through the water. But beneath the surface its legs are paddling furiously. When God asks you to wait, he has important work for you to do below the surface of your life. Your faith is growing as you learn to trust him.

Jesus went through the same grueling process of trusting God and pleading with him that you and I go through. This makes him a wonderful Savior. He has been tempted and tested in every way like we are, and with patience he endured. So he is able to help every one of us when we have to wait. Are we waiting today? We might be waiting for a job. We might be sick and waiting to get well again. We might be waiting for a husband or wife. Maybe we are waiting for a baby. We need to ask Christ to help us wait patiently for God to act in his timing.

Rescue

No one who waits for God is ever disappointed. In his timing God took action. In the second part of his testimony Christ tells everyone who will listen how God rescued him.

> [H]e inclined to me and heard my cry.
> He drew me up from the pit of destruction,
>   out of the miry bog,
> and set my feet upon a rock,
>   making my steps secure.
> He put a new song in my mouth,
>   a song of praise to our God.
> Many will see and fear,
>   and put their trust in the LORD. (40:1b–3)

When our Lord carried our sin on the cross, he was like a prisoner in a dungeon, thrown into a muddy pit or cistern and left to die. The pit is often used as a metaphor for death (e.g., Psalm 30:3); so "the pit" and "the miry bog" are pictures of death and the grave (40:2). With his feet stuck in the mud and clay, he looked up at the opening far above and waited for God to stretch down his hand.

God took action in five steps. First, he "inclined" (v. 1) toward Jesus. As Jesus was at his lowest point, God leaned over and bent down toward him. God the Father does not have a physical body to lean over literally, of course;

this is a figure of speech to show that God cared about what happened to Jesus and was concerned.

Several years ago I saw a young man lose control of his bike on a very steep hill. His tire lodged into the opening of a sewer grate, and he went over the handlebars. We quickly ran over to where he was lying motionless in the street, and we bent down over him. We inclined toward him because we wanted to see how he was. This is the picture of God inclining to Christ. It shows the Father's care and concern for the Son.

Next God "heard [his] cry" (v. 1). With his ear down to the opening of the cistern, God heard a cry coming from the muddy depths below. Then thirdly, God "drew [him] up from the pit" (v. 2). As Christ waited patiently in the grave, God pulled him out, and our Lord Jesus rose again to life.

Then God "set [his] feet upon a rock" (v. 2). Our Lord Jesus can never suffer again, and his enemies cannot touch him. He reigns forever in glory and has become our great High Priest "by the power of an indestructible life" (Hebrews 7:16). He always lives to serve us, to protect us, to pray for us. We do not have to worry that Christ will suffer a tragic accident or fall into the pit again. "[H]e is able to save to the uttermost those who draw near to God through him, since he always lives to make intercession for them" (Hebrews 7:25).

Finally, God put "a song of praise" in his mouth (v. 3). Christ opened his mouth and sang for joy. When Jesus and the disciples left the upper room on the night he was arrested, they sang a hymn, most likely Psalm 118. After the Resurrection, Jesus had a new and a better song. God put this song into his mouth by rescuing him. A new experience of God's grace calls for a new song of praise.

A Lesson

Christ ends his testimony with application.

> Blessed is the man who makes
>   the LORD his trust,
> who does not turn to the proud,
>   to those who go astray after a lie! (40:4)

The same God who rescued Jesus Christ will rescue everyone who trusts in him. There is blessing for everyone who waits patiently for God like Jesus did. The temptation, of course, is to give up hope as we wait for him to keep his promises. We see people who are proud because they are successful. They are not in a pit. They have done well for themselves, and they seem to have everything they want. So we turn to follow them instead of waiting for God.

But Christ wants us to lift our eyes and see how good God is.

You have multiplied, O LORD my God,
    your wondrous deeds and your thoughts toward us;
    none can compare with you!
I will proclaim and tell of them,
    yet they are more than can be told. (40:5)

When God sent us his Son, Jesus, he "multiplied" (v. 5) or "made great" his saving work and plans for us. Not even Christ himself can tell the full measure of the blessings God has given us in him.

How can this be? How can the blessings of God in Christ be more than Christ himself can communicate to us? The answer is simple, really. Jesus is more than just a human savior. He is fully God—"the radiance of the glory of God and the exact imprint of his nature" (Hebrews 1:3). "He is the image of the invisible God" (Colossians 1:15). In Christ "the whole fullness of deity dwells bodily" (Colossians 2:9). Everything that it means to be God—"the whole fullness of deity"—is in him. In Jesus, the infinite God took on flesh and became a man to be our Savior.

When God gave us Jesus, he gave us himself. When Christ came into the world, God did not just add to his mighty deeds in the Old Testament. Jesus is not simply another prophet like Moses or Elijah. God "multiplied" (v. 5) his wondrous deeds and made them great. He gave us himself. Christ cannot communicate the full blessings God has given us in his resurrection because he himself is our boundless, infinitely glorious God.

No matter how much we know of God's goodness to us in Christ, there is always more to know. This means that the Christian life is an endlessly joyful discovery. You will never get to the end of Christ. If you think to yourself, "Been there, done that" about Jesus, then you don't really see him. Jesus is big enough to take your breath away for the rest of your life. Sometimes people ask, "What will we do in Heaven forever? The idea of eternity makes me uncomfortable." We don't need to worry about being bored in Heaven. Christ is endlessly fascinating and eternally amazing. Christ will hold our attention for all eternity.

Christ's Mission

You can never get to the end of God's goodness to us in Christ. This becomes clearer in the second main section of Psalm 40. After his testimony Christ announces his mission.

Atoning for Sins

God sent Jesus to atone for our sins.

> In sacrifice and offering you have not delighted,
>   but you have given me an open ear.
> Burnt offering and sin offering
>   you have not required.
> Then I said, "Behold, I have come;
>   in the scroll of the book it is written of me:
> I delight to do your will, O my God;
>   your law is within my heart." (40:6–8)

What does this mean? The prophet Samuel rebuked Saul with words similar to these: "to obey is better than sacrifice" (1 Samuel 15:22). Saul had not waited patiently for Samuel but took matters into his own hands. The Old Testament also says in a number of places that God is not pleased with sacrifices when a man's heart is far from him.[4] Many scholars think that the point of verse 6 is that obedience from the heart is more important than sacrifices.

But in Psalm 40 there is not the slightest hint that a disobedient person is offering these sacrifices. If anything, the context is the outstanding faith, obedience, and patience of David and of Christ after him. Unlike Saul, Christ did wait "patiently" (40:1), and yet God is still not pleased by these sacrifices of bulls and goats.

To make an even stronger point, he says that God did not require sacrifices either. But in fact God did require these sacrifices in the Law of Moses. Verse 6 refers to the four kinds of sacrifices required in Leviticus 1–4,[5] namely "sacrifice," "offering," "burnt offering," and "sin offering." Together these represent all the sacrifices that the Law requires.

So how are we to understand this? Christ announces the end of the Old Testament system of sacrifices in these verses. Even in the best circumstances the blood of bulls and goats ultimately does not please God. And these are not what God requires for the forgiveness of sins. God is delighted with the willing obedience of Jesus Christ. Instead of offering the blood and carcass of animals for sin, Jesus offered his own body as a sacrifice for sin on the cross.

Jonathan Edwards reflected on the significance of this.

> Though many things had been done in the affair of redemption, though millions of sacrifices had been offered; yet nothing was done to purchase redemption before Christ's incarnation. No part of the purchase was made, no part of the price was offered till now. But as soon as Christ was incarnate, the purchase began. And the whole time of Christ's humiliation, till the morning

that he rose from the dead, was taken up in this purchase. Then the purchase was entirely and completely finished. As nothing was done before Christ's incarnation, so nothing was done after his resurrection to purchase redemption for men. Nor will there ever be any thing more done to all eternity.[6]

Verses 6–8 also give us a glimpse of the beautiful interaction of God the Father and God the Son for our salvation. The Father "delight[s]" in the Son and his obedience instead of sacrifice and offerings (40:6). The Son "delights" in doing the Father's will (40:8). Each delights in the other. The mutual joy and delight of the Father and Son is at the heart of our salvation.[7] To take this one step further, the Spirit inspired this psalm, and thus we can conclude that the Spirit delights in revealing the Son's and Father's delight in each other. This means that God's love for the world in saving sinners flows out of the love that flows between the members of the Trinity.

Our salvation is rooted in the love and joy God has in himself. The love of God flowing within the Trinity is like a nuclear reactor that overflows with power to save sinners. God's love for himself is the source of our salvation. Our redemption begins with God and his own love. This is why the Apostle John says, "In this is love, not that we have loved God but that he loved us and sent his Son to be the propitiation for our sins" (1 John 4:10).

We might run out of oil and natural gas someday. The world could conceivably run out of nuclear fuel in some far distant future. But the burning energy that fuels our salvation will never run out. God's love for himself is eternally powerful and self-sustaining—the Father, Son, and Holy Spirit will never stop loving and delighting in each other. If we are Christians, our salvation is solid and secure, rooted in the unchanging love of God.

Announcing Salvation

The second part of Christ's mission is to announce salvation.

> I have told the glad news of deliverance
>   in the great congregation;
> behold, I have not restrained my lips,
>   as you know, O LORD.
> I have not hidden your deliverance within my heart;
>   I have spoken of your faithfulness and your salvation;
> I have not concealed your steadfast love and your faithfulness
>   from the great congregation. (40:9, 10)

The word translated "told the glad news" (v. 9) is another way of saying "preached the gospel." Old Testament scholar Gerald Wilson says, "The psalmist's determination to proclaim Yahweh's righteousness to the congregation of the faithful is the practical equivalent to the New Testament proclamation of the gospel."[8]

Jesus proclaimed the gospel, the glad news of deliverance, from the beginning of his ministry (Mark 1:14, 15). And Christ continues to proclaim the gospel today. How so? Christ speaks through faithful preaching. In Ephesians 2:17 Paul says that Christ "came and preached peace to you who were far off and peace to those who were near." What is significant about this verse? Paul was writing to believers in Ephesus, a city in Greece that Jesus never visited. The gospel did not come to Ephesus until some twenty-five years after Christ ascended to Heaven. Paul and Apollos brought the gospel to Ephesus, yet Paul says that Christ came and preached peace to them.

The point is clear: when the gospel is announced today, Jesus himself is speaking. He sends preachers and evangelists to announce the good news as his mouthpiece. Christ is speaking when his Word is faithfully preached.

Christ's Prayer

After Christ's testimony and Christ's mission, Psalm 40 ends with Christ's prayer. Verses 11–17 are almost exactly identical to Psalm 70. Pieces and portions of the Psalms were reused and repurposed later in different settings and situations. That is the case with these seven verses.

Evidently Christ was still in the pit at the end of this psalm. At the beginning of the psalm, it seemed like he had been rescued already. But evidently when he testified to God's rescue in verses 1–5 he was speaking by faith, absolutely certain that it would happen. God had heard him and "take[n] thought for [him]" (40:17), and so his rescue was as good as done. In fact, Jesus did announce his resurrection before he went to the cross;[9] he knew for certain that God would rescue him. So the shape of this psalm fits with the pattern we have of Christ's life.

Mercy

David prays for mercy.

> As for you, O LORD, you will not restrain
>   your mercy from me;
> your steadfast love and your faithfulness will
>   ever preserve me!
> For evils have encompassed me
>   beyond number;
> my iniquities have overtaken me,

and I cannot see;
they are more than the hairs of my head;
   my heart fails me. (40:11, 12)

When we see this confession of sin, we might think that David can only be talking about himself and not about Christ—after all, Jesus himself was sinless. But the writer of Hebrews tells us unambiguously that the words of this psalm are the words of Christ.[10] Jesus Christ had no sin, but he was made sin for us. The transfer of sin to our Savior was real. We are joined to Christ so completely that he calls our sin his own. And by the same token his righteousness becomes our own. We are saved by this deep and intimate exchange. As a husband and wife are joined together to become "one flesh" (Ephesians 5:31), so Christ and the church are joined together in a unity so profound that the sinless Son of God took our sin.

If you consider the number of sins each one of us have committed without even knowing it, it is not too much for Christ to say that he is overwhelmed by sins that cannot be numbered. When someone begins a diet, often he will keep a log of the food he eats. The point is to show that all the little things we nibble on do add up. A cookie here and an extra serving there, and soon we are taking in lots of extra calories. Most people who keep a log are surprised at first at the amount they actually eat in a normal day.

We would be astonished if we could count up our sins for just one day. We sin with our thoughts, our words, our actions. But there is more. Whenever we do something God has forbidden, we also fail to do the right thing in that situation. So every sin of commission carries with it an opposite sin of omission. And the reverse is true as well. Whenever we fail or neglect to do the right thing, we also do the wrong thing. So every sin, whether omission or commission, is always double what we might think. But there is even more, because James multiplies all our sins by ten! Whoever fails in one point of the Law has broken all of it (James 2:10). So we can never break just one of the Ten Commandments by itself; every sin violates the whole Law.

And to make it even worse, we sin even in our best moments as we serve God. There has never been a single moment when we have loved the Lord our God with all our heart, soul, mind, and strength (Mark 12:29, 30). In our most sincere time of prayer, the pure eyes of our holy God see the unbelief, lukewarmness, spiritual pride, hypocrisy, and selfishness that is in our hearts. We grieve over the sins we see, but God sees far more. Our sins are like the dust on a gravel road. My sins and yours are beyond number.[11]

Christ took on himself all the sins of all his people—every one. He bore the countless sins of countless people. They swarmed around him so thickly that they blinded him. "[M]y iniquities have overtaken me, and I cannot see; they are more than the hairs of my head; my heart fails me" (Psalm 40:12). It was no small thing for Christ to be the sacrifice for our sin. When he took our sin, it was as if his heart stopped. He called out to God for mercy; the Father's covenant love and faithfulness was his only hope.

Deliverance

Christ ends with a prayer for deliverance from his enemies. Those who hate Christ will be ashamed, confused, and confounded.

> Be pleased, O LORD, to deliver me!
>   O LORD, make haste to help me!
> Let those be put to shame and disappointed altogether
>   who seek to snatch away my life;
> let those be turned back and brought to dishonor
>   who delight in my hurt!
> Let those be appalled because of their shame
>   who say to me, "Aha, Aha!"
>
> But may all who seek you
>   rejoice and be glad in you;
> may those who love your salvation
>   say continually, "Great is the LORD!"
> As for me, I am poor and needy,
>   but the Lord takes thought for me.
> You are my help and my deliverer;
>   do not delay, O my God! (40:13–17)

Christ's closing thought is the comfort of knowing that God the Father was thinking about him. The Father delights in the Son, and it was only a matter of time until he leaned toward him in the pit, heard his cry, and drew him up. His rescue was as good as done.

God did not delay, but at first light of the third day he rolled away the stone, and Christ rose again from the dead. Our great hope, our great joy, is that God rescued our Lord Jesus and pulled him up from the pit.

If you know him, you will be able to wait like he did. If you know him, you will thank him that your sins are forgiven. If you know him, you will delight in him forever. If you know him, you will say, "Great is the LORD!" (v. 16).

41

The Blessing of Christ

PSALM 41

ON A WEDNESDAY EVENING in late September 2013 about one hundred people gathered across from the only abortion facility in Tulsa to mark the start of the Forty Days for Life prayer campaign. This was one of many gatherings of churches and Christian ministries across the country to stand up for the lives of children in the womb.

Our commitment to protect weak and helpless children is not a new thing for Christians. In the early centuries of the church, Roman culture practiced infanticide. If a father did not want a child, he had the right literally to throw it away. Christians rescued newborn babies from garbage piles where they were left to die from scavengers or exposure.

This is not just distant history. My father-in-law grew up in Portland, Oregon, a port city with all the vices that you might expect. In the early 1900s one of the duties of the deaconesses at his church was to walk the boardwalks near the waterfront, looking for babies born during the night in a house of ill repute. Often these newborns would be put out by the swampy shore to die.

Christians have always been known for their compassion. When missionaries travel to undeveloped parts of the world, they sometimes start hospitals. Maynard and Dorothy Seaman built a hospital in remote Western Nepal, the only medical facility in the entire region. When they left Nepal after twenty-five years of ministry, they were currently treating three thousand patients for leprosy and another fifteen thousand for tuberculosis.

In December 2013 Kyle and Vanessa Jones dedicated a clinic among the Pokot tribe, several hours from the remote hospital where they work in Kapsowar, Kenya. Kyle is plenty busy at the main hospital, but his heart drew him to bring medical care to this tribe that is even farther away from any doctors.

An open heart toward the weak and poor is a quality that identifies God's people and brings God's blessing. David opens Psalm 41 with the beatitude, "Blessed is the one who considers the poor!" In Psalm 41 this blessing is the foundation of David's hope. Evidently David was very sick, and his enemies took this opportunity to plot against him. David's hope was that God would remember his care for the needy and bless him.

Psalm 41 is the last psalm in Book 1 of the Psalms. As you remember, the whole book of Psalms is organized in five smaller books. Now we come to the end of Book 1.

Significantly Psalm 41 begins with the important Hebrew word, "blessed."[1] This stands out because Book 1 began with blessing too. Psalm 1 begins, "Blessed in the man who walks not in the counsel of the wicked . . ." (Psalm 1:1). Psalm 2 ends with the same word; speaking of our response to Christ, the psalmist says, "Blessed are all who take refuge in him" (Psalm 2:12). Psalms 1 and 2 are tied together by this word "blessed" as they introduce Christ.

When we see this word "blessed" again at the end of Book 1 (41:1), we should think back to Psalms 1 and 2 and think about everything that we have read over the last forty psalms. Book 1 ends in the same place it began so that in a real sense the whole of Book 1 is the story of this blessed man, Jesus Christ. In Psalm 1 he is the ideal man who never sinned. In Psalm 2 he is the King whom God set on a throne. By the time we get to Psalm 41 we know that the Messiah is a vulnerable man whose enemies hate him and attack him.[2] The hostility and suffering he experienced is not a sign that God is displeased with him. In spite of his suffering—or because of his suffering—he is "blessed."

This was a reality that the Jews in Jesus' day could not accept. They thought the Messiah would come in triumph and victory. The idea of a Messiah who suffered, was rejected, and was crucified was "a stumbling block" for them (1 Corinthians 1:23). But this is exactly the kind of Messiah Book 1 of the Psalms teaches us to expect.

We can organize Psalm 41 in three sections. David starts by declaring his confidence that God will rescue him because of his care for the poor (vv. 1–3). He confesses his sin to God and asks for healing (vv. 4–10). And finally he experiences God's answer (vv. 10–12). In all this David is a prophet who is writing ultimately about Christ and his experiences.[3] Verse 13 is a concluding doxology to mark the end of Book 1.

Confidence

David declares his confidence in the first three verses. By faith David knew that God would deliver him and rescue him.

Blessed Are the Merciful

There are several important points to consider in the opening beatitude: "Blessed is the one who considers the poor!" (41:1a).

We can read this beatitude in two ways, and these two ways are related to each other.[4] On the one hand, this beatitude can refer to God himself. God himself considers the poor, and he is eternally blessed. Psalm 68 says,

> Father of the fatherless and protector of widows
>   is God in his holy habitation.
> God settles the solitary in a home;
>   he leads out the prisoners to prosperity. (Psalm 68:5, 6)

So one way of reading this is praise to God. "Blessed are you, O Lord, the one who considers the poor." Since David is weak and needy, he praises God and appeals to God's character.

On the other hand, this is a promise that God will bless people who care for the weak and poor. In that case the reason God will bless David in this psalm is because he has taken care of the needy in his kingdom. These two ways of reading this beatitude are, in fact, related to each other. God himself cares for the poor, and he blesses those who share his compassionate heart.

The word "poor" (41:1) can be translated "weak," "powerless," or "insignificant," depending on the context.[5] In fact, these possible translations are not far from each other. Those who are poor are usually weak and marginalized. Often they are sick because they may not have money for nutritious food or perhaps warm clothes. Money brings power and influence. Poverty closes doors of opportunity.

It is easy to overlook the poor. The blessed man not only sees a poor man, a poor woman, or a poor family—he also takes time to consider or regard them. The word "considers" means more than compassionate concern. The word implies careful thought and reflection in order to know the right thing to do for the poor.[6] Those who consider the poor do not just have warm feelings—they give the poor their time and attention to discover what should be done genuinely to help them. Spurgeon said,

> They do not toss them a penny and go on their way, but inquire into their sorrows, sift out their causes, study the best ways for their relief, and practically come to their rescue; such as these have the mark of divine favor plainly upon them, and are as surely the sheep of the Lord's pasture as if they wore a brand upon their foreheads.[7]

Philip Abode and the team at Crossover Community Impact in North Tulsa consider "the poor" (v. 1). They have studied hard to understand the community God has called them to serve. They attend conferences and read books. One of the men on staff earned his Master's from Harvard University in Urban Development precisely so he could consider "the poor" (v. 1). They are not serving the poor from a distance like a doctor trying to perform surgery over the Internet. They moved into the neighborhood so they could truly know the people they are serving. Considering the poor does not just mean a tear in the corner of our eye. It means PowerPoints and strategy meetings. It means researching the root causes of poverty. It means hard work and sacrifice.

God himself considered the poor when Christ came into the world. We were weak and helpless and insignificant, but God stooped down to us. He didn't help us from a distance but he sent his Son to become one of us, a vulnerable human being. The Bible says,

> For while we were still weak, at the right time Christ died for the ungodly. . . . God shows his love for us in that while we were still sinners, Christ died for us. (Romans 5:6, 8)

And again the Bible says,

> For you know the grace of our Lord Jesus Christ, that though he was rich, yet for your sake he became poor, so that you by his poverty might become rich. (2 Corinthians 8:9)

When God's people focus their attention on insignificant people at the fringes of society, we are imitating our Father in Heaven.

God Rescues the Merciful

David goes on to describe how God blesses those who show active, thoughtful compassion. The man or woman who cares for the poor can expect that God will care for him or her.

> In the day of trouble the LORD delivers him;
> the LORD protects him and keeps him alive;
>   he is called blessed in the land;
>   you do not give him up to the will of his enemies.
> The LORD sustains him on his sickbed;
>   in his illness you restore him to full health. (41:1b–3)

You might think that people who care for the weak and protect the helpless would not have enemies, but that is not the case. In January 1991 Christian author Randy Alcorn and several dozen others went on trial for peacefully protesting outside an abortion clinic, the Lovejoy Surgicenter near Portland, Oregon. It's hard to imagine a more inappropriate name for a facility that kills babies. Judge James Ellis was clearly hostile to the pro-life defendants. At various times he exploded with red-faced anger at defense witnesses or read his mail while they testified. Alcorn explains what happened next:

> The time came for Judge Ellis, who had been so overtly hostile toward us during the trial, to give his final instructions to the jury before sending them away for deliberations. His final words were "You must find these people guilty and you must punish them sufficiently to insure they'll never do this again." For our totally peaceful nonviolent actions, the jury awarded the abortion clinic $8.2 million dollars.[8]

Alcorn's conscience could not allow his wages to be garnished to pay an abortion clinic, so he resigned from his church. This was the way God moved him to start a separate ministry and become an author whose books have blessed many Christians. To avoid having his royalties garnished, the money from his books goes to the ministry to fund missions. God did not give Randy Alcorn up to the will of his enemies. Instead what others meant for evil, God meant for good (Genesis 50:20).

This was Jesus Christ's experience too. He came to this earth doing nothing but good. He healed the sick and cared for the poor. Yet his enemies hated him and wanted him dead. They thought they had defeated him by putting him to death on a cross, but God had other plans. God did not give Jesus up to the will of his enemies, but raised him on the third day in power and glory.

Grace: Forgiveness and Healing

After these words of faith and confidence, David turns to God. In verses 4–10 David appeals for grace so his enemies will not get the upper hand.

Confession

David starts by confessing his sin and asking God to heal him.

> As for me, I said, "O Lᴏʀᴅ, be gracious to me;
> heal me, for I have sinned against you!" (41:4)

We don't know when David was deathly ill like this. Whenever this was during his life, David clearly saw a connection between his sin and his sickness. Since the invention of the microscope, we generally accept the germ theory of disease. As scientifically-minded westerners, we often discount the idea that disease or illness could have a spiritual cause. To be clear, not all sickness is the result of personal sin.[9] But the Bible clearly indicates that some sickness is the result of personal sin.

Here is some evidence for you to consider. The Apostle Paul wrote to the believers in Corinth about the way they were dishonoring the Lord's Table. He warned them,

> Let a person examine himself, then, and so eat of the bread and drink of the cup. For anyone who eats and drinks without discerning the body eats and drinks judgment on himself. That is why many of you are weak and ill, and some have died. (1 Corinthians 11:28–30)

Evidently quite a few of the Christians in Corinth were sick because of their sin. They thought they honored the Lord by taking Communion, but they dishonored the body of Christ by the way they treated each other. God judged them with sickness, and some even died.

Or consider the words of James as he tells us to pray for the sick.

> Is anyone among you sick? Let him call for the elders of the church, and let them pray over him, anointing him with oil in the name of the Lord. And the prayer of faith will save the one who is sick, and the Lord will raise him up. And if he has committed sins, he will be forgiven. Therefore, confess your sins to one another and pray for one another, that you may be healed. (James 5:14–16)

The sick man calls the elders and confesses his sins to them. Then the elders pray for his forgiveness and healing.

Once again we need to say clearly that not all sickness is a result of sin. For example, Jesus met a man who was blind from birth.

> [H]is disciples asked him, "Rabbi, who sinned, this man or his parents, that he was born blind?" Jesus answered, "It was not that this man sinned, or his parents, but that the works of God might be displayed in him." (John 9:2, 3)

This is a case where our Lord himself says that a disease or disability was not caused by sin. God had other purposes in mind; that man's sickness was not caused by personal sin.

Having said that, we do need to recognize that *some* sickness is the result of personal sin. If you come down with a serious illness, the Holy Spirit might point out to you an area of sin in your life. Maybe it is a long-term sin that you are not willing to confess or give up. Maybe it is a grave sin that is bringing great hurt on others or shame to the Body of Christ. Don't let yourself worry that every cold you catch this winter is because of sin in your life—that would be going overboard. If God is disciplining you with sickness, he will make that plain to you because his whole purpose is to help you turn from sin and make you holy. So if the Holy Spirit does prompt you, David's words are an appropriate prayer for you to make your own: "O Lord, be gracious to me; heal me, for I have sinned against you" (Psalm 41:4).

Notice how the gospel is at the heart of this confession as well. David does not say, "Heal me because I have been so good." You might think this would have been a good time for David to remind God of all he had done for the poor and needy. "Heal me, because I have considered the poor."

That is how religious people come to God. They realize they need God's healing and forgiveness, so they come to him with the things they have done. They come with a resumé of their spiritual accomplishments: how much they give, how many hours they have served, the times they turned the other cheek, the missions trips they went on, the tract they gave someone at work, and so on.

But David does not do that. He doesn't say, "Heal me because I am so good." He says, "Heal me because I am so bad." This is the only way we can come to God. *I am a sinner, and I need your grace, your healing, your forgiveness. There is nothing I can do or say that makes me somehow worthy of your mercy. All I can bring you is my sin. I need you to heal me, body and soul.*

How can God forgive us when we come to him with our sin? As David wrote these words, he was not only speaking for himself, he was speaking for Christ. Jesus was perfectly sinless, yet he is joined to us as his people, and he took our sin as his own. He was perfectly innocent, but he carried our sin and could say to God the Father, "I have sinned against you." The spotless Son of God became sin for us so that we could be forgiven (2 Corinthians 5:21).

You can bring nothing to God but your sin. You can be forgiven because Jesus carried your sin. God considers the poor. "While we were still weak, at the right time Christ died for the ungodly" (Romans 5:6).

Opposition

David was desperate as he prayed because his enemies were cruel. They did not consider the weak and the poor. Instead David's sickness and trouble were a golden opportunity.

Imagine being in the hospital and the people who bring you flowers and balloons are secretly hoping you kick the bucket and die. You can hear them whispering in the hallway and trying to get more details at the nurses' station. This is how it was for David.

> My enemies say of me in malice,
>   "When will he die, and his name perish?"
> And when one comes to see me, he utters empty words,
>   while his heart gathers iniquity;
>   when he goes out, he tells it abroad.
> All who hate me whisper together about me;
>   they imagine the worst for me.
>
> They say, "A deadly thing is poured out on him;
>   he will not rise again from where he lies."
> Even my close friend in whom I trusted,
>   who ate my bread, has lifted his heel against me.
> But you, O LORD, be gracious to me,
>   and raise me up, that I may repay them! (41:5–10)

This betrayal was ultimately fulfilled as Judas turned against Jesus. Jesus quoted Psalm 41:9 at the Last Supper after he humbled himself by washing the disciples' feet (John 13:18). And just minutes later Judas went out into the night to betray him. I have been betrayed by people I have worked with, but never by a close friend. I can only imagine the pain.

Celebration

It is wonderfully fitting that Psalm 41, and Book 1 of the Psalms, ends on a strong note of faith. God heard his prayer and saved him! David ends with deep joy and assurance.

> By this I know that you delight in me:
>   my enemy will not shout in triumph over me.
> But you have upheld me because of my integrity,
>   and set me in your presence forever. (41:11, 12)

Many saw this sickness as a sign that God was against him. But David knew that God was pleased with him. In the same way, God the Father was pleased with Christ even as he suffered on the cross, surrounded by his enemies. God proved that he was pleased and delighted with Jesus by raising him from the dead. Although Christ took our sins as his own, God upheld him because of his perfect integrity. After he suffered, Christ was seated at God's right hand forever.

Book 1 of the Psalms is the story of Christ in David's life and words, centuries before Jesus was born. Christ is the ideal man of Psalm 1 and the King of Psalm 2. He was hated and attacked by his enemies. He identified with us and took our sin as his own. He called on God to save him because of his blameless life. And God heard him!

How fitting to end Book 1 of the Psalms with a doxology. In fact, all five books of the Psalms end with a doxology that is similar to verse 13.

> Blessed be the LORD, the God of Israel,
>   from everlasting to everlasting!
>   Amen and Amen.

When we read the Psalms, this is the natural response of our hearts. Our God is a God who saves. He considers the poor. He considers you and me. Blessed be his name.

Soli Deo gloria!

Notes

Introduction

1. Gerald Wilson, *Psalms*, The NIV Application Bible Commentary (Grand Rapids, MI: Zondervan, 2002), 1:23–26 has a helpful discussion of the origin of many psalms in temple worship.

2. Craig S. Keener, *Matthew*, IVP New Testament Commentary Series (Downers Grove, IL: InterVarsity, 1997), 1:369; Donald Carson, "Matthew," in *The Expositor's Bible Commentary*, rev. ed. (Grand Rapids: Zondervan, 2010), 9:604.

3. Hilton C. Oswald, "Introduction to Volume 10," in *First Lectures on the Psalms I: Psalm 1–75*, Luther's Works (St. Louis: Concordia, 1974), 10:*x*.

4. Such as the *Strasbourg Psalter* and the *Geneva Psalter*. Cf. Hughes Oliphant Old, *Worship: Reformed According to Scripture* (Louisville: John Knox, 2002), 43.

5. Willem A. VanGemeren, *Psalms*, The Expositors Bible Commentary, rev. ed. (Grand Rapids, MI: Zondervan, 2008), 5:79, 220.

6. Gerald H. Wilson, *"The Editing of the Hebrew Psalter," Society of Biblical Literature Dissertation* 76 (Chico, CA: Scholars, 1985), 207 says helpfully:

> While Ps 1 as introduction sets the "tone" for an approach to the Psalter, it indicates this is a collection to be read rather than performed; it turns attention away from the individual cultic setting of single compositions to the larger *literary* context of the whole; it stresses the importance of the approach (it is a matter of Life or Death).

7. The earliest psalm was written by Moses (Psalm 90, roughly 1400 BC); the last psalms written came after Israel returned from the exile (e.g., Ps. 126, written some time after 520 BC).

8. Or consider a line from Paul Verlaine's beloved French poem, *"Chansons d'Automne"*: *Les sanglots longs des violons de l'automne / Blessent mon cœur d'une langueur monotone*. It's beautiful in French, but falls flat on its face through translation: *The long sobs of the violins of autumn / Wound my heart with a monotonous languor*. In English we get the idea, but it's no longer evocative or moving.

9. W. H. Lewis, ed., *Letters of C. S. Lewis* (New York: Harcourt, Brace & World, 1966), 188.

10. The New Testament commands us to speak/sing to one another with psalms (Ephesians 5:19; Colossians 3:16), and the very term *psalm* indicates that they are songs to be accompanied by a harp. Not only so, but quite a few psalms call for musical instruments to be used either in the superscript or the body of the psalms. Accordingly, it is hard to see how musical instruments could be inappropriate for Christian worship.

11. C. S. Lewis, *Reflections on the Psalms* (New York: Harcourt, Brace & World, 1958), 2, 3, says:

> What must be said . . . is that the Psalms are poems, and poems intended to be sung: not doctrinal treatises, nor even sermons. . . . Most emphatically the

Psalms must be read as poems; as lyrics, with all the licenses and all the formalities, the hyperboles, the emotional rather than logical connections, which are proper to lyric poetry. They must be read as poems if they are to be understood; no less than French must be read as French or English as English. Otherwise we shall miss what is in them and think we see what is not.

12. John Piper, "*Songs That Shape the Mind and Heart*," (sermon) May 25, 2008, accessed August 11, 2012, http://www.desiringgod.org/resource-library/sermons/songs -that-shape-the-heart-and-mind.

13. See John Goldingay, *Psalms*, Baker Commentary on the Old Testament (Grand Rapids, MI: Baker, 2006), 1:22.

14. Now Crown College in St. Bonifacius, Minnesota.

15. For a discussion of the evidence of editorial shaping in the Psalter, see Gerald H. Wilson, "The Structure of the Psalter," in *Interpreting the Psalms: Issues and Approaches*, ed. Philip S. Johnston and David G. Firth (Downers Grove, IL: InterVarsity, 2005), 230–34; "Shaping the Psalter: A Consideration of Editorial Linkage in the Book of Psalms," in *Shape and Shaping of the Psalter*, ed. J. Clinton McCann Jr., *Journal for the Study of the Old Testament* 159 (Sheffield, UK: Sheffield Academic, 1993), 72–92.

16. Craig A. Evans, "Praise and Prophecy in the Psalter and in the New Testament," in *The Book of Psalms: Composition and Reception*, ed. Peter W. Flint, Patrick D. Miller, *Testamentum Supplements* 99 (Leiden: Brill, 2005), 551 notes:

> The Psalter was understood in early Christian circles as prophetic, much as it was at Qumran, whose scholars produced commentaries (or *pesharim*) on several Prophets and Psalms. Indeed, the Risen Christ in Luke 24 instructs his disciples concerning all that is written in "the Law and the Prophets and Psalms." Luke's grammar here suggests that "Psalms" are closely linked with "the Prophets."

The grammatical point to which Evans refers is that the word *Psalms* does not have the definite article in Luke 24:44. Thus Luke 24:44 should read, "in the Law of Moses and the Prophets and Psalms . . ." Evans concludes, "We do not have here an instance of the tripartite canon (i.e. the Law, the Prophets, and the Writings), but only the first two divisions—the Law and the Prophets, the latter of which was understood to include the Psalms."

17. Marvin E. Tate, "Rethinking the Nature of the Psalter," in *Psalms 1–50*, Word Biblical Commentary, 2nd ed. (Nashville, TN: Thomas Nelson, 2004), 19:454 says of Psalms 1 and 2:

> When the two psalms are read together, these persons become the same: the king is to be a person devoted to torah. . . . The king in Ps 2, exalted and empowered as a son of Yahweh, is at the same time supposed to be the righteous person of Ps 1, who turns away from the company of the wicked and delights in the torah of Yahweh.

18. Jamie Grant, "The Psalms and the King," in *Interpreting the Psalms: Issues and Approaches*, ed. Philip S. Johnston and David G Firth, 108, says, "Therefore, it is probably better to see Psalm 2 not so much as part of a narrative of the rise and fall

of the Davidic Covenant but as part of the introductory hermeneutical paradigm for the interpretation of the whole book of Psalms."

19. VanGemeren, *Psalms*, 5:89.

20. Derek Kidner, *Psalms 1–72* (London: Inter-Varsity, 1973), 24.

21. Ibid., makes the point that the New Testament repeatedly assumes that several Psalms refer to Christ although they seem to fit David's life perfectly without the need for a supernatural figure in the future. E.g., John 13:18; 15:25; Romans 15:9; Hebrews 2:13. See also John Calvin, *Commentary on the Book of Psalms*, Calvin's Commentaries (Grand Rapids, MI: Baker, repr. 1979), 4:11.

22. Psalm 43 seems originally to have been part of Psalm 42.

23. We need to remember that ancient Israel was a literate civilization with more books than just the Old Testament writings. For instance, there is a secretary listed among David's officials in 2 Samuel 8:17; three separate chronicles of David's reign and history are listed in 1 Chronicles 29:29, 30; and Solomon's writings in 1 Kings 4:32, 33 are quite extensive, far more than that which was included in Holy Scripture. So it is perfectly plausible for psalms written by Moses, David, and others to have been preserved for centuries before they were incorporated into the Psalms as we have them. In the case of Psalm 90, a psalm of Moses was apparently preserved for almost one thousand years before being used as the first psalm of Book IV.

24. See J. Clinton McCann, "Books I–III and the Editorial Purpose of the Psalter," in *Shape and Shaping of the Psalter*, ed. J. Clinton McCann Jr., *Journal for the Study of the Old Testament Supplement* 159 (Sheffield, UK: Sheffield Academic, 1993), 95–100.

25. This matches the concerns of Ezra 9, 10 and Nehemiah 13 from that time period.

Chapter One: Blessed Is the Man

1. Michael L. Brown, *New International Dictionary of Old Testament Theology and Exegesis*, ed. Willem A. VanGemeren (Grand Rapids, MI: Zondervan, 1997), 1:570–72.

2. John Piper, *"Songs That Shape the Mind and Heart,"* (sermon), May 25, 2008, accessed August 11, 2012, http://www.desiringgod.org/resource-library /sermons/songs-that-shape-the-heart-and-mind.

3. Franz Delitzsch, *Psalms*, in C. F. Keil and F. Delitzsch, *Commentary on the Old Testament* (Grand Rapidsm MI: Eerdmans, repr. 1991), 5:85 says, "The *perff.* in ver. 1 describe what he all along has never done, the *fut.* what he is always striving to do."

4. Willem A. VanGemeren, *Psalms*, The Expositors Bible Commentary, rev. ed. (Grand Rapids, MI: Zondervan, 2008), 5:79 (italics his).

5. Augustine, *Expositions on the Book of Psalms*, NPNF I, ed. Philip Schaff (Peabody, MA: Hendrickson, repr. 2004), 8:1.

6. James Boice, *Psalms: 1–41* (Grand Rapids, MI: Baker, 1994), 1:19.

7. VanGemeren, *Psalms*, 77 says that through this ideal man presented in Psalm 1, the Psalter instructs us to learn from David's frailty and long for the ideal Davidic king.

8. Ibid., 1:82.

9. Alex Luc, *New International Dictionary of Old Testament Theology and Exegesis*, ed. Willem A. VanGemeren (Grand Rapids, MI: Zondervan, 1997), 3:804.

Chapter Two: Let Earth Receive Her King

1. Alastair Gale, "For South Korea, More Controversy. For North, more Gold," Korea Realtime (blog), *The Wall Street Journal*, July 31, 2012, accessed August 24, 2012, http://blogs.wsj.com/korearealtime/2012/07/31/for-south-korea-more-controversy-for-north-more-gold.

2. See "PTC Finds Shocking Spike in Full Nudity on Broadcast TV," August 20, 2012, accessed August 24, 2012, http://www.parentstv.org/PTC/news/release/2012/0820.asp.

3. James Montgomery Boice, *Psalms: 1–41* (Grand Rapids, MI: Baker, 1994), 1:26.

4. See Willem A. VanGemeren, *Psalms*, The Expositors Bible Commentary, rev. ed. (Grand Rapids, MI: Zondervan, 2008), 5:89. The coronations recorded in 1 Kings 1 and 2 Kings 11:12 are absolutely silent regarding this psalm. The psalm itself has no superscription suggesting that it should be read in the context of the coronation of any Old Testament Davidic king.

5. Derek Kidner, *Psalms 1–72* (London: Inter-Varsity, 1973), 50.

6. Gerald Wilson, *Psalms*, The NIV Application Bible Commentary (Grand Rapids, MI: Zondervan, 2002), 1:109, 111, 112 acknowledges that there is no historical setting when Israel and Judah could claim world domination. He argues that worldwide rule was the official ideology of the Jerusalem monarchy, unlikely as it may seem to us historically, citing Psalm 72 as evidence. Yet Psalm 72 is often considered messianic, referring to David's great descendant, not to any Old Testament king. In fact, the Old Testament promises of a worldwide king seem to be messianic in character; cf. Isaiah 11:1–10; Micah 5:2; Zechariah 9:10. Second Samuel 7:12–16 promises the length of the Davidic King's rule ("forever"), not its breadth.

7. F. F. Bruce, "Messiah," in *The New Bible Dictionary*, quoted in Donald M. Williams, *Psalms 1–72, The Preacher's Commentary*, ed. Lloyd J. Ogilvie (Nashville, TN: Thomas Nelson, 1986), 13:33.

8. Charles Spurgeon, *The Treasury of David*, (Peabody, MA: Hendrickson, n.d.), 1:14.

9. These figures were reported to me by a well-informed Christian leader in the Middle East. I am withholding his name for his safety.

10. See Peter C. Craigie, *Psalms 1–50*, Word Biblical Commentary, (Nashville, TN: Thomas Nelson, 2004), 19:67.

11. John Calvin, *Commentary on the Book of Psalms*, Calvin's Commentaries, (Grand Rapids, MI: Baker, repr. 1979), 4:17.

12. Boice, *Psalms*, 1:26.

13. VanGemeren, *Psalms*, 97.

Chapter Three: God Save the King

1. There is some debate whether the phrase "psalm of David" means it was written by David. The Hebrew preposition *le-* which is used in this phrase (*ledawid*, that is, "of David") is inconclusive. It has a range of meaning, including "of, by, for, to, concerning, about." The specific nuance must be determined from context. Thus the superscription on its own could mean the psalm was written by David, for David, to David, about David, etc. The English translation "of David" preserves a similar range of meaning.

We conclude that "of David" means it was written by David based on the evidence from the Old and New Testaments. David's skill as a musician is established when he first enters the Biblical record (1 Samuel 16:14–23). In 2 Samuel 23:1 David is memorialized as "the sweet Psalmist of Israel." In Matthew 22:43, 44 and its parallels, Christ quoted Psalm 110, "a Psalm of David," to argue that he is David's greater son. His argument hinges on the point that David himself spoke the words of Psalm 110:1, calling the Messiah his own Lord.

2. Gerald Wilson, *Psalms*, The NIV Application Bible Commentary (Grand Rapids, MI: Zondervan, 2002), 1:129.

3. Fernando Ortega, "Sleepless Night," *Fernando Ortega* (Curb Records, 2004).

4. Wilson, *Psalms*, 1:128 comes close to this very question.

5. Tertullian, *On the Flesh of Christ*, in *Ante-Nicene Fathers*, ed. Alexander Roberts and James Donaldson (Peabody, MA: Hendrickson, 1994), 3:538.

6. Charles Spurgeon, *The Treasury of David* (Peabody, MA: Hendrickson, n.d.), 1:22.

7. Augustine, *Expositions on the Book of Psalms*, Nicene and Post-Nicene Fathers, Series I, ed. Philip Schaff (Peabody, MA: Hendrickson, repr. 2004), 8:4.

8. Franz Delitzsch, *Psalms*, in C. F. Keil and F. Delitzsch, *Commentary on the Old Testament* (Grand Rapids, MI: Eerdmans, repr. 1991), 5:109.

Chapter Four: Trusting God in a Bad Economy

1. See Gerald Wilson, *Psalms*, The NIV Application Bible Commentary (Grand Rapids, MI: Zondervan, 2002), 1:149, 150; Craig C. Broyles, *Psalms* (Grand Rapids: Baker, 1999), p. 53; Willem A. VanGemeren, *Psalms*, The Expositors Bible Commentary, rev. ed. (Grand Rapids, MI: Zondervan, 2008), 5:107 lists several possible historical backgrounds for this psalm.

2. So, for instance, in Psalm 62:9, the same Hebrew phrase is translated "those of high estate."

3. Broyles, *Psalms*, 53 says, "Thus, the fundamental issue of this Psalm is probably not the private issue of false accusation but the corporate issue, to what deity should people appeal for agricultural produce?"

4. Charles Spurgeon, *The Treasury of David* (Peabody, MA: Hendrickson, n.d.), 1:34.

5. John Goldingay, *Psalms*, Baker Commentary on the Old Testament (Grand Rapids, MI: Baker, 2006), 1:118n4 comments, "A second noun in the genitive regularly functions as an adj. in Hebrew, with any personal pronoun applying to the whole phrase."

6. Willem A. VanGemeren, *Psalms*, The Expositors Bible Commentary, rev. ed. (Grand Rapids, MI: Zondervan, 2008), 1:108; see also Broyles, *Psalms*, 53.

7. Wilson, *Psalms*, 153.

8. Ibid., 155; VanGemeren, *Psalms*, 111; Goldingay, *Psalms*, 121 translates this as "committed."

9. Goldingay, *Psalms*, 121n10.

10. Exodus 8:22; 9:4; 11:7; 33:16.

11. VanGemeren, *Psalms*, 110.

12. C. S. Lewis, *The Weight of Glory* (San Francisco: Harper Collins, repr. 2001), 26.

Chapter Five: The God Who Hears Prayer

1. See Gerald Wilson, *Psalms*, The NIV Application Bible Commentary (Grand Rapids, MI: Zondervan, 2002), 1:166, 174.

2. Ibid., 166.

3. See Willem A. VanGemeren, *Psalms*, The Expositor's Bible Commentary, rev. ed. (Grand Rapids, MI: Zondervan, 2008), 5:116.

4. Flannery O'Connor, *Wise Blood*, in *Three* (New York: Signet, 1964), 10. This illustration is from Tim Keller's 2006 Ockenga Lectures at Gordon Conwell Theological Seminary.

5. See Peter C. Craigie, *Psalms 1–50*, Word Biblical Commentary (Nashville, TN: Thomas Nelson, 2004), 19:87.

6. Wilson, *Psalms*, 169.

7. Thomas Fuller quoted in Charles Spurgeon, *The Treasury of David* (Peabody, MA: Hendrickson, n.d.), 1:54.

8. James Montgomery Boice, *Psalms:1–41* (Grand Rapids, MI: Baker, 1994), 1:49.

Chapter Six: How Long, O Lord?

1. See Matthew Clark, "Pastor Youcef Nadarkhani Writes Moving Letter of 'Gratitude' after Release," *The Docket* (blog), ACLJ, September 20, 2012, accessed September 26, 2012, http://aclj.org/iran/pastor-youcef-nadarkhani-letter-gratitude-after-release.

2. This would fit with the opposition we expect to God's King based on Psalm 2:1–3.

3. See John E. Hartley, *New International Dictionary of Old Testament Theology and Exegesis*, ed. Willem A. VanGemeren (Grand Rapids: Zondervan, 1997), 2:443.

4. John Goldingay, *Psalms*, Baker Commentary on the Old Testament (Grand Rapids, MI: Baker, 2006), 1:135, 136. Job was in such pain that he assumed God was angry at him too.

> Surely now God has worn me out; he has made desolate all my company. And he has shriveled me up, which is a witness against me, and my leanness has risen up against me; it testifies to my face. He has torn me in his wrath and hated me; he has gnashed his teeth at me; my adversary sharpens his eyes against me. (Job 16:7–9)

5. Gerald Wilson, *Psalms*, The NIV Application Bible Commentary (Grand Rapids, MI: Zondervan, 2002), 1:179.

6. Martin Luther quoted in Goldingay, *Psalms*, 141.

7. R. Kent Hughes, *Liberating Ministry from the Success Syndrome*, 2nd ed. (Wheaton, IL: Crossway, 2008), 143.

8. Derek Kidner, *Psalms 1–72* (London: Inter-Varsity, 1973), 62.

9. See David W. Pao and Eckhart J. Schnabel, "Luke," in *Commentary on the New Testament Use of the Old Testament*, ed. G. K. Beale and D. A. Carson (Grand Rapids, MI: Baker Academic, 2007), 335; W. D. Davies and D. C. Allison, *A Critical and Exegetical Commentary on the Gospel According to Saint Matthew*, International Critical Commentary (Edinburgh: T & T Clark, 1988), 1:719.

Chapter Seven: A Prayer for Justice

1. Portions of this introduction are suggested by James Montgomery Boice, *Psalms:1–41* (Grand Rapids, MI: Baker, 1994), 1:60, 61.

2. Herman Melville, *Billy Budd* (New York: Pocket Books, repr. 2006), 82.

3. Franz Delitzsch, *Psalms*, in C. F. Keil and F. Delitzsch, *Commentary on the Old Testament* (Grand Rapids, MI: Eerdmans, repr. 1991), 5:143.

4. Ibid., 142; Donald M. Williams, *Psalms 1–72, The Preacher's Commentary*, ed. Lloyd J. Ogilvie (Nashville, TN: Thomas Nelson, 1986), 13:72.

Chapter Eight: How Majestic Is Your Name!

1. Terrence Fretheim, "Yahweh," in *New International Dictionary of Old Testament Theology and Exegesis*, ed. Willem A. VanGemeren (Grand Rapids, MI: Zondervan, 1997), 4:1296.

2. Gerald Wilson, *Psalms*, The NIV Application Bible Commentary (Grand Rapids, MI: Zondervan, 2002), 1:201.

3. Gerard Manley Hopkins, "God's Grandeur," in *The Oxford Anthology of English Literature: Victorian Prose and Poetry*, ed. Lionel Trilling and Harold Bloom (New York: Oxford University, 1973), p. 5:682.

4. John Piper, "The Peculiar Mark of Majesty, Part 1," (sermon), April 1, 2007, accessed October 11, 2012, http://www.desiringgod.org/sermons/the-peculiar-mark-of-majesty-part-1.

5. Franz Delitzsch, *Psalms*, in C. F. Keil and F. Delitzsch, *Commentary on the Old Testament* (Grand Rapids, MI: Eerdmans, repr. 1991), 5:151, 152; W. R. Domeris quoted in *New International Dictionary of Old Testament Theology and Exegesis*, ed. Willem A. VanGemeren (Grand Rapids, MI: Zondervan, 1997), 2:472.

6. Roger E. Olson, *The Story of Christian Theology* (Downers Grove, IL: InterVarsity, 1999), 579.

7. Delitzsch, *Psalms*, 152.

8. See Sermon Illustrations, s. v. "Humilty," accessed October 13, 2012, www.sermonillustrations.com/a-z/h/humility.htm.

9. See Wilson, *Psalms*, 204.

10. "Son of Man" also identifies Jesus as the man God raised up to rule over all nations (cf. Daniel 7:13, 14). The title also retains the sense it has in Psalm 8 of human weakness.

Chapter Nine: Praise Him for His Justice

1. In Brecht's *Der Kaukasische Kreidekreis*, the heroine is Grusha, the peasant girl who rescued baby Michael, rather than the birth mother, Natella.

2. There are several other differences too in the rest of the Psalter. Peter C. Craigie, *Psalms 1–50*, Word Biblical Commentary (Nashville, TN: Thomas Nelson, 2004), 9:42 gives this helpful chart to summarize the differences.

Hebrew Text	Septuagint
1–8	1–8
9–10	9
11–113	10–112

Hebrew Text	Septuagint
114–115	113
116	114–115
117–146	116–145
147	146–147
148–150	148–150

3. There are two main arguments for treating these two psalms as one. First, Psalm 9 is an acrostic psalm that covers the first half of the alphabet (*aleph—kaph*); Psalm 10 covers the second half of the alphabet (*lamed—taw*), suggesting that these two psalms were originally written as one acrostic. Second, Psalm 10 is one of the very few psalms in Book 1 that does not have a heading or superscript. This may indicate that the superscription of Psalm 9 originally stood as the heading for the one longer original psalm. There seem to be stronger reasons for reading these as separate psalms, however. For one thing, it is very significant that they are separate psalms in the Hebrew text; it seems reasonable to give the original language text priority over translations. Secondly, Psalm 10 is not the only psalm in the body of Book 1 that does not have a heading; Psalm 33 doesn't have a superscript either (Psalms 1 and 2 have no heading but are introductions for the whole Psalter). Third, the acrostic pattern is incomplete; the psalms skip several letters of the alphabet. Willem A. VanGemeren, *Psalms*, The Expositors Bible Commentary, rev. ed. (Grand Rapids, MI: Zondervan, 2008), 5:153 also observes that the verses in Psalm 10:1–8 "show little evidence of a clear acrostic. Many of the proposals to recover the acrostic pattern are based on changes in *cola* for reasons of balance (stichometric analysis)." Fourth, the content of the two psalms is different. Psalm 9 is a song of praise, while Psalm 10 is usually considered a lament. Each one is complete in itself. Most modern English translations have these as two psalms. For a discussion of these issues see Gerald Wilson, *Psalms*, The NIV Application Bible Commentary (Grand Rapids, MI: Zondervan, 2002), 1:223; VanGemeren, *Psalms*, 143.

4. The letter *daleth* is missing.

5. Wilson, *Psalms*, 226.

6. C. S. Lewis, *Reflections on the Psalms* (San Diego, CA: Harcourt, 1958), 93.

7. Ibid., 94, 95.

8. Wilson, *Psalms*, 227; VanGemeren, *Psalms*, 145, 146; Craigie, *Psalms 1–50*, 118 says, "The grounds for confidence lie in anticipation, rather than the present experience of deliverance."

9. Translators have a notoriously difficult time determining and conveying the relationship of Hebrew verbs to time. The Hebrew verbal system is not based on time but on *aspect*, that is, whether an event is being viewed as complete (perfective) or incomplete (imperfective). In the case of 9:4, an action may be viewed as a complete event (perfective) although it has not yet occurred and is, therefore, in the future. The relation of an action to time depends primarily on context, not verbal aspect. Verbs in English and other classical languages, by contrast, are based on tenses that express relationship to time (past, present, future, perfect, pluperfect, imperfect, etc.). See

the brief yet helpful discussion of Hebrew verbal aspect in Craigie, *Psalms 1–50*, 110–13 who states the following.

> From the kind of evidence summarized above, it is evident that there can be no simple rule of thumb with respect to the appropriate English tense which may be indicated by the forms of the Hebrew verb. In practice, the context is the principal guide to determining the most appropriate translation, but difficulties arise precisely because context, in nonhistorical poetic texts (which is the case with respect to the majority of the psalms), may leave room for considerable ambiguity and uncertainty.

10. It was the same with the Amalekites; see Exodus 17:14.
11. See the apostolic preaching in Acts 10:42, for instance.
12. Derek Kidner, *Psalms 1–72* (London: Inter-Varsity, 1973), 69.
13. James B. Conant, "What Is Man That Thou Art Mindful of Him?" (baccalaureate address, June 7, 1942), in *Vital Speeches of the Day*, 8:585–87; accessed December 4, 2013, http://www.ibiblio.org/pha/policy/1942/1942–06–07a.html.

Chapter Ten: God, Where Are You?
1. Gerald Wilson, *Psalms*, The NIV Application Bible Commentary (Grand Rapids, MI: Zondervan, 2002), 1:233.
2. See *Wikipedia*, s.v. "Gordon Gekko," accessed November 5, 2012, http://en.wikipedia.org/wiki/Gordon_Gekko.
3. W. H. Lewis, ed., *Letters of C. S. Lewis* (New York: Harcourt, Brace & World, 1966), 75.
4. Willem A. VanGemeren, *Psalms*, The Expositors Bible Commentary, rev. ed. (Grand Rapids, MI: Zondervan, 2008), 5:156.

Chapter Eleven: Faith or Flight?
1. Erik Eckholm, "As Victories Pile Up, Gay Rights Advocates Cheer 'Milestone Year,'" *New York Times* (November 7, 2012).
2. "Backgrounder: The New Federal Regulation on Coerced Abortion Payments," Secretariat for Pro-Life Activities, United States Conference of Bishops (April 11, 2012).
3. Jason DeParle and Sabrina Tavernise, "For Women Under 30, Most Births Occur Outside Marriage," *New York Times* (February 17, 2012).
4. In fact, the name Gibeah means "hill."
5. See John Goldingay, *Psalms*, Baker Commentary on the Old Testament (Grand Rapids, MI: Baker, 2006), 1:190; Gerald Wilson, *Psalms*, The NIV Application Bible Commentary (Grand Rapids, MI: Zondervan, 2002), 1:255; James Montgomery Boice, *Psalms:1–41* (Grand Rapids, MI: Baker, 1994), 1:91.
6. Derek Kidner, *Psalms 1–72* (London: Inter-Varsity, 1973), 72.
7. Wilson, *Psalms*, 249; Charles Spurgeon, "Preface," in *The Treasury of David* (Peabody, MA: Hendrickson, n.d.), 1:129.
8. Some of these examples of flight in a modern context are suggested by Wilson, *Psalms*, 262–64.
9. Willem A. VanGemeren, *Psalms*, The Expositors Bible Commentary, rev. ed. (Grand Rapids, MI: Zondervan, 2008), 5:163.

Chapter Twelve: Deliver Us from Deception

1. John Goldingay, *Psalms*, Baker Commentary on the Old Testament (Grand Rapids, MI: Baker, 2006), 1:197.

2. James Montgomery Boice, *Psalms: 1–41* (Grand Rapids, MI: Baker, 1994), 1:101.

3. See Peter C. Craigie, *Psalms 1–50*, Word Biblical Commentary (Nashville, TN: Thomas Nelson, 2004), 19:101; also Numbers 10:35.

4. Previous generations often said that God's word is *infallible*, meaning that the Scriptures are incapable of error. Since the very words of Scripture are inspired by God, it is impossible for them to contain the slightest fault—they are *infallible*. By the middle of the twentieth century, some theologians began to emphasize a different sense of the word *infallible*—that the Bible could not fail to accomplish what God intended. They believed that the Bible did contain errors in matters of science, archaeology, and history, but that God nevertheless used these flawed human words to do his work. This limited sense of *infallibility* reflects a departure from a historic belief in the complete truthfulness of the Bible.

5. The Chicago Statement on Biblical Inerrancy summarizes this doctrine in a short statement of five points.

(1) God, who is Himself Truth and speaks truth only, has inspired Holy Scripture in order thereby to reveal Himself to lost mankind through Jesus Christ as Creator and Lord, Redeemer and Judge. Holy Scripture is God's witness to Himself.

(2) Holy Scripture, being God's own Word, written by men prepared and superintended by His Spirit, is of infallible divine authority in all matters upon which it touches: it is to be believed, as God's instruction, in all that it affirms; obeyed, as God's command, in all that it requires; embraced, as God's pledge, in all that it promises.

(3) The Holy Spirit, Scripture's divine Author, both authenticates it to us by His inward witness and opens our minds to understand its meaning.

(4) Being wholly and verbally God-given, Scripture is without error or fault in all its teaching, no less in what it states about God's acts in creation, about the events of world history, and about its own literary origins under God, than in its witness to God's saving grace in individual lives.

(5) The authority of Scripture is inescapably impaired if this total divine inerrancy is in any way limited or disregarded, or made relative to a view of truth contrary to the Bible's own; and such lapses bring serious loss to both the individual and the Church.

The full version of the Chicago Statement includes nineteen affirmations and denials. The Chicago Statement can be accessed at http://library.dts.edu/Pages/TL/Special/ICBI.shtml.

6. Charles Spurgeon, *The Treasury of David* (Peabody, MA: Hendrickson, n.d.), 1:143.

Chapter Thirteen: How Long?

1. Charles Spurgeon, "Fear Not," (sermon 156, New Park Street Pulpit, October 4, 1857).

2. Willem A. VanGemeren, *Psalms*, The Expositors Bible Commentary, rev. ed. (Grand Rapids, MI: Zondervan, 2008), 5:170; Peter C. Craigie, *Psalms 1–50*, Word Biblical Commentary (Nashville, TN: Thomas Nelson, 2004), 19:142.

3. VanGemeren, *Psalms*, 172.

4. John Goldingay, *Psalms*, Baker Commentary on the Old Testament (Grand Rapids, MI: Baker, 2006), 1:208, 209.

5. VanGemeren, *Psalms*, 101, 173.

Chapter Fourteen: I Am the Problem

1. Willem A. VanGemeren, *Psalms*, The Expositors Bible Commentary, rev. ed. (Grand Rapids, MI: Zondervan, 2008), 5:140, 174. See also Gerald H. Wilson, *The Editing of the Hebrew Psalter*, Society of Biblical Literature Dissertation 76 (Chico, CA: Scholars, 1985), 294.

2. Matthew Henry, *Commentary on the Whole Bible* (New York: Fleming H. Revell, n.d.), 3:283.

3. Derek Kidner, *Psalms 1–72* (London: Inter-Varsity, 1973), 79.

4. Chou-Wee Pan, *New International Dictionary of Old Testament Theology and Exegesis*, ed. Willem A. VanGemeren (Grand Rapids, MI: Zondervan, 1997), 3:11, 12; Peter C. Craigie, *Psalms 1–50*, Word Biblical Commentary (Nashville, TN: Thomas Nelson, 2004), 19:147.

5. Susan Jacoby, "The Blessings of Atheism," Sunday Review, *New York Times*, January 5, 2013, accessed January, 8, 2013, http://www.nytimes.com/2013/01/06/opinion/sunday/the-blessings-of-atheism.html.

6. Glenn Tinder, "Can We Be Good Without God?" *The Atlantic,* December 1989, accessed January 12, 2013, http://www.theatlantic.com/magazine/archive/1989/12/can-we-be-good-without-god/306721/.

7. Craigie, *Psalms 1–50*, 148.

8. James Montgomery Boice, *Psalms: 1–41* (Grand Rapids, MI: Baker, 1994), 1:117.

9. Wilson, *Editing of the Hebrew Psalter*, 288.

10. Toby Mac, "Forgiveness," featuring Lacrae on *Eye on It,* Forefront Records, 2012.

11. C. S. Lewis, *The Weight of Glory* quoted in Kidner, *Psalms 1–72*, 80.

Chapter Fifteen: The Ultimate Question

1. God's "holy hill" could be the physical Mount Zion in Jerusalem, of course. But it is clear that the population of Jerusalem and the citadel of Zion did not live up to the standards of this psalm in David's day or afterward. This psalm is a farce if it is only talking about the holy hill in Jerusalem. David seems clearly to be referring to Zion, God's "holy hill," figuratively as Heaven, as is the case elsewhere in Book 1 and beyond (Psalm 2:6; 3:4; 43:3; 84:7).

2. See Franz Delitzsch, *Psalms*, in C. F. Keil and F. Delitzsch, *Commentary on the Old Testament* (Grand Rapids, MI: Eerdmans, repr. 1991), 5:211; Donald M. Williams, *Psalms 1–72, The Preacher's Commentary*, ed. Lloyd J. Ogilvie (Nashville, TN: Thomas Nelson, 1986), 13:126. Interpreters who follow Gunkel's form-critical approach see an entrance liturgy in Psalm 15. In that view pilgrims arriving to worship asked about the qualifications for entrance (v. 1); the priest responded by

specifying the requirements (vv. 2–5a) and conferring a blessing (v. 5b). This is a speculative historical reconstruction that arose from an attempt to locate each psalm in a cultic setting and interpret it in the context of a religious or ceremonial event. There is no real evidence that this psalm was used as an entrance liturgy, however. Peter C. Craigie, *Psalms 1–50*, Word Biblical Commentary (Nashville, TN: Thomas Nelson, 2004), 19:150 notes that Near Eastern parallels include ritual as well as moral qualities. Willem A. VanGemeren, *Psalms*, The Expositors Bible Commentary, rev. ed. (Grand Rapids, MI: Zondervan, 2008), 5:182 similarly observes that we would expect the priest's answer to include ceremonial requirements if this was an entrance liturgy. Craigie, VanGemeren, and others propose a wisdom setting for this psalm. Several other points are worth noting as well. The superscription doesn't provide any evidence for this historical reconstruction. The question is addressed to Yahweh, not to the priests. The priests could be answering for Yahweh, of course, but this seems unusual. And in my opinion the actual content of the psalm itself precludes the entrance liturgy interpretation. It seems implausible for pilgrims to ask to "sojourn" in the tabernacle, a word that implies an extended stay, not a visit to offer sacrifices. Also it sets a standard that is impossibly high for anyone to attain; if a worshiper examined himself honestly on the basis of this psalm, he would not enter (cf. Psalm 130:3; 143:2). Rather than guessing about a liturgical setting to interpret this psalm, the canonical setting of Book 1—with its focus on the King whom God sets on his holy hill (2:6)—seems like a much more fruitful and reliable line of approach.

3. Gerald Wilson, *Psalms*, The NIV Application Bible Commentary (Grand Rapids, MI: Zondervan, 2002), 1:297.

4. Delitzsch, *Psalms*, 210, 211.

5. Ibid., 298; VanGemeren, *Psalms*, 182.

6. See Wilson, *Psalms*, 299.

7. Craigie, *Psalms 1–50*, 152.

Chapter Sixteen: An Easter Psalm

1. John Goldingay, *Psalms*, Baker Commentary on the Old Testament (Grand Rapids, MI: Baker, 2006), 1:233 notes that the Hebrew literally says "pit," not "corruption." He argues that since burial leads inexorably to decay, it is implied that if a body is "in the pit," it is rotting and seeing corruption.

2. Donald M. Williams, *Psalms 1–72, The Preacher's Commentary*, ed. Lloyd J. Ogilvie (Nashville, TN: Thomas Nelson, 1986), 13:129, 130.

3. John Calvin, *Institutes of the Christian Religion*, 1.2.1, trans. Ford Lewis Battles, Library of Christian Classics (Philadelphia: Westminster, 1960), 12:40, 41.

4. Gerald Wilson, *Psalms*, The NIV Application Bible Commentary (Grand Rapids, MI: Zondervan, 2002), 1:310.

Chapter Seventeen: Lord, Hear My Prayer

1. Gerald Wilson, *Psalms*, The NIV Application Bible Commentary (Grand Rapids, MI: Zondervan, 2002), 1:23–26, 318.

2. James Montgomery Boice, *Psalms: 1–41* (Grand Rapids, MI: Baker, 1994), 1:139.

3. Wilson, *Psalms*, 323.

4. Ian Murray, *Evangelicalism Divided: A Record of Crucial Change in the Years 1950 to 2000* (Carlisle, PA: Banner of Truth, 2000), 255, quoted in C. J. Mahaney, "Is This Verse in Your Bible?" in *Worldliness: Resisting the Seduction of a Fallen World* (Wheaton, IL: Crossway, 2008), 28.

5. Mahaney, *Worldliness*, 29.

6. Greg Beale, *We Become What We Worship* (Downers Grove, IL: IVP Academic, 2008), 255.

7. Derek Kidner, *Psalms 1–72* (London: Inter-Varsity, 1973), 90; Willem A. VanGemeren, *Psalms*, The Expositors Bible Commentary, rev. ed. (Grand Rapids, MI: Zondervan, 2008), 5:200, 201.

Chapter Eighteen: The Lord Is My Rock

1. H. C. Leupold, *The Psalms: Exposition of the Psalms* (Grand Rapids, MI: Baker, 1977), 174, quoted in James Montgomery Boice, *Psalms:1–41* (Grand Rapids, MI: Baker, 1994), 1:158.

2. Donald M. Williams, *Psalms 1–72, The Preacher's Commentary*, ed. Lloyd J. Ogilvie (Nashville, TN: Thomas Nelson, 1986), 13:144.

3. Charles Spurgeon, *The Treasury of David* (Peabody, MA: Hendrickson, n.d.), 1:239.

4. John Goldingay, *Psalms*, Baker Commentary on the Old Testament (Grand Rapids, MI: Baker, 2006), 1:118n4, 260.

5. Ibid., 267.

6. This follows the pattern of Peter's logic as he interpreted Psalm 16 in Acts 2:31. Peter concludes that David could not have been referring to himself because he did, in fact, rot in the grave (Acts 2:39). We conclude here that David could not have been referring to himself because he did, in fact, sin.

7. See Peter C. Craigie, *Psalms 1–50*, Word Biblical Commentary (Nashville, TN: Thomas Nelson, 2004), 19:176.

8. Franz Delitzsch, *Psalms*, in C. F. Keil and F. Delitzsch, *Commentary on the Old Testament* (Grand Rapids, MI: Eerdmans, repr. 1991), 5:266.

Chapter Nineteen: The Skies and the Scriptures

1. See James K. Hoffmeier, "The Limits of General Revelation," *Trinity Journal* 21 (2000): 21.

2. The word "rewarded" in Psalms 18:20, 24, translates a different Hebrew root word than "reward" in 19:11, yet the essential concept is the same.

3. See Willem A. VanGemeren, *Psalms*, The Expositor's Bible Commentary, rev. ed. (Grand Rapids, MI: Zondervan, 2008), 5:213, 214.

4. "First Glimpse at a Black Hole's Spin," BBC, February 27, 2013, accessed March 2, 2013, http://www.bbc.co.uk/news/science-environment–21607945.

5. Gerhard von Rad, *Old Testament Theology* (San Francisco: Harper & Row, 1962), 1:239, quoted in Hoffmeier, "Limits of General Revelation": 19, 20.

6. Oliver Morton, "The World Falls," *Heliophage (blog)*, August 22, 2012, accessed March 2, 2013, https://heliophage.wordpress.com/2012/08/22/the-worldfalls/.

7. Derek Kidner, *Psalms 1–72* (London: Inter-Varsity, 1973), 99.

8. D. J. A. Clines, "The Tree of Knowledge and the Law of Yahweh," *Vetus Testamentum* 24 (1974): 8.

9. Gerald H. Wilson, *Psalms,* NIV Application Commentary (Grand Rapids, MI: Zondervan, 2003), 1:368, 369.

10. The pronoun *his* is not in the Hebrew.

11. The King James Version follows the Septuagint.

12. John Goldingay, *Psalms*, Baker Commentary on the Old Testament (Grand Rapids, MI: Baker, 2006), 1:294, 295.

13. Wilson, *Psalms*, 372, notes, "The wordplay employing the root *tmm* for both Torah and the hopeful psalmist is unmistakable." Wilson concludes that the psalmist's hope should be taken as a desire for completeness and wholeness. He notes that *tmm* is the foundational term that is the basis for all the other superlative characteristics of God's word in 19:7–9.

On what basis can we limit this term when applying *tmm* to the psalmist? There seems to be an intentional tension that points the reader forward to a servant in David's line who will obey perfectly. See VanGemeren, *Psalms*, 214. This is reinforced by the connections back to the strong declarations of righteousness and blamelessness in Psalm 18:20–24.

Chapter Twenty: The Faith of Israel

1. For instance, Psalm 2:1–3; 18:4, 5; 22:1–21a; 69:1–29; Isaiah 52:14—53:12; Zechariah 12:10; 13:7. This is not limited to direct predictions, though. The sacrificial system points forward to the greater sacrifice of Christ (cf. Hebrews 10:1–18). The sufferings of Job, Joseph, David, and other types of the Messiah also point forward to his greater suffering, as do their subsequent glory.

2. According to Galatians 3:16 the promises of Genesis 13:14–16; 15:6; 22:17; Psalm 2:6–12; 18:16–50; 22:21b–31; Isaiah 9:6; 61:1–3; Malachi 3:1–3 refer to Christ's abundant offspring.

3. See Wayne Grudem, *1 Peter*, Tyndale New Testament Commentaries (Grand Rapids, MI: Eerdmans, 1988), 74, 75.

4. Walter C. Kaiser Jr., "Is It The Case That Christ Is the Same Object of Faith in The Old Testament? (Gen. 15:1–6)," *Journal of the Evangelical Theological Society* 55 (2012): 294.

5. H. C. Leupold, *Exposition of Genesis* (Grand Rapids, MI: Baker, 1953), 1:477, 478. The fuller quote is instructive.

The very issue in this chapter had been Abram's seed. But Abram cannot as a spiritual man have thought of this seed only as numerous descendants; for already in 12:3b that seed had been shown as involving one who would bring salvation to mankind ("all families of the earth blessed"). How could Abram have overlooked or undervalued this chief item? The remark of Hunnius (quoted by Delitzsch) certainly is correct: . . . . Abram believed that God would send this Savior for his own good as well as for the whole world. Naturally, however, such faith may not possess full understanding of the details of redemptive work and the atoning sacrifice. Yet in essence it is trust in the Savior sent by God.

6. Willem A. VanGemeren, *Psalms*, The Expositors Bible Commentary, rev. ed. (Grand Rapids, MI: Zondervan, 2008), 5:223.

7. Peter C. Craigie, *Psalms 1–50*, Word Biblical Commentary (Nashville, TN: Thomas Nelson, 2004), 19:185. There is a description of a ceremony in 2 Chroni-

cles 20 when Jehoshaphat gathered Israel to seek the Lord before a great battle, but this psalm is not mentioned or alluded to. Craigie mentions several other possible historical settings for this psalm as well, but there is no substantial evidence for these.

8. John Calvin, *Commentary on the Book of Psalms*, Calvin's Commentaries (Grand Rapids, MI: Baker, repr. 1979), 4:334.

9. Jamie Grant, "The Psalms and the King," in *Interpreting the Psalms: Issues and Approaches*, ed. Philip S. Johnston and David G. Firth (Downers Grove, IL: InterVarsity, 2005), 108, says,

> Therefore, it is probably better to see Psalm 2 not so much as part of a narrative of the rise and fall of the Davidic Covenant but as part of the introductory hermeneutical paradigm for the interpretation of the whole book of Psalms.

10. See Gerald Wilson, *Psalms*, The NIV Application Bible Commentary (Grand Rapids, MI: Zondervan, 2002), 1:387.

11. John Goldingay, *Psalms*, Baker Commentary on the Old Testament (Grand Rapids, MI: Baker, 2006), 1:302. See also VanGemeren, *Psalms*, 223.

12. The word "distress" in Psalm 18:6 and "trouble" in 20:1 share the same Hebrew root, *sar*.

13. The word "sanctuary" is literally "holy thing," "holy place," or "holiness." This could mean the sanctuary in Jerusalem, of course, but verse 6 tells us that God's help comes from "his holy heaven."

14. Andrew A. Bonar quoted in Charles Spurgeon, *The Treasury of David* (Peabody, MA: Hendrickson, n.d.), 1:303.

15. Ann Tatlock, *I'll Watch the Moon* (Minneapolis, MN: Bethany, 2003), 371.

Chapter Twenty-One: Jesus' Joy

1. Both Psalm 20 and 21 focus on the king's salvation. The words "save" or "salvation" (which share the same Hebrew root) tie these psalms together (Psalm 20:5, 6, 9; 21:1, 5). In Psalm 20:4 the people ask God to grant the king his heart's desire. Psalm 21:2 says, "You have given him his heart's desire." In both psalms the king trusts in the Lord (Psalm 20:7; 21:7). God's power is also central, in particular his right hand (Psalm 20:6, 7; 21:1, 8, 13).

2. Targum of Psalms (TgPss). The date of TgPss is uncertain.

3. Quoted in James Montgomery Boice, *Psalms: 1–41* (Grand Rapids, MI: Baker, 1994), 1:187.

4. John Calvin, *Commentary on the Book of Psalms*, Calvin's Commentaries (Grand Rapids, MI: Baker, repr. 1979), 4:343.

5. Gerald Wilson, *Psalms*, The NIV Application Bible Commentary (Grand Rapids, MI: Zondervan, 2002), 1:399.

6. Ibid., although Wilson does not think this expression necessarily means eternal life as we commonly think of it.

7. This promise could mean either that God would maintain an unbroken succession of David's descendants on his throne forever or that God would raise up an eternal king. Since the Davidic line only ruled until the Babylonian Captivity, the promise could not have been fulfilled through the succession of his descendants. Rather, 2 Samuel 7 is promising an eternal king who would sit on David's throne.

8. Gerhard von Rad, *Old Testament Theology* (San Francisco: Harper & Row, 1962), 1:239.

9. Calvin, *Commentary on the Book of Psalms*, 348.

10. Martin Luther quoted in Peter Hammond, "Praying for Justice," *Frontline Fellowship*, accessed March 16, 2013, http://www.frontline.org.za/index.php?option =com_content&view=article&id=1658:praying-for-justice&catid=24:persecution -cat&Itemid=200.

11. David is also setting up a contrast between his offspring, the Messiah, and the offspring of God's enemies. God will establish David's great descendant, Jesus Christ, and those who belong to him. But he will destroy the descendants of his enemies.

12. Hammond, "Praying for Justice."

13. Ibid.

Chapter Twenty-Two: The Psalm of the Cross

1. Charles Spurgeon, *The Treasury of David*, (Peabody, MA: Hendrickson, n.d.), 1:324.

2. Richard D. Patterson, "Psalm 22: From Trial to Triumph," *Journal of the Evangelical Theological Society* 47, no. 2 (June 2004): 226n74, 229, 230. See also James Mongtomery Boice, *Psalms: 1–41* (Grand Rapids, MI: Baker, 1994), 1:203, 204.

3. Derek Kidner, *Psalms 1–72* (London: Inter-Varsity, 1973), 105.

4. The traditional order of the seven last words of Christ are:

1. Luke 23:34, "Father, forgive them, for they know not what they do."
2. Luke 23:43, "Truly, I say to you, today you will be with me in paradise."
3. John 19:26, 27, "Woman, behold, your son! . . . Behold, your mother!"
4. Matthew 27:46, "My God, my God, why have you forsaken me?"
5. John 19:28, "I thirst."
6. Luke 23:46, "Father, into your hands I commit my spirit."
7. John 19:30, "It is finished."

5. Boice, *Psalms*, 194.

6. Willem A. VanGemeren, *Psalms*, The Expositors Bible Commentary, rev. ed. (Grand Rapids, MI: Zondervan, 2008), 5:242.

7. The word "pierced" has been the subject of much controversy. Kidner, *Psalms 1–72*, 107, 108, gives a good summary,

They have pierced (16) or, simply, "piercing," is the most likely translation of a problematic Hebrew word. A strong argument in its favour is that the LXX, compiled two centuries before the crucifixion, and therefore an unbiased witness, understood it so. All the major translations reject the Massoretic vowels (added to the written text in the Christian era) as yielding little sense here (see margin of RV, RSV, NEB), and the majority in fact agree with LXX. The chief alternatives (*e.g.* "bound" or "hacked off") solve no linguistic difficulties which "pierced" does not solve, but avoid the apparent prediction of the cross by exchanging a common Hebrew verb (dig, bore, pierce) for hypothetical ones, attested only in Akkadian, Syriac and Arabic, not in biblical Hebrew.

8. Isaac Watts, "Alas! And Did My Savior Bleed?" (1707).
9. Kidner, *Psalms 1–72*, 108.
10. See Matthew 11:27.
11. Interestingly, the word "company" in Genesis 35:11 and "congregation" in Psalm 22:22 are the exact same word in Hebrew, *qahal*. He is promised a "congregation" of nations.
12. See also Genesis 17:4.
13. Spurgeon, *Treasury of David*, 333.

Chapter Twenty-Three: The Lord Is Christ's Shepherd
1. Gerald Wilson, *Psalms*, The NIV Application Bible Commentary (Grand Rapids, MI: Zondervan, 2002), 1:431, 432.
2. Douglas J. Green, "The Lord Is Christ's Shepherd," in *Eyes to See, Ears to Hear*, ed. Peter Enns, Douglas J. Green, and Michael J. Kelly (Phillipsburg, NJ: P & R, 2010), 42.
3. See ibid., 43, 44.
4. Haddon W. Robinson, *Psalm Twenty-Three* (Chicago: Moody, 1968), 13.
5. Phillip Keller, *A Shepherd Looks at Psalm 23* (Grand Rapids, MI: Zondervan, 1970), 35; quoted in James Montgomery Boice, *Psalms: 1–41* (Grand Rapids. MI: Baker, 1994), 1:209.
6. Wilson, *Psalms*, 432.
7. Green, "Lord Is Christ's Shepherd," 42.
8. Willem A. VanGemeren, *Psalms*, The Expositors Bible Commentary, rev. ed. (Grand Rapids, MI: Zondervan, 2008), 5:254.
9. Wilson, *Psalms*, 433.
10. Derek Kidner, *Psalms 1–72* (London: Inter-Varsity, 1973), 112.

Chapter Twenty-Four: The King of Glory
1. See Gerald Wilson, *Psalms*, The NIV Application Bible Commentary (Grand Rapids, MI: Zondervan, 2002), 1:23–26, 448.
2. William Shakespeare, *Macbeth*, 5.1.
3. David Gushee, "The Truth About Deceit," *Christianity Today* (March 2006): 68.
4. J. C. Ryle, *Expository Thoughts on the Gospels* (New York: Robert Carter and Brothers, 1879), 2:234, 235.
5. Charles Spurgeon, *The Treasury of David* (Peabody, MA: Hendrickson, n.d.), 1:377.
6. Willem A. VanGemeren, *Psalms*, The Expositor's Bible Commentary, rev. ed. (Grand Rapids, MI: Zondervan, 2008), 5:262 notes that this interpretation of returning to Heaven has support in Ancient Near Eastern usage.
7. Peter C. Craigie, *Psalms 1–50*, Word Biblical Commentary (Nashville: Thomas Nelson, 2004), 19:212; VanGemeren, *Psalms*, 257.
8. John Keble quoted in Spurgeon, *Treasury of David*, 388.

Chapter Twenty-Five: He Will Never Let You Down
1. Phillip J. Nel, *New International Dictionary of Old Testament Theology and Exegesis*, ed. Willem A. VanGemeren (Grand Rapids, MI: Zondervan, 1997),

613–15; James Montgomery Boice, *Psalms: 1–41* (Grand Rapids, MI: Baker, 1994), 1:223, 224.

2. Gerald H. Wilson, *The Editing of the Hebrew Psalter*, Society of Biblical Literature Dissertation 76 (Chico, CA: Scholars, 1985), 463.

3. Boice, *Psalms*, 226, 227.

4. Jonathan Edwards quoted in Charles Spurgeon, *The Treasury of David* (Peabody, MA: Hendrickson, n.d.), 1:406, 407.

5. Spurgeon, *Treasury of David*, 395.

6. Peter C. Craigie, *Psalms 1–50*, Word Biblical Commentary (Nashville, TN: Thomas Nelson, 2004), 19:222.

Chapter Twenty-Six: The Man of Integrity

1. John Berman, "Golfer J. P. Hayes Pays Price For Honesty," *ABC News*, November 8, 2008, accessed December 9, 2013, http://abcnews.go.com/WN/story?id=6300276&page=1.

2. Literally, "kidneys" and "heart." The Old Testament writers view the kidneys as the seat of emotions and moral character, while the heart is the center of essential personhood, thought, and decision-making.

3. Terry L. Brensinger, *New International Dictionary of Old Testament Theology and Exegesis*, ed. Willem A. VanGemeren (Grand Rapids, MI: Zondervan, 1997), 1:637.

4. I owe the basic insights for these paragraphs to James Montgomery Boice, *Psalms: 1–41* (Grand Rapids, MI: Baker, 1994), 1:233.

5. Gerald H. Wilson, *The Editing of the Hebrew Psalter*, Society of Biblical Literature Dissertation 76 (Chico: Scholars, 1985), 475 says, "This verse may open a vague window on the practice of worship in the temple."

Chapter Twenty-Seven: My Light and My Salvation

1. James Hastings, ed., *The Speaker's Bible* (Grand Rapids, MI: Baker, 1974), 9:394.

2. Gerald Wilson, *Psalms*, The NIV Application Bible Commentary (Grand Rapids, MI: Zondervan, 2002), 1:483.

3. Donald M. Williams, *Psalms 1–72, The Preacher's Commentary*, ed. Lloyd J. Ogilvie (Nashville, TN: Thomas Nelson, 1986), 13:221.

4. Iain H. Murray, *Jonathan Edwards* (Southampton, UK: Camelot, 1987), 441.

5. See Derek Kidner, *Psalms 1–72* (London: Inter-Varsity, 1973), 120, 121. John Goldingay, *Psalms*, Baker Commentary on the Old Testament (Grand Rapids, MI: Baker, 2006), 1:394, notes that the range of word pictures in verses 5, 6 suggest God was with him in battle. And significantly, the "temple" was not built until after David died. If David wanted physically to live in the place of worship, we would expect him to say "inquire in his tabernacle." So it seems likely that he longs to experience God's presence in his ordinary life.

6. John Piper, *God Is the Gospel* (Wheaton, IL: Crossway, 2005), 11.

Chapter Twenty-Eight: My Strength and My Shield

1. Gerald Wilson, *Psalms*, The NIV Application Bible Commentary (Grand Rapids, MI: Zondervan, 2002), 1:494, especially n. 3. See also Terrence Fretheim, in

New International Dictionary of Old Testament Theology and Exegesis, ed. Willem A. VanGemeren (Grand Rapids, MI: Zondervan, 1997), 2:204.

2. Derek Kidner, *Psalms 1–72* (London, Inter-Varsity, 1973), 122.

3. See Susan Berry, "DC Abortionist: Pro-Life Activists Are 'Terrorists,'" *Breitbart* (blog), April 30, 2013, accessed November 26, 2013, http://www.breitbart.com /Big-Government/2013/04/30/DC-Abortionist-Pro-Life-Activists-Are-Terrorists.

4. John Piper, *"The Final Divide: Eternal Life or Eternal Wrath, Part 1"* (sermon) November 29, 1998, accessed May 18, 2013, http://www.desiringgod.org /resource-library/sermons/the-final-divide-eternal-life-or-eternal-wrath-part-1.

5. Non-Christians cannot do good works because "whatever does not proceed from faith is sin" (Romans 14:23). Nothing they do comes from faith; therefore everything they do is sin. Why is this so? Serving/worshiping God is the standard by which our works are judged, not how nice or considerate or humane a specific action is. A man-centered approach to works judges them by the benefit to fellow man or society. Good works are about God, in that they are done as unto the Lord in fundamental obedience to him. How I relate to him is far more important than the way I relate to other human beings. If I shake my fist at God but give to the poor, I am not doing good works because God is infinitely more important and valuable. If I murder my neighbor but feed his cat, am I a good person? Of course not. In the same way, someone who hates God but is kind to humans is not a good person either. And furthermore, anyone who does not love God cannot love humans created in his image. Good works are only possible for those who believe in Jesus Christ. Indeed, faith in Christ is the first and great work. "This is the work of God, that you believe in him whom he has sent" (John 6:29).

Chapter Twenty-Nine: The Lord of the Storm

1. Charles Spurgeon, *The Treasury of David* (Peabody, MA: Hendrickson, n.d.), 1:29.

2. Gerald Wilson, *Psalms*, The NIV Application Bible Commentary (Grand Rapids, MI: Zondervan, 2002), 1:504.

3. John Goldingay, *Psalms*, Baker Commentary on the Old Testament (Grand Rapids, MI: Baker, 2006), 1:416.

4. Wilson, *Psalms*, 509, 510; Peter C. Craigie, *Psalms 1–50*, Word Biblical Commentary (Nashville, TN: Thomas Nelson, 2004), 19:245.

5. Craigie, *Psalms 1–50*, 246. See also Terrence Fretheim, *New International Dictionary of Old Testament Theology and Exegesis*, ed. Willem A. VanGemeren (Grand Rapids, MI: Zondervan, 1997), 2:292; Wilson, *Psalms*, 504.

6. Craigie, *Psalms 1–50*, 249.

7. William Booth, "Good Singing," Christian History, *Christianity Today*, 1990, accessed May 24, 2013, http://www.christianitytoday.com/ch/1990/issue26 /2630.html?start=2?.

8. Gerhard Von Rad, *Old Testament Theology* (San Francisco: Harper & Row, 1962), 1:239.

9. Derek Kidner, *Psalms 1–72* (London: Inter-Varsity, 1973), 126.

10. Willem A. VanGemeren, *Psalms*, The Expositor's Bible Commentary, rev. ed. (Grand Rapids, MI: Zondervan, 2008), 5: 294.

11. Wilson, *Psalms*, 505.

12. VanGemeren, *Psalms*, 295.

Chapter Thirty: Resurrection Song

1. The phrase "A Psalm of David" could mean that it was written by David, for David, about David, or even in the style of David. Yet both Jesus and Peter assume that "of David" indicates Davidic authorship. See the use of Psalms 16 and 110 in Acts 2:25–31 and Mark 12:36, 37 respectively.

2. Charles Spurgeon, *The Treasury of David* (Peabody, MA: Hendrickson, n.d.), 1:44.

3. Eugene H. Merrill, *New International Dictionary of Old Testament Theology and Exegesis*, ed. Willem A. VanGemeren (Grand Rapids, MI: Zondervan, 1997), 4:6.

4. The words "Sheol" and "pit" (or "corruption") appear in Psalm 16:10 and Psalm 30:3, 9.

5. Gerald Wilson, *Psalms*, The NIV Application Bible Commentary (Grand Rapids, MI: Zondervan, 2002), 1:516n7.

6. See John Goldingay, *Psalms*, Baker Commentary on the Old Testament (Grand Rapids, MI: Baker, 2006), 1:427. Note that although Goldingay takes the force of the words seriously, he seems to take this metaphorically.

7. The Masoretic text suggested different wording for verse 3, which the ESV mentions in a footnote, "You restored me to life, that I should not go down to the pit." This is why some of our English Bibles translate verse 3, "You have kept me alive" (NKJV, NASB). This reading changes the verse to mean that David was merely sick, not dead. The *Ketib* reading should be retained over the *Qere* emendation here. See Willem A. VanGemeren, *Psalms*, The Expositors Bible Commentary, rev. ed. (Grand Rapids, MI: Zondervan, 2008), 5:298; Wilson, *Psalms*, 516; Peter C. Craigie, *Psalms 1–50*, Word Biblical Commentary (Nashville, TN: Thomas Nelson, 2004), 19:251; and Goldingay, *Psalms*, 427.

8. See Goldingay, *Psalms*, 430, 431; Terrence Fretheim, *New International Dictionary of Old Testament Theology and Exegesis*, ed. Willem A. VanGemeren (Grand Rapids, MI: Zondervan, 1997), 2:203.

9. Goldingay, *Psalms*, 431.

Chapter Thirty-One: Be Strong and Wait for the Lord

1. See John Goldingay, *Psalms*, Baker Commentary on the Old Testament (Grand Rapids, MI: Baker, 2006), 1:437.

2. James Montgomery Boice, *Psalms: 1–41* (Grand Rapids, MI: Baker, 1994), 1:269.

3. Gerald Wilson, *Psalms*, The NIV Application Bible Commentary (Grand Rapids, MI: Zondervan, 2002), 1:528.

4. Charles Spurgeon, *The Treasury of David* (Peabody, MA: Hendrickson, n.d.), 1:58.

5. Wilson, *Psalms*, 530.

6. Goldingay, *Psalms*, 450.

7. J. J. Stewart Perowne quoted in Spurgeon, *Treasury of David*, 66.

8. Ibid., 59.

9. Goldingay, *Psalms*, 442 confirms that verse 9 "makes explicit that the suppliant still has the problem that v. 7 spoke of as if it were solved."

10. Boice, *Psalms*, 271.

11. Goldingay, *Psalms*, 450.

Chapter Thirty-Two: The Blessing of Forgiveness

1. Michael Card, "Traitor's Look," on *The Life,* Sparrow Records, 1988.
2. Peter C. Craigie, *Psalms 1–50,* Word Biblical Commentary (Nashville, TN: Thomas Nelson, 2004), 19:264 points out that *maskils* do not always appear to be teaching psalms. Yet Psalm 32 seems to be a case where the etymology of *maskil* (from the root, "to instruct") seems to fit the nature of the psalm particularly well (see 32:8).
3. Willem A. VanGemeren, *Psalms,* The Expositors Bible Commentary, rev. ed. (Grand Rapids, MI: Zondervan, 2008), 5:79.
4. James Montgomery Boice, *Psalms: 1–41* (Grand Rapids, MI: Baker, 1994), 1:278.
5. John E Hartley, *New International Dictionary of Old Testament Theology and Exegesis,* ed. Willem A. VanGemeren (Grand Rapids, MI: Zondervan, 1997), 2:303.
6. Erwin Lutzer, *Putting Your Past Behind You,* revised ed. (Chicago: Moody, 1997), 53.

Chapter Thirty-Three: Shout for Joy!

1. Gerald Wilson, *Psalms,* The NIV Application Bible Commentary (Grand Rapids, MI: Zondervan, 2002), 1:556.
2. Ibid., 555.
3. Tremper Longman III, *New International Dictionary of Old Testament Theology and Exegesis,* ed. Willem A. VanGemeren (Grand Rapids, MI: Zondervan, 1997), 3:1128.
4. John Goldingay, *Psalms,* Baker Commentary on the Old Testament (Grand Rapids, MI: Baker, 2006), 1:464.
5. Matt Redman, "10,000 Reasons," on *10,000 Reasons,* Sixstepsrecords/Sparrow, 2011.
6. Andrae Crouch, "Bless His Holy Name," Lexicon Music, 1973.
7. Tremper Longman III, *New International Dictionary,* 3:1081, 1082.
8. John Piper, "Is It OK To Say Amen! On Sunday?" (sermon) February 21, 1983, accessed December 10, 2013, http://www.desiringgod.org/resource-library/taste-see-articles/is-it-ok-to-say-amen-on-sunday.
9. Gerard Manley Hopkins, "God's Grandeur," in *The Oxford Anthology of English Literature,* ed. Lionel Trilling and Harold Bloom (Oxford: Oxford University, 1973), 682.

Chapter Thirty-Four: Taste and See

1. David skips the letter *waw* and repeats the letter *pe* as the final verse.
2. Gerald Wilson, *Psalms,* The NIV Application Bible Commentary (Grand Rapids, MI: Zondervan, 2002), 1:568.
3. Holly Dunn, "Daddy's Hands," on *Holly Dunn,* MTM, 1986.
4. Charles Spurgeon, *The Treasury of David* (Peabody, MA: Hendrickson, n.d.), 1:124.
5. See Wilson, *Psalms,* 573.

Chapter Thirty-Five: My Savior Will Defend Me

1. J. Carl Laney, "A Fresh Look at the Imprecatory Psalms," *Bibliotheca Sacra* 138 (1981): 36 lists Psalms 7, 35, 58, 59, 69, 83, 109, 137, and 139.

2. Ibid., 42.

3. James Boice, *Psalms: 1–41* (Grand Rapids, MI: Baker, 1994), 1:301.

4. Some of this shape is suggested by Boice in ibid., 302.

5. John Piper, "Let Them Be Like the Snail That Dissolves to Slime," Desiring God (blog), March 15, 2010, accessed August 10, 2013, http://www.desiringgod.org /blog/posts/let-them-be-like-the-snail-that-dissolves-to-slime.

6. It's worth noticing that verses 17, 18 echo Psalm 22:21, 22, the psalm of the cross, with his facing enemies like lions and his promise to praise God before the congregation of God's people. David, and Christ after him, serve God's people by exalting God after his deliverance.

7. Isaac Watts, "Psalm 35, Part 1," Christian Classics Ethereal Library, accessed August 10, 2013, http://www.ccel.org/ccel/watts/psalmshymns.Ps.81.html.

Chapter Thirty-Six: God's Steadfast Love

1. Chuck Colson, "The Terrifying Truth: We Are Normal," *Breakpoint* (July 1983), accessed August 15, 2013, www.breakpoint.org/search-library/search?view =searchdetail&id=1395.

2. Kent Hughes, *Mark: Jesus, Servant and Savior* (Wheaton, IL: Crossway, 1989), 1:27.

3. Ibid., 27, 28.

4. Several translations have been proposed for verse 1. A significant issue is that the word translated "speaks" typically refers to an oracle or prophetic utterance based on divine revelation. Some scholars think this implies that "transgression" is not personified as the one speaking here but rather that David is himself speaking a prophetic utterance. The grammar of Psalm 36:1 is very similar to Psalm 110:1, however, in which David says that Yahweh *speaks* to his Lord.

5. This is the reading of the Masoretic text and is reflected in a footnote in the ESV. Other ancient versions (e.g., LXX, Vulgate, Origen) read "his heart." Derek Kidner, *Psalms 1–72* (London: Inter-Varsity, 1973), 145 suggests that the more difficult reading "my heart" may have been emended at an early date. This is the principle of *lectio difficilior potior* (the more difficult reading is stronger). It is easy to see how a scribe could have changed "my heart" to "his heart" in order to smooth over the difficulty of David identifying himself as a wicked man. But it is hard to see why a scribe would have made the opposite change.

6. Jonathan Edwards, "The Vain Self-Flatteries of the Sinner," *Sermons, Series II, 1731–1732* (WJE Online, vol. 47), accessed August 15, 2013, www.jonathan-edwards.org/Self-Flatteries.html; viewed on August 15, 2013.

7. Ibid. These examples of flattery are adapted from Edwards.

8. "We are Young," on *Some Nights,* Fueled By Ramen, 2012.

9. James Stewart quoted in R. Kent Hughes, *1001 Great Stories* (Wheaton, IL: Tyndale, 1998), 386.

10. Donald M. Williams, *Psalms 1–72, The Preacher's Commentary*, ed. Lloyd J. Ogilvie (Nashville, TN: Thomas Nelson, 1986), 13:290.

11. Sam MacBratney, *Guess How Much I Love You?* (London: Walker, 2009).

12. James Montgomery Boice, *Psalms:1–41* (Grand Rapids, MI: Baker, 1994), 1:311.

13. Allen Johnson Jr., "Memories of Hiroshima," Gambit, *Best of New Orleans*, August 2, 2005, accessed November 29, 2013, http://www.bestofneworleans.com /gambit/memories-of-hiroshima/Content?oid=1244646.

14. Williams, *Psalms 1–72,* 290.

15. Charles Spurgeon, *The Treasury of David* (Peabody, MA: Hendrickson, n.d.), 1:160.

16. George W. Robinson, "I Am His, and He Is Mine," (1876).

Chapter Thirty-Seven: Don't Envy the Wicked

1. Many scholars do not see a definite structure to Psalm 37 beyond the twenty-two units of the acrostic. Gerald Wilson, *Psalms*, The NIV Application Bible Commentary (Grand Rapids, MI: Zondervan, 2002), 1:603 agrees that the repetition of "cut off" and "inherit the land" is structurally significant. Not counting the introduction of 37:1, 2 and the conclusion of 37:39, 40, these repeated phrases divide the psalm into five main sections.

2. C. S. Lewis, *The Weight of Glory* (New York: Harper Collins, repr. 2001), 26.

3. Charles Spurgeon, *The Treasury of David* (Peabody, MA: Hendrickson, n.d.), 1:171.

4. Tim LaHaye and Bob Phillips, *Anger Is a Choice* (Grand Rapids, MI: Zondervan, 2002), 19, 20.

Chapter Thirty-Eight: A King's Confession

1. John Calvin, *Commentary on the Book of Psalms,* Calvin's Commentaries (Grand Rapids, MI: Baker, repr. 1979), 5:53.

2. Augustine, *Expositions on the Book of Psalms*, Nicene and Post-Nicene Fathers, Series I, ed. Philip Schaff (Peabody, MA: Hendrickson, repr. 2004), 8:104.

3. Gerald Wilson, *Psalms*, The NIV Application Bible Commentary (Grand Rapids, MI: Zondervan, 2002), 1:616.

4. Charles Spurgeon, *The Treasury of David* (Peabody, MA: Hendrickson, n.d.), 1:198.

5. Propitiation flows from God's love for sinners with whom he was angry. John Stott, *The Cross of Christ* (Downers Grove, IL: InterVarsity, 2006), 174 makes this key point: "God does not love us because Christ died for us, Christ died for us because God loves us." John Murray, *The Atonement* quoted in J. I. Packer, *Knowing God* (London: Hodder and Stoughton, 1973), 189, says,

> The doctrine of propitiation is precisely this, that God loved the objects of his wrath so much that He gave his own Son to the end that He by His blood should make provision for the removal of his wrath.

6. See James Montgomery Boice, *Psalms: 1–41* (Grand Rapids, MI: Baker, 1994), 1:332; Derek Kidner, *Psalms 1–72* (London: Inter-Varsity, 1973), 154.

7. Spurgeon, *Treasury of David*, 200.

8. See Nestle-Aland, *Novum Testamentum Graece*, 26th ed. (Stuttgart: Deutsche Bibelgesellschaft, 1979), 785.

9. Boice, *Psalms*, 336.

Chapter Thirty-Nine: Waiting in Silence

1. Craig C. Broyles, *Psalms* (Grand Rapids, MI: Baker, 1999), 188, also sees this situation behind the psalm.

2. John Goldingay, *Psalms*, Baker Commentary on the Old Testament (Grand Rapids, MI: Baker, 2006), 1:556, points out that the verb *'ālam*, "to keep silent," is never used to describe voluntary silence except for Psalm 39:2 and Isaiah 53:7. Thus there is an intriguing verbal link between these passages.

3. See Derek Kidner, *Psalms 1–72* (London: Inter-Varsity, 1973), 156.

4. Charles Spurgeon, *The Treasury of David* (Peabody, MA: Hendrickson, n.d.), 1:215.

5. Goldingay, *Psalms*, 557.

6. Ibid., 559.

7. Psalm 38:1, 18; 39:8; 40:12; 41:4.

8. Gerald Wilson, *Psalms*, The NIV Application Bible Commentary (Grand Rapids, MI: Zondervan, 2002), 1:625.

Chapter Forty: He Set My Feet on a Rock

1. Tertullian, *On the Flesh of Christ*, in *Ante-Nicene Fathers*, ed. Alexander Roberts and James Donaldson (Peabody: Hendrickson, repr. 1994), 3:538.

2. Derek Kidner, *Psalms 1–72* (London: Inter-Varsity, 1973), 24, makes the point that the New Testament repeatedly assumes that several psalms refer to Christ although they seem to fit David's life perfectly without the need for a supernatural figure in the future. See e.g., John 13:18; 15:25; Romans 15:9; Hebrews 2:13.

3. Hengstenberg quoted in Charles Spurgeon, *The Treasury of David* (Peabody, MA: Hendrickson, n.d.), 1:242.

4. For instance, Psalm 50:7–15, Isaiah 1:10–17.

5. John Goldingay, *Psalms*, Baker Commentary on the Old Testament (Grand Rapids, MI: Baker, 2006), 1:573.

6. Jonathan Edwards, "History of Redemption," in *Works of Jonathan Edwards* (Carlisle: Banner of Truth, repr. 1992), 1:572.

7. See Matthew 3:17; 17:5; John 3:35; 4:34; 5:20; 10:17; 13:31, 32; 14:13; 15:9, 10; 17:1, 20–26.

8. Gerald Wilson, *Psalms*, The NIV Application Bible Commentary (Grand Rapids, MI: Zondervan, 2002), 1:641. He points out that the verb *bśr* means "to bring news" (good news in this case), which is the meaning of *euangelion*, the Greek underlying the word "gospel." In fact, the LXX translates *bśr* with a form of *euangelizo* here.

9. See, e.g., Mark 8:31; 9:31; 10:34.

10. There is no obvious reason to separate verses 6–8 from the rest of the psalm and assign it to a different speaker. Thus, the testimony of Hebrews that these are the words of Christ applies to the whole psalm.

11. David Clarkson quoted in Spurgeon, *Treasury of David*, 250.

Chapter Forty-One: The Blessing of Christ

1. Gerald Wilson, *Psalms*, The NIV Application Bible Commentary (Grand Rapids, MI: Zondervan, 2002), 1:657 points out that the word "blessed" or its root appears at the end of each of the five books of the Psalter.

2. Ibid., 650, 651.

3. Charles Spurgeon, *The Treasury of David* (Peabody, MA: Hendrickson, n.d.), 1:255 makes a helpful introductory comment that is relevant to the interpretation of these Davidic psalms in general.

> A Psalm of David. This title has frequently occurred before, and serves to remind us of the value of the Psalm, seeing that it was committed to no mean songster; and also to inform us as to the author who has made his own experience the basis of a prophetic song, in which a far greater than David is set forth. How wide a range of experience David had! What power it gave him to edify future ages! And how full a type of our Lord did he become! What was bitterness to him has proved to be a fountain of unfailing sweetness to many generations of the faithful.
>
> Jesus Christ betrayed by Judas Iscariot is evidently the great theme of this Psalm, but we think not exclusively. He is the antitype of David, and all his people are in their measure like him; hence words suitable to the Great Representative are most applicable to those who are in him.

4. Ibid., 651.

5. See M. Daniel Carroll R., *New International Dictionary of Old Testament Theology and Exposition*, ed. Willem A. VanGemeren (Grand Rapids, MI: Zondervan, 1992), 1:951.

6. Wilson, *Psalms*, 652, points out, "The Hebrew word that underlies 'regard' is *maśkil*. . . . Rather than a sense of 'compassionate concern' that might be expressed with the Hebrew word *rḥm*, *maśkil* is a term associated with the wisdom tradition and reflects a perceptive ability to know the right response in a given situation."

7. Spurgeon, *Treasury of David*, 255.

8. Randy Alcorn, "How Did Eternal Perspectives Ministries Begin?" FAQs, *Eternal Perspective Ministries*, March 18, 2010, accessed September 28, 2013, http://www.epm.org/faq/question/how-did-eternal-perspectives-ministries-begin.

9. Sickness, disease, and death entered the world because of the fall (Genesis 3). Thus many Christians would affirm that sickness is the result of the presence of sin in the world in a general way. The point is that an individual's sickness may not be the result of his or her own personal sin. Rather they may be suffering because we live in a fallen world.

Scripture Index

General Index

Index of Sermon Illustrations

than having your student loans paid off or having a ticket taken off your record, 328

God's Majesty
Young mothers spend their days caring for children. Step back and see the big picture: God is making his name majestic in this world through them. God is establishing his strength in this world through children as they learn to praise him, 97

It is healthy to gaze at the vast beauty of the night sky and feel small. The greatest mystery, though, is not that I am so small but that God's love is so big. He is mindful of men and women who are mere microscopic specks in the universe, 99

God's Presence
If you're held hostage in a bank robbery, you will be happy to see the SWAT team when they come through the door. But the robbers will be terrified to see those very same men. This is how it is with God's face too, 161

C. S. Lewis said, "In the end that Face which is the delight or the terror of the universe must be turned on each one of us . . . either conferring glory inexpressible or inflicting shame that can never be cured or disguised," 161

Grace
Harry Ironside reassures an elderly man that the sins of his youth are forgotten by God, 265–66

Sometimes people wonder if we will get tired of praising God in Heaven. We think this way because we don't understand how amazing his grace is, 310

J. C. Ryle: "Above all, let us pray for a deeper sense of our own sinfulness, guilt and undeserving. This, after all, is the true secret of a thankful spirit. It is the man who daily feels his debt

to grace, and daily remembers [that] in reality he deserves nothing but hell—this is the man who will be daily blessing and praising God. Thankfulness [is] a flower which will never bloom well excepting upon a root of deep humility," 257

Heart
Emotions are not a sign of weakness; David was a man's man—he could take down any three of us in hand-to-hand combat—yet his heart was soft toward God. He was a scholar, soldier, and poet at the same time. So the Psalms challenge us men especially to be more fully ourselves, to be true men like David, 17

It is easy to be a moral person with a religious veneer of Christianity. God is not looking for people who are good at doing religious things. God is looking for men and women who love him and obey him sincerely from the heart, 59

The color of hydrangeas serves as a litmus test of the acidity of soil. It is the same with our hearts. If you want to know the soil of someone's heart, notice who they admire, 168–69

Heaven
Not long ago my nephew and his wife lost their little baby. I mentioned to my mother how comforting it was to know that Dad was there in Heaven to welcome his great-grandson, his namesake. She said to me, "Yes, that's true, but when we get to Heaven, we are going to see Jesus. The most wonderful thing will be to see him," 131

Holiness
If you have a cookout after church and spill barbecue sauce on the middle of your white shirt, it will stain. What happens when that same barbecue

sauce drops off a piece of meat onto the coals? Do the coals get dirty? No; the fire burns up the barbecue sauce. In the same way, when sin and impurity comes into God's presence, does God get dirty, like your shirt? No; his holiness consumes sin like fire, 255

Idolatry

John Calvin: "It will not suffice simply to hold that there is one whom all ought to honor and adore, unless we are also persuaded that he is the fountain of every good, and that we must seek nothing elsewhere than in him," 177

Jesus

Derek Kidner: "It would scarcely seem too much to infer . . . that wherever David or the Davidic king appears in the Psalter . . . he foreshadows in some degree the Messiah," 18

The Psalms are about Christ in several ways. On the one hand, they make specific predictions that were fulfilled in Christ. On a deeper level, the Psalms point forward to Christ through the life, words, emotions, and experiences of King David as a whole, 19

In Flannery O'Connor's novel *Wise Blood*, her main character, Hazel Motes, says at one point, "The way to avoid Jesus was to avoid sin, 69

We need to follow in Jesus' footsteps. Turn to God. Pour out your heart to him. If you are a Christian and it feels like God has abandoned you, don't believe your heart, 149

As a preacher, Jesus has committed himself to serve us. Jesus' first words to his Father were for you and me, for his church. I remember visiting a man in the hospital who was coming out of surgery. As he came to, his first question was about his wife. "How is she?" he asked me. I marveled at his love for his bride; he thought of her first, 239

Mayo Clinic is famous as a great hospital not because they can cure small things but because people come from around the world with the most desperate diseases. Jesus is like Johns Hopkins or MD Anderson Cancer Center, not the local urgent care clinic. He is not a Savior who can only handle small sinners; his blood has power to save great sinners, 266

Tertullian said about David, "He sings to us of Christ, and through his voice Christ indeed also sang concerning Himself." In the Psalms David points forward to Christ the way a model car points to a real car. David is a shadow of the reality that came in Jesus Christ, 407

Law

God blesses the man who both *delights* (heart) in his Law and *meditates* (head) on it. In fact, he mentions the heart first, suggesting that the reason a man thinks carefully about God's Word is because he has already come to love it. We treasure the Word before we ponder it and dwell on what it means, 15

Prayer

People who don't know God well have prayers that sound like a formula with set words and phrases. But if you know God, you can come to him without putting on your makeup. You pour out your unvarnished thoughts to him. If you had a good father, you talk to God the way you would talk to your dad—you are respectful but completely comfortable that he loves you and understands, 63

Redemption

Jonathan Edwards: "As nothing was done before Christ's incarnation, so nothing was done after his resurrection to purchase redemption for men. Nor will there ever be anything more done to all eternity," 411–12

Salvation

God will meet every need. David means more than knowing that his sins are forgiven, as wonderful as that is. He means complete salvation: comfort for his heart, for his mind, healing for his body, complete safety, perfect peace, 149–50

The love of God flowing within the Trinity is like a nuclear reactor that overflows with power to save sinners. God's love for himself is the source of our salvation, 413

Sin

G.K. Chesterton's answer to, "What is wrong with the world?" was "I am," 153

Harry Ironside reassures an elderly man that the sins of his youth are forgotten by God, 265–66

If your sin is a backpack of guilt and shame, Jesus took the backpack from your shoulders and carried it for you on the cross, 267

Steadfast Love

When a husband vows to love his wife "until death do us part," this is *chesed*, steadfast love. He will not always feel warm fuzzies for her; he might even be angry at her sometimes. But if he is a good man he will be committed to her and faithful to her and will care for her and love her. God has committed himself by covenant to his people like a husband to his bride, 149

God is like a father, always hoping his prodigal son will return, always ready to welcome him home. If you trust him to forgive your sins, his love will surround you, 335

Word of God

Author collected and refined in a fire lead bullets four times. David compares God's Word to silver refined in a crucible not four times but seven times, 140–41

God's promises are more reliable than a winning lottery ticket. Our hearts should start racing when we read what he has promised because we know it is going to happen. Christians who believe God's Word should say, "I think I'm going to have a heart attack!" 150

Sweet honey represents the pleasure of the senses—the finest tasting food, the best-smelling perfume, the most fashionable clothes, the fastest cars, the best new songs. The Bible is better, 209–10

Charles Spurgeon: "The Bible has passed through the furnace of persecution, literary criticism, philosophic doubt, and scientific discovery, and has lost nothing but those human interpretations which clung to it as alloy to precious ore. The experience of saints has tried it in every conceivable manner, but not a single doctrine or promise has been consumed in the most excessive heat," 141

World

Human beings across the globe are offended by the God of the Bible and rage against him, 36

The picture of eating bread is particularly graphic. Bread is a staple; we eat it every day. The world devours the righteous daily and constantly. Eating bread is also normal. We don't write postcards or tweet about eating a slice of bread; it is totally unremarkable. For the wicked, devouring God's people is a casual thing, an everyday occurrence, 160

Worldliness is not a matter of outward behavior. Outward behavior can be evidence of inner worldliness, but the real location of worldliness is internal, in our hearts, 188

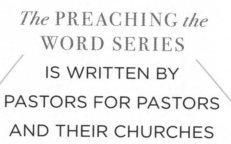

The PREACHING *the* WORD SERIES IS WRITTEN BY PASTORS FOR PASTORS AND THEIR CHURCHES